What's New in This Edition

The fifth edition of this book has been updated to keep pace with changes in the field of data communications. In this edition, the following topics have been revised or added:

Internet access and use

The TCP/IP protocol suite

The use of browsers

The File Transfer Protocol

The Hypertext Transmission Protocol

The operation and utilization of local area networks

100 megabit LAN operation, such as 100BASE-T, 100VG-AnyLAN, and FDDI

The operation of LAN switches

Asynchronous Transfer Mode (ATM)

SAMS
PUBLISHING

201 West 103rd Street
Indianapolis, IN 46290

Understanding
Data
Communications
Fifth Edition

**Second, Third, Fourth,
and Fifth Editions Revised by:**
   Gilbert Held

First Edition by:
   George E. Friend, M.S.;
   John L. Fike, Ph.D., P.E.;
   H. Charles Baker, Ph.D., P.E.;
   and John C. Bellamy, Ph.D.

With Contributions by :
   Gerald Luecke and
   Charles W. Battle

UNDERSTANDING

Publisher and President *Richard K. Swadley*

Acquisitions Manager *Greg Weigand*

Development Manager *Dean Miller*

Managing Editor *Cindy Morrow*

Marketing Manager *John Pierce*

Assistant Marketing Manager *Kristina Perry*

Acquisitions Editor
Grace Buechlein

Development Editor
Brian-Kent Proffitt

Production Editor
Cheri Clark

Technical Reviewer
Angela Murdock

Editorial Coordinator
Bill Whitmer

Technical Edit Coordinator
Lynette Quinn

Resource Coordinator
Deborah Frisby

Indexer
John Hulse

Formatter
Frank Sinclair

Editorial Assistants
Carol Ackerman
Andi Richter
Rhonda Tinch-Mize

Cover Designer
Tim Amrhein

Book Designer
Alyssa Yesh

Copy Writer
Peter Fuller

Production Team Supervisor
Brad Chinn

Production
Stephen Adams
Debra Bolhuis
Charlotte Clapp
Kevin Cliburn
Jason Hand
Daniel Harris
Chris Livengood
Paula Lowell
Casey Price
Laura Robbins
Bobbi Satterfield
Ian Smith

Overview

Contents

Preface

The communication of information of all kinds by means of binary signals—the ones and zeros that are used by computers—has gained such an important place in American society that it is fair to say that successful operation of the U.S. economy would be impossible without it. Information sent using data communications controls a major portion of the long-distance telephone network, enables the rapid authorization of credit purchases and cashing of checks, and provides for the inventory and ordering of goods in stores of all kinds, from fast-food franchises to photo finishers. Data communications technology allows the simultaneous printing in widely separated cities of national magazines and newspapers, whose entire text and picture copy is transmitted from a central source to the city in which the publications are to be printed daily.

A basic knowledge of such a pervasive force in our lives is as necessary for all of us as is some knowledge of the working of the automobile. I have attempted to cover the basic principles of data communications and to explain those areas of application that have a daily impact: communications between terminals and computers, including local area networks and packet networks; communication of telephone conversations and control of the telephone network; and the use of light rays and satellites for carrying the ever-increasing volume of data that helps make our lives more comfortable and sometimes a great deal more confusing.

This book is arranged somewhat like a textbook. Each chapter starts by saying what it covers, ends by saying what has been covered, and provides a short multiple-choice quiz on the chapter's contents. Like other books in the series, this book builds understanding step-by-step. Try to master each chapter before going on to the next one.

If your objective is to obtain general information about the subject, you can bypass the more detailed portions of the text and the quiz. This will enable you to absorb the information more easily and, hopefully, enjoy the style of presentation. If you need more basic information about the telephone system and telephone electronics, a companion book in the series, titled *Understanding Telephone Electronics,* should be helpful. For more detailed and more advanced information about data communications, refer to the books listed in the bibliography.

G.H.

An Overview of Data Communications

About This Book

This book is intended to explain how data communications systems and their various hardware and software components work. It is not intended to tell you how to build the equipment, nor will it tell you how to write computer programs to transmit data between two computers. What it can give you is a basis for understanding data communications systems in general, as well as some tips for setting up your own system to communicate between your personal or professional computer and another personal computer, a database service, an information utility, an electronic bulletin board, or a computer connected to the Internet.

To understand data communications, you need to have some understanding of the telephone channel, because it is the medium used by most data communications systems to move information from one place to another. Therefore, part of this book is devoted to describing the public telephone network and the equipment used to interface between it and a computer.

About This Chapter

This chapter presents some history of data communications and a general description of a data communications system. Explanations of bits, bytes, two-state communications systems, and codes help lay the foundation for further discussions in the remainder of the book.

What Is Data Communications?

Data communica-
tions is often
referred to as
computer communi-
cations due to the
ever-increasing use
of computers and
their support
equipment.

Data communications is the process of communicating information in binary form between two or more points. Data communications is sometimes called computer communications because a majority of the information interchanged today is between computers, or between computers and their terminals, printers, or other peripheral devices. The data might be as elementary as the binary symbols 1 and 0, or as complex as the characters represented by the keys on a typewriter keyboard. In any case, the characters or symbols represent information.

The field of data communications represents one of the most rapidly evolving technologies. Through the use of specialized semiconductors developed to perform signal processing and data compression, various multimedia applications are evolving that orient data communications to the transport of voice, data, and video information. Within a few years, you will be able to select a video from your telephone company and access the Internet via your cable television operator. Thus, the traditional use of data communications as a transport for moving data between terminal devices and computers is evolving into a mechanism to move voice, data, and video.

Why Is Data Communications Important?

It is important for us to understand data communications because of its significance in today's world. Data communications is commonly used in the world of business, and it is being used more and more in homes as well. Whether it is the transmission of bank-account information from a central computer to a convenient electronic teller machine, the selection of a pay-per-view cable TV program, or the downloading of a video game from a computer bulletin board to a home computer's memory, data communications is becoming an integral part of our daily activities. In fact, for many readers, hardly a day goes by without their being the recipient of an activity performed or enhanced through the use of data communications. For example, many traffic lights are controlled via the transmission of signals from computer systems, and large retailers routinely transmit sales information that allows timely distribution of warehouse inventory to retail locations. Thus, the more modern a society, the more dependent that society is on data communications.

The First Data Communications Systems

Modern data communications involves the use of electrical or electronic apparatus to communicate information in the form of symbols and characters between two points. Because electricity, radio waves, and light waves are all forms of electromagnetic energy, it is stretching things only a bit to say that early forms of communication, such as the puffs of smoke from the Indian's signal fire (see Figure 1.1), or reflections of sunlight from a hand-held mirror, also were forms of the same type of data communications. To carry this idea further, think of the puffs of smoke as discrete symbols, just as the symbols used in today's communications systems are discrete.

FIGURE 1.1.

Looks like trouble ahead.

The first data communications did not rely on electricity.

Early Uses of Electricity

The discovery and harnessing of electricity introduced many new possibilities for communications codes beyond the smoke signals, mirrors, signal flags, and lanterns in use in the 18th and 19th centuries.

One of the early proposals, submitted to a Scottish magazine in 1753, was simple but had profound implications for hardware. This idea was to run 26 parallel wires from town to town, one wire for each letter of the alphabet. A Swiss inventor built a prototype system based on this 26-wire principle, but the technology of wire making at that time eliminated that idea from serious use.

In 1833, Carl Friedrich Gauss used a code based on a 5-by-5 matrix of 25 letters (*I* and *J* were combined) to send messages by deflecting a needle from one to five times, right or left. The first set of deflections indicated the row; the second, the column.

●
Originally, data communications depended on codes transmitted by visual systems such as mirrors, flags, and smoke. Electrical data communications systems transmit codes by switching electrical current.

The Telegraph

Samuel F.B. Morse perfected the telegraph, the first mass data communications system based on electric power.

The next notable development in data communications occurred in the 19th century when an American, Samuel F.B. Morse, invented the electric telegraph. Although other inventors had worked on the idea of using electricity to communicate, Morse's invention was by far the most important because he coupled the human mind (intelligence) with the communications equipment.

A basic telegraph system is diagrammed in Figure 1.2. When the telegraph key at station A was pressed, current flowed through the system, and the armature at station B was attracted to the coil, clicking as it struck the stop. When the key was released at station A, it opened the electrical circuit, and the armature of the sounder at station B was forced to its open position by a spring, striking the other stop with a slightly different click. Thus, the telegraph sounder had two distinctive clicks. If the time between successive clicks of the sounder was short, it represented a dot; if longer, a dash. Morse developed a code, similar to the one shown in Figure 1.3, to represent characters by a series of these dots and dashes. The transmitting operator converted the characters in the words of a message to be sent into a series of dots and dashes. The receiving operator interpreted those dots and dashes as characters; thus, the information was transmitted from point A to point B.

FIGURE 1.2.

The basic telegraph system.

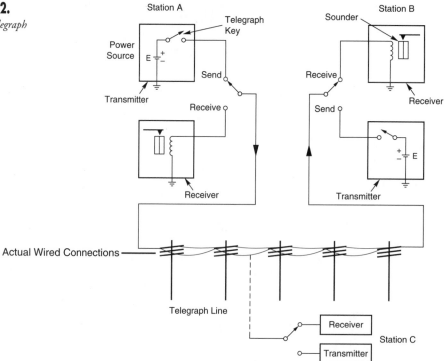

FIGURE 1.3.

International Morse code.

Telegraph Characters

Morse		Morse	
A	·—	T	—
B	—···	U	··—
C	—·—·	V	···—
D	—··	W	·——
E	·	X	—··—
F	··—·	Y	—·——
G	——·	Z	——··
H	····	,	——··——
I	··	.	·—·—·—
J	·———	1	·————
K	—·—	2	··———
L	·—··	3	···——
M	——	4	····—
N	—·	5	·····
O	———	6	—····
P	·——·	7	——···
Q	——·—	8	———··
R	·—·	9	————·
S	···	0	—————

Much of Morse termi-
nology is still in use
today.

When Morse developed his code, legend has it that he examined the quantity of type in boxes a typesetter used for storing English characters and digits. Morse assigned short codes to frequently occurring characters and digits, whereas he assigned longer codes to less frequently occurring characters and digits. This explains why a dot was assigned to the letter E, which is the most frequently occurring character in the English language, and a dash was assigned to the letter T, which is the second most frequently occurring character.

Morse first developed the telegraph in 1832, but it wasn't until much later that he successfully demonstrated its use. The best-known demonstration took place in 1844, when Morse transmitted, over a wire from Washington to Baltimore, the message "What hath God wrought!"

Because mail delivery by the Pony Express was the typical means of communication before the telegraph, the telegraph quickly became a success because of its much greater speed. The equipment was simple and rugged; the key and the sounder each contained only one moving part. Both the system's strength and its weakness (and its only real complexity) was the human mind—the transmitting and receiving operators. By the time of the Civil War, a telegraph line spanned the continent, crossing the prairies and deserts to connect California with the rest of the United States. It was from this historic technological breakthrough that the Western Union Telegraph Company made its legacy and indeed was named; its line connected the West with the Union. By the time the telephone was invented some 30 years later, the telegraph industry was large and prosperous, with many companies providing service to almost every city and town in the United States. In 1866, the telegraph connected the nations of the world with the laying of the trans-Atlantic cable between the United States and France.

●
The telegraph was the first electrically based communications system to connect the east and west coasts of the United States and both sides of the Atlantic.

Two-State Communications Systems

●

Much of the telegraph's terminology and many of the principles of operation are still used today. The most important of these principles is the two-state communications system.

The importance of the Morse telegraph is not just historical; it illustrates the simplicity of a complete data communications system. Much of the terminology that developed around the Morse system is still in use today. For example, consider the terms *mark* and *space*. If a device were arranged so that paper continually moved under a pen attached to the telegraph sounder armature, a mark would be made on the paper when the armature was attracted to the coil. Thus, we could refer to the state of current flow in the line as the marking state, and the state of no current flow in the line as the spacing state. Worldwide standards for data communications today still use the terms mark and space, with the idle condition on the transmission channel called the marking condition.

The wire (telegraph channel) between the operators, therefore, is in one of two states: current is flowing, or it is not. This illustrates a simple idea that has been repeated over and over again in the development of data communications systems. A two-state communications system is the simplest, the easiest to build, and the most reliable. The two states can be on and off (as in the telegraph), plus and minus (with current flowing in opposite directions), light and dark (as in turning a flashlight on and off to send code), 1 and 0 (the concept used in the computer), or some other design with only two possible values. A two-state or two-valued system is referred to as a binary system.

Bits and Bytes

●

Transmission codes in the binary system are made up of digits called bits. Each bit can have one of two possible states (high or low, on or off). Several bits combined in a uniform group are called a byte.

The numbers 0 and 1 are the symbols of the binary system. A binary digit is commonly referred to as a bit. The individual line changes in digital data (like the mark and space) are called bits, and each bit is assigned a value of 0 or 1.

The binary system uses positional notation, just as the familiar decimal system does, except that each position has only 2 possible values, rather than 10. For example, the number 345.27 in decimal means three hundreds plus four tens plus five ones plus two tenths plus seven hundredths. The weight of each position is a power of 10, thus:

$$345.27 = (3 \times 100) + (4 \times 10) + (5 \times 1) + (2 \times 1/10) + (7 \times 1/100)$$
$$= 3 \times 10^2 + 4 \times 10^1 + 5 \times 10^0 + 2 \times 10^{-1} + 7 \times 10^{-2}$$

Note the use of positive and negative exponents, and remember the definition that any number raised to the zero power is equal to 1. In the decimal system, as shown by the preceding example, 10 is the base, and the weight of each digit position is a power of 10.

Similarly, we can define powers of two in the binary positional system, in which the weight of each position is two times the weight of the one to the immediate right. A table of powers of two can be quite useful when you're dealing with binary numbers because most of us don't want to memorize them. Table 1.1 is such a table for powers of 2 up to 2^8, which will be sufficient for this book. Using this table makes it easy to convert a binary number to its decimal equivalent. For example:

```
1101001 = 1 x 2⁶ + 1 x 2⁵ + 0 x 2⁴ + 1 x 2³ + 0 x 2² + 0 x 2¹ + 1 x 2⁰
        = 64 + 32 + 0 + 8 + 0 + 0 + 1
        = 105 decimal
```

Table 1.1. The powers of two.

Power of Two	Positional Weight	9-Bit Binary Number
2^0	1	000000001
2^1	2	000000010
2^2	4	000000100
2^3	8	000001000
2^4	16	000010000
2^5	32	000100000
2^6	64	001000000
2^7	128	010000000
2^8	256	100000000

Computers are more efficient if their internal paths and registers are some power of two in length (2 bits, 4 bits, 8 bits, 16 bits, and so on). A commonly used grouping is 8 bits, and this 8-bit group is called a byte or an octet. From Table 1.1, you can see that a byte can represent 2^8, or 256, unique sequences of ones and zeros.

Communications Codes

A common characteristic of data communications systems is the use of an intelligent device to convert a character or symbol into coded form and vice versa. In the Morse system, the intelligent "devices" were the telegraph operators who converted the characters into dots and dashes.

Skilled telegraph operators were always in short supply, and the work was difficult and exhausting. An electrical or mechanical means of coding the characters was therefore needed. However, it was essentially impossible to automate the transmitting and receiving operations because of the varying duration of the dots and dashes in the Morse code and the fact that the codes for the characters were made up of different quantities of dots and dashes. Therefore, a code that had the same number of equal-duration signaling elements for each character was needed.

⬤
The use of simplified and standardized binary codes allowed information to be encoded and decoded by mechanical or electrical means and made it possible to automate data communications.

Some Definitions

A code is a previously agreed-on set of meanings that define a given set of symbols and characters.

Before we go any further, let's establish the following definitions in order to discuss communications codes:

Codes: Standard (agreed-on-in-advance) interpretations between signaling elements and characters. The key idea is *standard*. The codes used in data communications systems are already defined, and the code set is built into the equipment. About the only time the user might need to deal with codes is when interfacing two machines (such as computers and printers) from different manufacturers.

Characters are the letters, signs, and symbols on an input device's keyboard; some are used to control the system.

Characters: The letters, numerals, spaces, punctuation marks, and other signs and symbols on a keyboard. (Remember that the space character is just as important as any other, even though we tend to think of it as "nothing" or "blank.") For example, "A 7#" is a sequence of four characters. Communication systems also use control characters that do not print, but these characters also must be coded. Some of these control characters (such as Carriage Return or Tab) are also on a keyboard, but many are not.

Signaling elements are the representations of characters that are transmitted over transmission lines. It is easier to design and build machines to recognize signaling elements than to build them to recognize characters.

Signaling Elements: Something that is sent over a transmission channel and used to represent a character. The dots and dashes (or marks and spaces) of the Morse code are signaling elements, as are the ones and zeros in this sequence:

```
01000001010 0000001011 0111011011 0110001001
```

This is the way "A 7#" might look when transmitted between a personal computer and another computer or printer. You will see later that the code is ASCII, with even parity and one start and one stop bit.

The definitions for characters and signaling elements illustrate why machines and people need different ways to represent information. People quickly and reliably recognize printed characters by their distinctive shapes, but that is difficult and expensive for a machine to do. On the other hand, machines can easily handle long strings of two-valued signaling elements such as marks and spaces or ones and zeros, but that is hard for a person to accomplish with any accuracy.

Baudot Code

Emile Baudot developed one of the more successful codes suited for machine encoding and decoding. It was limited, however, because it used only five signaling elements per character.

As stated before, the Morse code was unsuitable for machine encoding and decoding because of the problems caused by the varying lengths of the codes for the characters. Early in the 20th century, when interest developed in replacing human telegraph operators with machines, several suitable codes already existed. The most prominent of these had been invented in the 1870s by a Frenchman named Emile Baudot. Because Baudot's code, similar to the one shown in Figure 1.4, used the same number of signaling elements (marks and spaces) to represent each character, it was better suited to machine encoding and decoding.

Code Signals (• Denotes Positive Current)							LTRS Shift	FIGS Shift	
Start	1	2	3	4	5	Stop		CCITT Standard International Telegraph Alphabet No. 2 Used for Telex	North American Teletype Commercial Keyboard
	•	•				•	A	—	—
	•			•	•	•	B	?	?
		•	•	•		•	C	:	:
	•			•		•	D	Who Are You?	$
	•					•	E	3	3
	•		•	•		•	F	Note 1	!
		•		•	•	•	G	Note 1	&
			•		•	•	H	Note 1	#
		•	•			•	I	8	8
	•	•		•		•	J	Bell	Bell
	•	•	•	•		•	K	(	(
		•			•	•	L	)	)
			•	•	•	•	M	.	.
			•	•		•	N	,	,
				•	•	•	O	9	9
		•	•		•	•	P	0	0
	•	•	•		•	•	Q	1	1
		•		•		•	R	4	4
	•		•			•	S	'	'
					•	•	T	5	5
	•	•	•			•	U	7	7
		•	•	•	•	•	V	=	;
	•	•			•	•	W	2	2
	•		•	•	•	•	X	/	/
	•		•		•	•	Y	6	6
	•				•	•	Z	+	"
						•		Blank	
	•	•	•	•	•	•		Letters Shift (LTRS)	
	•	•		•	•	•		Figures Shift (FIGS)	
			•			•		Space	
				•		•		Carriage Return	
		•				•		Line Feed	

Notes:
1. Not allocated internationally; available to each country for internal use.

FIGURE 1.4.

Five-level teleprinter code.

Unfortunately, the number of signaling elements was limited to five by problems in timing the electromechanical devices. The five-bit code could generate only 32 possible combinations, not enough to represent the 26 characters of the alphabet, the 10 decimal digits, the punctuation marks, and the space character. To overcome this limitation, Baudot used two shift-control characters—the letters (LTRS) shift and the figures (FIGS) shift—to enable the code set to represent all the characters that seemed necessary at the time. The shift codes do not represent printable characters; instead, they select one of two character sets, each composed of 26 to 28 characters.

Receipt of the letters shift code (11111) causes all following codes to be interpreted as letters of the alphabet; receipt of the figures shift code (11011) causes all the following characters to be interpreted as numerals and punctuation marks. Notice that the LTRS and FIGS codes, as well as the other control codes and the space character, always have the same interpretation no matter which shift mode the machine is in. Although Baudot's invention did not immediately revolutionize telegraphy (because of the difficulty that human operators had in sending equal-length codes), it did provide a basis for the later development of the teleprinter.

Modern Codes

There was a need for new codes that could represent all characters, check for errors, and leave room for further expansion.

The Baudot code and variations of it were the backbone of communications for almost half a century, but they clearly left much to be desired. Persons in the newspaper industry found the lack of differentiation between upper- and lowercase letters to be a problem. They devised a six-level code to designate the difference between upper- and lowercase letters. This was just one example of general need; modern communications required a code that could represent all printable characters and still leave room for error checking and format operations. Concerning format operations, a code should support linefeed and carriage-return characters, as well as formfeed and horizontal and vertical tabulation, because the use of those characters enables terminal operations to be conveyed as they occur. The code had to enable decoding without reliance on correct reception of previous transmissions, and also had to enable decoding by machine. Perhaps most important of all, the new code needed to be expandable.

During the 1960s, various data transmission codes were developed. Most of these have fallen by the wayside, leaving three predominant codes: a single five-bit code (CCITT International Alphabet No. 2), still used for telex transmission; the Extended Binary-Coded-Decimal Interchange Code (EBCDIC, pronounced "eb-see-dik"), developed by IBM and primarily used for synchronous communication in systems attached to large mainframe computers; and the American Standard Code for Information Interchange (ASCII, pronounced "as-key"), defined by the American National Standards Institute (ANSI) in the United States and by the International Organization for Standardization (ISO) worldwide.

EBCDIC

EBCDIC is a modern code using eight bits to represent 256 characters. It was developed by IBM to provide a standard code for its own products.

When a clear need arises for standardization, standards come into existence in two ways. In one way, a single manufacturer (especially a dominant one) can define a standard for its own products, and the rest of the industry can follow. This is what IBM did. It created the EBCDIC eight-bit code, enabling 256 characters to be represented. The world would probably be better off if EBCDIC had become the standard, because it included enough unique characters to allow almost any representation. However, only IBM and firms that build IBM-compatible equipment adopted EBCDIC. Because EBCDIC is primarily used in large IBM-compatible computing systems, it is not used in most of the examples in this book.

ASCII

The other, more common method of creating a standard is through a committee, which serves as a forum for examination of needs, discussion between interested parties, and compromise. This process produced the ASCII seven-bit code, formally known as ANSI Standard X3.4-1977. ASCII can depict 128 characters, but not all of them represent printed symbols. Included in the character set are all the letters of the English alphabet (both uppercase and lowercase), the numerals 0–9, punctuation marks, and many symbols. This standard code set is used in virtually all small computers and their peripherals, as well as in large computers in most of the world.

● ANSI developed the seven-bit ASCII data communications code that is in general use today. It can represent 128 characters.

A variation of ASCII, commonly referred to as "extended ASCII," gained wide acceptance with the introduction of the IBM Personal Computer of 1981. The IBM PC supports an eight-bit code, with the first seven positions supporting the ANSI standard. The additional bit position extends the computer's ASCII, enabling an additional 128 characters to be represented. This extension enables software developers to use extended codes for such functions as end-of-paragraph markings and bold printing indicators in a word processing system.

Figure 1.5 shows the ANSI standard ASCII characters and their associated codes. Compare this chart to the Morse code in Figure 1.3 and the five-bit teleprinter code in Figure 1.4. The Morse code had a varying number of elements (dots and dashes) for each character and was quite restricted—only letters, numerals, and a few punctuation marks. The five-bit code had a constant number of elements and a few more special characters, but it still couldn't distinguish between upper- and lowercase letters.

● The ASCII format is arranged so that lowercase letters can be changed to uppercase by changing only one bit. Bits 4 through 7 of the numeric characters also are the BCD value of the number.

ASCII not only has upper- and lowercase, but also has a great deal of regularity that might not be readily apparent. For example, to convert any uppercase alphabetic character (A through Z) to lowercase, it is necessary only to change bit 6 from zero to one! Another feature is that bits 4 through 7 of the numeric characters (0, 1, 2, 3, 4, 5, 6, 7, 8, and 9) are the binary-coded-decimal (BCD) value of the character. Another advantage of standard ASCII is that 128 different characters can be represented by the seven bits used in the code, rather than only 32 characters from the five-bit code.

The two leftmost character columns in the chart of Figure 1.5 represent the nonprinting control characters that can be used to control the operation of the receiving device. For example, the control codes for carriage return (CR) and linefeed (LF), which are commonly used on a typewriter, are shown. Other control codes include formfeed (FF), bell (BEL), horizontal tab (HT), and vertical tab (VT). These control codes were designed for printing or display devices, although some manufacturers have used the control codes for all manner of special functions. Also, some codes control how a receiving device will interpret subsequent codes in a multiple-character function or command. Two shift characters, called Shift In (SI) and Shift Out (SO), are used to shift between ASCII and character sets other than those used in English. ANSI standards X3.41-1974 and X3.64-1979 expand the definition of the escape (ESC) control code for even greater flexibility. Other

● ASCII also has several control codes that, in addition to their defined control functions, have been used by some manufacturers to represent specialized functions.

control codes delimit text, such as start of text (STX) and end of text (ETX). These codes are used primarily in block or synchronous data transmission. You'll see more of them in later chapters.

FIGURE 1.5.

American Standard Code for Information Interchange (ASCII).

Nonprintable Control Characters

Sample of Control Characters (Bold)
STX=Start of Text
EOT=End of Transmission
CR=Carriage Return
HT=Horizontal Tabulation

Examples:
1000011=C
0110011=3
1010000=P
0110000=0 (Zero)
0100000=SP (space)

The Escape Character

Escape sequences are code sequences made up of noncontrol characters that are to be interpreted as control codes.

The escape (ESC) character designates that the codes that follow have special meaning. Characters received in an escape sequence are not interpreted as printing characters, but as control information to extend the range of the "standard" character set by allowing other definitions. The escape character has the effect of making all character codes available for control of a device. Graphics characters, foreign-language character sets, and special applications sets have been developed that are accessible via escape character sequences; thus, they allow for a much richer variety of displayed symbols than is otherwise normally possible.

The CRT terminal and later the personal computer monitor are two hardware devices that have benefited most from the escape sequence. The serial communications link to these terminals and personal computers is the same as for a teleprinter, and ordinarily, any characters received via this channel are displayed on the terminal or monitor screen, as expected. But the people who developed the ASCII standard did not foresee (thus did not make provision for) capabilities for character and line deletion and display enhancements that are available on the CRT terminal and computer monitors, such as inverse video, under-lining, and blinking. Unfortunately, little standardization of these sequences existed until the ANSI X3.64 standard came out in 1979. Before then, and without standardization, designers felt free to exercise their creativity. For example, one major feature now found on most video display terminals is absolute cursor positioning. The computer can send a command to the terminal that places the cursor anywhere on the screen. This capability is important for many types of form-filling operations. Unfortunately, there are almost as many escape sequences to do cursor positioning as there are terminal manufacturers. Even different models in a manufacturer's line might use different escape sequences to perform the same action.

The result of this "creativity" with the character set is that some manufacturers' equip-ment will not operate correctly with that of most of the rest of the world. An example is a printer that automatically inserts a linefeed after receiving a carriage return. Because most computers send both a carriage return and a linefeed in response to only a carriage return input, the printout will not be spaced as desired because of the extra linefeed supplied by the printer.

To promote compatibility, many terminal and personal computer manufacturers provide implicit or explicit support of the ANSI standard. Explicit support of that standard in-cludes those terminals and personal computers designed explicitly to support the ANSI X3.64 standard. Implicit support is provided by terminals and personal computers that have the capability to load a program and read the contents of a predefined memory area or memory cartridge to enable support of the ANSI X3.64 standard.

Perhaps the most commonly available device capable of supporting the ANSI X3.64 stan-dard is the IBM PC and compatible personal computers. Those computers, which use the Microsoft MS-DOS or PC DOS operating system, can be configured to use device driver ANSI.SYS. ANSI.SYS is a file on the operating system diskette that will be loaded into memory during subsequent startups after it's specified. On most MS-DOS or PC DOS computers with a hard drive, you would add the statement `DEVICE = C:\DOS\ANSI.SYS` to your CONFIG.SYS file to automatically execute the ANSI.SYS device driver on a power-on or system reset, assuming that it is stored under the DOS directory on drive C. The execution of that file results in the personal computer becoming an ANSI-compatible ter-minal, including support for standardized escape code sequences.

Teleprinters

The teleprinter was the next major step after the telegraph in data communications. Tele-printer equipment has been the backbone of nonvoice business communications for over half a century. As recently as the mid-1970s, a teletypewriter (TTY), which is a teleprinter with a keyboard for input, was the standard terminal for small and medium-sized com-puters. Many companies had nationwide and even worldwide private teleprinter networks, although the fax machine and public and private computer-based electronic mail systems

●
The technology and techniques used in teleprinting have provided the basis for asynchronous data communica-tions.

resulted in most of those networks being replaced by more modern technology. Two nationwide public teleprinter networks are the TWX and TELEX services; TWX was merged into TELEX during the 1980s. Several common carriers will transmit telex messages to any teleprinter in the United States, and companies called "international record carriers" will deliver them to any teleprinter in the world. A company's telex number can be found in a directory similar to a telephone directory.

Like the telegraph, teleprinters are important not only in their own right because they were the principal data communications method for almost 50 years, but also because most of the standards and terminology for low-speed or asynchronous data communications came from the world of teleprinters. We'll discuss asynchronous transmission more thoroughly in Chapter 2, "Terminal Devices." For now, it is sufficient to realize that the transmission of each coded character begins with a "start" symbol and ends with a "stop" symbol. Although this technique permitted synchronization of teleprinter equipment thousands of miles apart, it also added to the already high overhead (in terms of extra time) required for transmission of each character.

Teleprinter equipment was inherently limited to slow transmission speeds because it was electromechanical: Solenoids had to be energized to attract armatures; motors had to start, turn, and stop; and clutches had to engage and disengage. All of these mechanical operations limited the maximum speed at which teleprinters could operate reliably to fewer than 30 characters per second. International telex operates even slower—fewer than 10 characters per second! Either speed is much too slow for a computer to communicate efficiently with another computer, or even with a modern printer or CRT terminal.

Data Communications in Computing

The introduction of the electronic computer provided greater speed and capabilities to the data communications system.

Further improvements in data communications were necessitated by the widespread use of electronic computers, introduced in the early 1950s. These computer systems were capable of storing large quantities of information and processing it quickly. Input and output equipment was much improved over the teletypewriter and teleprinter, so it could operate much faster. As more computers were used, it became necessary for computers to communicate with each other. Because this communication did not need any electromechanical equipment, data transfer theoretically could occur at extremely fast rates. Practically, however, data transfer rates are limited by the transmission medium—primarily the public telephone network.

The 1950s

The typical computer system of the 1950s, shown in Figure 1.6, used punched cards for input, printers for output, and reels of magnetic tape for "permanent" mass storage. There was little or no data communications in these systems because the input devices, output devices, and computer were all located close together and were directly connected by short cables. Information was processed on a "one job at a time" or "batch" basis.

FIGURE 1.6.

A typical data processing system of the 1950s.

For example, a wholesale grocery company would receive orders by mail and telephone during the day. At the end of the day, these would be collected and punched into cards, which were then assembled as a batch. The data on the cards were read into the computer for processing at night. During the processing, the computer would do such things as check the customer's credit. If the credit was satisfactory, the computer would generate a pick list for the warehouse so that the order could be filled and shipped the next day. The quantity ordered for the different types of items would be deducted from the quantity on hand, and the invoices and various warehouse tickets would be printed. This system worked well except that the person taking the order from the customer during the day, whether on the phone or at the customer's premises, was never certain whether the ordered items were available in the warehouse. Although an updated inventory report was available each morning, a running inventory was not kept during the day as orders were received.

●

The first computer systems had little need for data communications because they were located close together, input/ output was usually direct, and information was processed in discrete batches.

The 1960s

Batch processing systems such as the one just described are the most efficient in the use of computer time and equipment. They are relatively inefficient, however, in the use of the order clerks, salespeople, and other resources of the company. While the costs of employing people were increasing, the solid-state revolution caused the cost of computer logic and memory to decrease sharply. This meant that companies could invest in more computer equipment to reduce the costs of personnel, as well as to make themselves more competitive in business.

●

In the 1960s, the use of outlying, online terminals required communications links to connect them to the main computer.

In the 1960s, batch processing was largely replaced by online processing (see Figure 1.7). In the example of the wholesale grocery company, the clerks took the orders over the phone and used online terminals to enter the orders into the computer at the same time. Some of these terminals were directly connected to the computer by parallel communication channels, but many of the terminals were teleprinter devices that used serial data communications over dedicated private cables to the computer.

FIGURE 1.7.

A typical data processing system of the 1960s.

As the order was entered, the computer checked the inventory to see whether the goods were on hand. If so, the customer was given a delivery date; if not, he was told that the goods were out of stock and was given the option of placing a back order or selecting another item. Although more expensive than batch processing in terms of computer time and equipment, this method of doing business made the wholesale grocery company more competitive because it gave the customer better service.

The 1970s

In the 1970s, the introduction of the minicomputer and the very portable microcomputer required that these units have increased communications with their mainframe computer.

The 1970s changed this process still further (see Figure 1.8). Other computers, sometimes called minicomputers, could communicate with the larger computer in the wholesale grocer's central office. The online order terminals were not necessarily in the room next to the computer; they were sometimes on a different floor, in a different building, or even in a different city. Toward the end of the decade, even smaller computers, called microcomputers or personal computers, began to be seen not only in the homes of some of the employees, but also on their desks at the office. Sometimes the employees would communicate with the main computer through these smaller computers. The company salesmen began carrying portable computer terminals with them on their sales calls. They could enter their orders from the customers' offices directly into the main computer over a standard telephone line.

FIGURE 1.8.
A typical data processing system of the 1970s.

True data communications was everywhere in the system. There was more equipment around than anyone would have thought possible in the 1950s—more computers, more terminals, more communications channels—and businesses were run more efficiently because of it.

The 1980s

As the wholesale grocery company grew, it decided to produce some of the food products that it sold, so it set up producing operations in California, Texas, and Florida. Because its wholesale business is primarily in the northeast, it has major warehouse facilities in New Jersey, Pennsylvania, and Ohio, and sales offices in Chicago, Philadelphia, and New York City. The company headquarters is also in New York City.

With the expansion to the south and west, the company's data communications system also needed expansion. The company decided to use the relatively new satellite communications to tie the New York office with the Texas and California operations. (Satellite communications are discussed in later chapters.) The satellite could be used for other points as well, but the company (for various reasons) uses leased terrestrial circuits to the Florida, Chicago, and Philadelphia sites. The smaller sales offices in the states where the company operates are tied together with a network of low-speed teletypewriter-like terminals that allow order entry and some communication with the home office. The company's salesmen still carry portable terminals, but advances in technology have reduced the size of the terminal while increasing its capabilities. A typical terminal is shown in Figure 1.9.

●
Advances in technology increased the capabilities of computers, reduced the size and power requirements of computers, and provided a new communications link—the satellite.

FIGURE 1.9.
A TI 703KSR teleprinter.

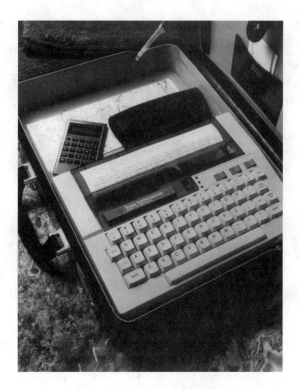

As low-cost personal computers became more widely available during the mid-1980s, many managers acquired them for departmental use. Although the original intention was to use the local processing capability of personal computers for such tasks as budgeting with spreadsheet programs and word processing, corporate managements quickly began to integrate personal computers into their company communications networks. Some personal computers replaced CRT terminals and served as both terminals and local processing devices. Other PCs were linked into a local area network (LAN), which enabled users to share peripheral devices and provided the capability of sending electronic messages to other users on the network.

Introduced in mid-1981, more than 10 million IBM PC and compatible computers had been manufactured by 1987, when the Personal System/2 Model 30 computer replaced the IBM PC. Figure 1.10 illustrates the major components of an IBM PC computer system. Today, the personal computer is as prevalent in many organizations as was the office typewriter.

FIGURE 1.10.
An IBM PC system.

The 1990s

The growth in the distribution of personal computers throughout organizations during the 1980s was linked to a requirement to provide communications capability between these devices. In addition, many personal computer uses required access to corporate mini- and mainframe computers, further increasing requirements for communications between different types of computers.

For the grocery company previously discussed, personal computers were installed in the sales offices in Chicago, Philadelphia, and New York City. The PCs were initially used for various functions ranging from what-if computations using spreadsheets to word processing and the maintenance of small databases of sales and marketing information. Eventually, however, it was recognized that productivity could be increased by providing a capability for various PC users within each office to communicate with one another. Through the installation of an appropriate adapter card in each personal computer (see Figure 1.10), as well as cabling and software, local area networks were installed in each sales office. This specialized type of network enabled persons within a building or campus to communicate with one another, share peripheral devices such as laser printers and plotters, and share access to common software programs and database information residing on special types of personal computers known as file servers.

As the grocery company continued to grow, it was recognized that LANs were essentially islands of information isolated from one another. Commencing in the late 1980s and gaining momentum in the 1990s, vendors introduced several internetworking products consisting of software and hardware that enabled diverse LANs to be connected to one another and information to flow between devices connected to one another and between devices connected to different LANs and other computer systems. Taking advantage of this technology, the wholesale grocery company installed devices known as gateways, bridges, and routers.

Gateways

Gateways enabled personal computers on selected LANs to access a corporate mainframe computer. Here the corporate mainframe acted as a central repository for large databases and intensive computing programs that are not suitable for execution on personal computers. For example, database information, including inventory, customer accounts, and historical ordering and pricing information, could require billions of characters of storage, whereas most personal computers are limited to hundreds of millions of characters of storage. Concerning intensive computing applications, the grocery company now used the mainframe for execution of linear programs that optimize delivery schedules based on an analysis of thousands of variables. Although personal computer users can access the linear programming results produced on the mainframe via gateways, the execution of this type of program on a personal computer might require 10 or 20 hours, whereas the execution might take 15 minutes when performed on a mainframe.

Bridges

Bridges enable data to be transmitted between two LANs, allowing electronic messages, data files, and programs to be sent between users on different networks. A bridge examines the destination address of data flowing on a LAN to determine whether its destination is on that LAN. If it is, the bridge simply functions as a transparent device and allows the data to continue to flow on the LAN to its destination. If the data destination is a different LAN, the bridge then transmits the data via a communications facility to a distant LAN, where another bridge functions in a similar manner.

Routers

With a need to add automation to the company's warehouse facilities, also served through the installation of LANs, sales personnel on occasion needed to access information from personal computers connected to warehouse LANs. In fact, the number of LANs installed within the grocery company would have required the establishment of a mesh network with many long-distance lines if only bridges were used. Fortunately, the development of routers, which examine data destination addresses and route data over different circuits based on those addresses, enabled a smaller number of lines to be used for interconnecting many LANs.

Figure 1.11 illustrates in a block diagram format the relationship of bridges, routers, and gateways for internetworking. In this example, a pair of bridges interconnects two sales office LANs, and a router is used to provide a link from one LAN to many warehouse

LANs. The gateway provides a mechanism that enables LAN users to access the mainframe computer. In fact, when sophisticated hardware and software are used, it might be possible for a PC user attached to the LAN at the top of Figure 1.11 to be "bridged" to the second LAN and provided, via the gateway, access to the mainframe—a key goal of internetworking. As we move toward the year 2000, we can reasonably expect that this broad term that defines the connection of diverse equipment and network facilities will represent the method by which organizations integrate their data transmission requirements.

FIGURE 1.11.

Internetworking using bridges, routers, and gateways.

Although the use of LANs by business, government, and academia represents one of the fastest growing areas in the field of data communications, a second rapidly expanding area concerns the use of the personal computer as a multifunctional terminal. In this role, the addition of hardware and software turns the PC into a LAN workstation, a conventional mainframe computer terminal, a fax machine, or another type of communications device. Through the use of modern graphical user interface (GUI) operating systems, such as Microsoft's Windows and IBM's OS/2, you can readily switch from one application to another and, in the case of Windows 95 and OS/2, execute two or more applications simultaneously due to the multitasking capability supported by each operating system. For example, under OS/2, you can execute a spreadsheet program while transmitting or receiving a fax.

The key to the capability of the personal computer to function as a multipurpose terminal was the development of specialized microprocessors and integrated circuits. This technology enabled functions that previously required tens to hundreds of individual computer chips to be performed by one chip or a few chips. This in turn enabled vendors to design adapter cards for insertion into an expansion slot in the system unit of a personal computer, which added the functionality of a standalone device to the PC. Figure 1.12 shows a modem/fax adapter card that enables a personal computer to transmit and receive faxes as well as communicate with other computers, bulletin board systems, and information utilities when used as a data modem.

FIGURE 1.12.

A fax/modem adapter card for insertion into a PC. (Courtesy of Practical Peripherals, Inc.)

Changes in the Industries

● Besides affecting the technological revolution, the breakup of the Bell System changed the way business used and paid for communications.

The hardware and software are not the only things changing. Both the computer industry and the communications industry have changed in ways that would have been unimaginable 20 years ago. The rise of the minicomputer, and later the microprocessor in personal computers, and programmable controllers for equipment created a situation in which computing power was rather inexpensive. The suppliers of mainframe computers, such as IBM, UNISYS, and Amdahl, were joined by companies such as Texas Instruments, Apple, AST, Compaq, Dell, and Hewlett-Packard that had not previously made computers. With many more computers used by many more people to create and use much more data, interest in data communications increased. In communications, the advent of satellites followed by optical-fiber transmission offered the promise of far greater bandwidths (range of usable frequencies), thus, faster data transmission speeds.

Due to advances in the miniaturization of portable computer components, modern note-book computers can be obtained with 300MB disk storage, a color display, and commu-nications support in a package weighing less than four pounds. Fitting into an attaché case, modern notebooks have significantly enhanced the ability of executives, salespersons, stu-dents, and teachers to work at home and when traveling, as well as to obtain access to information utilities and corporate networks. For the grocery company previously discussed, sales personnel can now visit clients and check on the status of inventory, place orders, and confirm product shipments during a sales call. Although most notebook computers have a limited expansion capability through the use of a PC Card slot, several vendors recognized the requirements of notebook computer users to communicate both when trav-eling and when in the office.

Figure 1.13 illustrates a combination Ethernet adapter and a data/fax modem, fabricated as a PC Card designed for insertion into a PC Card slot built into most modern notebook computers. Through the use of this type of combination adapter, mobile communications are significantly enhanced. The grocery salesperson, after communicating via the use of the modem portion of the adapter when visiting clients, can return to the office and then connect his notebook to the corporate Ethernet local area network.

FIGURE 1.13.

A combination Ethernet and data/fax modem fabricated on a PC Card for insertion into a PC Card slot commonly built into modern notebook computers. (Courtesy of Xircom, Inc.)

The revolution in computing and data transmission was paralleled by an upheaval in the structure of the communications industry. The telephone company's monopoly of almost a century disappeared forever, beginning in the late 1960s and accelerating until the Bell System was broken up in 1984. For the first time, not only could other firms compete with the telephone companies in offering long-distance service, but they also could sell equipment, including data communications devices, to be connected to the telephone network.

These two forces, the advent of the microprocessor-based personal computer and the increase in competition in both the computing and the communications industries, brought about dramatic changes and accelerated technological advances in the communications field. They also brought communications and computing closer together. In the example wholesale grocery company of the 1980s, it is hard to say where communications stops and computing begins. Are the salesperson's portable terminal and the manager's personal computer communications devices or are they computers? The answer, of course, is that they are both, because they do whatever combination of tasks is required for the job at hand.

●

The merging of voice, video, and data into computer-based applications requires the transmission of information several orders of magnitudes beyond text-based data, providing the driving force for the development of high-speed communications.

By examining current and evolving computer-based applications, we can predict to a fair degree of accuracy future developments in communications. For example, in a LAN environment, many organizations are replacing mainframe computers through the use of client-server applications, a process referred to as downsizing. In addition, these organizations are adding graphical applications in the form of images stored within a database; using multimedia for training employees in which voice, data, and video are merged for instruction; and using digitized voice messages to add verbal information to electronic mail.

Each of these emerging applications has one common feature: a requirement to transmit and store information many orders of magnitude above what conventional text-based applications require. Thus, a screen filled with text data is represented by 80×24 or 1920 eight-bit characters, whereas an image on a VGA monitor that is displayed in a resolution of 640×350 pixels in 256 colors would require 640×350×8/8 bits per byte, or 224,000 characters of storage. This means that the transmission of the previously described image would require more than 100 times the time for the transmission of a screen of text data. Because people's patience cannot be expected to grow by a factor of 100 as applications use images and as digitized audio and video are developed, you can reasonably predict the development of new types of communications systems to accommodate emerging computer-based applications.

In fact, this is exactly what is happening in both local and wide-area networking. Concerning LANs, the introduction of Fiber Distributed Data Interface (FDDI), Fast Ethernet, and VG-AnyLAN enabled organizations to construct LANs that operate at 100 Mbps, in comparison to the current popular operating rates of 10 Mbps for Ethernet LANs and 16 Mbps for token-ring LANs. In the wide-area networking environment, which can be defined as the infrastructure that connects geographically separated areas, a new technology referred to as Asynchronous Transfer Mode (ATM) is expected to be widely available by the year 2000. ATM is designed to transport voice, data, and video at operating rates of up to 2.488 Gbps.

In modern computer-communications systems, we can interconnect equipment of many different sizes and capabilities from various suppliers. One of the purposes of this book is to explain how to interconnect, or interface, these different kinds of equipment so that they all work together in a system.

A General Description of a Data Communications System

A data communications system can be described simply in terms of three components: the transmitter (also called the source), the transmission path (usually called the channel, but sometimes called the line), and the receiver (occasionally called the sink). In two-way communications, however, the source and the sink can interchange roles; that is, the same piece of equipment can transmit and receive data simultaneously. Therefore, it is easier to think of a data communications system between point A and point B (see Figure 1.14) in terms of the Universal Seven-Part Data Circuit, which consists of the following parts:

●
The most accurate way to separate a data communications system's parts is in terms of the Universal Seven-Part Data Circuit.

- The data terminal equipment (DTE) at point A.
- The interface between the DTE and the data circuit-terminating equipment or data communications equipment (DCE) at point A.
- The DCE at point A.
- The transmission channel between point A and point B.
- The DCE at point B.
- The DCE-DTE interface at point B.
- The DTE at point B.

a. Block Diagram

FIGURE 1.14.
The Universal Seven-Part Data Circuit.

b. Pictorial

In the Seven-Part Data Circuit, the DTE can be a terminal device or computer part; the DCE can be a modem if an analog channel is used or a Data Service Unit (DSU) if a digital channel is used.

The function of the various parts of the data communications system, both hardware and software, now can be described more easily. The DTE is the source, the sink, or both in the system. It transmits and/or receives data by utilizing the DCE and data transmission channel. Don't be misled by the name "data terminal equipment"; these could indeed be CRT or Teletype terminals, but they also might be personal computers, printers, front-end processors for mainframe computers, or any other device that can transmit or receive data. The whole purpose of the data communications system is to transmit useful information between point A and point B; the information can be used directly by the DTE, or the DTE can process and display the information for use by human operators.

The Form and Content of Information

The data communications system is concerned only with the correct transmission of data, in its coded form, between two points.

The DCE and the transmission channel perform the function of moving the data from point A to point B. In general, they neither know nor care about the content of the information transmitted; it could be stock market quotations, a display for a video game, or recipes for Aunt Martha's fudge.

This brings us to an important point about data communications—the difference between the form and the content of the information transmitted. The form of the information might be English language text represented by code for a telegram; the content might advise you that a rich uncle has just left you a million dollars. Clearly, the ordinary user of data communications is much more interested in the content of the information and really is not concerned about the mechanics of the communications process as long as the information is received correctly. It would be rather disappointing if, in fact, your uncle had left you only $100.00, but because of errors in transmission, the telegram you received stated that you had inherited $1,000,000.00.

The data communications system itself is concerned only with the correct transmission between points A and B of the information given it; the system does not operate on the content of the information at all. This means that where I talk about the "correctness" of the transmitted information in this book, I mean only that the information received has the identical form of the information transmitted. If someone gave a message to the telegraph operator stating that your uncle had left you a million dollars when he had left you only a hundred dollars, the inaccuracy of that information would probably not be the fault of the telegraph operator or the data communications equipment.

Protocol is the name given to the hardware and software rules and procedures for making sure that any transmission errors are detected. These might be as simple as transmitting an extra bit of information in each character to detect errors, as used with personal computers, or as complex as some systems use for satellite data communications. The satellite system sends extra information not only to allow the receiver to detect transmission errors, but also to correct the errors and to make the receiver appear to be in the room next to the DTE, rather than about 50,000 transmission miles away.

The DTE-DCE Interface

The DTE-DCE interface has been mentioned several times as though it is something special. It is. The interface consists of the input/output circuitry in the DCE and in the DTE, and the connectors and cables that connect them. In most systems, this interface conforms to the RS-232 standard as published by the Electronic Industries Association (EIA) in the United States. (The RS-232 and other standard DTE-DCE interfaces are discussed later in this book.) The RS-232 interface, and other serial interfaces that use some of the RS-232 specification but depart from it in some important way, are by far the most commonly used interfaces in data communications. The RS-232 standard specifies the rules by which data is moved across the interface between the DTE and the DCE and, therefore, ultimately from point A to point B. The word *serial* means that the bits cross the interface one at a time in series.

DTEs are a very important part of the process of moving data between points A and B. Not only are basic input and output capabilities important, but today's intelligent electronic terminals can perform many complex software-driven functions whose goal is to ensure better performance and accuracy of the data transfer. We'll look at these functions in several of the chapters to follow.

Similarly, although a great deal of discussion will be devoted to the interface between the DTE and the DCE, less time will be spent on the interface between the DCE and the communications channel. This is because the latter interface is quite simple (either 2 wires or 4 wires, rather than 2 to 24 as in the RS-232 interface) and because there is not a problem with the sequencing of the electrical signals across this interface.

We won't spend a great deal of time discussing the transmission channel either, even though it is obviously crucial to the data communications system. The various electrical characteristics of the channel itself (such as its bandwidth, the relative delay at various frequencies, and other parameters) usually conform to published specifications, and these specifications are often contained in the tariffs published by the telephone companies or other carriers. We have very little control over the transmission channel itself (except to hang up and redial), and the equipment used for data communications is tolerant of a wide range of some of the problems; but unless the data transmission rate is at a very high speed, the communications channel usually does not cause any trouble.

So we really don't care much about how the channel works, as long as a standard voice-grade channel between points A and B is available. A standard voice-grade channel is a telephone line that normally would be used for voice communication, that is, a telephone conversation. Thus, a fundamental problem in data communications is that the transmission of digital data must be accomplished over facilities that were designed for voice (analog) communications. The modem, a type of DCE used to convert digital data to an

●
The DTE-DCE interface consists of the input/output circuitry in the interface, as well as the cables and connectors that link DTE and DCE.

analog form (such as speed or tones) for transmission over the telephone channel, is described later in this book.

The Effect of Telecommunications Reform

In the future, we will probably need to know more about the operating characteristics of different transmission systems due to the telecommunications reform bill passed in 1996. Under this bill, cable TV companies will be able to offer voice-grade services, and telephone companies will use various technologies to provide high-speed access to the home and office over ordinary twisted-pair wire. In fact, by the time you read this edition, you might be able to obtain video-on-demand movies via your telephone and connect to the Internet via your cable TV operator. Recognizing the evolution in communications requires a degree of knowledge about the operating characteristics of different transmission media. Those characteristics are described at appropriate points in this book.

What Have You Learned?

Now that the fundamental secrets of data communications have been revealed, let's briefly review the problem, the terms, and the parts of the system:

1. Problem: To encode information using some kind of standard code, convert it to a form that can be transmitted over the existing telephone network, transmit it between point A and point B without introducing errors, and reverse the process at the receiving end to recover the original information.

2. Channel: A transmission facility connecting points A and B. It's usually a voice-grade telephone channel provided by the telephone company. The channel can be established for the duration of a call (dial up) or from a permanent connection (leased line).

3. Data Terminal Equipment (DTE): At one end, the source of the data to be transmitted; at the other end, the sink that receives the transmitted data.

4. Data Circuit-Terminating (or Communications) Equipment (DCE): The conversion equipment between the DTE and the transmission channel. One type of DCE, the modem, converts the data into tones for transmission over the voice channel.

5. RS-232 Interface: The interface wiring and electronics between the DTE and the DCE equipment at either end of the system. Although other important interface standards exist, this is the most common.

6. Information: The data to be transmitted between points A and B. It could be as simple as a command to turn on an indicator light, or as complex as the commands for drawing a multicolor illustration on a CRT display. In either case, the communications system itself is concerned only about moving the data between A and B without any error. The data communications system does not respond to, nor act on, the content of the data transmitted.

7. Internetworking: Hardware and software that enables information to flow between devices connected to different LANs and other computer systems.

8. Protocol: The rules for transmission of information between two points. They include rules for handling such questions as what to do if a transmission error occurs, or how to determine whether the receiver is ready to receive the transmission.

9. LAN and WAN: A local area network (LAN) interconnects devices within a building or campus, whereas a wide-area network (WAN) interconnects devices within a city or in different cities.

10. Telecommunications reform: The 1996 telecommunications reform bill promotes competition by enabling telephone companies to offer video-on-demand and other services traditionally offered by cable TV operators, and those operators can now offer telephone services.

Quiz for Chapter 1

1. Which is not an example of data communications?

    a. A Teletype printing news bulletins.

    b. A computer transmitting files to another computer.

    c. An automatic teller machine checking account balances with the bank's computer.

    d. A salesman telephoning orders to the office.

2. Two-state (binary) communications systems are better because:

    a. They can interface directly with the analog telephone network.

    b. The components are simpler, less costly, and more reliable.

    c. People think better in binary.

    d. Interstate calls are less costly.

3. Which is not a positional notation system?

    a. Roman (MCMXXXVII).

    b. Binary (01111110).

    c. Decimal (1492).

    d. Hexadecimal (3A2B).

4. Codes are always:

    a. Eight bits per character.

    b. Either seven or eight bits per character.

    c. Agreed on in advance between sender and receiver.

    d. The same in all modern computers.

5. The Baudot code:
    a. Was invented by the Baudot brothers, Mark and Space.
    b. Requires the escape character to print numbers.
    c. Requires shift characters to provide sufficient combinations.
    d. Was invented by Emile's sister, Brigitte.

6. The standard ASCII:
    a. Is version II of the ASC standard.
    b. Has 128 characters, including 32 control characters.
    c. Is a subset of the 8-bit EBCDIC code.
    d. Is used only in the United States and Canada.

7. Extended ASCII:
    a. Adds extra digits to standard ASCII.
    b. Provides 128 additional character definitions beyond standard ASCII.
    c. Doubles the bit length of each ASCII character.
    d. Provides extra characters that you define.

8. Escape sequences:
    a. Use the ESC character to indicate the start of a special control sequence.
    b. Are used to switch (escape) between ASCII and EBCDIC codes.
    c. Are a popular daydream for inmates.

9. The principal difference between batch processing and online processing is that:
    a. Computer resources are used more efficiently for online processing.
    b. Teleprinters are used for batch processing; CRTs are used for online processing.
    c. Transactions are grouped for batch processing; transactions are processed as needed for online processing.

10. The key difference between current and emerging computer-based applications with respect to their communications requirements is that:
    a. Emerging applications will use graphics that require less transmission time.
    b. The use of voice will reduce the necessity to transmit text.
    c. Emerging applications will require additional data storage, which will result in additional transmission time.
    d. The integration of voice, video, and data will reduce transmission time.

11. DCE and DTE:
    a. Mean "digital communications equipment" and "digital termination and equipment."
    b. Are connected by either two or four wires.
    c. Refer to the modem and the computer or terminal, respectively.

12. The correctness and accuracy of the transmitted message content is:

  a. Verified by the modem.

  b. Determined by the sender and receiver, not by the communications system.

  c. Ensured by the use of digital techniques.

13. The telecommunications reform bill of 1996 promotes:

  a. Competition among different industry groups.

  b. Two-wire services.

  c. The use of digital transmission.

Terminal Devices

About This Chapter

Having defined data communications in an overall sense, we now begin describing the various equipment and software that make up the system. We'll start with the part of the system that is most visible to the user: the terminal. Terminals are one of the most dynamic areas of the computer industry; they are associated with convenience, speed, and glamour. The great majority of data terminals used through the early to mid-1980s fell into two categories: teleprinter terminals and CRT terminals. Growing additions to the latter category are small business computers and personal computers used as terminals. In fact, by the early 1990s, more personal computers were used as terminals than teleprinters and CRT terminals combined. By the mid-1990s, advances in the design of semiconductors and disk drives resulted in the manufacture of millions of lightweight notebook and palmtop computers yearly. These devices, as well as conventional desktop personal computers, represent modern terminal devices that include an intelligent processing capability. We'll discuss both the older teleprinter terminals and the newer CRTs, as well as the components of a personal computer that enable desktop, notebook, and palmtop computers to function as a multipurpose communications terminal.

Teleprinters

The device that was invented to replace the Morse telegrapher was called the teleprinter. It was actually a form of specialized telegraph that used the five-bit character code. An early teleprinter is shown in Figure 2.1. The largest manufacturer of teleprinters in the United States was the Teletype Corporation, and thus the word *Teletype* has been commonly used to refer to any teletypewriter or teleprinter. This usage is improper, however, because Teletype is a trademark of Teletype Corporation.

A teleprinter can be defined as any device that combines a low-speed printer with a serial communications interface. Although a keyboard is an important component of most teleprinters, it is not required to fit this definition (which is used in the commercial marketplace). Thus, the common line printer qualifies if it has a serial interface.

Teleprinter Communications

Teleprinters use start-stop asynchronous transmission, which is the most widely used method of data communications for a serial interface. It is the simplest technique, but it's also the least efficient (the price paid for simplicity).

Teleprinters transmit at a speed much lower than the capacity of a telephone voice grade line. Common teleprinter speeds in North America are 75 and 110 bits per second (bps). Common speeds elsewhere in the world are 100 and 200 bps. The international teleprinter (telex) network and many European lines operate at 50 bps. Teleprinter signals are formed simply by switching an electrical current on and off or by reversing its direction of flow. The current is either 20 or 60 milliamperes, and the equipment is called current-loop equipment. (Most teleprinters today use RS-232 as the external interface, but current-loop circuitry still can be used internally.) The on and off pulses form a code that is interpreted by the receiving device. Single-current teleprinter signaling, also known as neutral or unipolar signaling, is common in the United States. Double-current signaling, also called polar or bipolar signaling, is more common in Europe. We'll discuss current-loop signaling more in Chapter 4, "Asynchronous Modems and Interfaces."

Teleprinter Terminals

Two types of teleprinters are available: those with typewriter-style keyboards (called keyboard send-receive, or KSR), and those without keyboards (called receive-only, or RO). The typical teleprinter is capable of printing from 10 to 30 characters per second (cps) or from 100 to 300 words per minute (wpm), which is much faster than most typists. However, because much of the terminal's time might be devoted to printing output from a computer instead of entering data, it is usually desirable to have the fastest possible printing mechanism. Thus, teleprinters are available with printing speeds of up to 120 cps.

In the usual operation of a teleprinter, a user enters inputs to the computer via the keyboard. The inputs are transmitted back (in what's called an echo) from the computer character-by-character to the printer and are printed to verify receipt. Output originating in the computer or another source is printed as it is received. Thus, a "hard copy" of both the inputs and the outputs is available. Although many teleprinters are used in this way, some are strictly online printing devices and thus don't require a keyboard.

The classic and perhaps best application for teleprinter terminals is in interactive sessions with a computer, such as timesharing or bulletin boards. Here the comparative slowness of the teleprinter is not restrictive, and the printed copy is often quite useful. The slow speed of operation is not as noticeable as in other applications because much of the operator's time is spent in thinking, rather than in waiting for output. Another application for which teleprinters were popularly used during the 1960s through the 1970s was in regional weather information networks. In this type of network, weather forecasts and related information were broadcast from a central computer to teleprinters connected to the computer via the installation of leased lines. Because the transmission of information was always from the computer to the teleprinter and no response was required or sought, this was one of the primary applications for the use of RO teleprinters.

More modern teleprinters, such as the one shown in Figure 2.2, use various printing techniques and operate at many print speeds. They provide features such as programmable format control, adjustable forms control, upper- and lowercase printing, interchangeable character styles (fonts), bidirectional printing and paper feeding, selectable character and line spacing, status indicators, portability, and additional keys such as a numeric keypad.

Manufacturers incorporated the microprocessor into teleprinters to reduce design, development, and production costs while providing a variety of applications that can be implemented by either the vendor or the user. The microprocessor delays the time when a particular teleprinter design will become obsolete because future applications can be accommodated by reprogramming the microprocessor to perform other jobs. From the user's point of view, microprocessor technology also offers the major advantage of lower cost because the manufacturer's cost savings resulting from using microprocessors are passed on to the customer.

●
The speed of the teleprinter's printing mechanism is very important in applications in which most of its time will be spent in receiving and printing incoming data.

●
Teleprinters that use microprocessors can be programmed for various applications. This has reduced their cost and extended the machine's life.

FIGURE 2.2.
A TI 820 KSR teleprinter.

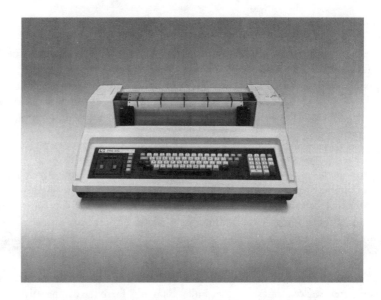

Compared to total terminal sales, few new teleprinter units are sold outside of the traditional record services markets (telex, twx, and private teleprinter network). Even most of these are specialized. An example is the portable printing terminal often used by a traveling businessperson whose needs are satisfied by a small, lightweight (three to eight pounds), hand-carried terminal.

The rapid decrease in the price and size of portable computers means that they now can be used for applications that previously were reserved for portable terminals. Not only can portable personal computers communicate with large corporate computers, but these portables also enable the traveling businessperson to compose memorandums and letters and to analyze business decisions with spreadsheet programs. Although portable terminals communicating with corporate computers could perform such functions, the personal computer can complete these tasks in a local mode of operation, which eliminates many long-distance communication sessions. In addition, through the development of miniaturized fax/data modems, it is now extremely convenient for persons working at home or traveling to use their portable computer to send electronic mail messages, surf the Internet, or communicate with the corporate mainframe.

The first type of portable computer was more appropriately referred to as transportable, due to its weight, which ranged from 20 to 30 pounds. Fortunately for the executive who travels, as well as for students and employees who work at home, advances in the development of integrated circuits and disk drives resulted in three new types of personal computers that became available in the late 1980s and early 1990s: laptops, notebooks, and palmtops.

Laptops, so named because they could literally be placed on a person's lap, normally weigh less than 12 pounds, and many can fit into an attaché case. Notebooks, so named because they are similar in size to an 8½×11-inch notepad, easily fit into an attaché case and usually weigh less than four pounds. Palmtops, so named because they can be lifted by closing one's hand around the device, usually weigh less than 2 pounds. All three types of portable computers can perform most, if not all, computing functions associated with conventional personal computers while providing a high level of portability.

The chief drawbacks of portable computers include a compressed keyboard, in which multiple keystrokes might be required to generate some of the key functions for normal keyboards, and poor screen readability. The first problem, that of a compressed keyboard, was alleviated by IBM with the introduction of a new series of Thinkpad notebook computers from that vendor referred to as Butterfly computers. Opening the cover of a Butterfly Thinkpad model results in the popping out of two halves of a keyboard, expanding the keyboard beyond the dimensions of the computer carrying case. Unfortunately, the difficulties associated with the readability of screens continue to represent a problem. Although considerable advances in screen technology have occurred over the past decade, many portable computer screens must be viewed from a certain angle to be readable. This viewing requirement is based on the reflection of light from the screen or the angle by which light is generated by a backlighted screen.

Figure 2.3 illustrates the interface of a Hewlett-Packard HP95XL palmtop computer to a U.S. Robotics Worldport fax/data modem. The HP95XL was one of the first palmtop computers to be sold. It included a copy of Lotus Development Corporation's popular 1-2-3 electronic spreadsheet program built into read-only memory (ROM). The Worldport fax/data modem enables an HP95XL user to transmit and receive text and fax messages at data rates up to 14,400 bits per second. By examining the size of the HP95XL, the modem, and the hands of the person holding both devices, you will note that the HP95XL and the Worldport modems both can easily fit into the palm of one's hand. Hence, both the computer and the modem are referred to as palmtop devices.

FIGURE 2.3.

An HP95XL palmtop computer connected to a U.S. Robotics Worldport palmtop fax/data modem. (Courtesy of U.S. Robotics)

In the early 1990s, a new type of computer became available that has the potential to revolutionize the method by which we transmit and receive information. This device is commonly referred to as the Personal Digital Assistant, or PDA. Although similar in size to palmtops, PDAs are being marketed with integrated cellular communications capability to include data and fax modems designed to transmit and receive information via a cellular telephone connection. When acquired with this capability, the PDA enables a user to bypass the necessity of connecting his device to a telephone to communicate. This can be a major benefit for travelers, because connecting a portable computer to a telephone-line jack can be difficult or impossible in many hotels, motels, and airports.

Teleprinters Versus CRT Terminals

A teleprinter's disadvantages are slower speed, little or no variability in format, and limited reliability due to mechanical wear.

The drawbacks to teleprinters involve speed, formatting, and reliability. Teleprinters are far slower in operation than CRT terminals; even their highest print speed doesn't compare to the 300 or 1200 characters per second on the CRT. Because teleprinters are designed primarily for message communications, they do not provide sophisticated capabilities for data editing or formatting. It is quite difficult to create a form on a teleprinter, and of course such attributes as blinking, highlighting, and similar enhancements that are available on a CRT terminal are impossible on a teleprinter. Although teleprinters are quite reliable, they nevertheless are electromechanical devices that are subject to wear and misalignment. CRT terminals, on the other hand, generally have higher reliability because of far fewer parts, most of which do not move.

Serial Printers

Teleprinter terminal serial printers, either impact or non-impact, print one character at a time sequentially.

Teleprinter terminals use serial (or character) printers, so named because they print one character at a time. Such printers can be classified into two categories: impact printers, which mechanically strike the paper to produce a printed image, and nonimpact printers, which produce an image by some other means. Impact printers are further divided into two subcategories: those that produce a fully formed character, in which the character is created by impact from a single piece of type, and dot-matrix printers, in which the character image on the paper is formed by a matrix of dots. Nonimpact teleprinters form characters by the dot-matrix method only, using an electrothermal, an ink-jet, or a laser printing method.

Impact Printers

Impact printers are those that use mechanical action to strike a ribbon against the paper to print the desired character, either completely formed or in a dot matrix.

Impact printing mechanisms include replaceable type-ball elements (as used on the IBM Selectric typewriters), daisy wheels (a flat disk with petal-like projections for the character elements), elements shaped like a cup with finger-like projections, moving type belts with the characters engraved on the belt, a rotating cylinder containing the characters, and a type block with characters embedded in the block. All of these mechanisms share the same advantages of fully formed characters in almost any style and shape, and also have the capability to make "carbon" copies. They also share the same disadvantages of low speed and mechanical complexity. No matter how the character is mounted or engraved on the type element, it must be positioned in front of the platen and then struck against an inked ribbon and paper to produce an image. This process limits the speed of the printer to a maximum of 120 cps (but it's usually much lower), and it creates a large amount of noise in the process.

This speed limitation was an incentive for printer manufacturers to seek a different approach that would extend the upper limit of printing speed for serial impact printers. Their search led to the development of the dot-matrix printer. Dot-matrix printers are a compromise (and often a successful one) between decreased character quality and substantially higher print speeds of 180 cps or more. The printed image is formed from a rectangular matrix of dots, which was initially nine dots high by seven dots wide. Printing is performed by moving a print head containing a column of nine pins across the paper and selectively actuating the pins at seven successive intervals to form each character. Developments in dot-matrix printer technology increased the number of pins that could be placed on the print head, resulting in the availability of 18- and 24-pin print-head printers. Dot-matrix printers with these high-density print heads result in the printing of characters whose pin dots overlap to produce a nearly solid character format. This type of printing, which provides the appearance of an impact printer output, is referred to as near letter quality. Although dot-matrix printers contain comparatively few moving parts, they are subject to much wear and heat within the print head as a result of the succession of pin movements required to create each character.

Dot-matrix teleprinters are typically less expensive than similarly featured fully formed character teleprinters. With the improved print quality that's now available with high-resolution dot-matrix printing, most teleprinter users are satisfied with dot-matrix printers.

Another development that improves speed in teleprinters was the bidirectional print head with logic-seeking control. The print head can print while moving in either direction (left to right or right to left). The logic-seeking control circuitry determines the shortest horizontal distance to move the print head to print the next line. Thus, on full pages of text, one line is printed left to right, the next is printed right to left, and so forth. This feature, available on both fully formed character printers and dot-matrix printers, eliminates the time required for a full carriage return to the left side for every line.

Nonimpact Printers

The nonimpact types of teleprinters employ various electronic, optical, and chemical techniques to produce printed images. All nonimpact teleprinters currently on the market use dot-matrix character formation. Some of the printing techniques have been developed from xerography and facsimile communications techniques. Others were specifically developed for use in high-speed printing applications in which print speeds of more than 2000 lines (that's *lines,* not *characters*) per minute are not uncommon. Still others were designed to meet a specific goal, such as quiet operation.

●
Nonimpact printers use electrothermal, ink-jet, or laser printing techniques. They are more reliable, quieter, and faster than impact printers.

The electrothermal printing technique is one nonimpact method. The print head applies heat through the matrix pins to chemically coated paper. The heat causes a chemical reaction, which produces a matrix of colored dots that form the character. It is quiet and efficient but requires special paper, to which some persons object.

The ink-jet technique uses a stream of electrically charged ink droplets sprayed onto ordinary paper to produce the characters, as shown in Figure 2.4. Dot placement is accomplished by electrostatic deflection plates that control the direction of the charged ink droplets, in much the same manner as electron beam position is controlled within a cathode ray tube. By electronic control of switching between reservoirs of different colored ink, instant color changes can be made as the printer operates. Ink-jet printers were originally very expensive, but prices have decreased substantially in the past few years.

FIGURE 2.4.

The basic ink-jet printing technique.

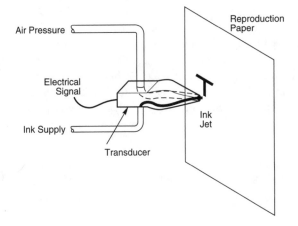

Laser printers create images of entire pages by "recording" on a rotating drum with a laser beam and imparting these images to paper. The laser beam focuses on a minute spot that continually scans along the length of the light-sensitive coated drum. Turning the scanning beam off and on creates the pattern that is transferred to paper. The spot (or dot) resolution is as high as 600×600 per square inch.

Reliability of nonimpact printers is high compared to that of impact printers because they have few mechanical parts. Their incapability to produce more than one copy at a time (no carbon copies) might sometimes be a disadvantage, but their rapid, quiet, and reliable operation is certainly an advantage.

CRT Terminals

The cathode ray tube (CRT) terminal, also called a video display terminal (VDT), is a common interface between people and computers. The CRT terminal was originally developed as an alternative to teleprinter terminals. Its introduction in 1965 revolutionized the data communications environment, in which the teleprinter had been the only interface device. Although many companies entered the marketplace, prices remained high due to low-volume production and the cost (price and assembly labor) of discrete components. The advent of the integrated circuit, followed by large-scale integration, brought prices down, although they were still out of reach of the ordinary individual. Then came the microprocessor, which replaced much of the integrated circuit logic and drove prices still lower. The result was high-quality, high-performance, and relatively low-cost CRT terminals that even the hobbyist can afford. A CRT terminal designed for businesses is shown in Figure 2.5.

● In many applications, the CRT terminal has replaced the teleprinter terminal as the interface between computers and people.

FIGURE 2.5.
A TI 931 CRT terminal.

ASCII Terminals

In the computer industry, the term *ASCII display terminal* usually refers to a CRT terminal that operates without a separate controller, uses the ASCII code, and transmits and receives asynchronous data. This term originated with CRT terminals (the glass Teletype) designed to replace Teletype ASR 33/35 teleprinter terminals, and ASCII terminals are still described as being TTY or Teletype compatible. ASCII terminals are available in a wide range, from low-end dumb units that do little more than emulate a teleprinter (or

● A CRT terminal that can operate without a separate controller and can transmit and receive asynchronous data using the ASCII code is called an ASCII terminal.

that emulate another CRT terminal, such as the ADM-3, which emulates a teleprinter) up to 132-column split-screen editing terminals with several pages of electronic memory storage.

CRT terminals have three capabilities in common:

- A keyboard that can generate a full alphanumeric character code set.
- A CRT monitor that can display the characters of that code set.
- The capability to send and receive data via communications lines to a remote host computer.

CRT terminals fall into one of three categories: dumb, smart, and user-programmable. Of course, there is some overlap between categories, but I'll define them here:

- Dumb terminals are Teletype compatible and offer a limited number of functions—perhaps none beyond keyboarding and display. They are the lowest cost, but often the difference in price between them and the smart terminals is small compared to the difference in performance and features.
- Smart terminals offer extended functions, such as editing and formatted data entry. The user might be able to tailor the terminal to fit the application through limited programming, such as format creation, parameter definition, or input checking.
- User-programmable (or intelligent) terminals feature software support. The manufacturer provides an operating system (an assembler, a compiler, or an interpretive programming language), subroutines (I/O utilities; one or more protocol emulators), and one or two application programs, such as data entry and text editing. They provide some form of program storage and more memory for text.

> ● CRT terminals can be classed in one of three categories: dumb terminals, smart terminals, and user-programmable terminals.

Dumb Versus Smart Terminals

The description of the capabilities of teleprinters also applies to the capability of the dumb CRT terminals except for print speed. These terminals essentially consist of a CRT, video (display), memory, and interface electronics. Few truly dumb terminals are still manufactured; virtually all CRT terminals currently manufactured are microprocessor controlled, making them smart terminals according to our definition. The microprocessor chips cost only a few dollars, which is less than the cost of the logic they replace.

> ● Microprocessor control has given CRT smart terminals the flexibility and capabilities to perform many operations beyond simple display and keyboarding.

The microprocessor programs (firmware) reside in read-only memory (ROM) or programmable ROM (PROM). ROM-resident programs control those features that are "permanent," whereas PROM-resident programs are typically produced in smaller quantities and implement customized or modifiable features. Either type can be replaced by a different type with a different program by removal of the old chip and insertion of a new one, although this feature is more talked about than actually used. In addition to controlling basic terminal functions, the microprocessor can provide protocol emulation, define the character code sets to be generated by the keyboard, implement special features, set control parameters, and so forth. Moreover, the microprocessor delays obsolescence, because future needs can be implemented via reprogramming.

In addition to the capability to simply display alphabetic and numeric characters, microprocessor control provides the capability to highlight characters by means of underscoring, reverse video, blinking, differing levels of brightness, and combinations of these attributes. One of the most impressive capabilities of these terminals is the capability to display a predefined form and let the operator "fill in the blanks" while checking the entries as they are made.

Many CRT terminals can display double-size characters, and most have a graphics character set for creating forms and formats. Some also support business graphics; for example, bar, column, and pie charts to graphically show sales, income and expense, inventory levels, and so forth. Interactive or engineering graphics, on the other hand, is a highly specialized area usually requiring a completely different, high-resolution graphics terminal.

User-Programmable Terminals Versus Personal Computers

Taken separately, the words *programmable* and *terminal* are precisely definable. But when combined to describe one class of equipment, their meanings become vague and difficult to define with precision. In 1979, a popular periodical defined a user-programmable terminal as a terminal that permits local file updating and accommodates user-written applications programs. At that time, this definition stirred up quite a bit of controversy because such a terminal would have to provide for the following features in addition to the basic terminal functions:

● Because of the need for increased requirements, the emphasis has shifted to using microcomputers for terminal functions.

- The availability of, and the support and documentation of, at least one general-purpose programming language for development of programs by customer personnel.
- Entry of programs via the terminal keyboard.
- The capability to access and retrieve programs stored in the host computer memory, and the capability to execute (use) those programs at the terminal.

Much of the value of user-programmable terminals is in their off-line processing capability provided by the previously listed items. All user-programming terminals have built-in main memory that the user can employ to store and execute programs, but the capacity varies from as little as 1 kilobyte (usually written as 1K or 1KB), which accommodates only a very small program, to as much as 512KB (which accommodates a large program and much data). Most, although not all, user-programmable terminals also provide for local mass storage using floppy, hard, or cartridge disks, or cassette or cartridge magnetic tape.

With disks, tapes, memory, an operating system, and a programming language, the user-programmable terminal sounds a lot like a personal computer, doesn't it? This is the revolution in the terminal market. Dumb terminals and low-end smart terminals are rapidly being squeezed aside by personal computers, which relegate terminals to specialized tasks. Most office workers now have a personal computer on their desks, which either can be used stand-alone, as a computer connected to a local area network for client-server computing where the PC represents the client computer, or can be placed online to the large host computer. Files can be up- and downloaded and processed wherever it makes the most sense to do so. All because of data communications and the microprocessor!

Emulation

When the personal computer operates a communications program that enables the computer to duplicate the attributes of a terminal, the software is known as a terminal emulator program. Such programs permit the personal computer to communicate with mainframe application programs developed to work with predefined types of terminals.

Depending on the terminal emulation software marketed for the personal computer, you might be able to replace several types of terminals with one computer. For an example, consider the organization that has both Hewlett-Packard (HP) and Digital Equipment Corporation (DEC) mainframe computers. With HP 2645 and DEC VT100 terminal emulation software, one can use a personal computer to emulate common Hewlett-Packard and Digital Equipment Corporation terminal devices and thereby get full screen access to two different computer systems designed to operate with two specific types of terminals.

Non-ASCII Terminals

This section describes CRT terminals that do not fit the ASCII label, together with some specialized terminals that use other displays. Of these, the most important type is the batch or cluster type.

Batch Terminals

Two different methods of terminal-computer communications, interactive and batch, effectively mesh user needs with the communications techniques.

Communications between terminal devices to include personal computers and other computers tend to fall into two basic categories, interactive and batch, which are distinguished by the types of functions to be performed. Interactive communications support conversational inquiry/response, interactive data entry, and other such applications. Batch communications, on the other hand, support either remote job entry or remote batch data communications. Remote job entry (RJE), in which the terminal device acts as a remote console for the central computer, enables local users to load and execute application programs. For remote batch data communications, the terminal acts as a remote input/output device for an application program being performed in the host.

The reasons for these distinctions are efficiency and accuracy. An interactive terminal designed to communicate in asynchronous character-by-character mode is not very efficient for transmitting large blocks of data as required in the batch mode, nor is the error checking (if any) adequate to ensure correct transmission. On the other hand, it would be wasteful to tie up a complete remote batch terminal just to enable one user to use the keyboard to ask questions about particular data stored in the host computer with the answers sent back by the computer.

Although batch terminals were commonly used to access a remote computer during the 1960s and 1970s, the personal computer also affected the use of this type of terminal device. The widespread use of personal computers during the 1980s resulted in the development of hardware and software that enables many types of personal computers to function as remote job entry type terminals.

Clustered Terminals

When a remote location generates a large amount of data via key entry, the use of a clustered system might be indicated. This is typical in large-scale data processing installations in which it is common practice to control many peripheral units, such as CRT terminals, at one location with a single control unit. Data entered through the keyboard devices is stored in a buffer for transmission. Then the output of many operators is transmitted in one block to the main computer at much higher speed than that used by teleprinters and ASCII CRT terminals. In addition to the key entry devices, storage, and controller, the cluster might include printers and mass storage. This type of architecture is fundamental to modern data processing. A widely used example is the IBM 3270 series.

●
Clustered terminals are generally used in remote, high-volume, key-entry locations to facilitate the transfer of large quantities of data to a main computer.

IBM 3270 Series

The IBM 3270 is not a terminal per se but is a designation for a family of devices designed for use in clusters. The 3270 series has had a strong impact on the synchronous terminal market since its introduction in 1971. The first generation, which was discontinued in 1982, included the 3271/3272 control units, 3275 display station, 3277 display, and 3284/3286/3288 printers. In 1977, the product line was expanded and updated with the 3274 control unit, 3276 control/display, 3278 display, and 3287/3289 printers. In 1979, color displays and printers were added. In 1983, IBM made some long-awaited changes and enhancements to the 3270 product line. Added were the 3178 display station, a new 3274 control unit, the 3290 information panel (a gas plasma display), and the 3299 terminal multiplexer.

●
The 3270 series represents a family of terminals connected in groups or clusters to control units.

In 1986, a few years after the introduction of the new 3274, IBM announced its 3174 control unit. The device in some respects is similar to a personal computer because it can be customized through the addition of special adapter cards. Three of the key functions that can be added to a 3174 control unit are asynchronous ASCII terminal support in which the control unit performs protocol conversion and Ethernet and token-ring interfaces. The latter two interfaces enable devices on an Ethernet or token-ring LAN to access a mainframe via the 3174, which then functions as a gateway.

The 3299 multiplexer is normally used to reduce the amount of cable required to connect terminals to a control unit when the distance between the location of the terminals and the control unit exceeds a few hundred feet. Up to eight terminals can be connected to a 3299, with only one cable required to connect the 3299 to a control unit.

Newer terminals in the 3270 series include the 3179 color display station, the 3279G color graphics display station, the 3180 and 3191 monochrome display stations, and the 3192 and 3194 color display stations. The latter two are most notable for their design, which minimizes the desk space they require compared to earlier terminals in the 3270 series.

In the area of personal computer connectivity to the 3270 series, IBM has introduced many products. The more significant products include a new control unit, as well as adapter cards that are installed into a system expansion slot of a computer in the IBM PC and PS/2 series. The adapter card permits direct connection of the personal computer to a control unit, which enables the PC to function as a 3270 terminal. With this configuration, personal computer users also can transfer files and do local processing, both of which are beyond the capability of conventional 3270 terminals. As previously mentioned, in 1986, IBM introduced the 3174 control unit, which features an optional Ethernet or token-ring gateway. This feature enables one member of the IBM PC series to be cabled to the 3174 as a gateway device on an Ethernet or token-ring local area network. Other personal computers are then connected to the gateway personal computer, enabling many personal computers on the network to get access via one personal computer.

●

The IBM 3270 family of clustered synchronous terminals is receiving strong competition from microcomputers.

In providing the PC interface, IBM finds itself in an interesting quandary. The 3270 line has been quite profitable over the years; now it faces competition from personal computers, especially those manufactured by IBM! As personal computing becomes the rule rather than the exception in most major corporations, the terminal industry is on the verge of the biggest change since the introduction of the CRT.

The many other firms that offer 3270-compatible products must likewise compete with personal computers. To remain competitive, these companies have traditionally offered some combination of lower prices, improved performance, and shorter delivery times to penetrate the IBM "plug compatible" market. In addition to the 3270-compatible vendors, some ASCII terminal manufacturers have invaded the 3270 market through protocol conversion. On a 3270 network, synchronous terminals can be replaced with asynchronous terminals coupled with "black boxes" that convert the asynchronous data to synchronous form with the proper headers, check bits, and so forth. These devices allow an ASCII terminal to support the functional characteristics of the 3270 terminal. The advantage of this strategy is that ASCII terminals are considerably less expensive than their 3270 counterparts.

The capability to support LAN connectivity considerably expanded the functionality of the 3174 control unit and extended the use of IBM's proprietary 3270 networking technology to include the support of standardized client-server networks. This in turn has enabled many organizations to continue to use their 3270 networks well into the late 1990s.

Figure 2.6 illustrates in schematic format communications in a modern 3270 network in which a 3174 control unit provides connectivity to a mainframe from computers connected to a LAN, as well as for individual terminals directly connected to the control unit. In many organizations, the 3270 terminals shown cabled directly to the 3174 control unit were replaced by personal computers with emulation boards during the late 1980s and early 1990s. The 3745 communications processor represents a specialized minicomputer designed to perform communications processing, offloading those functions from the mainframe computer so that its processing can be focused on executing application programs.

●
The addition of LAN support to 3174 control units has extended the use of 3270 networks into the late 1990s.

FIGURE 2.6.

Communications connectivity in a modern 3270 network.

Other Types of Terminals

Most terminals manufactured today employ a keyboard and a CRT. The popularity of this combination stems from its flexibility, high character capacity, and relatively low cost. Specialized needs, however, led to the development of a broad range of other terminals, which include optical bar code readers, voice response units, portable terminals, and the ordinary tone dialing telephone. In addition, such things as supermarket cash registers, portable communicating terminals for inventory management, and a host of other types of equipment now employ data communications. By the DTE/DCE definition, all of these are terminals.

Parts of a Terminal

Having discussed the various types of terminals, we'll now discuss the components of a typical CRT terminal. Note that the discussion is also applicable to personal computers because that device represents an intelligent terminal. But first, we'll talk about one of the current buzzwords in the terminal business: ergonomics.

Ergonomics

ANSI standards define ergonomics as "a multidisciplinary activity dealing with the interactions between man and his total working environment, plus such traditional environmental aspects as atmosphere, heat, light, and sound, as well as the tools and equipment of the workplace."

Terminal manufacturers have become increasingly aware of the need to consider ergonomics in the design of their equipment. The trend toward making CRT terminals more "operator friendly" began in Europe, and most people agree that European manufacturers still lead in this area. Recent developments in terminals, such as sloped keyboards and green or amber displays, have come about because of ergonomic considerations.

Keyboards

Although terminal keyboards have been improved for user comfort and utility (ergonomics), little has been done to improve and standardize the keyboard layout.

Most display terminals now have keyboards that are detached or detachable. Most of these are connected to the terminal's console or, in the case of a personal computer, to the PC's system unit via a coiled cable. This type of cable is usually three to six feet long, which enables the operator to place the keyboard in a comfortable position while using the terminal. A more recent development is the "light-link" or cordless keyboard, in which an infrared transmitter/receiver replaces the cable to allow even more freedom of movement.

Another design factor is the slope and thickness of the keyboard. Most keyboards today are either sloped or stepped, with the angle being 5 to 15 degrees. Most recent terminals have sculptured key caps rather than flat key caps, which speeds data entry and improves operator comfort. Audible keyboard feedback might be provided by a beep or key click from a speaker, and tactile feedback might be provided by a unique "feel" when the stroke is registered. Like most other ergonomic considerations, the previous features are not, in themselves, the most important criteria for choosing one terminal over another; what they do indicate is the manufacturer's commitment to providing equipment that is up-to-date and easy to use.

Keyboard Layout

The layout of the keyboard is a primary concern of ergonomics. The de facto standard typewriter key layout is that of the IBM Selectric typewriter illustrated in Figure 2.7. A keyboard that has this arrangement of the alphabetic keys is called a QWERTY (pronounced "kwer-ty") keyboard because these are the first six letters of the top row of alphabetic keys. The QWERTY keyboard is far from the best layout. In fact, the QWERTY keyboard layout was designed for early mechanical typewriters to arrange the key hammers to reduce key hang-ups. This arrangement also slowed the typist so that he or she could not key faster than the early typewriters could operate! In the 1890s, there were more than a hundred different typewriter keyboards because almost every company that made a typewriter used a different keyboard. These keyboard types included the Crandall (ZPRCHMI), the American (CJPFUBL), the Hall (KBFGNIA), and the Morris (XVGWSLZ).

FIGURE 2.7.

The IBM Selectric typewriter keyboard layout.

Various attempts have been made to improve keyboard layout. Some had the letters of frequently used words close together. One proposed by Dr. August Dvorak put the five vowels under one hand and the five most common consonants under the other hand. There were circular keyboards, semicircular keyboards, keyboards with six rows, and keyboards with one long row. The idea of a shift key didn't come along until 1875; before that, upper- and lowercase letters were on different keys.

Despite numerous attempts to improve keyboard layouts, the QWERTY keyboard remains the industry standard. In fact, a comparison of the IBM Selectric typewriter keyboard, a product introduced in the 1950s (illustrated in Figure 2.7), with the keyboard of the IBM PC Convertible, a product introduced in the 1980s (illustrated in Figure 2.8), indicates the high degree of similarity between keyboard layouts. The basic QWERTY keyboard structure remains the same some 30 years later, with keyboard changes related to the incorporation of computer-operation-related keys on the PC Convertible keyboard. Those keys include the Alt, Ctrl, cursor position, function, Print Screen, and other specialized keys. Today, the primary difference between personal computer keyboards relates to the position of the function keys (across the top of the keyboard or located in two columns on the left), the inclusion or absence of a numeric keypad, and the placement of cursor-positioning keys.

FIGURE 2.8.

The IBM PC Convertible portable computer keyboard layout. (Courtesy of IBM Corporation)

Programmable Keyboards

●

The capability to program the keyboard provides the opportunity to rearrange the layout or key functions to suit personal taste.

You might be thinking that the operator has no choice but to adapt because the keyboard is built-in and the key arrangement is fixed. Ten years ago that was true, but now it's not always true. Alternative keyboard arrangements (including the Dvorak) are available from some manufacturers, either as standard equipment or as add-on devices for several terminals and computers. More important, many keyboards are programmable. The processor in the terminal considers each key depression simply as a contact closure in a matrix of contacts. The matrix location represented by that row and column is used by the processor to look up the character in the corresponding location in a table in memory. Thus, the keyboard layout can be changed by simply reprogramming the table; that is, the C key could be defined in the table so that a *?* is printed rather than a *C*. The process of changing the assignments of keys on a personal computer is more formally referred to as keyboard remapping. This process facilitates the use of a personal computer as a specialized terminal device, such as a 3270 type terminal, which can have 20 or more additional keys beyond those on a PC keyboard. With the mapping of pairs of keys, such as Shift+function keys, to generate predefined codes, the 101 keys on a PC keyboard can be assigned values that correspond with 120 or more keys on a 3270 terminal keyboard.

Numeric Keypads

Most terminals have some form of numeric keypad with the numerals 0 through 9 grouped like those on a 10-key adding machine to provide faster entry of numeric data. Other keys such as +, −, and . also might be included. The numeric keypad might be entirely separate from the main keyboard, or it might be implemented through an alternative definition of alphabetic keys (usually the "IOP" and "KL;" and "M,." groups). Using the main keyboard's number keys to enter numbers requires the use of both hands. Thus, number entry is faster with a numeric keypad because all the numerals are under the fingers of the right hand.

Other Keys

In addition to the alphabetic and numeric keys, terminal keyboards offer various special keys that are unique to computer input. Unfortunately, there is no standard arrangement of these keys. These keys might include the Ctrl (control) key (which allows input of some or all of the ASCII control characters), Tab (usually programmable), Esc, arrow keys (which control cursor movement), and programmable F (function) keys.

●
Special keys provide access to functions unique to computer input. No uniformity exists as to the positioning of these keys on the keyboard.

For example, on the Wyse WY-50 terminal, the Line Delete key sends ESC R. Some keys send different codes in the shifted and unshifted positions. Thus, the unshifted Page key means scroll one page forward, and the shifted Page key means scroll one page backward. The eight function keys are capable of producing 16 code sequences when used with the Shift key. When power to the terminal is turned on, these keys are set to Ctrl+A@ through Ctrl+AO, but they can be changed by the computer program, which sends the terminal a series of escape sequences. For example, the sequence Esc z A DIR B: CR Del will reprogram the F2 key to send DIR B: followed by a carriage return. Each function key can be programmed with up to eight characters. Like most modern terminals, the WY-50 has the capability to display function key labels on the bottom line of the CRT screen.

Those users who think *The more keys the merrier* should be very merry indeed because many terminals now have more than 100 keys. However, the keys sometimes are not laid out in the most useful way. For example, the cursor arrow keys might be in a row, rather than in a diamond pattern in which their direction can be felt. These additional keys might be packed closely around the regular keyboard or arranged in logical groups and slightly separated from the main keyboard. When keys have unusual or unexpected placement, the operator is likely to press them by mistake. The result can be devastating.

Other Input Devices

Alternatives to keyboard input, which can make entry of specialized data easier, include light pens, touch-sensitive screens, graphics tablets, a "mouse" (a cursor-positioning device), and even speech input. Proponents of all of these devices, and more, suggest that they will eventually replace the keyboard for most input. Don't bet on it. Buy the most comfortable, best designed, easiest-to-use keyboard that you can find; it and the display are your window into the computer. The other devices can be quite useful (especially the mouse), but most input probably will be through the keyboard for a long time to come.

Display

There has been more discussion about CRT displays, including personal computer monitors, than about any other part of the terminal or PC. Some researchers have noted eyestrain, headaches, dizziness, back pains, nausea, and nervous symptoms in workers whose jobs require that they operate CRT terminals for long periods. Eyestrain and fatigue are considerations that designers must deal with when designing a CRT display screen. Most CRTs are etched or contain a bonded faceplate to reduce glare; tilt and swivel adjustments are also popular for the same reason. The swivel and tilt features also enable the operator to place the screen at the most comfortable viewing angle. The phosphor color and character size are important too. White, green, or amber phosphors are generally used in the United States, with green probably being the most popular.

Most display terminals use the dot-matrix technique to form characters. The more dots that are contained in the character cell, the better defined the character will appear on-screen. For years, 5×7-dot characters were standard, but today, 7×7, 7×9, and 9×11-dot characters are more common. Some manufacturers use high screen-refresh rates and noninterlaced scanning to reduce image flicker and improve legibility. The size of the characters generated depends on the size of the screen and the display format used. Characters are larger on 15-inch screens than on 12-inch screens; likewise, characters are larger in an 80-character-per-line format than in a 132-character-per-line format. Display enhancements such as double-height and double-width characters can make characters larger, but these are intended for highlighting important data, not for routine use.

Most CRT terminals display 24 text lines of 80 characters each. Many also provide a 25th line, which is used for labels, status, or other terminal- or program-related information. The status line sometimes is displayed in reverse video.

Memory-Mapped Displays

Most ASCII terminals use a technique called memory-mapped video. An advantage of the memory-mapped technique is that the microcomputer can write to and read from the video memory in the same way as ordinary memory because a portion of the ordinary memory is used for the video memory. The difference is that whatever characters are stored in video memory are displayed on the CRT when addressed by the microprocessor.

An 8-bit microprocessor uses 2 bytes (16 bits) for a memory address; thus, it can directly address 2^{16}, or 65,536, memory locations. If each memory location can hold one character (which is the usual arrangement), and if the display size is 80 characters by 24 lines, then 1920 character locations are needed in video memory. If the program memory is restricted to addresses below 63,615, memory locations from 63,615 through 65,535 could be used for video memory to store an array of characters for the display.

The display provides the visualization of the terminal inputs and outputs. Most use dot-matrix character formation with 24 text lines having 80 characters per line.

When memory-mapped displays are used, the microcomputer can write into and read from the video memory just as from ordinary memory.

Assume that the upper-left corner of the CRT display receives the character from the first location (63,615) in video memory, the next horizontal position on the CRT receives the character from the second location (63,616), and so forth. Thus, if the first video memory location contains *J*, the second *O*, the third *H*, and the fourth *N*, the upper-left corner of the CRT displays *JOHN*.

Memory-mapped displays are fast and inexpensive. Because the character set is translated into dots within the dot matrix using a table lookup technique, it is also possible to redefine the character set by changing the table entries (if the table is user accessible). Line insertion and deletion, scrolling, and other effects are easily accomplished by moving data around in video memory, or even simpler, by changing starting addresses. The principal disadvantage of memory-mapped video of the type described is that it takes up space in the memory used to store programs and data. This usually is not a problem for terminals, but for computers, video memory is now usually separate. Also, computer video memory now is often bit-mapped rather than character-mapped, as discussed in the preceding paragraphs. With bit-mapping, each dot on the screen has a separate memory location. This feature allows high-resolution graphics displays, but it requires much more video memory.

Other Types of Displays

Although the CRT is the dominant display device today, there are other devices for displaying information. These include solid-state devices such as light-emitting diodes and liquid crystal displays, and plasma (gas discharge) matrices such as those used in the IBM 3290. These alternative types of displays provide extremely sharp images, but the dominance of the CRT remains unchallenged for now.

PC Terminals

The growth in the use of personal computers resulted in its adoption as a standard terminal device by many organizations. Some organizations, including several airlines, purchased tens of thousands of IBM PC and compatible personal computers for use with their online reservation systems during the 1980s. Other organizations use personal computers for both terminal emulation and local processing functions and have PCs coexisting with conventional terminals. Still other organizations connect personal computers to a local area network through the installation of an appropriate adapter card and the cabling of the adapter card to a network cable. This type of connection results in the personal computer becoming a workstation terminal device on the LAN. Regardless of the application or utilization, the processing capability of the personal computer can be used with appropriate hardware and software to provide terminal capabilities not available through the use of conventional terminals.

Figure 2.9 shows an IBM PS/2 Model 30 computer with keyboard and graphics monitor. This computer is similar to other members of the PS/2 family in that it contains a built-in serial port. The connector for this port, which is located at the rear of the computer, can be cabled to a modem. When appropriate communications software is loaded into the computer, it can then function as an asynchronous terminal.

Through the addition of different types of adapter cards that are inserted into expansion slots within the system unit of a personal computer, you can alter the functionality and capability of the computer. For example, the addition of an internal fax/data modem enables the computer user to transmit and receive both text and fax messages. Figure 2.10 illustrates the GammaLink GammaFax CPi adapter card, which when inserted into a system expansion slot of an IBM PC or compatible personal computer provides a fax/data transmission capability. This type of adapter card removes the necessity for a separate external fax/data modem. Because it uses the power of the computer and does not require a separate housing, it is usually less expensive than a stand-alone device. In addition, its use conserves space on the desktop. In some offices, desktop space is at a premium because the computer, telephone, and calendars compete for a fixed amount of space, and the addition of a stand-alone modem would further reduce the amount of space available for other use.

For synchronous transmission, IBM and third-party vendors manufacture various adapter cards that can be installed in system expansion slots in the system unit of that computer. Some adapter cards enable the PS/2 to be attached directly to IBM 3174 or 3274 control units. When terminal emulation software is loaded, the computer then functions as a 3278- or 3279-type terminal, providing the user with full screen access to mainframe computer applications. Other hardware adapter cards can be used to provide the PS/2 with batch terminal emulation capability to enable it to emulate various IBM and non-IBM remote job entry devices.

FIGURE 2.10.

A GammaLink GammaFax CPi adapter card. (Courtesy of GammaLink Corporation)

Perhaps the most popular type of communications adapter card used in a business environment is a LAN adapter card. Figure 2.11 illustrates the first LAN adapter card marketed by IBM for connecting personal computers to a broadband local area network in which transmission occurred by the radio frequency (rf) modulation of digital data. That is, the adapter card converted the binary ones and zeros of digital data into analog frequency tones for transmission on the network. The adapter card illustrated in Figure 2.11 represented an interim local area network used by IBM that was superseded by its token-ring network, which enables data to flow end-to-end in a digital format and whose operation is described later in this book.

FIGURE 2.11.

An IBM broadband LAN adapter card and cable. (Courtesy of IBM Corporation)

Although the type of adapter card inserted into the expansion slot of a personal computer governs its functionality and capability, note also that most PCs can support the installation and operation of multiple types of adapter cards. In fact, many modern operating environments, such as Microsoft Corporation's Windows and IBM's OS/2, enable you to switch easily between application programs that use different adapter cards. For example, you could first send a message to another user on the LAN through the use of an electronic mail program that communicates with the network by using a LAN adapter card. You then could switch to the use of a communications program that transmits data to a distant bulletin board through an internal modem card. Perhaps the most important thing to note concerning the use of communications adapter cards is that their use turns the personal computer into a multipurpose terminal. That is, with appropriate hardware and software, the PC can function as a LAN workstation, emulate a specific type of vendor terminal, function as a remote batch terminal, or perform another communications-related activity.

The use of a personal computer as a terminal enables hardware and software manufacturers to take advantage of the processing capability of the computer to provide additional capabilities. For example, by using a portion of the memory of the computer for temporary printer data storage, the personal computer can be programmed to accept a mixed data stream of video and printer destination data. This method enables the personal computer operator to maintain interactive transmission with a mainframe computer while a print job is routed to the PC, stored in memory, and dumped from memory to the printer.

A second advantage of using personal computers as terminals includes the expandability and upgradability of PCs. For example, additional memory can easily be added to most personal computers. Concerning upgradability, many personal computers get their display capability from the use of display adapters in a system expansion slot in the computer's system board. When a new video standard gains acceptance, most personal computers can have their existing video display adapters removed and a new adapter that supports the new standard installed. If video support was acquired from the use of a chip set installed on the system board, the installation of a video display adapter normally overrides the chip set, enabling the personal computer to support the new video standard.

The Ubiquitous Terminal

Rapid advances in the development of personal computer hardware and software, coupled with the evolution of communications technology, resulted in the PC becoming a ubiquitous terminal. In actuality, there is no standard PC because the personal computer includes desktop systems, laptops, notebooks, palmtops, and PDAs, each based on the use of a microprocessor and software that enables the computer to perform different types of processing, including the capability to communicate with other computers.

Figure 2.12 illustrates a Windows 95 screen display occurring on a notebook computer that could also represent the display on other types of computers. Windows 95 includes support for multitasking operations, which enables users of this operating system to perform several tasks at one time.

Through the use of a multitasking operating system, a computer user can enhance her productivity by switching between different tasks.

In Figure 2.12, three tasks are being performed, each represented by an open window. In the largest window, which is labeled Wp and represents a foreground operation, a word processing program is being used to type a memorandum. In the background window in the upper-right corner of the display, a communications program is operating, and the window in the upper-left corner of the display provides the computer user with the ability to easily access information stored on different floppy and hard disks and a CD-ROM. By simply clicking on a window or a window label at the bottom of the screen, the computer user can switch between windows. Although you can operate in only one window at a time, you can invoke an operation in one window, such as a file transfer, and then switch to a second window and continue writing a memorandum. Windows 95 from Microsoft Corporation and OS/2 from IBM Corporation represent two multitasking operating systems whose use enables personal computer users to enhance their productivity by eliminating the user's need to wait for one activity to terminate before performing another activity.

FIGURE 2.12.

The Windows 95 desktop after three tasks were initiated.

By the mid-1990s, the use of laptops, notebooks, palmtops, and PDAs provided tens of millions of persons with the ability to exchange electronic mail, access the corporate mainframe, check the price of stocks or bonds, determine the availability of a product, compose memorandums, and perform different types of computer operations regardless of their location. Although the miniaturization of computer hardware was important in providing this capability, equally important were advances in modem technology that reduced the size of the modem to that of a credit card.

Figure 2.13 illustrates the Courier PC Card from U.S. Robotics, which provides an operating rate of 28,800 bps for data transfer, as well as a fax transmission and reception capability. This modem is designed as a Type II PC Card, which can be inserted into a PC Card slot built into most modern portable personal computers.

Through the use of portable computers with modem PC cards and cellular telephones, there is virtually no limit to the ability of persons on the go to communicate. Advances in computer and communications technology has truly revolutionized the manner in which many persons live and work. For many persons, the ability to communicate on the go enables them to have a virtual office without walls, whereas for other persons, such as students, it provides the convenience of being able to work at their own pace without having to get up early on the weekend to gain access to the university computer.

FIGURE 2.13.

The U.S. Robotics Courier PC Card modem. (Courtesy of U.S. Robotics)

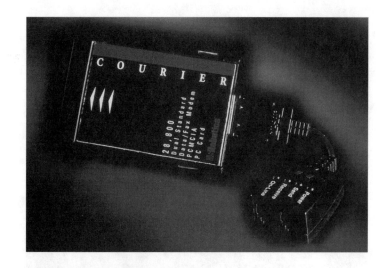

Data Transmission

Data can be transmitted by two methods: serial transmission and parallel transmission.

Serial and Parallel Transmission

In parallel data transmission, each bit of a character is sent over its own wire. In serial transmission, all bits travel over the same wire one after another.

Data is commonly transferred between computers and terminals by changes in the current or voltage on a wire or channel. Such transfers are called parallel if a group of bits moves over several lines at the same time, or serial if the bits move one by one over a single line. Figure 2.14 illustrates parallel and serial data transmission.

In parallel transmission, each bit of a character travels on its own wire. A signal, called the strobe or clock, on an additional wire indicates to the receiver when all the bits are present on their respective wires so that the values can be sampled. Computers and other digital systems that are located near one another (within a few feet) normally use parallel transmission because it is much faster. As the distance between equipment increases, not only do the multiple wires become more costly, but also the difficulty of transmitting and receiving pulse signals on long wires increases.

Serial transmission is used for transmission over long distances. The conversion from parallel to serial and vice versa is accomplished with shift registers. Transmission of serial data is called synchronous if the exact sending or receiving time of each bit is determined before it is transmitted or received. It's called asynchronous if the timing of the bits in a character is not determined by the timing of a previous character.

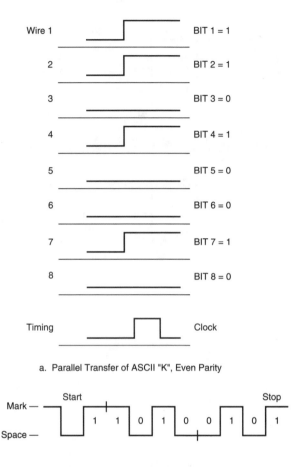

FIGURE 2.14.

*Parallel and serial
data transfer.*

a. Parallel Transfer of ASCII "K", Even Parity

b. Serial Transfer of ASCII "K", Even Parity

Timing

Figure 2.15 illustrates a series of bits transmitted serially over a line. Note that although both the sender and the receiver use the same nominal clock rate, the receiver must somehow determine a more exact clock for decoding the data. This is one of the fundamental problems of data communications. In this case, the receiver retimes its clock on the negative-going edge of the transition (change) from one to zero of the start bit, then uses its new timing to find the middle of the start bit as shown in Figure 2.15a. Notice in Figure 2.15b that although the receiver clock is slightly fast, it doesn't cause an error because the sample strobe still occurs within each bit time.

●
Bit timing is critical
to the accurate
transmission and
reception of data.

FIGURE 2.15.

Clocking asynchronous data.

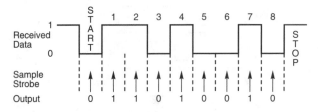

a. Ideal Sampling at Midpoint of Each Bit

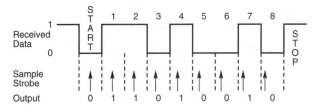

b. Sampling When Received Clock Is Slightly Fast

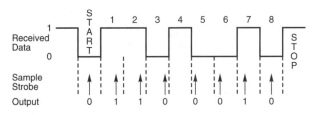

c. Sampling When Received Clock Is Too Slow

Figure 2.15c shows a different situation. Here, the receive clock is so much slower than the transmit clock that the sample strobe does not sample bit 4 at all; thus, an error occurs in the output. The communications system must somehow ensure that the receive clock is timed so that errors do not occur. Although bit timing is very important, it alone isn't enough to complete the communications process.

> The framing method used in asynchronous transmission defines a character by using start and stop bits to separate it from other characters.

Framing

Framing is the next step in timing after bit timing. In the example of Figure 2.15, it could be called character timing, because the start and stop bits frame one character for the receiver. This is the framing used in asynchronous data transmission, which is discussed in association with teleprinter operation in the next section. Synchronous data communications systems use different methods of framing, which are discussed in later chapters.

Asynchronous Transmission

Asynchronous communications systems evolved before electronic systems. Electromechanical systems therefore had to be used. The problem in those systems was the synchronization of the operation of two electromechanical devices (motors), one at each end of the line, whose speeds could not be easily adjusted. The timing and framing problem was solved by resuming each character using the edge of the start bit, which was required to be the first bit on the line. Nevertheless, if the difference in motor speeds was too great, the bit timing would drift with each successive bit until the sampling of the last received data bit in the character could be incorrect. Thus, five bits became the standard for the low-speed teleprinter code because the chance of error increased significantly if more bits were used.

Imagine an operator keying a teleprinter keyboard to produce characters for transmission. The framed character generated by each key depression begins with a start bit and ends with one or two stop bits. The stop condition is a mark or positive voltage on the line (negative voltage with double-current signaling). The positive voltage remains on the line until the next character starts because the line idle condition is internally defined as current flow or mark, rather than no current or space. When a space (start bit) is detected, the receiving device starts, and it will be in synchronization with the transmitting device.

> The first asynchronous communications systems used electric motors driving rotating contacts at each end. The rotation of the motors had to be synchronized.

Electromechanical Method

The diagram in Figure 2.16 illustrates the operation of an electromechanical start-stop teleprinter machine. The sending device and the receiving device both have an armature, A, which rotates at a constant speed when a clutch connects it to an electric motor in the machine. Contacts on the armature connect an outer ring of contacts, B, to the transmission line. In the diagram, the armature is in its stop position. Current from the battery in the sender flows through the contact labeled STOP, through the armature, and through the line to the receiver. This current causes the receive relay to remain energized, keeping the clutch disengaged, the armature stationary, and the teleprinter in the idle condition.

> Current pulses, placed on the line by the sender's rotating armature, select the character to be printed through the synchronized receiver contacts.

Sender   Receiver

FIGURE 2.16.

Electromechanical start-stop coding and decoding.

Now suppose that an operator at the sending device presses the H key on the keyboard. In accordance with the five-bit code shown back in Figure 1.4, data contacts 3 and 5 close to encode the H, and the start contact at the sending machine closes. This action energizes the start magnet to engage the clutch to turn the armature of the sending device counterclockwise. The armature connects the contacts on the outer ring to the line in sequence: start, 1, 2, 3, 4, 5, stop. Notice that the start contact and data contacts 1, 2, and 4 do not conduct current.

As soon as the armature of the sender travels to its start contact, the current through the line and the receive relay ceases. The receive relay is de-energized, and current flows through the other set of relay contacts and through the start magnet of the receiver. This action engages the clutch, and the receiver armature begins turning counterclockwise at approximately the same speed as the sender armature. When the sender armature is over data contact 3, current flows through the line and the receive relay. The receive relay is energized, and as the armature of the receiver passes over data contact 3 on the outer ring, current flows through select magnet 3.

Select magnet 5 is operated similarly. The operation of these two magnets causes the letter H to be selected on the type mechanism of the receiver. When the sender armature reaches its stop contact, the receiver armature passes over contact C, current flows to the print magnet, and the letter H is printed. Both armatures then come to rest in the position shown in the illustration, unless the sender is ready to transmit another character immediately.

Note that the start and stop elements have those exact functions; that is, they start and stop the armature rotation. As you can visualize, if there were much variation in the rotational speeds of the sending and receiving armatures, the armatures would not be in synchronization, and the character would be decoded incorrectly. As discussed previously, this is one reason that the Baudot code was limited to five symbols.

Bit timing within a character must be precise to prevent errors. However, the timing between characters is not of importance for accuracy.

With start-stop transmission, a new character can begin at any time after the stop bits of the preceding character have been received. The time between one character and the next is indeterminate, but within a character, the timing is precisely defined. For that reason, it might be better to call this technique self-synchronized or internally synchronized, rather than asynchronous, meaning "not synchronized." (The lack of a continuous synchronous agreement between the transmitter and the receiver—specifically, the lack of a clocking signal within or accompanying the data channel—is the reason for the name "asynchronous.")

Electronic Receiving Circuit

The electromechanical arrangements of the early teleprinters were replaced with electronic circuits. Because these can be synchronized within closer tolerances, an eight-bit code can be used. An electronic circuit for receiving asynchronous serial data in an eight-bit code is shown in Figure 2.17. It utilizes a clock that runs at 16 times the symbol rate of the incoming data. This rapid rate is used to detect the 1 to 0 transition (when the start bit begins) as soon as possible after it occurs. The circuit that detects the 1 to 0 transition enables a spike detection circuit. Eight "ticks" of the 16X clock (one-half a bit time) are counted, and then the line is checked to see whether it is still in the 0 state. If it is not, it is assumed that the initial 1 to 0 transition was due to noise on the line, the spike detection circuit is reset, and no further action is taken.

FIGURE 2.17.

An asynchronous receiver.

If the line is still at 0, a valid start signal has arrived. A counter is enabled that divides the 16X clock by 16 to produce a sampling clock that ticks once per bit time for the shift register. This tick occurs roughly at the center of the bit being sampled. The off-center error can be made smaller by sampling at 32 times the bit rate, and even further reduced by sampling at 64 times the bit rate. However, when higher sampling rates are used, the counter in the spike detection circuit and the counter in the bit sampler circuit must count proportionately higher.

The bit sampler circuit strobes the shift register eight times to sample the state of the line to get the eight bits into the serial-to-parallel shift register. Then a signal, called a flag, is sent to the computer or controller with which it is associated to announce that a character has been received. The computer then signals the shift register to transfer the eight bits in parallel into the processing circuits.

A problem with using only a shift register (called a single-buffered interface) is that when characters are arriving continuously, the computer has only the duration of the stop bit to read the received character before the next character begins entering the register. A simple improvement is to provide a holding register into which the received character can be parallel transferred as soon as the eighth bit has been sampled. A character-available flag is sent to the computer when the parallel transfer occurs, and the receiving register becomes available for the next character. This arrangement, called a double-buffered interface, is shown in Figure 2.18. In either case, the arrival of a character that cannot be handled because the

●

A single-buffered interface requires the receiving computer to read each character as soon as it is received, with no break before the next one begins.

preceding character has not been read is called data overflow. If overflow occurs, most receiver circuits overwrite the old character with the new one (the old one is lost) and place an error signal on a separate lead to the computer.

FIGURE 2.18.
A double-buffered interface.

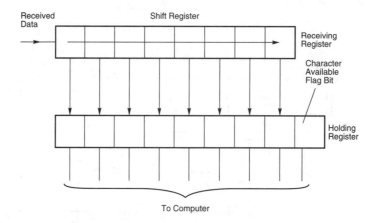

Received Data — Shift Register — Receiving Register

Character Available Flag Bit

Holding Register

To Computer

Stop Bits and Timing Errors

A double-buffered interface provides a holding register to hold the character for reading, and the next character received fills the receiving register.

With a double-buffered interface, the stop bit arrival time is no longer the only time available to the computer for reading the character, so there is time for circuitry to check the stop bit (sometimes called the ninth bit) to confirm that it is a 1. If it is not a 1, one of the following conditions exists: The communications channel path is broken, the receiver timing is confused, or the transmitting station is sending a special signal. The existence of one of these conditions typically provides an error signal on a lead in the asynchronous receiver.

Such an error occurs when the receiver has lost track of which zeros in the transmission are the start bits and which are just zeros in the data. If, for some reason, the receiver treats a data bit as a start bit, it assembles the next eight bits as a character. Because these eight bits are really parts of two characters (the end of one and the beginning of another), the ninth bit to arrive will not be the stop bit, but rather a data bit from the second character. If it is a zero, the error-checking circuit detects an error. Because framing is the process of deciding which groups of eight bits constitute characters, and this error is due to a failure in that process, it is called a framing error.

Failure in the framing process generally can be avoided. The idle line condition is a mark condition, and any amount of idle time more than a character time corrects this condition. Even if characters are sent continuously, the receiver eventually becomes realigned to the correct start elements, no matter which zero bit is chosen as the start bit. Of course, the characters received while the framing is not in alignment are decoded incorrectly.

The UART

The electronic circuitry previously described has been reduced through the use of very large-scale integrated circuitry onto a communications chip referred to as a UART (Universal Asynchronous Receiver Transmitter). A UART in its transmit mode converts the bits received in parallel, which represent a character within a computer, into a serial data stream and then transfers each bit onto the serial interface at an appropriate time. In addition, the UART frames the character to include the addition of start and stop bits and optionally add a parity bit before transmitting the bits in a serial sequence. When in its receive mode, the UART samples the line for incoming bits; forms a stream of bits into a character after removing the start, stop, and parity bits; and transfers the received character to the computer. The use of a parity bit for error detection is covered later in this book.

Through the use of UARTs that are no bigger than a thumbnail, it became possible to provide every type of personal computer, ranging in size from a desktop to a personal digital assistant, with a serial port. The UART normally is included on the motherboard of modern computers and connected to the physical connector that represents the interface to the serial port. Although most readers are probably familiar with 15- and 25-pin connectors labeled "serial port" on many computers, the actual work in which parallel data inside the computer is converted into a serial bit sequence transmitted through the connector is performed by a UART inside the computer.

When the IBM PC was introduced in 1981, the computer's serial communications capability was obtained via the installation of a serial adapter card that included a National Semiconductor 8250 UART. That UART, which was used in motherboards of other computers during the 1980s and early 1990s, did not include an internal buffer. This limited its data transfer capability to 19,200 bps before data loss might occur. Today, most computers, as well as modems fabricated on adapter cards, use the more capable 16550 UART.

The UART contains a built-in 16-byte buffer that enables higher-speed data transfers before data loss might occur. The 16550 can support data transfers up to 115,200 bps, which makes it suitable for transferring data to 28,800 bps modems employing data compression and obtaining an average compression ratio of 4:1. Because many personal computers manufactured through the mid-1990s include the 8250 UART, that chip should be replaced if you want to effectively use high-speed modems with those computers. Fortunately, the more capable 16550 UART will fit into the socket used by the 8250, which can be easily removed if it is not soldered into the motherboard. As an alternative, the use of a modern modem fabricated on an adapter card for insertion into a computer will include a 16550 UART that supports the high-speed data transfer required to effectively use the modem.

●
To support high-speed data transfer beyond 19,200 bps, the 8250 UART used in older personal computers should be replaced with the more capable 16550 chip.

Other Types of Transmission

Large data communications systems normally do not use asynchronous transmission because the start-stop codes take too much time, and error detection and correction methods are impractical.

Asynchronous transmission is the most common in data communications simply because there are more terminals and small-computer applications in which it is used. Large systems and networks usually use methods other than asynchronous. This is because of the large overhead penalty of 20 percent associated with start-stop codes; that is, 2 (the start and stop bits) out of the 10 bits transmitted are for control rather than for information. This is not a problem in many other types of interactive applications, in which more time is spent looking at the screen than transferring a file of 500,000 characters (4 million bits) at 9600 bps.

A second problem in such large transfers is error checking. A file-transfer user originally had to check the input and output for errors by looking at the screen and rekeying or asking for retransmission of portions that contained errors. Such a procedure is clearly impractical for long file transfers that occur at fast rates and often without an operator present. Although transmission protocols have been developed to provide error-free asynchronous transmission, the use of this type of communications is oriented for relatively short transmission requirements. Applications requiring large-volume, high-speed data transfers necessitate a different method of data transfer. This method is called synchronous transmission.

In synchronous transmission, start and stop bits are not used. Characters are sent in groups, called blocks, with special synchronization characters placed at the beginning of the block and within it, to ensure that enough 0-to-1 or 1-to-0 transitions occur for the receiver clock to remain accurate. Error checking is performed automatically on the entire block. If any errors occur, the entire block is retransmitted. This technique also carries an overhead penalty (nothing is free), but the overhead is far less than the 20 percent for blocks of more than a few dozen characters. Figure 2.19 compares asynchronous and synchronous transmission of a sequence of characters.

FIGURE 2.19.

A comparison of asynchronous and synchronous data transmission.

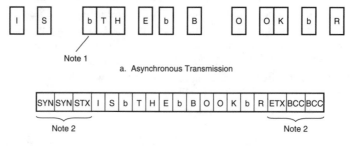

Note 1

a. Asynchronous Transmission

Note 2　　　　　　　　　Note 2

b. Synchronous Transmission

NOTES:
1. b means blank (space character)
2. Transmission control characters

In addition to asynchronous and synchronous transmission methods to achieve receiver timing, there is now a third method called isochronous transmission. This technique is used in a few computer networks. It involves timing that is controlled by the network rather than the DCE or DTE, as is true for synchronous and asynchronous transmission. Synchronous and isochronous data transmission are discussed later in this book.

What Have You Learned?

1. Compared to CRT terminals, teleprinters are much slower in printing, have limited formatting capability, don't have enhancements such as blinking and highlighting, and are less reliable in operation.

2. A serial or character printer prints one character at a time. The printer can be either an impact or a nonimpact printer. An impact printer can produce fully formed characters or characters formed by a dot matrix. A nonimpact printer usually uses a thermal, optical (laser), or ink-jet method.

3. CRT terminals can be classified as dumb, smart, and user-programmable. A dumb terminal is essentially the same as a teleprinter except for printing speed. A smart terminal has capabilities such as editing, formatting, highlighting, and blinking. A user-programmable terminal has a built-in programming language and the capability to store and execute programs.

4. As applied to terminals, ergonomics has to do with the color, character size, and nonglare surface of the display, and with the shape, position, and layout of the keys. It also is concerned with the physical position of both the display and the keyboard with respect to the operator.

5. The communications functionality and capability of a personal computer is altered through the addition of different types of adapter cards and the use of appropriate software.

6. In serial transmission, the bits are transmitted one at a time over a single wire. In parallel transmission, each bit of a group moves over its own wire, and all bits of the group move at the same time.

7. Both bit timing and framing are necessary to maintain synchronization for proper decoding in data communications. Bit timing usually is accomplished by clocking the bits. Framing usually is accomplished by inserting special bits or characters in the data stream just for that purpose.

8. In asynchronous transmission, each character is sent by itself and is framed by a start bit and stop bit. This is the transmission method used by teleprinters and ASCII terminals.

9. The UART receives data from a parallel format within a computer, frames the data by the addition of start and stop bits and an optional parity bit, and transmits the data one bit at a time serially.

10. In synchronous transmission, many characters are sent together in groups called blocks. Each block is framed by special synchronization characters.

Quiz for Chapter 2

1. Teleprinters:
   a. Are only for printing at remote locations, not for input.
   b. Offer both high-speed operation and various formatting controls.
   c. Have a printer for output and might have a keyboard for input.

2. Impact printers:
   a. Strike a ribbon against the paper to produce character images.
   b. Include ink-jet and thermal devices.
   c. Are rapidly becoming obsolete.

3. Glass Teletypes:
   a. Are among the most recent developments in CRT terminals.
   b. Were so named because they had the same interface as teleprinters.
   c. Are teleprinters designed to interface with fiber-optic transmission systems.

4. Electromechanical teleprinters:
   a. Use a complex mechanical buffer to match speed between transmitting and receiving machines.
   b. Use start/stop codes to synchronize sending and receiving equipment.
   c. Are rarely used today.

5. ASCII terminals are generally defined as:
   a. Terminals using synchronous transmission in EBCDIC.
   b. Terminals using synchronous transmission in ASCII.
   c. Terminals using asynchronous transmission in ASCII.
   d. Any terminals having an American (dollar-sign) keyboard.

6. One drawback associated with laptop and notebook computers is:
   a. Pop-out keyboard.
   b. Screen viewing angle.
   c. Portability.
   d. Weight.

7. "3270" terminals refer to:

    a. Asynchronous terminals made by IBM.

    b. Any terminal that is painted blue.

    c. Synchronous terminals that interface with an IBM-type cluster controller.

8. The use of IBM's proprietary 3270 networking technology was extended by:

    a. The standards committee.

    b. The use of mainframes.

    c. The addition of LAN connectivity.

    d. Graphics terminals.

9. A multipurpose terminal refers to:

    a. A terminal with a serial port.

    b. A computer with both serial and parallel ports.

    c. A terminal with a UART.

    d. A computer to which communications functionality is added through the addition of hardware and software.

10. The difference between timing and framing is that:

    a. Timing is concerned with the individual bits, whereas framing is concerned with the boundaries between characters.

    b. Timing refers to serial transmission, whereas framing refers to parallel transmission.

    c. Timing is concerned primarily with asynchronous systems, whereas framing is concerned with synchronous systems.

11. Escape codes are so called because:

    a. In effect, they provide a means to temporarily "escape" from the standard meanings of the character set.

    b. They initiate operation of the escapement mechanism in teleprinters.

    c. They cause the cursor to escape from the boundaries of the CRT screen and roam around in memory.

12. The QWERTY keyboard:

    a. Is still considered to be the layout allowing the greatest typing speed.

    b. Is the most popular keyboard, but not necessarily the best.

    c. Is a key layout that is rarely used.

13. Memory-mapped displays:

    a. Are associated with electromechanical teleprinters.

    b. Have the advantage that they do not take up memory space.

    c. Allow direct addressing of display locations by the processor.

14. The major differences between personal computer keyboards are:

    a. In the use of QWERTY versus other key layouts.

    b. In the use of the Shift key.

    c. In the position of function keys and the inclusion or omission of a numeric keypad.

    d. In the placement of the numeric keys on the keyboard.

15. Serial printers:

    a. Are used to transmit grain prices.

    b. Are faster than CRT terminals and offer more flexibility.

    c. Print one character at a time.

    d. Usually use serial interfaces.

16. Nonimpact printers:

    a. Are normally quieter than impact printers.

    b. Generate carbon copies easily.

    c. Produce fully formed characters.

17. CRT terminals:

    a. Are the most widely used hard-copy terminals.

    b. Offer high-speed display and formatting flexibility.

    c. Do not normally use microprocessors.

18. User-programmable terminals:

    a. Are replacing personal and professional computers.

    b. Offer more flexibility at lower cost.

    c. Are being replaced by personal and professional computers.

19. A multitasking operating system enables:

    a. Several windows to be displayed.

    b. Communications between computers.

    c. The use of the UART.

    d. Several tasks to be performed at the same time.

20. Ergonomics:

    a. Involves the interface between people and machines, such as terminals.

    b. Is the application of ergo-economics to communications.

    c. Utilizes three-level ergo-coding for transmission over certain channels.

21. Serial and parallel transmission:

    a. Differ in how many bits are transferred per character.

    b. Are used in synchronous and asynchronous systems, respectively.

    c. Differ in whether the bits are on separate wires or all on one wire.

22. Memory-mapped displays:

    a. Are used for high-resolution graphics, such as maps.

    b. Use ordinary memory to store the display data in character form.

    c. Store the display data as individual bits.

23. Asynchronous transmission:

    a. Is less efficient than synchronous, but simpler.

    b. Is much faster than synchronous transmission.

    c. Is another name for isochronous transmission.

24. Single-buffering:

    a. Is more efficient than double-buffering.

    b. Is less efficient than no buffering.

    c. Provides very little time to unload the incoming character from the register.

25. Most terminal keyboards:

    a. Provide numerous additional specialized keys.

    b. Are strictly typewriter style, with few extra keys.

    c. Use the Dvorak layout.

Messages and Transmission Channels

About This Chapter

Useful communication requires four elements, as shown in Figure 3.1: a message (information) to be communicated, a sender of the message, a medium or channel over which the message can be sent, and a receiver. Messages usually are information that is useful to people, but the sender and receiver might or might not be human. The medium must be one suitable to convey the type of message. In this chapter, we will examine in more detail the types of messages and the media that carry them.

UNDERSTANDING

FIGURE 3.1.

The elements of communication.

MESSAGE   RECEIVER

What Is Information?

To help you understand the following discussion, I'll first lay the groundwork by establishing what information is.

Information as a Quantity

The unit of information used in data communications is the bit, which has only two possible values, 1 and 0. Seven bits are needed to select any one of 128 different symbols in ASCII.

"Information," according to one definition, "is the communication or reception of knowledge or intelligence." Information is also "a numerical quantity that measures the uncertainty in the outcome of an experiment to be performed." This second definition has an application in the sending of messages. For example, suppose that we have a machine that can send only two symbols, A1 and A2. We can then say that the "experiment" is the accurate recognition of the two symbols (A1 and A2) being sent from one machine to another. As far as the receiving machine is concerned, it is just as likely to receive one symbol as the other. So we can say that the "numerical quantity" in this experiment is a unit of information that allows a selection between two equally likely choices. This quantity, or unit of information, is usually called a bit (a contraction of *binary digit*), and it has two possible values, 0 and 1. If these two values are used to represent A1 and A2, then A1 could be represented by the bit value 0, and A2 by the bit value 1. The number of bits per symbol is 1, but we still need a way of selecting which symbol (bit) we want to use. A machine that needs only two symbols needs only a 1-bit select code (0 and 1).

A machine that uses only two symbols is not of much use for communication, but suppose that the machine used 128 symbols (like the standard ASCII character set). Then the number of equally likely choices to be handled is 128, and the number of bits (information) required to represent each of those 128 symbols is seven (refer to Table 1.1 in Chapter 1, "An Overview of Data Communications"). You can see, then, that if the knowledge (or intelligence) to be communicated can be represented by a set of equally likely symbols, the amount of information required per symbol to communicate that knowledge is necessarily dependent on the total number of bits of information. The standard ASCII character set is particularly useful for selecting the information to be communicated because it can select one of 128 ASCII symbols with only one 8-bit byte, a common bit grouping in computers (the eighth bit is not used in this case). The extended ASCII character set that uses all 8 bits per byte supports 256 symbols, doubling the number of ASCII symbols.

Information Content of Symbols

In many information systems, not every symbol is equally likely to be used in a given communication. The English language is a good example. In a message written in English, the letter *e* is 12 times more likely to occur than the letter *s*. This uneven distribution is also characteristic of particular groups of letters and of words. What this means, then, is that each of the 128 symbols in ASCII or 256 symbols in extended ASCII is not likely to occur an equal number of times in any given communication. For example, notice that the uses of the letters *e* and *g* and the letter combinations *th* and *er* are unequal in this paragraph.

In 1949, Claude Shannon published a book titled *The Mathematical Theory of Communication*. In this book, he discusses the uncertainty or amount of disorder of a system, which he called entropy. The entropy of a set of equally likely symbols (such as the digits 0–9 in a table of random numbers) is the logarithm to the base 2 of the number of symbols in the set. The entropy of the English alphabet, which contains 26 letters and a space, is then $\log_2(27) = 4.76$ bits per symbol. Because of the uneven use of letters in the English language, however, its entropy was estimated by Shannon as 1.3 bits per symbol. This means that the language is about 70 percent redundant and that it should be possible to reconstruct English text accurately if every other letter is lost or changed due to noise or distortion. Obviously, redundancy is desirable to raise the chances of receiving a good message when the medium is noisy. (The words *noise* and *noisy* in this book refer to electrical noise—that is, an electrical signal that is not supposed to be present.)

● Redundancy is the measurement of the probability of occurrence of any particular character in a character set.

Using Redundancy in Communications

So, you wonder, what does all this have to do with the real world of data communications? Quite a bit, because almost every scheme in current use for sending data uses redundancy in an attempt to verify that the data has been received exactly as sent—that is, no errors have been introduced by the sending mechanism, the transmission medium, or the receiver. The redundant information might consist simply of a retransmission of the entire original message. Although simple to implement, retransmission is not efficient.

● Redundancy can be used to reconstruct a message even if part of the message is lost during transmission. It is very important in verifying data accuracy.

Special techniques are therefore used to generate redundant information that is related to the message in a way that is known to both the sender and the receiver. The sender generates the redundant information during transmission and sends it with the message. The receiver regenerates and checks the redundant information when the message is received. This scheme is represented in Figure 3.2. Verification usually occurs at the end of each link in the chain making up the transmission path. The details of this process and various methods in current use are described in Chapter 11, "Architectures and Packet Networks."

FIGURE 3.2.

Error-checking points.

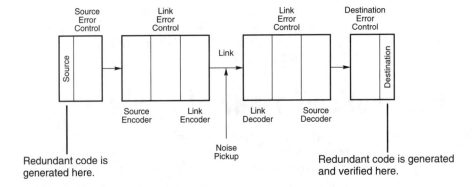

What Carries the Message?

• Bounded data channels confine the signals within wires, coaxial cable, or optical-fiber cable. Unbounded channels enable the signal to radiate in all directions.

The physical channels (the media) that carry data are of two types: bounded and unbounded. In a bounded medium, the signals are confined to the medium and do not leave it (except for smaller leakage amounts). A pair of wires, coaxial cable, waveguide, and optical-fiber cable are examples of bounded media. The atmosphere, the ocean, and outer space are examples of unbounded media, in which electromagnetic signals originated by the source radiate freely into the medium and spread throughout it. The unbounded media are used by various radio frequency transmitting schemes to carry messages. The main feature of unbounded media is that when the signal is radiated from the transmitter, it radiates equally in all directions (unless restricted) and continues forever onward. As it moves farther from the source, the energy is spread over a larger area, so the level continually gets weaker at greater distances. As the wave moves through the medium, it is affected by natural disturbances, which can interfere with the signal.

Wire Pairs

• Wire pairs are the simplest type of bounded carrier. The two wires that provide the go and return signal path, when balanced to ground, provide the most protection from induced noise.

The simplest type of a bounded medium is a pair of wires providing a go and return path for electrical signals. Early telegraph systems used the earth itself rather than a wire for one of the paths, as shown in Figure 3.3a. Repeaters were inserted along the line to reduce the effects of noise and attenuation (loss of signal strength). This scheme did not work well, however, because the earth is not always a good conductor, and the path was susceptible to large noise currents induced by lightning. Losses were reduced by using two wires, as shown in Figure 3.3b, but because the line was still unbalanced to ground, it was subject to picking up noise from almost every noise-producing device. Finally, the balanced two-wire line, shown in Figure 3.3c, was used to greatly reduce noise pickup.

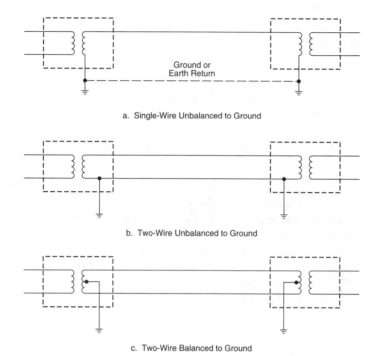

a. Single-Wire Unbalanced to Ground

b. Two-Wire Unbalanced to Ground

c. Two-Wire Balanced to Ground

FIGURE 3.3.

Types of transmission circuits.

The most common type of bounded medium consists of wire pairs twisted together and made into cables of from 4 to 3000 pairs. Because a wire acts as an antenna, several techniques are used to reduce electromagnetic interference (EMI). Most wires are shielded, and some wires are also twisted at 90-degree angles every so often. The twists additionally suppress EMI. The size of the wire used varies from 16 AWG (American Wire Gauge) with a wire diameter of 0.05082 inch to 26 AWG with a diameter of 0.01594 inch. AWG wire sizes are inversely proportional to the diameter of the wire. That is, the lower the AWG, the thicker the wire, whereas a higher AWG indicates a thinner wire. In modern cables, each wire is insulated with a polyethylene or polyvinyl chloride (PVC) jacket; however, a large quantity of older cable is still in use in which the insulation for each wire is paper.

Open-wire lines have a low attenuation of voice frequencies due to the large size of the wire and the relatively large distance between the two wires when mounted on a crossarm of a utility pole. A typical value of attenuation for 104 mil (0.104 inch) diameter open wire lines is 0.07 decibel (dB) per mile, whereas 19-gauge (0.03589 inch diameter) twisted wire pairs in a multipair cable have a voice frequency attenuation of about 1 dB per mile.

The size of the wires used and the distance between them affect the attenuation. Twisted wire pairs are limited to a maximum frequency of about 1 MHz.

The attenuation of twisted wire pairs rises rapidly with increasing frequency, and the amount of crosstalk between adjacent pairs also increases with frequency. The maximum usable frequency for wire pairs in cables is around 1 MHz without special treatment.

The Effect of Inductance

A concept that might not be obvious about paired wire circuits is that the addition of inductance in the line can help reduce attenuation at voice frequencies. The line impedance (AC resistance) is increased so that a given amount of power can be transmitted with less current but at a higher voltage. The result is a reduction in the series losses and an increase in the shunt losses. Because the series losses are usually the most severe, there is a net reduction in attenuation until the inductance rises to the point where series and shunt losses are equal.

When a circuit is loaded with added inductance, attenuation can be reduced at higher frequencies so that the circuit response is relatively constant over the voiceband.

Adding inductance to wire pairs is called loading, and a circuit to which inductance has been added is called a loaded line or loaded circuit. The effect of loading is illustrated in Figure 3.4. The typical frequency-versus-attenuation performance is shown for a nonloaded 19-gauge cable pair and a 19-gauge cable pair loaded with 88 millihenrys of inductance every 6000 feet. (The standard notation for this is 19H-88 loaded pair.) Figure 3.4 shows that the attenuation of the loaded circuit is less than that of the unloaded one and that it changes very little with increasing frequency up to a certain point above 3 KHz. This point is called the cutoff point or cutoff frequency.

FIGURE 3.4.

Effect of inductance loading.

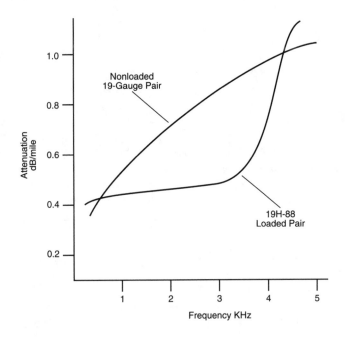

Loading was introduced around 1900 on long-distance open wire lines to reduce losses due to attenuation, because there were no amplifiers for the signals.

Electronic Amplifiers

In 1883, Thomas Edison discovered the rectifying properties of the thermionic vacuum tube. A thermionic vacuum tube is one in which a stream of electrons is emitted by an incandescent substance. Edison's device was a two-element tube (called a diode) consisting of a cathode (the incandescent substance) and an anode.

The principle of thermionic vacuum tubes lay unused, however, until 1904. At that time, Sir John Ambrose Fleming, an English physicist and engineer, adapted the diode for use as a demodulator (detector) of radiotelegraph signals for the Marconi Wireless Telegraph Co. In 1906, Lee DeForest introduced a third element, called a control grid, to the diode and created the triode. By 1912, the triode and its associated circuits were developed for use as an amplifier.

When the use of the DeForest triode as an amplifier began in 1914, it was no longer necessary to load long-distance circuits, because the losses in the line could be compensated for by amplification. However, loading is still used on longer local loops (from the telephone office to the customer) because it is cheaper than adding active components for amplification. The presence of loading on local circuits has a considerable effect on their capability to carry high-frequency data signals, which causes problems for some new types of telephone service.

Electronic amplifiers eliminate the requirement to load long-distance circuits because amplification can compensate for the line losses.

Coaxial Cable

To make telephone service economical, a way had to be found to put more than one conversation onto a channel. Indeed, the invention of the telephone arose out of Alexander Bell's experiments on a "harmonic telegraph," an attempt to put more than one telegraph signal on a channel. Putting more conversations or more data on a single channel requires a larger bandwidth (capability to carry more frequencies), which, as a practical matter, means higher frequencies. Because the practical frequency limit for wire pairs is around 1 MHz, some other method had to be developed.

Some significant and interesting effects occur in the vicinity of a wire carrying an alternating current signal. One of these effects is that both an electric field and a magnetic field are created around the conductor. The magnetic field can induce the signal it is carrying into adjacent conductors. (In communications, the induced and unwanted signal is called crosstalk.) However, if one conductor of the pair is the ground side of the circuit and is made to surround the other conductor, both the radiated electric field and the magnetic field can be confined within the tube formed by the outer conductor, as illustrated in Figure 3.5.

To put more data transmissions onto one channel at the same time, the transmissions must be at frequencies higher than those practical for wire pairs. Coaxial cables can be used for signals with frequencies of 10,000 MHz.

FIGURE 3.5.

Structure of coaxial cable.

Outer Conductor
(Shield)

Confines the electric and magnetic fields inside the tube.

Insulator
(Plastic)

Center Conductor
(Solid or Hollow)

This medium is called a coaxial cable, because the two conductors have a common axis. The self-shielding works well at frequencies above about 100 KHz, but at lower frequencies, the "skin depth" of the current is comparable to the thickness of the outer conductor, and the shielding becomes ineffective. The resistive loss of coaxial cable increases in proportion to the square root of the frequency, making coaxial cable generally usable at frequencies of up to 2000 MHz, although some types can be used up to 10,000 MHz.

Waveguide

If the frequency of transmission is high enough, the electric and magnetic components of a signal can travel through free space, requiring no solid conductor. However, to avoid interference and losses due to signal spreading and to be able to route the signal as desired, it is sometimes useful to confine these waves to another bounded medium called a waveguide.

Waveguides can be used at frequencies of 2000–110,000 MHz.

Waveguides are commonly used at frequencies from 2000 MHz up to 110,000 MHz to connect microwave transmitters and receivers to their antennas. Waveguides are pressurized with dry air or nitrogen to drive out moisture from inside the waveguide because moisture attenuates the microwaves. Older waveguides were constructed with a rectangular cross section, but common practice today is to make the guides circular, as shown in Figure 3.6. Waveguides remain in use as a conductor of high-power, high-frequency signals, but optical-fiber cables are being used in newer systems.

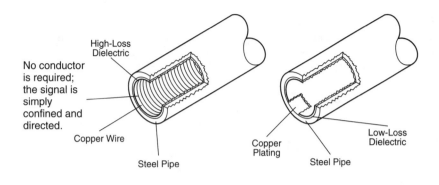

FIGURE 3.6.
Circular waveguides.

No conductor is required; the signal is simply confined and directed.

High-Loss Dielectric

Copper Wire

Steel Pipe

Low-Loss Dielectric

Copper Plating

Steel Pipe

a. Helix

b. Dielectric Lined

Fiber-Optic Systems

The capacity of a transmission system is a direct function of the highest frequency it can carry. Progress in transmission technology has therefore been measured by the bandwidth of the media available to carry signals. Recent developments in the use of glass fibers to carry binary signals have shown these systems to be extremely well-suited to high-data-rate applications. Fiber-optic systems are attractive for several reasons:

● The low transmission loss, as compared with wire pairs or coaxial cable, allows much greater separation between repeaters. A fiber-optic system with no repeaters has been demonstrated that transmits 420 megabits per second (Mbps) over a span of 75 miles with an error rate several times lower than that of high-quality coaxial cable systems.

● Because the optical fibers carry light rays, the frequency of operation is that of light. The transmission wavelength used for current single-mode fibers is 1.2 micrometers, equivalent to a frequency of around 800 terahertz (800 trillion Hz). Such frequencies allow data transmission rates of 20,000 Mbps over short distances.

● Optical-fiber cables do not radiate energy, do not conduct electricity, and are noninductive. They are essentially free from crosstalk and the effects of lightning-induced interference, and they present no security problem from an inductively coupled "wire tap."

● Because optical-fiber cables transport light energy, they can be routed through most hazardous areas, such as oil refineries, grain elevators, and similar locations where the use of cables carrying electricity are either barred or represent a potential danger.

●
Fiber-optic systems can handle high-capacity, high-frequency transmissions economically because they have low loss, are free of electromagnetic interference, are nonconductive, are noninductive, and do not radiate energy.

● Optical-fiber cables are smaller, lighter, and cheaper than metallic cables of the same capacity. It is economically feasible to provide several unused fibers in a cable for spares and for future growth. A cross section of a typical optical-fiber cable is shown in Figure 3.7.

FIGURE 3.7.

A typical optical five-fiber cable for direct burial.

¹Kevlar is a trademark of E.I. Du Pont de Nemours and Co.

One standard fiber-optic system currently in service is the AT&T FT3 lightwave system, which can carry 80,000 two-way voice conversations at the same time. The cable for this system is one-half inch in diameter and contains 144 fibers. Each fiber pair operates at 90 Mbps for a total data rate of about 6000 Mbps. The system provides one spare fiber for every operating one, and switchover to a spare is automatic on loss of signal in a fiber. A more detailed discussion of fiber-optic systems is given in Chapter 7, "Fiber-Optic and Satellite Communications."

Building Cabling Standards

Although American Wire Gauge numbering governs the thickness of a conductor, other properties govern the capability of twisted pair to transport information. Recognizing the requirement to standardize cabling used within buildings for the transportation of voice, as well as for data on local area networks, the Electronic Industries Association (EIA) and the Telecommunications Industry Association (TIA) jointly developed a standard that specifies various building cabling parameters. Formally referred to as the EIA/TIA-568 standard, this standard specifies cabling parameters ranging from backbone cabling used to connect a building's telecommunications closets to an equipment room, to horizontal cabling used to cable individual users to an equipment closet. This standard defines the performance characteristics of both backbone and horizontal cables, as well as different types of connectors used with different types of cable.

> ●
> The EIA/TIA-568 standard specifies backbone and horizontal cabling parameters.

Backbone Cabling

Four types of media are recognized by the EIA/TIA-568 standard for backbone cabling. Table 3.1 summarizes the backbone media cabling options to include the maximum cabling distance support by each type of media.

Table 3.1. EIA/TIA-568 backbone cabling media options.

Media Type	Maximum Cabling Distance
100 ohm unshielded twisted pair (UTP)	800 meters (2624 feet)
150 ohm shielded twisted pair (STP)	700 meters (2296 feet)
50 ohm thick coaxial cable	500 meters (1640 feet)
62.5/125 μm multimode optical fiber	2000 meters (6560 feet)

Backbone cabling is commonly used to connect network devices known as hubs to form the backbone of a local area network. That connection can occur between hubs located on different floors or hubs located on the same floor. Thus, backbone cabling can consist of vertical and horizontal cabling. In comparison, restrictive horizontal cabling provides the connection from individual workstations to a port on a hub. Because most hubs are located in a telecommunications or wiring closet, the EIA/TIA-568 standard for horizontal cabling governs the cabling from a telecommunications closet to a user's work area. Figure 3.8 illustrates the relationship between backbone and horizontal cabling, as well as their use to interconnect hubs and workstations. Later in this book, we will discuss the operation and utilization of different types of hubs in detail.

FIGURE 3.8.
Building cable relationship.

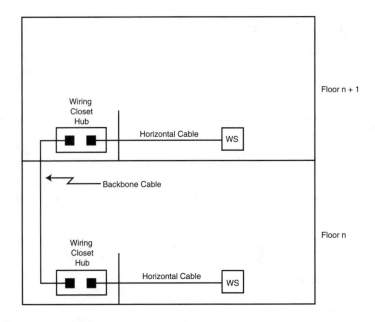

Horizontal Cabling

The EIA/TIA-568 maximum horizontal cabling distance is 100 meters from equipment in a wiring closet to a workstation.

Under the EIA/TIA-568 standard, horizontal cable connects equipment in a telecommunications or wiring closet to a user's work area. The media options supported for horizontal cabling are the same as those specified for backbone cabling with the exception of coaxial cable, for which 50 ohm thin cable is specified. However, the cabling distance for each type of cable is restricted to 90 meters in length from equipment in the telecommunications or wiring closet to a telecommunications outlet located in a user's work area. This cabling distance permits the use of a patch cord or drop cable up to 10 meters in length to be used to connect a workstation to the outlet, resulting in the total length of horizontal cabling restricted to a maximum of 100 meters.

This 100 meter horizontal cabling restriction is associated with many LAN technologies that are based on the use of unshielded twisted pair (UTP) cabling. Recognizing that different types of LANs use different signaling rates, the EIA/TIA-568 standard classified UTP cable into five categories. Those categories and their suitability for different types of voice and data applications are indicated in Table 3.2.

Table 3.2. EIA/TIA-568 UTP cable categories.

Cable Category	Description
Category 1	Voice or low-speed data up to 56 Kbps; not useful for LANs
Category 2	Data rates up to 1 Mbps

Cable Category	Description
Category 3	Supports transmission up to 16 MHz
Category 4	Supports transmission up to 20 MHz
Category 5	Supports transmission up to 100 MHz

In examining the entries in Table 3.2, note that UTP Categories 3, 4, and 5 support transmission with respect to indicated signaling rates. This means that the capability of those categories of UTP to support different types of LAN transmission depends on the signaling method used by different LANs. Category 3 cable is typically used for Ethernet and 4 Mbps Token-Ring LANs. Category 4 is normally used for 16 Mbps Token-Ring LANs, and Category 5 cable supports 100 Mbps Ethernet and the emerging ATM to the desktop at a 155 Mbps operating rate. A detailed discussion of LANs is provided in Chapter 10, "Alternatives in Local Area Networks."

High-Frequency Radiotelephone

By convention, radio transmission in the frequency band between 3 MHz and 30 MHz is called high-frequency (HF) radio. Frequency bands within the HF spectrum are allocated by international treaty for specific services, such as mobile (aeronautical, maritime, and land), broadcasting, radio navigation, amateur radio, space communications, and radio astronomy. HF radio has properties of propagation that make it less reliable than some other frequencies. HF radio does, however, allow communications over great distances with small amounts of radiated power.

HF radio waves transmitted from antennas on the earth follow two paths, as indicated in Figure 3.9, when they leave the antenna. The groundwave follows the earth's surface, and the skywave bounces back and forth between the earth's surface and various layers of the earth's ionosphere. The groundwave is useful for communications up to about 400 miles, and it works particularly well over water. The skywave propagates signals for up to 4000 miles with a path reliability of about 90 percent. Data signals are carried on HF radio systems as continuous wave (CW) radio telegraphy at about 15 bits per second (bps), and frequency shift keyed (FSK) single sideband signals are carried on HF at 75 bps. Higher data bit rates (up to 4800 bps) are converted to standard 3 KHz voice channel analog signals by modems, and these analog signals are transmitted on voice frequency (VF) carrier systems using HF radio.

●
High-frequency signals radiate from an antenna over two paths: a groundwave following the earth's surface and a skywave that bounces between the earth and the ionosphere.

FIGURE 3.9.

The paths of HF radio waves.

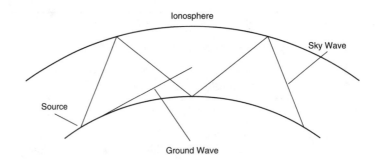

Microwave Radio

Microwave radio is used by line-of-sight carrier systems to carry large quantities of voice and data signals. It is affected adversely by atmospheric conditions and solid objects.

The tall towers with large horns or the dish antennas that you see while driving through the countryside are the repeater stations for line-of-sight (LOS) microwave radio systems (sometimes called radiolink systems). Such systems can carry large quantities of voice and data traffic for several reasons:

- They require no right-of-way acquisition between towers.
- They can carry very large quantities of information per radio system, due to their high operating frequency.
- They require the purchase or lease of only a small area of ground for installation of each tower.
- Because the wavelength of the transmitted signal is short, an antenna of reasonable size can focus the transmitted signal into a beam. This provides a much greater signal strength at the receiver without increasing transmitter power.

Radiolink systems are subject to transmission impairments that limit the distance between repeater points and cause other problems. The microwave signals are

- Attenuated by solid objects (including the earth), and in addition, the higher frequencies are attenuated by rain, snow, and fog.
- Reflected from flat conductive surfaces (such as water and metal structures).
- Diffracted (split) around solid objects.
- Refracted (bent) by the atmosphere so that the beam can travel beyond the line-of-sight distance and be picked up by an antenna that is not supposed to receive it.

In spite of these possible problems, radiolink systems are highly successful and until the late 1980s carried a substantial part of all telephone, data, and television traffic in the United States. Beginning in the early 1980s, most long-distance communications carriers installed tens of thousands of miles of optical fiber. Since the late 1980s, most long-distance transmission has been moved off microwave systems to fiber-optic transmission systems. The microwave range of radio frequencies is allocated for various purposes by international treaty. Some of the frequency assignments for the United States are shown in Table 3.3.

Table 3.3. Frequency assignments for microwave radiolink systems.

Service	Frequency, GHz
Military	1.710–1.850
Operational Fixed	1.850–1.990
Studio Transmitter Link	1.990–2.110
Common Carrier	2.110–2.130
Operational Fixed	2.130–2.150
Common Carrier	2.160–2.180
Operational Fixed	2.180–2.200
Operational Fixed (TV)	2.500–2.690
Common Carrier and Satellite (downlink)	3.700–4.200
Military	4.400–4.990
Military	5.250–5.350
Common Carrier and Satellite (uplink)	5.925–6.425
Operational Fixed	6.575–6.875
Studio Transmitter Link	6.875–7.125
Common Carrier and Satellite (downlink)	7.250–7.750
Common Carrier and Satellite (uplink)	7.900–8.400
Common Carrier	10.7–11.7
Operational Fixed	12.2–12.7
CATV Studio Links	12.7–12.95
Studio Transmitter Link	12.95–13.2
Military	14.4–15.25
Common Carrier	17.7–19.3

Most common carrier radiolink systems carry analog signals, principally frequency modulation (FM). A few systems, however, carry digital signals. Two examples in extensive service in the United States are the AT&T 3A-RDS radio system, which operates in the 11 GHz band, and the AT&T DR-18 radio system, which operates in the 18 GHz band. The 3A-RDS system carries DS-3 digital signals at 44.736 Mbps, and the DR-18 system carries DS-4 digital signals at 274.176 Mbps. The DS-3 and DS-4 signals, which are made up of several lower-bit-rate signals, are discussed in more detail later in this chapter.

Terrestrial radiolink systems are point-to-point; that is, the signal is transmitted in a beam from a source microwave antenna across the earth's surface to the antenna at which it is aimed. The width of the beam transmitted by a microwave antenna varies between 1 degree and 5 degrees as a function of the frequency of transmission and antenna size. As a

●
Although there are microwave systems that send data in digital form, most send data as analog signals.

result, the transmission is highly directional, which is desirable if the information is intended for only one destination (for example, a telephone conversation). For many applications, however, the information has multiple destinations (for example, TV broadcasts), which makes the satellite radiolink system more practical and desirable.

Satellite Radiolink Systems

A satellite radiolink consists of an uplink transmitter signal to the satellite and a downlink retransmitted signal to receiving stations on earth.

Figure 3.10 is a simple model of a satellite radiolink system. The satellite contains several receiver/amplifier/transmitter sections, called transponders, each operating at a slightly different frequency. Each of the 12 transponders on each satellite has a bandwidth of 36 MHz. Individual transmitter sites, called uplink earth stations, send narrow beams of microwave signals to the satellite. The satellite acts as a relay station. A transponder receives the signal from a single transmitter, amplifies it, and then retransmits it toward earth on a different frequency. Note that the transmitting earth station sends to only one transponder on a single satellite. The satellite, however, sends to all downlink receiving earth stations in its area of coverage, called its footprint.

FIGURE 3.10.

Satellite radiolink system.

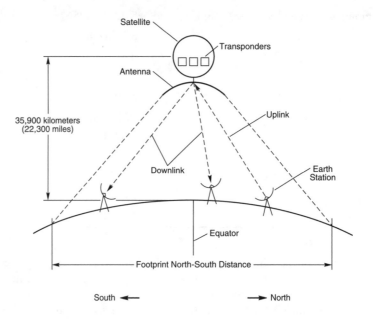

Commercial communications satellites are launched into geostationary orbit at an altitude of 35,900 kilometers (22,300 miles) above the equator. This means that the geostationary satellite is orbiting the earth at a constant speed and in the same direction as the earth's rotation about its axis. The orbiting speed is such that it causes the satellite to have a fixed location with respect to the earth. The earth station antennas, therefore, can be fixed in position and do not have to track a moving target in the sky. The angle of view for a geostationary satellite is almost 120 degrees wide. In principle, three such satellites equally spaced around the equator could cover the earth from 60 degrees north latitude to 60 degrees south latitude. In practice, the coverage angle is restricted to less than 110 degrees because the earth station's antenna must be elevated above the local horizon by more than 5 degrees.

Several types of signals are carried by satellite systems. For example, 6 MHz bandwidth standard TV programs, multiplexed 64 kilobits per second (Kbps) telephone channels, and high-speed data all can be carried simultaneously. One privately operated system, the Satellite Business System, which was merged with Hughes Network Systems, is all digital with each of the 10 transponders per satellite capable of carrying 43 Mbps of digital data.

Cellular Radio Systems

Americans have demonstrated an insatiable desire to communicate with each other any-where, at any time. It seems that no location is too private, too noisy, or too busy to ex-clude the installation of a telephone or a data terminal. Because Americans spend a lot of time in their cars, mobile telephones and data terminals are in great demand. Each tele-phone conversation requires a separate radio channel, and because only a limited number of such channels were available in the past, the demand for mobile telephone channels far outstripped the radio frequencies available to provide them. However, in 1982, a system allowing the reuse of channels within a metropolitan area, called the cellular radio system, began trial operation in Chicago. This system provides many more mobile telephone chan-nels. It rapidly gained acceptance throughout the United States in the late 1980s.

> ●
> The introduction of cellular radio systems effectively increased the number of radio channels available to mobile telephone systems.

A diagram of a simple cellular system is shown in Figure 3.11. A metropolitan area is di-vided into several cells, each of which is served by a low-powered transmitter and an asso-ciated receiver. The radio channels are suitable for data transmission up to 9.6 Kbps as well as voice. The number of radio channels assigned to each cell is sufficient for the pre-dicted number of users in that cell at any one time. When a caller makes a call, his mobile unit automatically seizes a free channel in his current cell. When the caller moves out of the cell, the cell controller automatically switches control of the call from the cell being left to the one being entered. Even a different radio channel can be used, but the caller doesn't have to do anything and is never aware of anything happening. The call is linked from the cell controller to a central switching system. The central switching system can link the caller via radio to another mobile user or can access the public telephone network for connection to any fixed telephone.

The original cellular radio system was based on analog technology. It results in the dedication of a cell channel to one caller while that caller is located within the cell. This constraint limits the number of simultaneous conversations that an analog-based cellular radio system can support. In the late 1980s, research and development efforts resulted in a prototype digital-based cellular radio system in which several callers can share the use of a cell channel by time, a technique referred to as time division multiplexing. Due to the tremendous growth in the number of cellular telephone subscribers and their use of cellular radio systems, it is expected that digital-based systems will be in widespread use by the late 1990s.

FIGURE 3.11.

A cellular radio system.

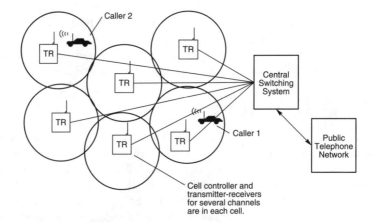

Cell controller and transmitter-receivers for several channels are in each cell.

Effects of Bandwidth on a Transmission Channel

All transmission channels of any practical interest are of limited frequency bandwidth. The limitations arise from the physical properties of the channel or from deliberate limitations on the bandwidth to prevent interference from other sources. For primarily economic reasons, most data communications systems seek to maximize the amount of data that can be sent on a channel.

Theoretical Information-Handling Capacity of a Channel

Claude Shannon proved that the maximum capacity of an ideal channel whose only impairments are finite bandwidth and noise randomly distributed over that finite bandwidth is as shown here:

```
C = W x Log₂[1 + (P/N)] bits per second
```

In this formula,

> P is the power in watts of the signal through the channel.
> N is the power in watts of the noise out of the channel.
> W is the bandwidth of the channel in hertz.

Neglecting all other impairments, some typical values for a voice-grade analog circuit used for data are W = 3000 hertz, P = 0.0001 watts (–10 dBm), and N = 0.0000004 watts (–34 dBm). According to Shannon's Law, the value of C is as shown here:

```
3000 x Log₂(1 + 250) = about 24,000 bits per second
```

Shannon's value of C is normally not achievable because there are numerous impairments in every real channel besides those taken into account in Shannon's Law. Also, there are no ideal modems. However, Shannon's Law provides an upper theoretical limit to a binary channel. It is important to note that, due to the nature of the function Log_2, the value of C in the formula can be increased more readily by increasing W than by increasing (P/N).

Readers familiar with the latest generation of modems might question how they achieve an operating rate of 33.6 Kbps when, according to Shannon's Law, the operating rate should be limited to approximately 24,000 bps. The answer to this question involves the actual bandwidth used by such modems. Figure 3.12 illustrates the amplitude-frequency response curve for a voice-grade telephone channel. At a zero decibel level (0db), the bandwidth is very close to 3,000 Hz; however, at lower levels, the bandwidth slightly increases, enabling a higher operating rate to be achieved.

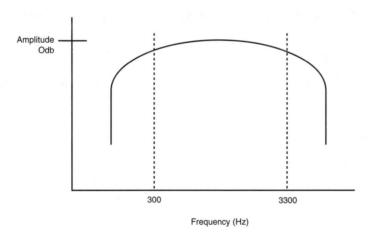

FIGURE 3.12.

The voice-grade channel amplitude-frequency response curve.

Intersymbol Interference Reduces Capacity

One of the factors that tends to reduce the achievable capacity of a channel below the value of C in the formula is a problem called intersymbol (or interbit) interference. If a rectangular pulse like that shown in Figure 3.13 is input to a bandlimited channel, the bandwidth limitation of the channel rounds the "corners" of the pulse, as shown in the output waveform, and causes an undesired signal to appear. The "tail" or overshoot part of the new signal interferes with previous and subsequent pulses, adding uncertainty to the signal; that is, the signal might be incorrectly interpreted at the destination.

FIGURE 3.13.

A pulse response through a bandlimited channel.

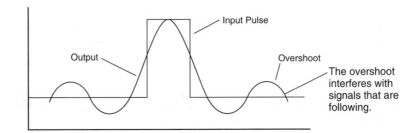

Harry Nyquist analyzed the problem of intersymbol interference and developed an ideal rounded pulse shape for which that impairment is minimized. Nyquist also did much theoretical research dealing with sampling of analog signals for representation in binary form. Nyquist's Sampling Theorem says that if an analog signal is sampled 2f times per second, the samples can be used to perfectly reconstruct the original signal over a spectrum f hertz. For example, if a signal is sampled at the rate of 8000 times per second, those samples can be used to reconstruct the original signal with perfect accuracy over the range of 0–4000 hertz.

> Theoretically, a channel's data rate can be increased as desired as long as the signal-to-noise ratio increases. The practical maximum data rate limit was defined by Nyquist's theory to be two times the bandwidth.

Bandwidth Requirements for Various Signals

The ratio at which information can be transmitted depends on the bandwidth of the transmission media.

Analog Signals

> As improved analog signal processing techniques continue to evolve, a given bandwidth can be used more efficiently.

Transmission rates for data communications seem to follow a corollary of Parkinson's Law; that is, data rates increase to fill the bandwidth available. A good example is the introduction of low-cost modems operating at 14,400 and 28,800 bps for personal computers, which are 48 and 96 times faster than the rate of 300 bps that was used for a long time. Large-scale integrated circuits made possible the remarkable increases in performance and decreases in price of these modems. In 1974, a 300 bps full-duplex modem cost $600 to $800. By 1988, a 1200 bps modem could be bought for under $100, whereas 2400 bps modems were then in the $175-to-$250 range. In 1988, 9600 bps modems designed for use on dial-up lines cost over $3000. By 1994, several vendors were selling such modems for under $125, and fax/data modems capable of operating at speeds up to 14,400 bps were readily available from numerous vendors for under $200. By late 1996, 14,400 bps modems were considered commodity items and cost less than $75; the latest generation of high-speed modems capable of data rates up to 33,600 bps could be obtained for less than $200.

The 300 bps full-duplex signals use two bands of frequencies, each occupying about 300 Hz. Thus, the total 600 Hz used out of the 3000 Hz available bandwidth is inefficient. The 1200 bps modems also are full-duplex and use most of the available bandwidth. Therefore, four times as much information can be sent in the same channel in a given time period. Modern modems operating at or above 9600 bps use a sophisticated echo canceling technique that enables both transmit and receive signals to flow on a common wire pair. Through sophisticated signal processing techniques, modems can even carry up to 33,600 bps using an analog signal over a voice channel.

Digital Signals

Transmission of signals in binary form can require considerably more bandwidth than an equivalent analog signal. For example, the transmission of 24 analog voice channels requires about 96 KHz (24×4 KHz). Transmission of these same 24 voice channels in digital form using the standard T1 time division multiplexing format requires about 776 KHz, or about eight times as much bandwidth (776 / 96). The advantages gained by sending the signals as binary data, however, more than offset the requirement for greater bandwidth. (For a discussion of the trade-offs and advantages, refer to another book in this series, *Understanding Telephone Electronics*.)

Carrier Systems

In general, carrier systems are mechanisms that provide a means to send signals from more than one source over a single physical channel. The bandwidth available to carry signals in a particular medium can be allocated in two ways: by frequency or by time intervals.

Analog Carrier Systems

The frequency spectrum represented by the available bandwidth of a channel can be divided into smaller bandwidth portions, with each of several signal sources assigned to each portion. This is the principle of frequency division multiplexing (FDM). FDM is still used in some simple data communications systems, and at one time it formed the foundation for the long-haul part of the public telephone network. Since the 1980s, communications carriers have invested tens of billions of dollars in converting their infrastructure to digital technology, resulting in the replacement of essentially all carrier FDM systems by time division multiplexing (TDM) systems. Chapter 6, "Multiplexing Techniques," covers multiplexing technology, including the operation of FDM and TDM systems. One common example of a frequency division multiplexing system is a standard low-speed (300 bps) modem, which divides the spectrum available in a voice channel into two portions—one for transmit and one for receive (this concept of frequency division is discussed in more detail in Chapter 6, "Multiplexing Techniques").

The electronic mechanisms that implemented FDM are called analog carrier systems. The carrier in an analog carrier system is a signal generated by the system, and the carrier is

---

● Digital signals require a greater bandwidth than an equivalent analog signal. The advantages offered by transmitting signals in digital form more than offset this disadvantage.

● In FDM, the total available channel bandwidth is divided into smaller bandwidth portions (subchannels), each with its own signal source.

modulated by the signal containing the information to be transmitted. Table 3.4 shows the standard analog carrier systems in use in the public telephone network. As previously noted, however, most communications carriers have replaced their analog-based FDM equipment with digital-based TDM equipment.

Table 3.4. Analog carrier systems.

Multiplex Level	No. of Voice Circuits	Frequency Band, KHz
Voice Channel	1	0–4
Group	12	60–108
Supergroup	60	312–552
Mastergroup	600	564–3,084
Jumbogroup	3600	564–17,548

Digital Carrier Systems

TDM is used in digital carrier systems because many bits can be packed into the very narrow time blocks allotted to each of several signal sources.

The second method of dividing the capacity of a transmission channel among several separate signal sources is to allocate a very short period on the channel in a repeating pattern to each signal. This technique is called time division multiplexing. It is well suited to binary signals consisting of pulses representing a one or a zero. These pulses can be made of very short duration and still convey the desired information; therefore, many of them can be squeezed into the time available on a digital carrier channel.

The original signal can be an analog wave that is converted to binary form for transmitting, as in the case of speech signals in the telephone network, or the original signal can already be in binary form, as in the case of a business machine. The electronic systems that perform this TDM process are called digital carrier systems. As with the analog carrier systems, there is a standard hierarchy of digital carrier systems in the public telephone network, as shown in Table 3.5. Refer to Chapter 6 for specific information concerning time division multiplexing and the operation and utilization of a T1 multiplexer that can be used with a DS-1 digital carrier system.

Table 3.5. Digital carrier systems.

Digital Signal No.	No. Voice Circuits	Bit Rate, Mbps
DS-1	24	1.544
DS-2	96	6.312
DS-3	672	44.736
DS-4	4032	274.176

In examining the entries in Table 3.5, note that the lowest operating-rate digital signal is indicated as DS-1, which consists of 24 voice circuits whose aggregate operating rate is 1.544 Mbps. Although the DS-1 digital signal is indeed the lowest operating-rate signal in the digital carrier hierarchy, it is not the lowest operating-rate digital transmission facility available for use. To understand why this is the case requires additional information about the DS-1 signal.

The DS-1 Digital Signal

In North America, the DS-1 is commonly referred to as a T1 line or circuit. That circuit was developed to relieve cable congestion in metropolitan areas by providing a transport mechanism for 24 digitized voice conversations to be simultaneously carried over one cable. To do so, each voice conversation is digitized using a technique called pulse code modulation (PCM). Under PCM, an analog voice conversation is digitized at 64 Kbps. To provide information that enables one conversation to be distinguished from another and switched into and out of a group of conversations requires framing bits to be added to the T1 data flow. Those framing bits operate at 8000 bps and carry control information, error detection information, and a limited data link capability. Such capability, for example, enables two private branch exchanges (PBXs) to communicate with one another while transporting 24 voice conversations on a T1 circuit interconnecting the PBXs.

The 24 channels, each operating at 64 Kbps, result in an operating rate of 1.536 Mbps. When the 8 Kbps framing information is added to the T1 line, its operating rate becomes 1.544 Mbps.

Each voice channel in a DS-1 digital signal, referred to as a DS-0 or digital signal level zero channel, represents the lowest operating rate digital circuit marketed by communications carriers for direct connection to a channel on their T1 lines. Communications carriers also offer low-speed digital services operating at data rates from 2.4 Kbps up to 56 Kbps, using time division multiplexers to group multiple low-speed digital circuits onto a 64 Kbps circuit. The 64 Kbps circuit in turn is connected to a channel on a carrier's T1 line, which represents the basic backbone infrastructure used for transporting voice, data, and video across North America.

Carrier Digital Offerings

The T1 circuit was originally limited to use by communications carriers to relieve the cable congestion in metropolitan areas. The successful use of this transmission facility resulted in AT&T and other communications carriers tariffing its use for commercial organizations and government agencies during the mid-1980s. Slower-speed digital transmission services, such as AT&T's Dataphone Digital Service (DDS), actually preceded the public offering of T1 service because DDS was introduced during the mid-1970s.

DDS is a leased-line digital transmission service with operating rates of 2.4, 4.8, 9.6, 19.2, and 56 Kbps. A switched 56 Kbps offering is also available in certain cities.

The economics associated with the T1 tariff resulted in the monthly cost of a T1 line being 4 to 8 times the cost of one 56 Kbps DDS circuit. Because a T1 line has more than 24 times the capacity of a 56 Kbps DDS circuit, most organizations that required the use of multiple 56 Kbps DDS lines between common geographical locations soon replaced those circuits with T1 lines. In addition to the economics associated with the use of T1 lines, their additional data transport capacity enabled organizations to merge voice, data, and video applications onto a common circuit. In fact, by the early 1990s, the T1 circuit formed the backbone for most corporate and government networks.

The difference between the maximum data rate supported by DDS and the operating rate of a T1 circuit left many organizations unsatisfied with respect to the traffic-handling capacity of communications carrier circuits. Recognizing the requirements of those organizations for the use of a fraction of a T1 line's operating rate, communications carriers introduced fractional T1 (FT1) service in the early 1990s. Today, most communications carriers offer FT1 service in operating rates from 64 Kbps to 768 Kbps in increments of 64 Kbps. Although an organization contracts for a specific FT1 operating rate, the carrier normally installs a T1 line from the serving office to the customer's premises. The customer either installs equipment or gets equipment from the communications carrier, which places the customer's data into a group of DS-0s that represents the contracted FT1 service.

Figure 3.14 illustrates an example of the digital multiplexing hierarchy used to transport FT1- and T1-based communications between cities. At the serving carrier office, data in the form of individual or groups of DS-O's from subscribers is removed (dropped) from some T1 lines and placed (inserted) onto other T1 lines. In this way, most if not all of the 24 DS-O slots on certain T1 lines are used. Next, groups of T1 lines are multiplexed onto a T3 or T4 line for the routing of voice and data that represents 672 or 4032 voice-grade circuits routed between long-distance communications carrier offices.

FIGURE 3.14.

The digital multiplexing hierarchy.

To illustrate the economics associated with the use of FT1, Table 3.6 lists AT&T's monthly Interoffice Channel Charges in effect in early 1996 for that carrier's Accunet Spectrum of Digital Services, that vendor's name for FT1 service. To put those monthly charges in perspective, readers should note that AT&T's 56 Kbps DDS service has monthly per-mile charges ranging from $7.13 to $1.10 based on the length of the circuit. In comparison, AT&T's T1 circuit, which provides a 1.544 Mbps operating rate, until recently had a monthly mile charge of $3.50 regardless of the length of the circuit. Since August 1994, the monthly recurring charges for high-speed services have utilized a city-pair pricing structure in place of a per-mile pricing structure. Table 3.7 lists five examples of T1 and T3 monthly circuit costs, and Table 3.8 lists AT&T's 56 Kbps DDS and T1 circuit mileage charges in effect in early 1996. In comparing the costs listed in Table 3.6 to the costs listed in Table 3.8, it is reasonable to conclude that most DDS usage will be replaced by FT1 service, whereas organizations that require slightly more than half the bandwidth of a T1 circuit will more than likely order a full T1 line.

Table 3.6. AT&T Accunet Spectrum of Digital Services Interoffice Channel Charges.

Channel Operating Rate	Monthly Charge Per Mile
64 Kbps	$0.27
128 Kbps	$0.49
192 Kbps	$0.71
256 Kbps	$0.93
320 Kbps	$1.13
384 Kbps	$1.33
448 Kbps	$1.51
512 Kbps	$1.68
576 Kbps	$1.85
640 Kbps	$2.00
704 Kbps	$2.14
768 Kbps	$2.27

Table 3.7. AT&T T1/T3 representative city-pair costs.

City Pair	Air Miles	T1 Monthly Cost	T3 Monthly Cost
Miami–Seattle	2722	$13,130	$160,421
LA–Washington	2293	$11,548	$138,343
Atlanta–Miami	601	$ 4,309	$ 51,264
Dallas–Memphis	418	$ 4,634	$ 41,846
Boston–Providence	42	$ 3,248	$ 22,495

Table 3.8. AT&T 56 Kbps DDS monthly circuit charges.

Circuit Miles	Cost Per Mile Per Month
1–50	$7.13
51–100	$4.57
101–500	$2.40
500+	$1.10

What Have You Learned?

1. Information is a numerical quantity that measures the randomness of a system.

2. Symbols such as letters have an information content. Not every symbol is equally likely to occur.

3. The redundancy of a system measures how likely symbols are to be repeated.

4. Data communications systems use redundancy to detect and correct errors in transmission.

5. Signals can travel through guided and unguided transmission media.

6. Adding inductance to pairs of wires is called loading. Loading is used to reduce high-frequency attenuation over the wire pair.

7. The EIA/TIA-568 standard specifies cabling parameters used to connect equipment in wiring closets to workstations.

8. Fiber-optic transmission systems send data signals as light rays. These systems have much higher bandwidth and have immunity from most external interference.

9. Transmission rates over channels are limited by the bandwidth of the channel, the signal-to-noise ratio, and the amount of intersymbol interference in the transmitted waveform.

10. The use of different types of digital transmission systems is based on bandwidth availability and economics.

Quiz for Chapter 3

1. The amount of uncertainty in a system of symbols is also called:

   a. Bandwidth.

   b. Loss.

   c. Entropy.

   d. Quantum.

2. The twists in twisted wire pairs:

   a. Reduce electromagnetic interference.

   b. Occur at a 30-degree angle.

   c. Eliminate loading.

   d. Were removed due to cost.

3. Redundancy measures:

   a. The transmission rate of a system.

   b. How likely symbols are to be repeated.

   c. The time between failure.

   d. The system cost.

4. An example of a bounded medium is:

   a. Coaxial cable.

   b. Waveguide.

   c. Fiber-optic cable.

   d. All the above.

5. Loading refers to the addition of:

   a. Resistors.

   b. Capacitors.

   c. Bullets.

   d. Inductance.

6. Coaxial cable has conductors with:

   a. The same diameter.

   b. A common axis.

   c. Equal resistance.

   d. None of the above.

7. Fiber-optic cable is suitable for:

   a. Routing through conduits.

   b. Use in most hazardous areas.

   c. Pulling connectors.

   d. Mobile video applications.

8. Fiber-optic cables operate at frequencies near:

   a. 20 MHz.

   b. 200 MHz.

   c. 2 GHz.

   d. 800 THz.

9. The EIA/TIA-568 standard:

   a. Specifies building design parameters.

   b. Specifies cabling parameters.

   c. Defines the method for interconnecting buildings.

   d. Was developed by the Electrical Integration Association.

10. The maximum horizontal cabling distance from equipment in a wiring closet to a workstation under the EIA/TIA-568 standard is:

   a. 100 feet.

   b. 90 meters.

   c. 100 meters.

   d. 90 feet.

11. HF radio waves follow how many basic paths on leaving the transmitter?

   a. Two.

   b. Four.

   c. One.

   d. Many.

12. Digital cellular radio systems:

    a. Expand the number of cells.

    b. Enable multiple subscribers to share the use of cells.

    c. Enable multiple subscribers to share the use of a common channel within a cell.

    d. Extend the transmission distance of subscribers within a cell.

13. The area of coverage of a satellite radio beam is called its:

    a. Beamwidth.

    b. Circular polarization.

    c. Footprint.

    d. Identity.

14. Transmission of binary signals requires:

    a. Less bandwidth than analog.

    b. More bandwidth than analog.

    c. The same bandwidth as analog.

    d. A license from the FAA.

15. The standard first-level digital multiplex system in the United States operates at:

    a. 2.048 Mbps.

    b. 44.736 Mbps.

    c. 1.544 Mbps.

    d. 9600 bps.

16. The use of Dataphone Digital Services:

    a. Can be expected to increase.

    b. Provides a higher operating rate than FT1 service.

    c. Can be expected to be replaced by FT1 service due to the lower cost of that service.

    d. Provides a higher operating rate than T1.

Asynchronous Modems and Interfaces

About This Chapter

Having laid the groundwork by describing the form of the data (codes), the source of the data to be transmitted (terminals), and the transmission media, we now can discuss how the data is transmitted. This chapter explains how modems work in terms of frequency, bandwidth, and modulation, and it describes the data terminal equipment/data communications equipment (DTE/DCE) interface. Due to the role of the microprocessor in adding intelligence to modems, this chapter also covers smart-modem features. Features described and discussed in this chapter include command sets, error detection and correction, data compression, and the Microcom MNP protocol.

Why Data Can't Be Transmitted Directly

Digital information cannot be transmitted directly over the switched telephone network because the portion of the network beyond the central office cannot carry direct current.

Although it might not have been obvious at the time, the reasons that modems are necessary were discussed in Chapter 3, "Messages and Transmission Channels." Remember that the switched telephone network uses various transmission methods from wire pairs to microwave, but only in the local area (primarily within the area served by a Central Office) does an actual metallic path (wire) exist from one telephone to another. This means that we cannot transmit data in its original form as a series of pulses much farther than from our telephone to the Central Office (CO). Actually, if loading coils are used in the local loop, we can't even transmit the data that far. As discussed in Chapter 3, the bandwidth (the passband) of the telephone channel beyond the CO after it has been filtered and amplified is approximately 300 to 3400 Hz, as shown in Figure 4.1. Because direct current (zero Hz) is below 300 Hz, it is not within the passband. Thus, data in its original pulsed DC or "baseband" form cannot be transmitted over this channel.

FIGURE 4.1.

The telephone channel bandwidth.

Solving the Problem with Modems

A transmitting modem changes the digital signals produced by computers to an analog signal with a frequency bandwidth that can be transmitted over the telephone network.

Because we are interested in transmitting data beyond the CO using the existing telephone network, we need to change the data pulses to another form that can be transmitted over the telephone channel. Because the telephone network is designed and optimized for transmission of analog signals in the voiceband, why not make the data look like these analog signals for transmission? This is exactly the function of a modem. The ones and zeros of the data stream from the DTE are converted to tones (or analog waveforms resembling tones) having frequencies within the 300 to 3400 Hz range. Thus, the modem is nothing more than a rather complex interface device.

At the transmitting end, incoming pulses from the DTE are converted to tones and transmitted over the telephone channel; at the receiving end, the tones are converted back to pulses, which are passed to the DTE. In other words, the transmitting modem modulates an analog signal, called a carrier, with the data (more about modulation in the next section) and uses the analog signal to carry to the other end of the telephone circuit. The receiving modem demodulates the analog signal to recover the data in its original pulse form and passes it to the receiving DTE. In fact, the name "modem" is a contraction of the words *modulator-demodulator*. One important fact to remember is this: A modem does not operate on the content of the data; it merely changes the form for transmission. The data compression capability of modern smart modems is discussed later in this chapter. In actuality, software in the form of instructions burned into read-only memory (ROM) and referred to as firmware controls a microprocessor in the modem that operates on data before its modulation. Although many articles and books note that modems operate on data, technically it is the microprocessor in the modem that does so. The modem's internal circuitry merely changes the form of the data for transmission.

> ●
> A receiving modem converts the analog signal back to its original digital form so that the receiving computer can use the data.

Telephone Channel Restrictions on Modems

In addition to the bandwidth limits, another restriction of the telephone channel that affects modem design is inherent in any analog transmission facility; that is, the transmission is best at frequencies near the center of the passband and poorer at frequencies toward the upper and lower limits of the passband. High-speed modems use almost all the voiceband for one channel. Therefore, most high-speed modems in North America use a carrier frequency of 1700 to 1800 Hz because these frequencies are very near the middle of the voiceband. Low-speed modems, because of their narrower bandwidth requirements, can use more than one carrier frequency within the voiceband and still operate in the "good" portion of the band.

Still another restriction of the telephone channel is that certain frequencies cannot be used. The telephone network uses the transmission channel for passing information and control signals between the switching offices. This process, called in-band or in-channel interoffice signaling, uses tones at frequencies within the voiceband. A modem cannot use these same frequencies because the network might interpret them as control tones, with disastrous results to the call.

> ●
> Modems cannot use the frequencies in the transmission channels that are used for telephone network signaling.

Modem Interfaces

A modem has an interface to the telephone network and an interface to the DTE. The one to the telephone network is the simpler because that interface consists of only two wires, called the "tip" and "ring." As long as the modem adheres to the voltage, current, power, and frequency rules of the telephone company, the telephone channel is really just a pipe to move analog tones from one place to another.

A protocol establishes the procedures used by the transmitting and receiving equipment in establishing and maintaining communications. "Handshaking" ensures that the equipment is ready to go.

The interface wiring between the modem and the DTE is more complex and is governed by standards discussed later in this chapter. This interface also requires that certain procedures (called a protocol) be observed in establishing communications between the two ends. First, the DTE and the modem at the transmitting end must establish communication with one another. The DTE indicates to the modem that it wants to transmit, and this modem signals to the modem at the other end of the circuit to see whether it is ready to receive. Because, in general, modems do not store data, the receiving modem must contact its DTE to see whether it is ready to receive. (This communication between the equipment often is referred to as "handshaking.") After the transmitting modem knows that the receiving modem and DTE are listening on the line, it notifies the transmitting DTE, which then begins passing data to the transmitting modem for modulation and transmission. On the receiving end, the receiving modem demodulates the incoming signal and passes the received data to the receiving DTE.

In half-duplex transmission (only one direction at a time), when the transmitter is finished and wants a reply from the other end, the channel must be "turned around." To do this, much of the handshaking must be done again to establish transmission in the opposite direction, and this turnaround handshaking must occur each time the direction is changed. In full-duplex transmission (both directions simultaneously), the transmission uses two different carrier frequencies. Thus, the handshaking is necessary only for the initial setup.

Analog Modulation

Modulation is the process of using some medium as a carrier to carry information between two points. For example, you could send Morse code by turning a flashlight on and off to modulate the light beam. Reflection on this process reveals that you would be changing some property of the carrier to represent the data—in this instance, that property is the intensity of the beam. (You might more easily understand this if you imagine using a bright light for a mark and a dim light for a space. In this case, you would be modulating the brightness or "amplitude" of the light beam to send data.)

A sine wave signal often is used as the carrier in an analog modulation process. A sine wave can easily be generated by electromechanical generators and electronic oscillators.

A sine wave that might be used as a carrier in a modem is illustrated in Figure 4.2. Sine waves not only are mathematical functions, but also are fundamental phenomena of the physical universe. Sine waves are generated by devices such as electromechanical generators and electronic oscillators.

A man named Fourier discovered that any series of pulses, sounds, voltages, or similar waves can be broken down into a series of sine waves of varying frequencies and amplitudes. This means that human speech, in the air or on a telephone wire, can be analyzed in terms of the sine waves it contains. That is not to say that the human larynx creates speech by combining sound waves at different frequencies; it simply means that Fourier analysis is a fundamental and useful tool for analyzing the characteristics of any transmission channel or device, whether it be a modem or the speakers of a high-fidelity sound system.

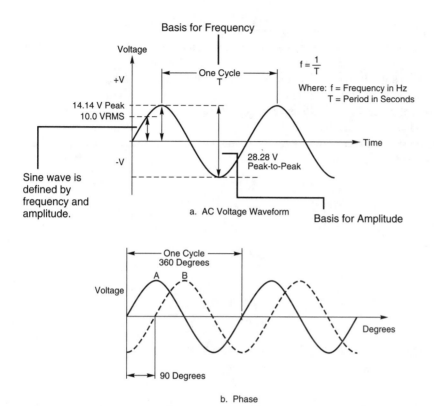

FIGURE 4.2.

The sine wave fundamentals.

a. AC Voltage Waveform

b. Phase

As illustrated in Figure 4.2a, a sine wave can be defined by its frequency and amplitude. Frequency is measured in cycles per second with the unit of measurement termed the Hertz (Hz). That is, one cycle per second equals one hertz. Amplitude can be measured in units of volts peak-to-peak, volts peak, and volts root mean square (rms), as indicated in the illustration.

Another parameter of a sine wave is the phase of the wave, but it has meaning only in reference to another wave of the same frequency. Two different sine waves having the same frequency can be compared by the amount by which one leads or lags the other. Because one complete cycle of a sine wave occurs in 360 degrees, we can consider the difference between the two waves in terms of degrees, as indicated in Figure 4.2b. The amplitudes of the two waves compared do not have to be the same, but the frequencies must be exactly the same.

Because the frequency, amplitude, and phase completely characterize a sine wave, these are the only parameters of the carrier sine wave that can be changed to modulate the carrier for transmitting information from one modem to another. All modems, therefore, use amplitude, frequency, or phase modulation, or some combination of these parameters.

●
Frequency, amplitude, and phase are the characteristics of a sine wave that can be varied to achieve modulation.

The modem converts the ones and zeros of the data stream into an analog signal that is within the telephone voiceband so that data can be transmitted over the telephone network.

Figure 4.3 illustrates amplitude, frequency, and phase modulation. Notice that the same sequence of ones and zeros of the data stream affect the carrier in different ways. After modulation, the pulses are represented by an AC signal having frequencies within the voiceband. Thus, the information can be transmitted over telephone channels. Actually, simple amplitude modulation is not used for data communications because it is very susceptible to electrical noise interference, which can cause errors in the received data. Low-speed modems use frequency modulation, higher-speed modems use phase modulation, and the very highest-speed modems for voiceband transmission use a combination of phase and amplitude modulation.

FIGURE 4.3.

The types of analog modulation.

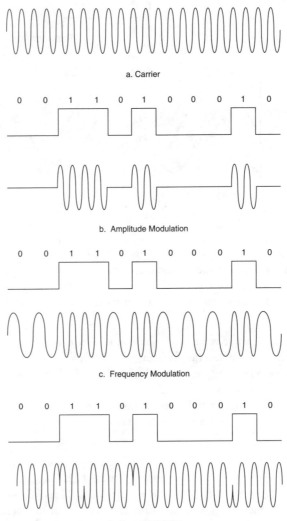

a. Carrier

b. Amplitude Modulation

c. Frequency Modulation

d. Phase Modulation

Low-Speed Modem Operation

With this background, we can describe how a standard 0–300-baud low-speed modem works. Figure 4.4 shows the voiceband divided into two sub-bands for transmission in both directions simultaneously. Recall that such two-way transmission is called full-duplex, meaning that the same bandwidth is available in both directions at the same time.

FIGURE 4.4.

Frequencies used for 300-baud full-duplex transmission.

For some people, the process of transmitting data over one channel in two directions at the same time might be hard to visualize. One could think of it as being similar to two people talking on the same local call simultaneously. Both people can talk and hear at the same time, although they might have trouble understanding each other because the entire bandwidth of the channel is available to both parties in both directions. However, the modems completely separate the data into the two bands shown, one for each direction, so that each can understand the other.

The separation is accomplished when one modem is set to the originate mode and the other is set to the answer mode, by a switch on each modem or through the issuance of commands to each modem from attached DTEs. The terms *originate* and *answer* come from the use of low-speed modems in dial-up computer applications in which a user calls a computer. The calling modem is usually in the originate mode, and the called modem is in the answer mode (makes sense, doesn't it?). This way, the marking tone of the answer modem (the high-pitched "whistle" heard when it answers) also disables any echo suppressors (which interfere with data transmission) that might be in the circuit.

In Figure 4.4, notice that the originate modem transmits zeros (spaces) at 1070 Hz and ones (marks) at 1270 Hz. The answer modem also transmits spaces and marks, but at 2025 and 2225 Hz, respectively. This type of modulation is called frequency-shift keying (FSK). (The term *keying* means turning a transmitter on and off.) The appropriate mark or space frequency is simply turned on and off by the transmitting modem as it wants to send a one or zero. If you listen on a telephone line that is carrying low-speed FSK modem transmissions, you might hear a warbling sound as the frequencies shift back and forth.

●

By separating channel bandwidths, modems can transmit and receive data simultaneously. The calling modem is set to the originate mode, and the answering modem is set to the answer mode.

●

FSK is a simple, economical modulation technique used in low-speed modems. The mark and space each are assigned a particular frequency, then transmitted simply by switching the appropriate frequency on and off.

If the originating modem transmits zeros at 1070 Hz and ones at 1270 Hz, at what frequency does it receive zeros and ones? For compatibility with the answer modem that transmits zeros and ones at 2025 and 2225 Hz, the originating modem receives zeros and ones at those frequencies. Similarly, the answer modem receives zeros and ones at 1070 Hz and 1270 Hz, to maintain transmission compatibility with the originating modem.

The FSK modem just described is more commonly known as a Bell System 113–type device. Originally, the Bell System supplied all modems that could be attached to the switched telephone network. By the time other vendors were permitted to sell modems for use on the switched network, the Bell System's monopoly had created a large base of telephone company devices, which encouraged vendors to manufacture modems compatible with Bell System products.

In Europe, the Consultative Committee for International Telephone and Telegraph (CCITT), now known as the International Telecommunications Union-Telecommunications Standardization section (ITU-T), developed a series of standards that govern the operation of modems. This series is commonly referred to as the V-series, because the letter prefix "V" is used to denote modem-related standards. One such standard that governs the operation of an FSK modem is known as V.21. The V.21 standard uses different originate and answer frequencies for marks and spaces in comparison with the Bell System 113–type device, due to the requirement to avoid control frequencies used on European telephone networks. The V.21 modem uses 980 Hz for a mark and 1180 Hz for a space in its originate mode, whereas it is designed to receive a mark and space at 1650 and 1850 Hz, respectively. Due to the differences in operating frequencies, a Bell System 113 and V.21 modem are incompatible with one another.

High-speed modems use phase modulation because it requires less bandwidth for the same data rate.

FSK is a straightforward and economical modulation method that works well over telephone channels, so the logical question is this: "Why not use it for higher-speed modems?" The answer is "between the lines" (no pun intended) of Figure 4.4. Higher data rates require more bandwidth. Thus, if we wanted to transmit at higher speeds, the mark and space frequencies for each sub-band would have to be farther apart, and the two sub-bands would have to be separated further to provide enough bandwidth. Soon we would be outside of the telephone channel; in other words, we would require more bandwidth than is available. Therefore, higher-speed modems use some form of phase modulation, because phase modulation requires the least bandwidth of the three analog modulation methods.

Bell System 212A and V.22 Modems

Until the mid-1980s, the Bell System 212A modem was the most popular upgrade for Bell System 113–type modem users. The 212A modem can be considered two modems in one because it employs FSK modulation using the Bell System 113 frequency assignments at 300 bps. At its higher 1200 bps rate, it uses dibit phase shift keyed (DPSK) modulation. Under DPSK modulation, two bits at a time are encoded into one phase shift or signal change. Thus, the modem's signal rate (commonly known as its baud rate) is 600, or one-half of its 1200 bps data rate. The phase shift encoding of the 212A-type modem is illustrated in Table 4.1.

Table 4.1. The 212A-type modem phase shift.

Dibit	Phase Shift (Degrees)
00	90
01	0
10	180
11	270

When a 212A modem operates at 1200 bps, it can transmit data either asynchronously or synchronously. One key advantage to using 212A-type modems is that when connected to a computer, they can receive transmissions from terminal devices operating at either 300 or 1200 bps.

The V.22 standard is similar to the 212A at 1200 bps. However, at the 212A's lower data rate, the two modems are incompatible. The V.22 modem's second data rate is 600 bps, compared with the 212A's lower data rate of 300 bps. A second major difference between the lower speeds of the two modems is in the method of modulation used. The 212A uses FSK modulation at 300 bps, whereas the V.22 uses two-phase PSK at 600 bps. Fortunately, the V.22 modem is used primarily in Europe, whereas the 212A-type modem is used primarily in North America.

V.22bis

The V.22bis (*bis* meaning "second" in Latin) received widespread acceptance throughout the United States and Europe during the late 1980s. It represents one of the few modems that can be used for worldwide communications. The V.22bis recommendation governs modems designed for asynchronous data transmission at 2400 bps over the switched telephone network, with a V.22 fallback method of operation. When the V.22bis modem operates in its fallback mode, incompatibility problems can arise because of the different methods used to manufacture this modem.

In the United States, most if not all V.22bis modems follow the Bell System 212A specifications for fallback operations—DPSK at 1200 bps and FSK at 300 bps. In Europe, most V.22bis modems follow the V.22 specifications for fallback operations, which include two-phase PSK at 600 bps. Thus, at their lowest fallback rate, V.22bis modems manufactured for use in North America are incompatible with those manufactured for use in Europe.

Modem Features

Most modern modems include 30 to 100 or more built-in features. Although some of those features might represent proprietary technology, most of those features represent the incorporation of de facto or de jure standards, such as the support of several types of modulation schemes. Two of the most common features now incorporated into modems designed for use on the switched telephone network are data compression and error detection and correction.

Modems incorporating compression really operate at variable data rates because throughput depends on the susceptibility of the data to the compression algorithms in the modem. As an example of how a modem can compress data, consider the sequence ACCOUNT*bbbbbbb* AMOUNT, in which *b* indicates a blank or space character. This sequence could represent the column headings of a report; it's similar to most accounting reports that contain columns of data with each column separated by spaces from the next column. If the modem uses a special character denoted as S_c to show space compression, the sequence is transmitted as ACCOUNT S_c7 AMOUNT between modems. At the receiving modem, the character S_c indicates the occurrence of space compression, and the number 7 indicates the number of space characters compressed. This information provides the receiving modem with the capability to decompress the data into its original form.

To prevent the natural occurrence in the data stream of a character indicating space compression and thus falsely affecting the modem at the opposite end of the data link, the originating modem is programmed to stuff an extra space-compression-indicating character into the transmission sequence. Thus, if the data stream into the modem is XYZS$_c$ABC, the modem transmits the sequence XYZS$_c$S$_c$ABC. At the receiving modem, the occurrence of the first S_c character causes the modem to examine the next character. When the receiving modem finds a second S_c character following the first, it disregards the second S_c character, restoring the data stream to its original form while preventing a false decompression of the data.

Until 1990, most compression modems used a mixture of compression algorithms. Although the actual throughput is variable, the net effect of compression is roughly double the data transfer rate of the device. In 1990, the ITU-T (formerly known as the CCITT) promulgated its V.42bis recommendation. V.42bis defines a modified Lempel-Ziv compression algorithm for use in modems. This data compression technique was adopted by more than 20 modem vendors by the beginning of 1991 and by 1996 was incorporated into most intelligent modems.

Two competitive data compression methods are MNP Class 5 and Class 7. Microcom Corporation licensed MNP Class 5 compression to more than 50 modem vendors during the 1980s. Later, Microcom licensed its enhanced data compression incorporated into MNP Class 7 to other modem manufacturers. Due to the large base of MNP-compatible modems that were manufactured before the development of the V.42bis compression standard, most modem manufacturers incorporate support for both MNP and V.42bis. This dual compression support enables modern modems to have compression compatibility with older modems that support only MNP compression as well as newer modems that either support both MNP and V.42bis or support only V.42bis compression. The MNP modem protocol is discussed later in this chapter.

V.42bis

V.42bis compression is based on the theoretical work of Professors Lempel and Ziv at the Technion in Haifa, Israel, and the effort of the Englishman Terry Welch, whose modifications to Lempel and Ziv's string compression algorithm resulted in the LZW algorithm. The LZW algorithm, which has its mnemonics in honor of the two Israeli professors and the Englishman, forms the heart of the V.42bis compression standard.

●

The LZW algorithm forms the basis for compression performed by the V.42bis standard.

Under the LZW algorithm, the character set is initially selected as 256 individual dictionary entries whose codes range from 0 to 255. Then, the algorithm operates on a character at a time in the input string to be compressed according to the following two-step method:

1. If the character is in the dictionary, get the next character.

2. If the character is not in the dictionary, output the last known string's encoding, and add the new string to the table.

Under the LZW algorithm, characters to be compressed are read and used to progressively form larger and larger strings until a string is formed that is not in the dictionary. When this situation occurs, the last known string's encoding is output, and the new string is added to the dictionary. The LZW algorithm uses a numeric code as a token to indicate the position of a string in the dictionary's string table. If we call the string previously read the prefix of the output string, while the last byte read becomes the suffix, then the algorithm can be defined in the following way:

```
prefix + suffix = new string
```

After a new string is formed, the suffix becomes the prefix, or this:

```
prefix = suffix
```

To illustrate an example of LZW encoding, let's assume that the input string of data flowing into a modem is "ababc". Initially, each character in the character set that forms the dictionary is assigned a numeric code value equivalent to its character code. Thus, in ASCII, an "a" would have the code value 97, "b" would have the code value 98, and so on.

Under the LZW algorithm, the first operation assumes that the prefix has a value of the null string, which I will indicate by the symbol Δ. Thus, the first operation results in the addition of the null string to "a", which forms the new string "a". Because "a" is in the dictionary, the algorithm does not output anything. However, because the suffix becomes the prefix, "a" now becomes the prefix for the next operation. This is indicated at the top of Table 4.2.

Table 4.2. LZW encoding of the string "ababc".

Prefix	Suffix	New String	Output
Δ	a	a	-
a	b	ab	97
b	a	ba	98
a	b	ab	-
ab	c	abc	256
c	Δ	c	99

Now let's consider the second character in the input string "b". Processing that character according to the LZW algorithm results in the addition of the prefix ("a") and the suffix ("b") to form a new string ("ab"). Because the new string ("ab") is not in the dictionary, rule 2 is followed. That is, the last known string's encoding, which is 97, is output for the character "a", and the new string ("ab") is added to the dictionary. Because codes 0 to 255 representing the individual characters in an 8-bit character set were previously used, the next available code, 256, is used to represent the string "ab". Note that doing so requires the number of bits used to form a token to increase, with the initial token size negotiated between modems during the V.42bis negotiation process.

Returning to the input string to be compressed, "b", which was the suffix when generating the string "ab", becomes the prefix for the next operation. This is indicated in line 3 in Table 4.2.

Because the next character in the string to be encoded is "a", it functions as the suffix in creating the new string "ba". Because that string is not presently in the dictionary, the last known string ("b") is output using its ASCII code value of 98. Next, the string "ba" is added to the dictionary, using the next available code, which is 257. Because "a" was the suffix in creating the string "ab", it now becomes the prefix for the next string operation, as illustrated in line 4 in Table 4.2. The fourth character in the input string ("b") is now processed as the suffix to form a new string. This results in the new string "ab", which was previously added to the string table. Because it is already in the string table, no output is generated, and the string "ab" becomes the prefix for creating the next string.

The creation of the next string is shown in line 5 in Table 4.2. Here, the previously created string "ab", which was in the string table, becomes the prefix for generating the next string, and the last character in the input data string ("c") becomes the suffix in forming the next string. The resulting string ("abc") is not in the dictionary. Thus, the last known string, "ab", has its code value output. Because "ab" was previously assigned the value 256, that value is output, and the suffix ("c") becomes the prefix for the creation of the next string. Because "c" was the last character in the input string, its code value of 99 is output.

In addition to specifying the use of LZW string compression, the V.42bis standard defines several compression-related parameters, such as the size of the dictionary and how the dictionary is emptied or flushed. Although some parameters are negotiated during the initial modem call setup process, other parameters, such as flushing the dictionary, can occur at any time during the transmission session.

For further information covering data compression techniques and applications, refer to the book *Data and Image Compression, 4th Edition,* by Gilbert Held. Published by John Wiley & Sons in 1996, this book explains 15 compression algorithms and contains BASIC and C++ language programs that can be used to compress and decompress data.

Error Detection and Correction

When a modem compresses data before its modulation, the effect of a single bit error can be far more pronounced than when no compression occurs. To illustrate this effect, assume that the data sequence AAAAAAAA occurred. Assume that the modem is programmed to replace a string of more than three repeated characters by a special compression-indicating character followed by the number of characters that were compressed and the character that was compressed. Further assume that the special compression-indicating character is represented by the bit sequence 11111111 and that the character A is represented by the bit sequence 01000001.

The effect of a bit error is more pronounced on compressed data than on noncompressed data.

Figure 4.5 illustrates the potential effect of a bit error on a compressed sequence of bits. In Figure 4.5a, the original repeated character sequence of eight As is shown. In Figure 4.5b, that sequence is compressed into the character sequence S_c8A, in which S_c is the previously discussed compression-indicating character. Figure 4.5c indicates the compressed binary sequence. That sequence of 24 bits in effect represents 40 bits, because the three-compressed-character sequence represents eight noncompressed characters.

a. Repeated character sequence: AAAAAAAA

b. Compressed character sequence: S_c 8   A

c. Compressed binary sequence: 11111111 00001000 01000001

d. Occurrence of bit error: 11111111 00001000 01000011

e. Received compressed character sequence: S_c 8   C

f. Decompressed character sequence: CCCCCCCC

FIGURE 4.5.

The potential effect of a bit error on compressed data.

In Figure 4.5d, it was assumed that a bit error occurred that changed the next-to-last bit in the 24-bit sequence. The effect of that bit error is to change the binary value of the third character in the compressed character sequence from decimal 65 to decimal 67. This results in the character being changed from an A to a C, as indicated in Figure 4.5e, which when decompressed results in a string of eight Cs replacing the original noncompressed sequence of eight As.

If the bit error occurred in the repeat character indicator position, the number of characters decompressed would be in error. If the bit error corrupted the compression-indicating character, the receiving modem would not recognize that compression had occurred. In this situation, the compression-indicating character would be received as some other character, and the modem's decompression algorithm would not know that it was supposed to operate on the following two characters. Thus, the original string of eight As would be received as the three-character sequence X8C, in which X would represent the character resulting from a bit error corrupting the compression-indicating character.

As indicated by the preceding examples, the effect of a bit error on compressed data can be significantly more pronounced than the effect of a bit error on noncompressed data. This is the rationale for the inclusion of an error detection and correction feature built into every modem that has the capability to perform data compression.

Although a modem's error detection and correction feature can be set to operate on noncompressed data, it is automatically placed into operation whenever the modem is set to perform compression. This ensures that the integrity of compressed data is maintained.

In an error detection and correction mode of operation, the originating modem first groups data to be transmitted into blocks of characters. A mathematical algorithm is performed on each block that results in the generation of one or more check characters that are appended to each block. For example, the modem might treat each data block as one long binary number and divide that number by a fixed polynomial, resulting in a quotient and remainder, with the remainder used as a check character. The modem then transmits each block to include its check character or characters. The receiving modem performs a similar operation on each received data block. That is, the receiving modem might treat the block as one long binary number and divide that number by the same fixed polynomial used to generate the checksum.

When the division process is complete, the receiving modem would use the remainder as a locally generated checksum and compare that checksum to the checksum appended to the received data block. If the two checksums match, the data is assumed to be received without error, and the receiving modem transmits an acknowledgment to the transmitting modem. The acknowledgment informs the transmitting modem that it can discard the previously transmitted block because it was received without error. If the two checksums do not match, the receiving modem assumes that one or more bit errors occurred that altered the composition of the data block. The receiving modem discards the block and transmits a negative acknowledgment to the transmitting modem, which serves as a request for that modem to retransmit the preceding block. Thus, error correction is performed by retransmission.

Because modems performing error detection and correction must store a previously transmitted block until a receiving modem indicates that it was accepted, modems with this feature must have buffer storage. The actual amount of storage required is based on the method used to perform error detection and correction. The most popular method of error detection and correction used by modems is MNP Class 4. With the development of V.42bis data compression, the ITU-T promulgated the V.42 error detection and correction standard.

The V.42 error detection and correction standard actually defines two methods of error detection and correction: LAPB and MNP Class 4. LAPB (link access protocol balanced) represents the error detection and correction method used by the Higher Level Data Link Control (HDLC) protocol used at the network layer. LAPB is the primary method of modem error detection and correction specified by the V.42 standard; MNP Class 4 represents a secondary or alternative method. Due to the large base of MNP-compatible modems, many V.42-compatible modem users typically set the modem's error detection and correction mode to MNP Class 4. Later in this chapter, I discuss how such modem features as data compression and error detection and correction are enabled and disabled.

Interface and Signaling Standards

There are many "standards" and "recommended practices" used to define data communications interfaces and signaling. In fact, the entire problem of data communications can be looked at as the task of passing information through a series of interfaces and transmission channels without loss of meaning.

The interface that is of the greatest interest is the one between the equipment that originates and/or receives the data (the Data Terminal Equipment) and the equipment that handles the problem of transmitting the data from place to place (the Data Communications Equipment). Computers are called Data Terminal Equipment (whether or not they look or act like a CRT or another terminal). Modems are called Data Communications Equipment (also called data circuit-terminating equipment or data sets) because their function is to communicate the data rather than consider, compute, or change the data in any way.

●
Correct interfacing between equipment is of utmost importance to achieve error-free data communications. The most common interface standard is RS-232.

Terms such as RS-232, V.24, RS-422, RS-423, RS-449, X.21, X.25, and current loop are the designations of the various standards and recommendations designed to make the task of connecting computers, terminals, modems, and networks easier. As you'll see, manufacturers have in many cases used the standardized interfaces for functions that were never intended. This method helps by not increasing the number of interfaces, but it adds to the confusion of the user.

In terms of the present computer and communications world, the Electronic Industries Association (EIA) RS-232 is the standard. I'll therefore describe it and use it as a way to explain interfaces in general. I'll consider some of the limitations of RS-232, and I'll discuss some of the newer developments that eventually might replace RS-232.

The RS-232 and V.24 Interface

● The RS-232 standard covers the mechanical and signal interface between data terminal equipment and data communications equipment employing serial binary data interchange.

The proper name of RS-232 is "Interface Between Data Terminal Equipment and Data Communication Equipment Employing Serial Binary Data Interchange." Currently, the most popular version of RS-232 is revision C, which is formally referred to as RS-232C. In the late 1980s, revision D was introduced, which was followed by revision E in the early 1990s. The latest version will eventually supersede RS-232C and RS-232D. All three versions of the RS-232 standard have a large core of common functions and operating features that will collectively be referred to as RS-232. We will designate an appropriate revision to describe specific functions associated with each version of RS-232. What is written here also applies to ITU-T Recommendation V.24, which is almost identical to RS-232, but the electrical signal characteristics are specified separately in ITU-T Recommendation V.28.

In addition to explanatory notes and a short glossary, the RS-232 standard covers four areas:

- The mechanical characteristics of the interface (which has some surprises)
- The electrical signals across the interface
- The function of each signal
- Subsets of signals for certain applications

The Mechanical Interface

● Connector shape and pin arrangement are not covered in the standard, but the assignment of signals to connector pins, the connector gender, and cable length and capacity are covered.

As with any standard, the purpose of RS-232 is primarily as a reference for designers of equipment; therefore, it is not a tutorial, and not particularly easy reading. (Perhaps that explains why it seems that many people who write about RS-232 have never read it.) Almost anyone in the computer or communications field, including authors, will tell you that the DB-25 connector is defined in the standard. That is simply not true when referencing RS-232C. It wasn't until reference D was introduced that the 25-pin interface connector was formally specified. Until RS-232D, all that the mechanical section covered was the assignment of signals to the connector pins (discussed in the next section), which piece of equipment has the female connector (the DCE), the recommended maximum cable length (50 feet), and the maximum cable capacitance (2500 picofarads).

Because the DB-25 connector became almost universally associated with RS-232C, its pin arrangement is shown in Figure 4.6. However, it was not defined in the standard until revision D, and some manufacturers (notably IBM) use a different connector on some of their equipment. That connector is referred to as a DB-9, which, as its nomenclature indicates, defines a nine-pin connector. This connector is normally used as a serial port interface on notebook and laptop computers as well as on many desktop computers that combine serial and parallel ports onto a single adapter card. The DB-9 connector requires less mounting space on the rear of a computer and provides manufacturers with a mechanism to reduce the size of a computer while still providing a built-in serial port connection. A later portion of this chapter describes the RS-232 circuits carried within a DB-9 connector and their relationship to the circuits carried within a DB-25 connector. RS-232D additions and changes to RS-232C are indicated in parentheses in Figure 4.6.

FIGURE 4.6.

A typical RS-232 female connector.

Secondary Transmitted Data — 14
Transmit Clock — 2/15
Secondary Received Data — 3/16
Receiver Clock — 4/17
Unassigned (Local Loopback) — 5/18
Secondary Request to Send — 6/19
Data Terminal Ready (DTE Ready) — 7/20
Signal Quality Detector — 8/21
Ring Indicator — 9/22
Data Rate Select — 10/23
External Clock — 11/24
Unassigned (Test Mode) — 12/25/13

Protective Ground (Shield) — 1
Transmitted Data — 2
Received Data — 3
Request to Send — 4
Clear to Send — 5
Data Set Ready (DCE Ready) — 6
Signal Ground — 7
Data Carrier Detect — 8
Reserved — 9
Reserved — 10
Unassigned — 11
Secondary Data Carrier Detect — 12
Secondary Clear To Send — 13

RS-232D Additions/Changes to RS-232C Indicated in Parentheses

Electrical and Functional Interfaces

Although it doesn't make much sense to say that one part of a standard is more important than another, the heart of RS-232 is certainly the electrical and functional sections. The electrical portion covers the all-important voltage and current specifications for each pin, along with such features as the requirement that the equipment not be damaged if any two pins are shorted together (which is not to say that the equipment would still work, but it's not supposed to burn up). The functional portion, perhaps the most important of all, defines the sequencing of the signals and the action taken by the DTE and DCE in response.

Although the RS-232 standard defines the procedures for automatic answering by the modem and for reversing the transmission direction in half-duplex communications, it does not define automatic dialing. This is covered in EIA Standard RS-366. As you will see later, many newer modems incorporate automatic dialing in ways that the authors of RS-232 and RS-366 did not imagine.

●
The standard covers the specifications for current and voltage, special electrical considerations, and the sequencing of signals across the interface.

A Pin-by-Pin Tour of RS-232

In Figure 4.7, the signals are numbered and named according to three standard systems, plus a fourth that isn't a standard but that many people use. The first is by pin number, which is the way that people who deal regularly with the interface think of the signals: pin 2, pin 3, pin 5, and so forth. The second is the EIA designation: BA, BB, CB, and so forth. The third is the CCITT (now known as the ITU-T) designation: 103, 104, 106, and so on. The fourth is an abbreviation of the signal description: TD for Transmitted Data, RD for Received Data, CTS for Clear To Send, and so forth. A given signal often has more than one of these abbreviations because they aren't standard. Now we'll take a pin-by-pin tour and look at the signals by category and function.

FIGURE 4.7.

RS-232 pin designations.

PIN NO.	EIA CKT.	CCITT CKT.	Signal Description	Common Abbrev.	From DCE	To DCE
1	AA	101	Protective Chassis Ground (Shield)	GND		
2	BA	103	Transmitted Data	TD		X
3	BB	104	Received Data	RD	X	
4	CA	105	Request to Send	RTS		X
5	CB	106	Clear to Send	CTS	X	
6	CC	107	Data Set Ready (DCE Ready)	DSR	X	
7	AB	102	Signal Ground/Common Return	SG	X	X
8	CF	109	Received Line Signal Detector	DCD	X	
9			Reserved			
10			Reserved			
11			Unassigned			
12	SCF	122	Secondary Received Line Signal Detector		X	
13	SCB	121	Secondary Clear to Send		X	
14	SBA	118	Secondary Transmitted Data			X
15	DB	114	Transmitter Signal Element Timing (DCE)		X	
16	SBB	119	Secondary Received Data		X	
17	DD	115	Receiver Signal Element Timing		X	
18			Unassigned (Local Loopback)			X
19	SCA	120	Secondary Request to Send			X
20	CD	108/2	Data Terminal Ready (DTE Ready)	DTR		X
21	CG	110	Signal Quality Detector	SQ	X	
22	CE	125	Ring Indicator	RI	X	
23	CH	111	Data Signal Rate Selector (DTE)			X
23	CI	112	Data Signal Rate Selector (DCE)		X	
24	DA	113	Transmitter Signal Element Timing (DTE)			X
25			Unassigned (Test Mode)		X	

RS-232D Additions/Changes to RS-232C Indicated in Parentheses

Pins 1 and 7, Protective Ground (GND) and Signal Ground (SG)

Two grounds are provided: chassis (frame) ground (pin 1) for the system, and a reference signal ground (pin 7) for the signals on all the other pins.

If provided, pin 1 is connected to the chassis of the equipment and is intended to connect one end of the shield if shielded cable is used. Shielded cable can be used to minimize interference in high-noise environments. Never connect the shield at both ends of the cable. Pin 7 is the common reference for all signals, including data, timing, and control signals. Pin 7 must be connected at both ends for the DTE and DCE to work properly across the serial interface. Under RS-232D, pin 1's use is modified to provide shielding, and this conductor is referred to as the shield.

Pin 7 is the reference signal ground for all the other pins and thus is very important. The interface will not work without it because none of the signal circuits would be completed. One difficulty of RS-232 is the use of two separate grounding wires; grounding of distributed analog systems is often difficult, and having two ground paths doesn't help. For example, suppose that there is an RS-232 cable between two pieces of equipment and that the Protective Ground is open (or not connected) but the Signal Ground is connected to the power outlet ground at both ends. However, due to problems in the building's ground circuit, the two ends are at different ground potentials. This causes a current to flow through the Signal Ground Wire, and the resistance in the wire causes a difference in potential to develop between pin 7 at one end and pin 7 at the other end. If this potential is large enough, it could cause the data to be received incorrectly.

Pins 2 and 3, Transmitted Data (TD) and Received Data (RD)

At last we're getting down to the nitty-gritty. These are the pins that count; if it weren't for the data that passes through these pins, all the rest would be unnecessary. One important point to remember is that all signal names in the RS-232 standard are as viewed from the DTE. Thus, the DTE transmits on pin 2 and receives on pin 3, but the DCE transmits on pin 3 and receives on pin 2. If you imagine yourself as a computer (easier than imagining yourself as a modem), the names are easier to understand.

For people accustomed to more modern electronic interfaces, RS-232 signal levels might be a bit surprising because they are not TTL levels. In RS-232C, a positive voltage between 5 and 15 volts on pin 2 or 3 with respect to pin 7 represents a logic 0 level, and a negative voltage between −5 and −15 volts on either pin represents a logic 1. These are levels for data; the voltage polarities are reversed for logic 0 and 1 on the control lines. Under RS-232D and RS-232E, the ON and OFF voltage ranges were extended to +25 V and −25 V, respectively.

Pins 4 and 5, Request to Send (RTS) and Clear to Send (CTS)

Terminals cannot transmit until Clear to Send (CTS) is received from the DCE. For private-line transmission, CTS is usually linked to Request to Send (RTS). In such cases, the DTE can use RTS to turn on the modem transmission carrier if the modem is so optioned. In this type of application, the relationship between RTS and CTS is usually a simple count-down timer that is optioned when the DCE is installed. The time delay will be set to such a value as to allow time for the carrier to turn on and become stable before CTS is returned to the DTE. If the DCE is optioned for constant carrier (without regard to RTS), the RTS/CTS delay is usually set to zero.

Pins 6 and 20, Data Set Ready (DSR) and Data Terminal Ready (DTR)

Data Set Ready (DSR)—that is, Modem Ready—is used to indicate that the modem is powered on and is not in test mode. In dial-data applications, Data Terminal Ready (DTR) is used to create the equivalent of an off-hook condition. When the modem is in auto-answer mode, DTR can be asserted in response to the ring indicator to tell the modem to answer the incoming call. Under RS-232D, the signal on pin 6 was renamed DCE Ready, and the signal on pin 20 was renamed DTE Ready.

●
The voltage polarities transmitted and received on the data lines (pins 2 and 3) range from 5 to 15 volts positive for a logic 0 level and from 5 to 15 negative for logic 1, and they are reversed on the control lines.

●
The signals on pins 4, 5, 6, and 20 are the handshaking signals that establish the communications link.

Pin 8, Received Line Signal Detector (DCD or CD)

The Received Line
Signal Detector is
asserted when the
modem receives a
carrier of sufficient
strength for reliable
communications.

The Received Line Signal Detector signal is usually called Data Carrier Detect (DCD) or Carrier Detect (CD). The term CD should be avoided, however, because it can be confused with the EIA designation of CD for pin 20. The modem asserts DCD whenever it receives a signal on the telephone line that meets its internal criteria for amount of energy at the carrier frequency. Many DTEs require this signal before they will transmit or accept data. For this reason, in applications in which no modem is present, pin 8 usually is tied to pin 20, which in most cases is asserted whenever the DTE is turned on.

Pin 22, Ring Indicator (RI)

When the DCE
detects a ringing
signal on pin 22, it
tells the DTE that the
phone is ringing.
The DTE tells the
modem to answer
the phone by
asserting pin 20.

The Ring Indicator (RI) signal is the means by which the DCE tells the DTE that the phone is ringing. Virtually all modems that are designed to be directly connected (via an FCC-approved modular plug) to the telephone network are equipped for auto answer. This means that the modem can recognize the standard ringing voltage, indicate the ringing to the DTE, and answer (take the line off-hook) when told to do so by the DTE. Pin 22 is asserted by the DCE in time with the cadence of the ringing signal on the line. Thus, when the ringing voltage is present, RI is true (on); between rings, RI is not true (off). The DTE tells the modem to answer the phone by asserting pin 20, DTR.

The 10 pins and signals in the foregoing descriptions are by far the most often used of those defined in RS-232 and V.24. It is very unlikely that equipment or cables for the small-computer market will be equipped with any other proper RS-232 signals, although sometimes (unfortunately) other pins are used in nonstandard ways that can cause problems when equipment is interconnected. I will now quickly cover the functions of the remaining pins in the specification.

Pins 15, 17, 21, and 24

Pins 15, 17, and 24
are used by syn-
chronous modems to
control bit timing.
Pin 21 indicates that
the quality of the
received carrier is
satisfactory.

Synchronous modems use the signals on pins 15, 17, 21, and 24. Because the transmitting modem must send something (a 1 or 0) at each bit time, the modem controls the timing of the bits from the DTE. Similarly, the receiving modem must output a bit and associated timing when received. Pin 15 (Transmitter Signal Element Timing—DCE source) and pin 17 (Receiver Signal Element Timing—DCE source) are used for these purposes. In instances in which the transmitter timing comes from a source other than the transmitting modem (such as another modem in a multiplexing situation), pin 24 (Transmitter Signal Element Timing—DTE source) is used. Pin 21 (Signal Quality Detector) indicates that the received carrier meets some predetermined criterion for quality.

Pin 23, Data Signal Rate Selector

Pin 23 looks for two pins in the chart of Figure 4.7, but actually it is either Data Signaling Rate Selector (DTE source) or Data Signaling Rate Selector (DCE source). Some modems, called dual-rate or "gearshift" modems, allow switching between two transmission speeds. Sometimes the speed is selected automatically by the modem during the training (initializing) sequence, or it might be selected by the transmitting DTE. The signal on pin 23 controls whether the modem uses the high or low speed. Usually the modem at the calling end sets the speed for the connection and informs its DTE. The calling modem signals the speed to the answering modem, which informs the called DTE by asserting Data Signaling Rate Selector (DCE source).

Secondary Channels: Pins 12, 13, 14, 16, and 19

Some modems are equipped with both primary and secondary channels. The five secondary signals—Secondary Transmitted Data, Secondary Received Data, Secondary Request to Send, Secondary Clear to Send, and Secondary Received Line Signal Detector—allow control of the secondary channel in the same way as described for the primary channel. In these modems, the primary transmission channel usually has the higher data rate, and the secondary channel transmits in the reverse direction with a much lower data rate (for example, 75 bps).

●
In modems equipped with primary and secondary channels, the secondary channels carry signals in the reverse direction and at a much lower data rate.

Some Examples of RS-232 Connections

Now that you understand the functions of the various signals, I'll give you some examples of RS-232 interfaces. I'll begin with a simple example in which the interface is used in the proper way. Later, I'll discuss how the interface is used in ways for which it was not intended.

Computer to Modem Interface

When you call from your home computer to another computer over telephone lines, you are using the Universal Seven-Part Data Circuit that was defined in Chapter 1, "An Overview of Data Communications," and illustrated in Figure 1.14. Your computer is connected to a modem through an RS-232 interface, and the modem is connected to the telephone network. At the far end, whether it is a local or long-distance call, the other computer is similarly connected to a modem through an RS-232 interface. Figure 4.8a shows the absolute minimum RS-232 interface for the "normal" DTE-DCE connection.

●
Not all the RS-232 pins are used in every application, but the minimum DTE-DCE interface connections are transmitted data, received data, signal ground, and frame ground.

FIGURE 4.8.

The minimum RS-232 interface.

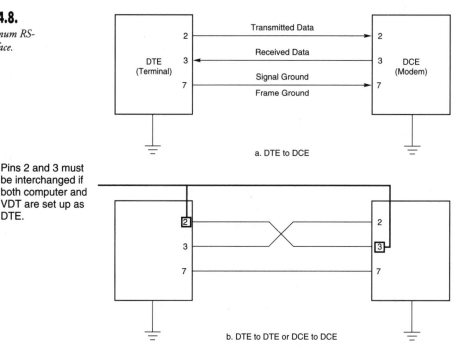

Pins 2 and 3 must be interchanged if both computer and VDT are set up as DTE.

Asynchronous Modem Control

The major problem with the four-conductor interface illustrated in Figure 4.8a is the lack of control circuits routed between the modem and the terminal. For example, after you establish a connection to a distant modem, you likely would want a method to alert you to the fact that your communications connection with the distant modem was broken. This would require your terminal to monitor pin 8, which provides a carrier detect signal. As previously noted, intelligent modems include built-in buffer memory to hold data blocks until a distant modem acknowledges the correct receipt of the block. Because buffer memory is finite, the modem must have a method to inform the terminal device to suspend transmission to the modem until its buffer is emptied to the point where the modem can again receive data. This process, known as flow control, can be implemented in several ways to include a toggling of the Clear to Send signal by the modem. Later in this chapter, flow control is described in detail.

Another control circuit missing from Figure 4.8a is Ring Indicator (RI) on pin 22. Its omission precludes the automatic answering operations.

To enable a terminal to inform an attached modem that it is operational and ready to receive data requires the inclusion of the Data Terminal Ready signal on pin 20. Similarly, for the modem to provide an indication to the terminal that it is powered on requires the inclusion of the Data Set Ready circuit on pin 6. Last but not least, for the terminal device to inform the modem that it has data to transmit requires the inclusion of the Request to Send circuit on pin 4.

The inclusion of the preceding control circuits results in a core set of 10 circuits required for an asynchronous intelligent modem. Because it is common practice to strap frame ground to signal ground, this reduces the number of RS-232 circuits required for asynchronous intelligent modem operations to 9 and explains why computer manufacturers incorporated DB-9 connectors as the interface to serial ports on many desktop computers and almost all laptop and notebook computers.

Table 4.3 compares the DB-9 and DB-25 pins with respect to the DB-9 connector. In examining the entries in Table 4.3, it becomes obvious that a special type of cable is required to connect the serial port of a computer with a DB-9 connector to the DB-25P (P for plug) connector that will be plugged into a DB-25S (S for socket) connector built into almost all modems. That cable must cross pin 1 at the DB-9 connector to pin 8 at the DB-25 connector end of the cable. Similarly, pin 2 at the DB-9 connector end of the cable must be crossed to pin 3 at the DB-25 connector end of the cable, and so on.

Table 4.3. DB-9 to DB-25 pin correspondence.

DB-9	Conductor Circuit	DB-25
1	Carrier Detect	8
2	Receive Data	3
3	Transmitted Data	2
4	Data Terminal Ready	20
5	Signal Ground	7
6	Data Set Ready	6
7	Request to Send	4
8	Clear to Send	5
9	Ring Indicator	22

Computer to Video Display Terminal Interface

The video display terminal (VDT) uses the simplest possible interface, as Figure 4.8 shows. If both the computer and the VDT are set up as DTE, pins 2 and 3 must be interchanged at the VDT end of the cable, as Figure 4.8b shows. Otherwise, each would expect to transmit data on the same wire.

This interchange usually is done at one of the cable connectors. However, an adapter with the wiring interchange done between its back-to-back connectors can be inserted between one end of a standard cable and the equipment. This adapter, often called a modem eliminator or null modem, enables the standard cable wiring to be left as is. These adapters are available in any combination of connector gender, that is, male-to-male, male-to-female, and female-to-female.

Computer to Serial Printer Interface

●

When an RS-232 cable is used to connect peripheral equipment to a computer, it might have to be modified.

The label on the box for your new printer says, "Serial interface connects directly to the RS-232 port of your computer." When you open the box, you see a connector on the back of the printer that looks just like the RS-232 connector on your modem. (The manufacturer also charges you quite a bit extra for the absolutely essential printer cable, but that's another story.) So it appears that the RS-232 interface on your computer does double duty: it can connect to a modem or to a printer.

But the RS-232 was never intended for connecting peripheral devices such as printers to DTEs such as computers. It's not that it won't work; the problem comes in the confusion of identities. The computer is almost always (when you're talking about RS-232, it pays to say "almost always") internally wired as a DTE, and modems are always wired as DCEs (yes, always, because the role of the modem is defined precisely in the standard)—but what about the poor printer? Is it DTE or DCE, fish or fowl? Does it use the same signals (and pins) that the modem uses, or are some different? Can you get by without buying that expensive special printer cable—can you use your modem cable, which, after all, looks just like the printer cable and even has the same connectors?

Nonstandard Use of a Standard

●

Modified RS-232 cables often have pins that are not connected, or they are interchanged or jumpered to adapt the cable for the desired interface connections.

You probably have already guessed that the answer is bad news, or you wouldn't be reading about it. The RS-232 and other standards are intended to define the interface between DTEs and DCEs for communications over networks, usually telephone facilities. They don't address the idea of using the interface as a general serial input/output port. The wiring and control of a peripheral device in the same room, such as a printer (or another computer), is simply not considered in the standard. This means that the manufacturers are presented with a useful solution to the interfacing problem but have few guidelines (and no hard-and-fast rules) on how to apply it. The result is a certain amount of confusion in the marketplace. The purpose of this section is to help clarify what happens across the interface to aid in solving the problem if necessary.

One source of the confusion is that printers and similar peripherals simply don't do the same things that modems do, and they therefore don't need the same control signals. The printer doesn't need to send and receive some of the signals that the modem needs, and it needs some signals that the modem doesn't. One question is whether pin 2 or pin 3 of the RS-232 connector will be used for data transfer. In the sense of the standard, both the computer and the printer are DTE, and when a DTE is connected directly to another DTE, most of the signals defined in RS-232 are unnecessary. Although the manufacturer's special printer cable looks like an RS-232 cable, some of the pins aren't connected at all, and some of the pin connections are interchanged or jumpered together to adapt the interface on both ends. So the printer manufacturer's claim that its product is "RS-232 compatible" really means that the equipment accepts and generates only a small fraction of the RS-232 signals and (probably) doesn't violate any other parts of the standard.

Flow Control

Imagine that you decide to write your own software (called a printer driver) to pass data through the RS-232 port to the printer. You've bought the manufacturer's cable, and you've checked things such as bit rate, parity, number of stop bits, and character code. Suppose that the printer is set up for ASCII seven-bit characters, odd parity, and one stop bit. The printer manual says it can operate at 9600 bits per second, and because that's the fastest your computer can output serial data, you'll use that speed. Now you send a page of text to the printer, using your driver program. What happens? After the first line or two, there are more missing characters than printed characters. It looks as though they never made it to the printer! There doesn't seem to be any rhyme or reason, but every time you try to print using your program, data is lost. Why?

Let's compare data rates. Asynchronous ASCII uses 7 bits for the character code, 1 for the parity bit, 1 for the stop bit, and 1 for the start bit, for a total of 10 bits per character. Because the computer is transmitting 9600 bits per second to the printer, the character rate must be 960 characters per second.

Digging out the printer manual one more time, you see that the printer's maximum rate is 80 characters per second. That means you are sending 12 times as much data as the printer can accept. No wonder the data was getting lost. The printer buffer would fill up, and then data would be lost until buffer space became available again. What you need is a simple handshake mechanism to stop the computer from sending data when the buffer fills up and to turn it on again when the buffer empties. This is called flow control, and RS-232 is bound to have it, right? Wrong! RS-232 was designed for communicating between computers over telephone channels; the assumption is that any flow control mechanism needed is built into the software at either end. As you'll see next, various schemes have been used for flow control with varying degrees of success.

●
The RS-232 assumes that the flow control needed by modems would be furnished by the software at either end of the communications network.

Methods Used for Flow Control

From the previous discussion about RTS and CTS (pins 4 and 5), it would seem that these signals could be used for flow control. Although they often are used in this way, they shouldn't be, for many reasons. The problem is that the DCE is not allowed to drop Clear to Send until the DTE drops Request to Send. RTS and CTS are indeed handshake lines; the problem is that they indicate something besides that the DCE is ready to accept data. The RTS and CTS signals are intended to allow the terminal to request control of the

●
The RTS and CTS lines should not be used for flow control because it is very likely that data will be lost.

communications link from the modem. The terminal assumes that it will keep the link as long as it needs it, and the DCE cannot arbitrarily drop Clear to Send whenever it wants to do so. This means that CTS cannot properly be used by the DCE as a flow control indicator; the DCE (or equipment such as a printer posing as DCE) can't raise and lower Clear to Send to tell the DTE to pause or restart transmission. Put another way, the DTE and the communications link are handshaking, not the DTE and the DCE. The handshake is for the purpose of establishing message transmission, not character-by-character or line-by-line acknowledgment for a printer.

Suppose that you decide to use RTS and CTS for flow control anyway (as some manufacturers who should know better have done). If the printer drops Clear to Send in the middle of a character transmission, what does that mean? If the transmitter stops immediately in the middle of the character, that character is sure to be garbled because timing is important in serial communications. If the transmitter waits until the character is transmitted and then stops, there might be no room in the printer's buffer for the last character. Because this possibility is not considered in the standard, the success of RTS-CTS as a flow control mechanism cannot be predicted without studying the manuals for both of the devices involved. Even taking that action is no guarantee of success, but the odds are better.

Some manufacturers avoid the conflict by using the Data Terminal Ready or Data Set Ready (DTR or DSR) pins, depending on whether their printer thinks it is DTE or DCE. For example, if pin 6 (DSR) is used to provide flow control, the printer turns off pin 6 when it can accept no more data and turns it on again when its buffer is nearly empty. Still, there is no assurance that the device on the other end of the cable will recognize the signal or interpret it correctly because these lines were not intended to be used for flow control.

A way to achieve flow control is for the peripheral equipment to send special characters to the computer, which uses software to recognize the characters.

Another method for flow control is for the printer to send special characters for pause and return over the data line (pin 3, RD) to the computer. The software driver recognizes the special characters and controls the terminal output according to the character received. ASCII codes DC1 and DC3 (device controls 1 and 3) are often used, but they usually are called XON and XOFF. On the standard keyboard, these characters correspond to Ctrl+Q (resume) and Ctrl+S (pause). The printer logic transmits Ctrl+S when its buffer is approximately 80 percent full and Ctrl+Q when the buffer is less than 20 percent full.

Some printer manufacturers use both the DSR line and the RD line (XON/XOFF). However, problems might occur with either method. In instances in which the printer is connected to a modem (perhaps a short-haul modem on another floor of the building), there is no connection between the DSR circuits at the opposite ends (nor between RTS/CTS), so use of other pins is impossible. XON/XOFF should work fine in this instance, provided that the software recognizes it, and provided that the printer logic anticipates buffer overflow in time. Problems also can occur if several terminals are multiplexed together because the reverse characters are stored for a short time in the multiplexer.

Of course, these problems occur because RS-232 was never intended for flow control or for DTE-to-DTE connections. We should not be surprised when individually arranged flow-control methods don't always work; they simply are not part of the standard. In spite of the most intelligent modem, manufacturers support the use of RTS and CTS control signals as a mechanism for enabling flow control from the DTE to the modem and the modem to the DTE. Fortunately, most of those modems also support XON/XOFF flow control and might also support other characters that can be used as a flow control mechanism.

In summary, RS-232 is not very reliable for flow control because it was not designed for this application.

Limitations of RS-232

It would seem that the lack of a flow control mechanism is the major drawback of RS-232, but actually that isn't the case. Flow control is handled much better through software than through hardware, and that is the direction in which new systems are moving. Small-computer peripherals just haven't gotten there yet. RS-232 does have some limitations that restrict its use, however. After discussing these limitations, I'll look at some standards that don't have these limitations and that offer other advantages as well.

Distance Limitations

The principal problem with RS-232 is its distance limitation of 50 feet. With all but the highest data rates, much longer cable runs can be successful, but they never seem quite long enough, and there's always a risk of losing data. The distance restriction is not a serious disadvantage when the modem is close to the computer or terminal and the long-haul transmission to a remote computer takes place over telephone lines. In local applications, however, RS-232 cables often are used to connect terminals directly to computers because it is convenient to use the same terminal and computer interface whether or not a modem connection is used. (Also, the RS-232 connector is probably the only one provided.) For these connections, the 50-foot limit becomes restrictive.

An RS-232 transmitter generates a voltage between +5 and +25 volts for one of the two possible signal states (space), and a voltage between −5 and −25 volts for the opposite state (mark). Unfortunately, these voltage levels are not the same as those inside the computer and terminal, which use standard TTL and MOS logic. This means an additional power supply (usually ±12 volts) is required for the RS-232 levels. As Figure 4.9 shows, an RS-232 receiver circuit recognizes voltages above +3 V as spaces, and voltages below −3 V as marks. When a signal changes from one condition to the other, the specification limits the amount of time in the undefined region to 5 percent of a bit period. This requirement determines the maximum amount of stray capacitance allowable in the cable because capacitance limits the rise time (or transition time) of the signal. RS-232 specifies that the capacitance must not exceed 2500 picofarads (pF). Because the cables generally used for RS-232 have a capacitance of 40 to 50 picofarads per foot, RS-232 limits cables to 50 feet (2500/50 = 50).

The RS-232 standard of 2500 picofarads for stray capacitance can be restrictive in direct computer-to-terminal connections.

FIGURE 4.9.

*RS-232 data signal
levels at the receiver.*

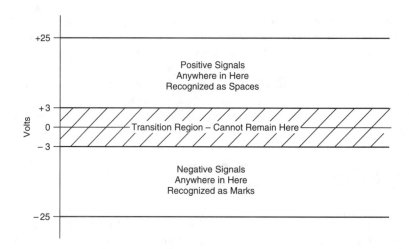

Speed Limitations

A second limitation is the maximum transmission speed of 20,000 bps, although this is not usually a disadvantage in applications between computers and terminals. The data rate between a computer and a terminal is usually less than or equal to 19,200 bps at best. When a PC is cabled to a modern high-speed modem that can operate at up to 33.6 Kbps without performing data compression, the transfer of data to the modem via an RS-232 cable violates the standard's maximum transmission rate. This violation becomes possible by use of a cable considerably shorter than the 50-foot cable limit specified by the RS-232 standard, with most modem manufacturers recommending a maximum cabling distance of 12 feet or less. When a high-speed modem is placed in its compressed mode of operation, you usually want to transfer data to the modem from two to four times its operating rate to effectively use its compression capability. This means you would set the serial port of your PC to 67.2 Kbps or 134.4 Kbps if you were using a modem operating at 33.6 Kbps. Unfortunately, at data rates above 115.2 Kbps, the UART built into PC serial ports can lose data during sustained data transfer operations. To overcome this problem, some modem vendors require the use of an "enhanced" serial port in the PC, whereas other modem vendors include a parallel port in their product and special software that uses that port for high-speed data transfer to and from the modem.

Ground Limitations

Improper grounding
of control and data
signal grounds can
cause signals to be
misinterpreted.

The third disadvantage of RS-232 is, as discussed previously, its grounding method. The problem is not so much with the protective (chassis) ground as with the control and data signals; all are referenced against the same signal ground wire (pin 7). This method, called unbalanced transmission, works satisfactorily most of the time. If, however, there is a difference in ground potential between the two ends of the cable (quite likely for long runs), the transition region between a space and a mark is narrowed. When this situation occurs, the possibility exists that a signal will be misinterpreted, as Figure 4.10 shows. Just as the various parts of the standard work together (speeds within the standard usually work fine over cables that are also within the standard), so the various restrictions interact. If you try to drive cables that are too long at speeds that are too high, all these problems tend to bite you at once.

FIGURE 4.10.

Problems because of differing ground potentials in RS-232.

Other Interfaces

Although RS-232 is the most commonly used interface, several additional interfaces are frequently used to connect data terminal equipment to data communications equipment. Those interfaces include RS-444A, RS-422A, and RS-449.

An Old Standby: The Current Loop

RS-232, for all its faults, at least defines connector pins and signal levels. No such standards exist for teleprinters. The serial transmission format is defined, with start and stop bits, data bits, and parity bits, but the electrical interface varies with the manufacturer, and control signals are unknown. In teleprinters, the signal interface is called the current loop. Rather than positive and negative voltages representing logic ones and zeros, the current loop uses presence or absence of current. Presence can be either 20 or 60 milliamperes, depending on the teleprinter model and manufacturer. No standard connector or standard pinouts exist for current-loop operation.

●
When the serial data transmission format is defined by the presence or absence of current, the signal interface is called a current loop.

The idea of the current loop is to switch a current on and off. The active side of the transmission line generates the current, and the passive side switches or detects it. Because either the receiver or transmitter can be active, there are four possibilities: active receiver, active transmitter, passive receiver, and passive transmitter. Because of the convenience of locating the power supply at just one end of the link (usually at the computer), all four of these signals are found in a single computer-to-terminal connection.

Despite the lack of standards, designers of serial devices for computers like to include current-loop interface capability. It's a useful interface because teleprinters are still a cost-effective solution as a combination printer and terminal, and many devices other than teleprinters use it. Where RS-232 is limited to a 50-foot cable, a current loop can be up to 1500 feet long and handle data rates of up to 9600 bps without a special power supply. Unfortunately, the current-loop interface is completely incompatible with RS-232 and requires either hardware that has both interfaces built-in or interface boxes. The interface boxes can be built to adapt to any of the four possible interfaces. For example, if two microcomputers that are to be connected both contain the active interface, an active-to-active converter is required to directly connect them. Similarly, to connect a passive terminal directly to another passive terminal, a passive-to-passive converter is required. Fortunately, the converters can be easily constructed using an optoisolator. The active-to-active converter does not even need a power supply, although the passive-to-passive must have one to generate the current.

> ●
>
> Data rates up to 9600 bps can be handled using current loops, even when cable lengths are longer than those allowed for RS-232 interfaces.

RS-422A, RS-423A, and RS-449

Useful though the current loop might be in some cases, most of the world is not moving away from RS-232 back to teleprinters. Instead, the movement is toward three types of interfaces. Two are similar to RS-232, but with some of the warts removed; the other is quite different, with hardware functions replaced by software. I'll examine the ones more like RS-232 first.

In the early 1970s, the EIA introduced the RS-422A, RS-423A, and RS-449 standards to overcome the defects of RS-232 while at the same time incorporating and improving on the advantages of the current-loop interface. A major change was to unbundle the electrical, mechanical, and functional specifications of RS-232 into separate documents. RS-422A and RS-423A cover only electrical specifications; RS-449 covers control functions.

RS-422A

> ●
>
> By using balanced transmission based on the RS-422A standard, greater speed in data transmission is achieved, and ground potential problems are eliminated.

To allow transmission at high data rates, RS-422A uses two separate wires for each signal. This technique, called balanced transmission, doubles the number of wires in the cable but enables very high data rates and minimizes the problem of varying ground potential. Because ground is not used as a voltage reference, RS-422A grounding requirements are much less critical than those of RS-232, and the use of the Signal Ground wire is optional with RS-422A.

Another major difference between RS-422A and RS-232 is the transition region between mark and space states. With the elimination of the ground potential problem, the transition region can be much narrower. In RS-422A, the difference between the voltages on the two wires determines whether a mark or a space is sent. This difference is only 0.4 V in RS-422A, whereas it is 6 V (+3 V and –3 V) in RS-232. If the difference signal between the two wires is positive and more than 0.2 V, the receiver reads a mark; if it is negative and more than –0.2 V, the receiver reads a space. These voltage values allow suitable transmitters and receivers to be implemented with the ±5 V power supply commonly available in computers.

RS-423A

RS-423A transmits at lower speeds and uses one wire as a common return path for all signals in a given direction (unbalanced transmission like RS-232, but with two return wires). The RS-423A standard operates in both RS-232 and RS-422A environments. It provides users of existing RS-232 interfaced equipment with a way to move to the new RS-422A regime, including a defined RS-232 to RS-422A adapter connector.

Because of the much smaller transition region, RS-422A transmitters do not drive RS-232 receivers correctly. RS-423A equipment, on the other hand, interfaces with RS-232 signals. Each direction of transmission uses a common return path that is connected to ground only at the transmitter end. The receiver determines whether a mark or a space is present by examining whether the signal wire is negative or positive with respect to the common return. Because this return path does not connect to ground in the receiver, the problem of ground currents does not arise.

In an RS-423A transmitter, the voltage difference between the signal line and the common return must be at least 4 V—positive for a space and negative for a mark. This gives an 8 V transition region, which is compatible with RS-232 receiver circuitry but which presents the same power supply problem that occurs with RS-232. Because the RS-423A receiver must properly respond to the same 0.4 V transition region as an RS-422A receiver, an RS-422A transmitter can be used with RS-423A receivers.

> ●
> The RS-423A standard defines an adapter for use between RS-232C and RS-422A that enables RS-232C equipment to interface with RS-422A equipment.

RS-449

RS-449 is the intended successor to the functional portion of RS-232, including the mechanical specification of the plugs and sockets. Apart from its improved speed and distance specifications, RS-449 offers some minor functional enhancements over RS-232 in automatic modem testing and provision for a standby channel, but it still does not incorporate outward dialing. The acceptance of RS-449 in the marketplace seems questionable at this time.

Figure 4.11 shows the RS-449 signals with the corresponding RS-232 and V.24 signals. Notice the similarity between the new and old standards. The major differences are in the grounding arrangements (Send Common and Receive Common) and testing facilities.

> ●
> The RS-449 standard, which uses two connectors rather than one, is intended to replace the functional portion of RS-232. Even so, it has no provision for automatic dialing.

Apart from these, only a few miscellaneous signals have been added. All signals use the RS-423A transmission standard except those that can optionally use the RS-422A for higher speed links. (Two wires are specified for each of these.) The signals are divided between a 37-pin and a 9-pin connector, and the ground and common signals are handled separately for each cable. Many applications will not need the smaller cable because it contains only signals relevant to the secondary channel.

FIGURE 4.11.

Comparing RS-449 with RS-232 signals.

RS-449		RS-232*		CCITT Recommendation V.24	
SG	Signal Ground	AB	Signal Ground (Shield)	102	Signal Ground
SC	Send Common			102a	DTE Common
RC	Receive Common			102b	DCE Common
IS	Terminal in Service				
IC	Incoming Call	CE	Ring Indicator	125	Calling Indicator
TR	Terminal Ready	DC	Data Terminal Ready (DTE Ready)	108/2	Data Terminal Ready
DM	Data Mode	CC	Data Set Ready (DCE Ready)	07	Data Set Ready
SD	Send Data	BA	Transmitted Data	103	Transmitted Data
RD	Receive Data	BB	Received Data	104	Received Data
TT	Terminal Timing	DA	Transmitter Signal Element Timing (DTE Source)	113	Transmitter Signal Element Timing (DTE Source)
ST	Send Timing	DB	Transmitter Signal Element Timing (DCE Source)	114	Transmitter Signal Element Timing (DCE Source)
RT	Receive Timing	DD	Receive Signal Element Timing	115	Receiver Signal Element Timing (DCE Source)
RS	Request to Send	CA	Request to Send	105	Request to Send
CS	Clear to Send	CB	Clear to Send	106	Ready for Sending
RR	Receiver Ready	CF	Received Line Signal Detector	109	Data Channel Received Line Signal Detector
SQ	Signal Quality	CG	Signal Quality Detector	110	Data Signal Quality Detector
NS	New Signal				
SF	Select Frequency			126	Select Transmit Frequency
SR	Signaling Rate Selector	CH	Data Signaling Rate Selector (DTE Source)	111	Data Signaling Rate Selector (DTE Source)
SI	Signaling Rate Indicator	CI	Data Signaling Rate Selector (DCE Source)	112	Data Signaling Rate Selector (DCE Source)
SSD	Secondary Send Data	SBA	Secondary Transmitted Data	118	Transmitted Backward Channel Data
SRD	Secondary Receive Data	SBB	Secondary Received Data	119	Received Backward Channel Data
SRS	Secondary Request to Send	SCA	Secondary Request to Send	120	Transmit Backward Channel Line Signal
SCS	Secondary Clear to Send	SCB	Secondary Clear to Send	121	Backward Channel Ready
SRR	Secondary Receiver Ready	SCF	Secondary Received Line Signal Detector	122	Backward Channel Received Line Signal Detector
LL	Local Loopback	(LL)	(Local Loopback)	141	Local Loopback
RL	Remote Loopback			140	Remote Loopback
TM	Test Mode	(TM)	(Test Mode)	142	Test Indicator
SS	Select Standby			116	Select Standby
SB	Standby Indicator			117	Standby Indicator

*RS-232D Additions/Changes to RS-232C Indicated in Parentheses

One of the major problems that prevented more than a token acceptance of the RS-449 standard is its use of two connectors, with each connector differing in size and conductor connection from the RS-232 connector used with tens of millions of DTEs and DCEs. Recognizing that RS-449 would probably not fulfill its intended role, the EIA announced the RS-530 standard in the late 1980s as the successor to RS-449. Both RS-442 and RS-423 standards will continue to exist, and both are referenced by the RS-530 standard.

RS-530

RS-530 is similar to RS-449 in that it provides equipment with the capability to transmit data above the RS-232 limit of 20 Kbps. Like RS-232, RS-530 uses the nearly universal 25-pin D-shaped interface connector.

The RS-530 standard gets its capability to transmit data above 20 Kbps by the use of balanced signals in place of several RS-232 secondary signals and the Ring Indicator signal. This balanced signaling technique is accomplished by the use of two wires with opposite polarities for each signal to minimize distortion.

Table 4.4 summarizes the RS-530 interchange circuits based on their pin assignments. Although no equipment conforming to this new standard was marketed at the time this book revision was prepared, its elimination of the Ring Indicator signal suggests that its use will be reserved for non-PSTN applications.

Table 4.4. RS-530 interchange circuits.

Pin Number	Circuit	Description
1		Shield
2	BA	Transmitted data
3	BB	Received data
4	CA	Request to send
5	CB	Clear to send
6	CC	DCE ready
7	AB	Signal ground
8	CF	Received line signal detector
9	DD	Received signal element timing (DCE source)
10	CF	Received line signal detector
11	DA	Transmit signal element timing (DTE source)
12	DB	Transmit signal element timing (DCE source)
13	CB	Clear to send
14	BA	Transmitted data
15	DB	Transmitter signal element timing (DCE source)
16	BB	Received data
17	DD	Receiver signal element timing (DCE source)
18	LL	Local loopback
19	CA	Request to send

continues

Table 4.4. continued

Pin Number	Circuit	Description
20	CD	DTE ready
21	RL	Remote loopback
22	CC	DCE ready
23	DC	DTE ready
24	DA	Transmit signal element timing (DTE source)
25	TM	Test mode

RS-366

The RS-366 standard is different because it deals with automatic dialing under computer control.

None of the RS standards discussed provides for automatic dialing of calls by a computer. RS-232 and RS-449 provide specifications for answering calls, but not for dialing. A different standard, RS-366, covers automatic calling units. The reason is that until the late 1980s, equipment for placing calls under computer control was expensive because the actions required in making a telephone call can be quite complicated. The dialing equipment must be able to determine whether the line is free, take the phone off hook (in effect), wait for and recognize a dial tone, dial the number, and understand and respond to the various call progress tones (such as the busy signal) the telephone system provides to indicate the status of a call.

The principal use of RS-366 automatic dialing equipment in data communications is for dial backup for private-line data circuits, and for automatic dialing of remote terminals to allow them to transmit data. For example, a company's central computer could be programmed to automatically dial the computer in each branch office each evening and to cause (via software) the day's transactions to be transmitted to the main office.

The growth in availability of low-cost intelligent modems that respond to commands generated by DTEs has considerably reduced the use of RS-366–based automatic dialing equipment. Although RS-366 is still used to control the operation of synchronous modems, the use of RS-366 is expected to further decline because many modem manufacturers now are incorporating a synchronous dial control capability into their products.

The CCITT standards are aimed toward direct digital data communications. CCITT X.21 covers both automatic dialing and answering, and it uses full-duplex synchronous transmission.

CCITT X.21

The CCITT has charted a course different from the RS-standards, a course that was predicated on the eventual availability of direct digital connection to a digital telephone network. Then all data transmission will be synchronous, and the communications equipment will provide bit and byte timing signals. The CCITT X.21 recommendation, introduced in 1976, includes the protocol for placing and receiving calls and for sending and receiving data using full-duplex synchronous transmission. Byte-timing signals are an option, but one that nearly all digital telephone exchanges will almost certainly provide. In sharp contrast to RS-232, RS-449, and RS-530, X.21 uses only six signals. The electrical specifications are contained in recommendations X.26 (corresponding to EIA RS-422A) and X.27 (corresponding to EIA RS-423A).

The eventual maximum line speed under X.21 is likely to be 64,000 bps, the data rate now used to encode voice in digital form in the telephone network. In Europe, British Telecom offers X.21 customer data rate access to its Kilostream digital service at 2.4, 4.8, 9.6, 48, and 64 Kbps. Customer data rates up to 9.6 Kbps are converted to a line rate of 12.8 Kbps, whereas data rates of 48 and 64 Kbps both use a line rate of 64 Kbps for transmitting through the Kilostream network.

The circuits used in X.21 are given in Table 4.5. The first two circuits listed provide the voltage reference and ground connections. The computer sends data to the modem on the transmit line, and the modem returns data on the Receive line. The Control and Indication circuits provide control channels in two directions. The Signal Element Timing line carries the bit timing, and the Byte Timing line carries the byte timing. Although the Control and Indication lines are control lines, most of the controlling information uses the Transmit and Receive lines. The computer changes the state of Control when it wants to place a call, just as you lift the handset when you want to dial. To end the call, the computer changes Control back to the idle state. Similarly, the modem changes the state of Indication when the remote telephone is answered and changes it back if it shuts down. All the dialing information travels on the Transmit line in coded form, and all the information about tones comes back on the Receive line.

Table 4.5. CCITT X.21 signals.

Interchange Circuit	Name	To DCE	From DCE
G	Signal Ground or Common Return	(Note)	
Ga	DTE Common Return	X	
T	Transmit	X	
R	Receive		X
C	Control	X	
I	Indication		X
S	Signal Element Timing		X
B	Byte Timing		X

Note: See Recommendation X.24.

The major advantage of X.21 over RS-232, RS-449, and RS-530 is that the X.21 signals are encoded in serial digital form. For example, when a dial tone is received, a continuous sequence of ASCII "+" characters is sent to the computer on the Receive wire. In effect, this is a digital dial tone. The computer dials the number by transmitting it as a series of ASCII characters on the Transmit line, one bit at a time. After dialing the call, the computer receives call progress signals from the modem on the Receive wire. These signals indicate such things as number busy, access disallowed, and network congestion.

By using serial digital coding rather than dedicated wires for special functions, X.21 establishes a basis for providing special services in computer communication. A short-code-dialing or repeat-last-call facility would be extremely useful, for example, to reconnect a call every time you complete a line of typing at the terminal. (Some European nations are trying this approach to networking right now.) If the line could be disconnected while you are typing, long-distance calls would be much cheaper. Of course, this would also depend on the tariff policies of the telecommunication carriers. Using X.21 could allow many of the advantages of telecommunications by the packet-switching technique without the associated complexity.

> X.21, with its signal encoded in serial digital form, permits a few signal lines to accomplish all functions.

Although X.21 is defined as the lowest (or "physical") level of the international X.25 packet-switching protocol, it is far ahead of its time because direct digital connection to public telephone networks is hardly possible now. For this reason, CCITT offers the X.21bis recommendation as an interim measure to connect existing computer equipment to packet communication services. X.21bis is virtually identical to CCITT V.24 and RS-232. (Packet switching and CCITT protocols are discussed more in Chapter 11, "Architectures and Packet Networks.")

Types of Modems

Next, we'll cover the types of modems available, including the asynchronous (300 or 300/1200 baud) auto-answer modem, the full-duplex asynchronous private line modem, the half-duplex asynchronous private line modem, and smart modems.

Asynchronous (300 or 300/1200 Baud) Auto-Answer Modem

> The asynchronous 300 or 300/1200 baud auto-answer modem is normally used with unattended personal computers that are connected to dial-up circuits.

Asynchronous 300- or 300/1200-baud modems are usually used with personal computers. The signals needed for these modems, as well as for more modern higher-operating-rate asynchronous devices, are Protective Ground, Signal Ground, Transmitted Data, Received Data, Request To Send, Clear To Send, Data Terminal Ready, Ring Indicator, Received Line Signal Detector, and possibly Data Set Ready. Pin 20 (DTR) indicates that the computer is ready to receive calls, and pin 22 (RI) indicates that the modem is receiving the telephone ringing signal, going high and low as the ringing current goes off and on. (This is the way a modem can count how many rings to wait before answering.) If the computer leaves pin 20 (DTR) on all the time, the modem answers incoming calls without delay. If DTR is off, the computer turns it on in response to receiving an RI signal to tell the modem to answer the call. At the completion of the call, the computer turns off pin 20 (DTR) to cause the modem to disconnect the line (go on hook).

The following sequence of events is one possible set that can happen when a computer receives a call from another computer via a low-speed asynchronous modem and manual modem operations are employed. When the modem detects ringing, it turns on pin 22 (RI), the DTE responds by asserting pin 20 (DTR), and the modem goes off hook to answer the phone. The answering DTE asserts pin 4 (RTS), which commands the modem to turn on its transmitter. After the RTS-CTS delay, the modem responds by asserting CTS. At the other end of the line, the computer operator hears the carrier signal and either pushes the data button or puts the telephone handset into the acoustic coupler. Now the calling modem's transmitter turns on, producing its own carrier tone. When the modem at the receiving computer hears this carrier, it turns on pin 8 (DCD). On receiving this signal, the receiving computer begins transmitting data to tell the sending computer to log on, and so forth. Some operating systems wait for the caller to transmit a special character to begin the logon process.

At the end of the session, the caller logs off, causing the receiving computer to terminate the call. It turns off pin 4 (RTS), which causes the receiving modem to turn off its carrier signal. The receiving computer then drops pin 20 (DTR), causing the modem to go on hook to "hang up" the telephone line. At the calling end, pin 8 (DCD) goes off, the operator replaces the handset, and the action is complete.

When modems with an automatic answering capability are used, the previously described operations occur automatically and without operator intervention. If you can envision a typical data center or even a modern bulletin board system, you can get an appreciation for the use of automatic answering modems. Without this capability, one or more operators would be required to be on duty to place receiving modems into their data mode in response to incoming calls generating ringing signals. In fact, data centers during the late 1950s and early 1960s relied on the use of operators to place modems into their data mode in response to incoming calls. Fortunately for operators whose level of job satisfaction in those days was probably equivalent to watching paint dry, the development of automatic answering modems enabled computers to be programmed to answer incoming calls automatically. This formed the basis for the emergence of unattended bulletin board systems, which began to appear during the late 1970s and early 1980s and which today number in the tens of thousands.

Full-Duplex Asynchronous Private Line Modem

The full-duplex asynchronous modem could be used on private lines as well. It is called a private line modem because it is not equipped for automatic answer. The signals used are Protective Ground, Signal Ground, Transmitted Data, Received Data, Received Line Signal

A private line modem does not have the capability for automatic answering because it's not needed; the modem is always online.

Detector (pin 8), and Data Set Ready (pin 6). Pin 8 (DCD) says, in effect, "I hear something like a modem talking to me"—in other words, that another modem is trying to make contact on the line. Pin 6 (DSR) usually is not used in asynchronous modems, but it could indicate that the modem is ready and not in voice or test mode.

Half-Duplex Asynchronous Private Line Modem

The signals used in the half-duplex asynchronous modem are Protective Ground, Signal Ground, Transmitted Data, Received Data, Request To Send, Clear To Send, Received Line Signal Detector, and possibly Data Set Ready. Pins 4 and 5 (RTS and CTS) control the transmission direction in the half-duplex operation. The computer asserts pin 4 (RTS) when it wants to transmit. The modem responds by turning on pin 5 (CTS) to indicate that it is ready to receive characters to be transmitted. There is a built-in delay (typically 200 milliseconds) between the Request To Send and the Clear To Send response because the modem must generate the carrier waveform and allow it to stabilize. When transmission is completed in that direction, the computer drops pin 4 (RTS), causing the modem to turn off the transmitter and to drop CTS. The process of determining who transmits when, and how to tell when the other end is finished, is the responsibility of the software protocol, which is outside the modem and the RS-232 interface.

Smart Modems

> By combining a microprocessor with a modem, both data communications and automatic dialing can be realized in one unit—a "smart modem."

The so-called "smart" or "intelligent" modem combines a standard modem and a microprocessor to provide both data communications and automatic dialing in one unit. (One of the first intelligent modems to be marketed was the Smartmodem 1200 made by Hayes Microcomputer Products, Inc.) A smart modem accepts commands in ASCII form over the same RS-232 interface used for data transmission and can respond over the same interface with either status codes or sentences. For example, the computer operator would turn the modem on and load the terminal software, then type a code such as AT DT1-800-772-5942. This code tells the modem to take the phone line off hook, wait for a dial tone, then tone dial (using DTMF tones) the number 1-800-772-5942. The modem will attempt to do this. If the number is busy, the modem's response, "number busy," would appear on the computer's screen. Modems of this type usually can redial the last number entered, and many of these modems can be programmed to automatically keep trying a number at preset intervals if they encounter a busy signal. Some modems can store a list of frequently called numbers (such as the preceding one) that the user can select by entering only a two- or three-digit code.

The smart modem contradicts our previous statement that modems don't look at the data that passes through them, because it does examine some of the information coming over the RS-232 interface for its commands. Smart modems have essentially replaced the use of non-intelligent or "dumb" modems for use on the switched telephone network, and many software products support these modems. Virtually all the numerous developed communications software products support the basic Hayes modem command set, which has become a de facto standard. Thus, if you are considering the purchase of a smart modem, it would be wise to consider one that is compatible with the Hayes commands.

The Hayes command set consists of a basic set of commands and command extensions. The basic commands, such as placing the modem off hook and dialing a number, are applicable only to modems designed to transmit and receive data at that speed.

Commands in the Hayes command set are initiated by transmitting an attention code to the modem, followed by an appropriate command or set of commands. The attention code is the character sequence AT, which must be input by the user or sent to the modem by a software program in all uppercase or all lowercase letters. The requirement to prefix all command lines with the code AT has led many modem manufacturers to denote their modems as Hayes AT compatible or simply AT compatible.

A Hayes Smartmodem can hold up to 40 characters in its command buffer, permitting a sequence of commands to be transmitted to the modem on one command line. This 40-character limit does not include the attention code, nor does it include spaces placed in a command line to make it more readable. Table 4.6 lists the major commands included in the basic Hayes command set.

Table 4.6. Major commands of the basic Hayes command set.

Command	Description
A	Answer call
A/	Repeat last command
B	Select the method of modem modulation
C	Turn modem's carrier on or off
D	Dial a telephone number
E	Enable or inhibit echo of characters to the screen
F	Switch between half- and full-duplex modem operations
H	Hang up telephone (on hook) or pick up telephone (off hook)
I	Request identification code or request checksum
L	Select the speaker volume
M	Turn speaker off or on
N	Negotiate handshake options
O	Place modem online
P	Pulse dial
Q	Request modem to send or inhibit sending of result code
R	Change modem mode to "originate-only"

continues

Table 4.6. continued

Command	Description
S	Set modem register values
T	Touch-tone dial
V	Send result codes as digits or words
W	Select negotiation progress message
X	Use basic or extended result code set
Z	Reset the modem

Although communications software that supports the basic Hayes command set operates with this modem, such software might not be capable of supporting many of the advanced features incorporated into modems manufactured by other vendors. In fact, communications software that supports only the basic Hayes command set might not be sufficient to use most of the advanced features incorporated into both Hayes and other vendor modem products developed over the past five years. Those features, such as error detection and correction, data compression, fax/data mode selection, and operating rates above 2400 bps, are usually enabled through the use of extended command codes or settings in predefined modem S registers. This explains why it is no trivial exercise to develop a communications program that supports the features of a large number of modems developed by different vendors. The section "Extended Command Sets," later in this chapter, examines a few of the extended commands used to enable different features built into several popular modems.

This is the basic format required to transmit commands to a Hayes-compatible modem:

```
AT Command[Parameter(s)]Command[Parameter(s)]..Return
```

Each command line includes the prefix AT, followed by the appropriate command and the command's parameters. The command parameters are usually the digits 0 or 1, which serve to define a specific command state. As an example, C1 is the command that tells the modem to turn on its carrier signal, whereas C0 is the command that causes the modem to turn off its carrier signal. Up to 40 characters can be entered into a command line, and each command line must be terminated by a carriage return character.

To illustrate the use of the Hayes command set, suppose that you want to automatically dial information for New York City. The number is 212-555-1212. First, you tell the modem to go off hook, which is similar to picking up a telephone handset. Then, you tell the modem the type of telephone system you are using—pulse or touch-tone—and the telephone number to dial. If you have a terminal or personal computer connected to a Hayes-compatible modem, the following commands would be sent to the modem:

```
AT H1
AT DT9,1,212-555-1212
```

In the first command, the 1 parameter used with the H command places the modem off hook. In the second command, DT tells the modem to dial a telephone number using touch-tone (T) dialing. The digits 9 and 1 are included in the telephone number because it is assumed that you had to dial 9 to gain access to an outside line through your company's switchboard and 1 for long distance. The commas between the outside line (9), long-distance access number (1), and the area code (212) cause the modem to pause for two seconds before dialing the area code. Usually, two seconds is long enough for you to hear the outside line and long-distance dial tones before the modem dials the next number.

Because a smart modem automatically goes off hook when dialing a number, the first command line is not required and is normally used for receiving calls. In the second command line, the type of dialing does not have to be specified if a previous call was made because the modem automatically uses the last type specified. Although users with only pulse dialing availability must specify P in the dialing command when using a Hayes Smartmodem, other vendors offer modems that can determine automatically the type of dialing facility that the modem is connected to, then use the appropriate dialing method without requiring the user to specify the type of calling.

Modem Registers

In addition to the support of the command set, the degree of compatibility between Hayes Smartmodems and non-Hayes modems is governed by the number, use, and programmability of registers contained in the modem. Although many modern modems can include 100 or more registers, most devices support the use of the first 13 S-Registers supported by all Hayes modems.

A Hayes-compatible modem supports the functionality specified by the first 13 S-Registers used by Hayes Microcomputer Products modems.

Table 4.7 lists the functions of the first 13 registers built into Hayes Smartmodems to include the default value of each register and the range of settings permitted. To read the value of register n, you would issue the following command:

ATSn?

To set the value of register n to x, you would use the following command format:

AT Sn = x

To illustrate the use of an S-Register setting, let's assume that you want to read the value in the S6 register. To do so, you would send the following command to the modem:

ATS6?

The modem's response to the preceding command would be a value between 2 and 255, indicating the amount of time in seconds the modem will wait for a dial tone. Suppose that your modem is located behind a PBX that requires three to four seconds from noting a line going offhook to issuing a dial tone. You would send the following command to your modem to set it to wait for four seconds for a dial tone:

AT S6 = 4

Table 4.7. S-Register control parameters.

Register	Function	Default Value	Range
S0	Ring to answer on *		0–255
S1	Count number of rings	0	0–255
S2	Escape code character	ASCII 43	ASCII 0–127
S3	Carriage Return character	ASCII 13	ASCII 0–127
S4	Line Feed character	ASCII 10	ASCII 0–127
S5	Backspace character	ASCII 8	ASCII 0–127
S6	Dial tone wait time in seconds	2	2–255
S7	Carrier wait time in seconds	30	1–255
S8	Pause time caused by comma in seconds	2	0–255
S9	Carrier detect response time in units of 1/10 second	6	1–255
S10	Time delay between loss of carrier and hang up in units of 1/10 second	7	1–255
S11	Touch-tone duration and spacing time in milliseconds	70	50–255
S12	Escape sequence guard time in units of 20 seconds	50	0–255

The MNP Protocol

Among the first modems to offer an error detection and correction feature were products manufactured by Microcom, Inc. This company created a revolution in modem technology by developing a modem protocol known as MNP, an acronym for Microcom Networking Protocol.

MNP is a communications protocol built into MNP-compatible modems that supports interactive and file transfer applications. In developing MNP, Microcom recognized that the first implementation of the protocol would not necessarily be the last and structured it to accommodate changes in its implementation. To accomplish this, the major functions of the protocol are divided into classes. When an MNP modem communicates with another MNP modem, the two devices negotiate with each other to operate at the highest mutually supported class of MNP service.

Table 4.8 summarizes the features associated with available MNP classes. Until 1990, Microcom licensed MNP only through Class 5 to other modem manufacturers. In that year, Microcom began to offer full MNP licenses. Thus, an MNP-compatible modem, although compatible with all other MNP modems, might be compatible with only a subset of available MNP classes unless a third-party vendor got a full license and incorporated all MNP classes into the product.

Table 4.8. MNP classes.

Class	Description of Functions Performed
Class 1	Uses asynchronous byte-oriented half-duplex transmission that provides an efficiency of approximately 70 percent. A 2400 bps modem using MNP Class 1 gets a throughput of 1690 bps.
Class 2	Uses asynchronous byte-oriented full-duplex data transmission that provides an efficiency of approximately 84 percent. A 2400 bps modem using MNP Class 2 gets a throughput of approximately 2000 bps.
Class 3	Strips start and stop bits from asynchronous data, enabling synchronous bit-oriented full-duplex transmission between modems. This provides an efficiency of about 108 percent, enabling a 2400 bps modem to get a throughput of approximately 2600 bps.
Class 4	Adds adaptive packet assembly in which packet sizes are dynamically adjusted based on the number of retransmission requests. Also adds Data Phase Optimization, which provides a mechanism to reduce protocol overhead. The efficiency of Class 4 is approximately 120 percent, enabling a 2400 bps modem to get a throughput of 2900 bps.
Class 5	Adds data compression to Class 4 service, which provides an average compression ratio of 1.6 to 1, meaning that every 16 characters are compressed into 10 characters for transmission. This increases the protocol efficiency of Class 5 to approximately 200 percent, enabling a 2400 bps modem to get a throughput of about 4800 bps.
Class 6	Adds Universal Link Negotiation and Statistical Duplexing to Class 5. Universal Link Negotiation enables MNP modems to begin operation at a common low-speed modulation method and negotiate the use of an alternative higher speed modulation method. At the end of a successful link negotiation for Class 6 operation, the two modems operate at 9600 bps using V.29 technology. Statistical Duplexing results in the monitoring of user traffic patterns to enable the dynamic allocation of V.29 half-duplex transmission to resemble full-duplex transmission. Under Class 6 9600 bps operations, MNP provides an average throughput approaching 19,200 bps.

continues

Table 4.8. continued

Class	Description of Functions Performed
Class 7	Adds an enhanced data compression capability to MNP based on a Huffman statistical encoding technique. Under Class 7, a compression ratio between 2.0 and 3.0 is achievable, which increases throughput from two to three times the modem's operating rate.
Class 8	Is no longer marketed.
Class 9	Adds support of V.32 modulation to Class 7, providing a throughput up to three times the 9600 bps full-duplex operating rate of a V.32 modem.
Class 10	Adds Adverse Channel Enhancement (ACE), which optimizes modem performance in environments with poor or varying line conditions, such as cellular communications, rural telephone service, and some international connections.

In examining the entries in Table 4.8, you will note the inclusion of such terms as V.29 and V.32. Both reference ITU-T modulation standards, with V.29 originally developed as a half-duplex 9600 bps modulation technique for use on leased lines. Microcom, as well as other vendors, modified that technology to work on the PSTN. In addition, using the intelligence of a microprocessor to monitor the direction of transmission, it became possible to quickly turn off the transmitter of one modem and turn on its receiver, enabling the half-duplex transmission mode to resemble full-duplex transmission. In comparison, a V.32 modem uses echo cancellation technology to enable transmission and reception of data to occur simultaneously on the PSTN, and it provides an inherent full-duplex transmission capability. Both V.29 and V.32 modulation are described in Chapter 5, "Synchronous Modems, Digital Transmission, and Service Units."

V.42 Recommendation

Although MNP error detection and correction is included in more than one million modems manufactured by Microcom and by more than one hundred third-party vendors, as previously discussed in this chapter, it is not the primary method of error detection and correction recommended for use in modems by the ITU-T. In 1990, the CCITT (now known as the ITU-T) promulgated its V.42 recommendation.

Unlike other V series recommendations that govern modern modulation techniques, the V.42 recommendation defines a protocol in which modems block data for transmission and generate and add a cyclic redundancy check (CRC) to each block for error detection. In recognition of the large installed base of MNP modems, MNP error detection and correction is supported as a secondary standard. That is, a V.42-compatible modem first attempts to communicate in its error-free mode using LAPB. If the distant modem does not support the V.42 protocol, the V.42 modem next attempts to communicate using MNP error control.

Data Compression

Although the V.42 recommendation supports MNP error control, the V.42bis recommendation, which is a data compression scheme that requires the use of the V.42 protocol, does not support a secondary method of compression. This theoretically means that for your V.42bis modem to operate in a compressed mode, it must communicate with another V.42bis-compatible modem. Fortunately, most V.42bis modems also include MNP support through Class 5, enabling you to communicate in both a data compressed mode and an error control mode with another MNP modem.

The key difference between V.42bis and MNP Class 5 or Class 7 is in their method of data compression. V.42bis uses the previously described Lempel-Ziv-Welch (LZW) algorithm, which can operate on single characters as well as on strings. In comparison, MNP compression primarily operates on single characters and is slightly less efficient. When using a V.42bis modem that incorporates V.32 modulation, the 9600 bps operating rate of the modem can achieve a throughput of up to 38,400 bps when data is very susceptible to compression.

Interface Versus Operating Rate

To effectively use data compression requires you to set your modem's interface data rate to exceed its operating rate and if supported by your serial port to four times its operating rate. To understand why this is required, consider Figure 4.12, which illustrates the relationship between the interface speed and the operating rate of a modem.

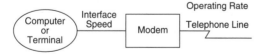

FIGURE 4.12.

The relationship between interface speed and modem operating rate.

If the interface speed equals the operating rate, data compression will not increase the throughput of the modem. To increase the modem's throughput, you must set the interface rate to at least twice the modem's operating rate. For example, if the modem operates at 9600 bps, you should set the interface rate to at least 19,200 bps. This setting allows more bits in the form of characters to enter the modem per unit of time than can be transmitted. Then, data compression can attempt to reduce the bits entering the modem so that they can be transmitted at the modem's operating rate, increasing the modem's throughput.

Flow Control

A second consideration you must take into account when using error control either by itself or with data compression is flow control. To see why flow control is necessary, consider Figure 4.12. Assume that the interface speed is set to 19,200 bps and that the operating rate is 9600 bps. If the modem cannot effectively compress data, perhaps due to the composition of the data, the rate at which data enters the modem will exceed the rate at which it is placed onto the line. Although the modem has a buffer, eventually it will overflow, and data will be lost. Hence, a method is required to regulate the flow of data into the modem. This method is called flow control.

Most modems support at least two methods of flow control, referred to as XON/XOFF and CTS/RTS. The XON/XOFF method of flow control results in the modem transmitting an XOFF character to your computer to disable transmission, and an XON character to enable transmission to resume. Because your computer might require a capability to regulate data from the modem if you are printing received data or performing another mechanical-related operation, you can also use XON and XOFF from your computer to the modem to enable and disable transmission from the modem to your computer.

The CTS/RTS method of flow control references the use of the Clear to Send (CTS) and Request to Send (RTS) control signals at the interface between the computer and the modem. When the modem regulates flow control, it drops the CTS signal to inform the computer to stop transmission and raises the CTS signal to inform the computer to resume transmission. When the computer regulates the flow of data from the modem, it toggles the RTS signal lead.

In setting flow control, you must ensure that your computer and modem are set to use the same method. Concerning which method to select, if you expect to transfer files that might contain control characters, including an XOFF, you should use the CTS/RTS method of flow control. Otherwise, the reception of an XOFF would inadvertently turn off your computer's capability to transmit data.

Extended Command Sets

Although the basic Hayes command set was sufficient for supporting most intelligent-modem operations during the early 1980s, by the late 1980s, many modem vendors were introducing advanced features that were not supported by the basic Hayes command set. Although Hayes Microcomputer Products introduced a series of extended commands to govern the operation of advanced features incorporated into that vendor's product line, other vendors did not wait for Hayes and introduced features into their modems that were controlled by extended commands they developed. The result of this action was the development of a series of extended command sets whose operation is applicable to only one or a few modems. To illustrate this fact, Table 4.9 lists the first 11 extended commands supported by two popular fax/data modems capable of transmitting at rates up to 14,400 bps, the Practical Peripherals 14400 FXMT and the U.S. Robotics Sportster 14400 FAX. Because extended commands are prefixed with the ampersand, another term used to reference those commands is ampersand commands.

Table 4.9. Comparing extended command operations.

Extended Command	Modem Function	
	Practical Peripherals 14400 FXMT	**U.S. Robotics Sportster 14400 FAX**
&A	Connect when autoanswering	ARQ results code
&B	V.32 automatic retrain	Data rate terminal to modem
&C	DSD signal operation	DCD signal operation
&D	DTE signal operation	DTE signal operation
&F	Undefined	Load factory settings
&G	Guard tone operation	Guard tone operation
&H	Undefined	Transmit data flow control
&I	Undefined	Received data software flow control
&K	Flow control	Data compression
&L	Dial/leased line mode	Undefined
&M	Synchronous mode selection	Error control

In examining the entries in Table 4.9, note that the general modem function controlled by the extended command is listed for each modem. In many cases, there are several extended commands based on a numeric value following the sequence *ampersand, letter.* For example, &B0 would disable V.32 automatic retraining on a Practical Peripherals 14400 FXMT modem, whereas &B1 would enable that feature.

In comparing the functions controlled by each extended command listed in Table 4.9, you will note that software developed to control one modem cannot issue the same extended commands to control features on the other modem.

This limitation explains why it is important to verify that a communications program you intend to purchase supports a particular modem that you have or that you anticipate purchasing. Otherwise, you might have to either manually enter appropriate commands to

●

It is important to verify that a communications program supports the extended commands recognized by the modem you use.

take advantage of many of the features built into the modem or forego using those features.

Although it is quite common for modem vendors to assign different functions to the same extended command, there are some extended commands that many vendors use in a similar manner. The series of &T commands used for modem testing represents the most common extended command that is almost universally used in a similar manner by different vendors.

Table 4.10 summarizes the functional assignment to the series of &T commands commonly used by most vendors.

Table 4.10. The &T extended command assignments.

Command	Function
&T0	Terminate test in progress
&T1	Initiate local analog loopback
&T2	Initiate local digital loopback
&T6	Initiate remote digital loopback
&T7	Initiate local digital loopback with self-test
&T8	Initiate local analog loopback with self-test

Most modems designed for use on the switched telephone network support a self-test and three loopback tests. The self-test, designed to verify the operation of the modem's internal circuitry, uses a pattern generator to produce a known sequence of data that is used by the transmitter.

Figure 4.13 illustrates the operation of a basic modem self-test. After a self-test is initiated, the modem's transmitter is tied to its receiver, breaking any prior connection to a communications line. Data modulated by the transmitter is demodulated by the receiver and passed to a pattern comparator which includes a section of ROM that contains the same data sequence generated by the pattern generator. Thus, the pattern comparator enables the demodulated data to be compared to the sequence generated when the self-test is initiated. If the received data does not match the contents of the pattern comparator, the modem's circuitry will cause a status indicator, typically labeled ER for error, to illuminate. This action informs you that the modem is defective and should be returned to the manufacturer.

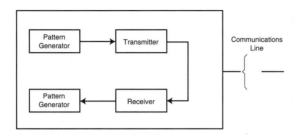

FIGURE 4.13.
A modem self-test.

Loopback Tests

Modems may be able to perform four types of loopback tests, with the position of each loopback indicated with respect to a modem pair illustrated in Figure 4.14. Although most leased-line modems can perform all four loopbacks, a modem used on the switched network cannot perform a remote analog loopback.

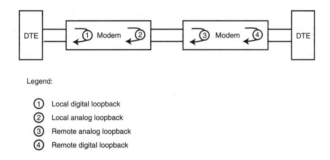

FIGURE 4.14.
Modem loopbacks.

The local digital loopback test is employed to test the operation of an attached DTE and the cable connecting the DTE to the modem. To do so, the local modem ties its transmitter and receiver circuits together, in effect bypassing its modulator and demodulator. Thus, input data received on pin 2 is routed to pin 3, which is the Receive Data conductor.

The local analog loopback test results in the local modem's modulator becoming tied to its demodulator. This tests both the analog and the digital circuits of the local modem.

The remote analog loopback results in a remote modem bridging the transmit and receive wire pairs of a leased line together. This enables you to use test equipment at the local site to test both the local modem and the quality of the line. Because modems designed for use on the switched network operate on a two-wire system, this loopback test is not included in switched network modems.

The remote digital loopback test results in the remote modem connecting its demodulator to its transmitter. This results in received data being demodulated and passed to its transmitter for remodulation back to the local modem. Thus, this test checks the circuitry of the local and remote modems, as well as the line connection between the modems.

●
Modems designed for use on the switched network can support three loopback tests, whereas modems that can be used on a four-wire leased line can support an additional loopback test.

Fax Modems

Although in the preceding section we compared the use of several extended commands between fax modems manufactured by two vendors, we did not actually discuss what a fax modem represents. In this section we will do so, obtaining an overview of the operation of this type of communications product.

In general, a fax modem is a modem that includes the capability to transfer fax image data over analog telephone circuits. To do so, the fax modem must support several fax standards. Two of the key standards governing fax transmission are the ITU-T T.4 and T.30 standards.

The T.4 standard defines how fax data is formatted. This standard states that each scan line in a document consists of 1728 dots and that scanning occurs left to right, line by line, until the right corner at the bottom of the page is reached. The T.4 standard also defines the vertical resolution of a document. The standard vertical resolution is 1143 lines per page, and an optional fine resolution of 2287 lines per page is defined. Concerning the higher resolution, most fax machines have a button labeled "fine" or "high resolution" that, when pressed, places the fax machine into its fine resolution mode.

The T.4 standard defines how fax data is formatted, whereas the T.30 standard governs the manner by which fax data is transmitted.

The second major standard governing the operation of fax modems is the T.30 standard. This standard governs the manner by which fax data is transmitted to include the initial call setup between two fax machines, during which information about the capability of each machine is exchanged.

Although the T.4 and T.30 standards govern the manner by which fax data is formatted and transmitted, they were developed for stand-alone fax machines. Thus, another standard was required to govern the interaction between a computer used to store or receive images and a fax modem used to transmit and receive images. That standard represents another extension to the AT command set in the form of fax modem commands.

Fax Modem Commands

Currently, three commonly used sets of commands govern the operation of fax modems. Each set, which is more formally referred to as a fax modem service class, is based on certain properties originally developed by Hayes Microcomputer Products AT command set.

Class 1 represents a core set of six commands that was approved by the American National Standards Institute (ANSI), the Telecommunications Industry Association (TIA), and the Electronics Industry Association (EIA) as the ANSI/TIA/EIA-578 standard in 1990. A Class 1 fax modem requires the computer to perform most of the work involved in transmitting and receiving data according to the T.30 protocol.

A Class 2 proposal, which consisted of more than 50 commands and moved T.30 support into the fax modem, reached the ballot stage but was never approved. During the time the Class 2 standard was developed, many vendors manufactured and continue to manufacture modems that support the unapproved Class 2 draft standard.

A third fax modem command standard is Class 2.0, which was approved as the EIA-572 standard. Although the Class 2.0 standard was based on the unapproved Class 2 draft, there are significant differences in the structure of commands that make the two incompatible. Although Class 2.0 is the officially approved standard, the unapproved Class 2 draft represents a more widely adopted fax command standard.

All fax modem commands begin with the prefix AT+F. The most basic fax modem command supported by each class is AT+FCLASS=?. That command is issued to the modem to determine what service class it supports. If the modem responds with 0,1,2, it supports data, Class 1 fax, and Class 2 fax. Most fax modems are sold with fax software that automatically issues appropriate fax commands based on the selection of menu entries displayed on the computer's screen. This insulates the computer user from having to know the function of individual fax commands; however, you might want to note a few fax commands in addition to the FCLASS command. Those commands, which are listed in Table 4.11 for Class 2 and Class 2.0–compatible fax modems, enable you to retrieve basic information about the modem that can be extremely valuable when you're attempting to configure software to work with a specific modem.

Table 4.11. Basic fax commands to retrieve modem information.

Description	Class 2	Class 2.0
Service Class	AT+FCLASS	AT+FCLASS
Manufacturer ID	AT+FMFR?	AT+FMI?
Modem ID	AT+FMDL?	AT+FMM?
Modem Revision ID	AT+FREV?	AT+FMR?

What Have You Learned?

1. A modem (modulator-demodulator) changes data pulses to analog tones that the telephone channel will pass.

2. Frequency-shift keying is the type of modulation used by most low-speed modems. Phase modulation or a combination of phase and amplitude modulation is used in high-speed modems.

3. Data terminal equipment (DTE) is the equipment that originates or receives the data in digital form.

4. Data communications equipment (DCE) is the equipment that converts the data from the DTE to the form required for the transmission channel. A modem is DCE.

5. The signal levels, signal identification, and wiring between the DTE and the DCE are governed by standards.

6. The RS-232 and CCITT V.24 standards for the DTE-DCE interface are the ones used most in the present computer and communications world.

7. The LZW algorithm forms the basis for compression performed by the V.42bis standard.

8. RS-422A, RS-423A, and RS-449 are relatively new standards that overcome the defects of RS-232. The widespread adoption of RS-449, however, will probably be superseded by the RS-530 standard.

9. A communications program that is limited to supporting basic Hayes commands might not be capable of using the advanced features built into most modern modems.

10. Without an appropriate method of flow control, a modem can lose data when its interface speed is set to a higher value than its operating rate.

Quiz for Chapter 4

1. Flow control is:

    a. What is done by people who open and close floodgates on dams.

    b. The process whereby the modem matches the rate of the receiver.

    c. The process of starting and stopping the terminal output to avoid loss of characters by the receiving device.

2. Buffering is:

    a. The process of temporarily storing data to allow for small variations in device speeds.

    b. A method of reducing the severity of communications headaches.

    c. Storage of data within the transmitting modem until the receiver is ready to receive.

3. Direct machine-to-machine transmission over long distances without modems is not practical because:

    a. Copper wire does not transmit DC efficiently.

    b. A DC path that will handle data in pulse form does not exist.

    c. Data comes from the computer in the form of tones, not pulses.

4. Modulation is the:

    a. Varying of some parameter of a carrier, such as its amplitude, to transmit information.

    b. Utilization of a single transmission channel to carry multiple signals.

    c. Transmission of pulses in DC form over a copper wire.

5. RS-232, RS-449, RS-530, V.24, and X.21 are examples of:

    a. Standards for various types of transmission channels.

    b. Standards for interfaces between terminals and modems.

    c. Standards for interfaces between modems and transmission facilities.

    d. Standards for end-to-end performance of data communications systems.

6. V.42 defines:

    a. Compatibility with MNP Class 5 data compression.

    b. A method of data storage.

    c. Two methods of error detection and correction.

    d. Compatibility with MNP Class 7 enhanced data compression.

7. The cable connecting a DB-9 connector at one end to a DB-25 connector at the other end must cross-connect pin 8 at the DB-9 side to which pin at the DB-25 side:

    a. 4.

    b. 22.

    c. 5.

    d. 2.

8. A smart modem can:

    a. Detect transmission errors and correct them automatically.

    b. Correctly answer multiple-choice quizzes.

    c. Accept commands from the terminal via the RS-232 interface.

9. RTS/CTS:

    a. Is the way the modem indicates ringing, and the way the terminal indicates that it is ready for the call to be answered.

    b. Is the way the DTE indicates that it is ready to transmit data, and the way the DCE indicates that it is ready to accept data.

    c. Are the pins that represent received transmissions and carrier transmissions.

10. Pin 7, the Signal Ground:

    a. Completes the circuit for control and data signals.

    b. Indicates a failure in the ground side of the transmission line.

    c. Completes the circuit for control signals but not data signals.

11. Pin 22, the Ring Indicator:

   a. Must be present on all modems connected to the switched network.

   b. Is used on acoustic-coupled modems but not on direct-connect types.

   c. Is asserted when ringing voltage is present on the line.

12. The reason that many cables have "RS-232" connectors with some wires crossed or connected to each other is:

   a. There are various RS-232 standards.

   b. Many computers and peripherals use RS-232 serial interfaces, but not as DTE-to-DCE.

   c. Asynchronous modems reverse the direction of transmitted and received data from the standard.

13. Extended command sets supported by modern modems:

   a. Are standardized.

   b. Are prefixed with the letter *E*.

   c. Use different commands to control many advanced modem features.

   d. Can be counted on to provide a high-speed data transfer capability without requiring flow control.

14. A local digital loopback tests:

   a. The local analog line.

   b. The local digital line.

   c. The operation of the local DTE and cable connecting the DTE to the modem.

   d. The remote modem.

15. Data rates above the 20,000 bps limitation of the RS-232 standard become possible by:

   a. Using the Signal Ground conductor.

   b. Extending the cable distance.

   c. Shortening the cable.

   d. Calling 911.

16. To set the S12 register to a value of 130, you would enter the command:

   a. `AT130`

   b. `ATS12130`

   c. `ATS12=130`

   d. `AT130=S12`

17. The T.4 standard:

   a. Defines the modem class.

   b. Defines how fax data is formatted.

   c. Defines how fax data is transmitted.

   d. Defines the connection to a fax modem.

18. A response of 1 to the command `AT+FCLASS=?` would indicate that:

   a. Your modem has a release date of 01/01/95.

   b. Your modem supports fax Class 1.

   c. Your modem supports fax Class 1.0.

   d. Your modem has a revision code of 1.0.

Synchronous Modems, Digital Transmission, and Service Units

About This Chapter

In this chapter, you will be introduced to the signaling methods used by synchronous modems, the American and International standards that apply to synchronous data modems, and the concepts used in higher-speed (above 19,200 bits per second) wideband devices. This will be followed by an examination of the techniques of direct transmission of binary signals without modems, called digital transmission. Because the transmission of binary signals over long distances without modems requires the use of devices known as service units, the operation and utilization of those devices will also be covered in this chapter.

Synchronous Signaling and Standards

Synchronous signaling permits data to be transmitted without gaps between characters, enabling higher data transfer rates to be achieved.

A Search for Higher Data Rates

Like the Olympic athlete whose motto is *alitus, cititus, fortitus,* the aims of the data communications systems designer in the development of high-technology products are to pack more data per channel, deliver it at a faster speed, and deliver it at a lower cost. The transmission of a larger quantity of data through a channel of a given bandwidth with smaller and cheaper devices is a natural target. Because in many cases the channel available is a standard voice-grade line, and the cost of the channel dominates the cost of the system, a large amount of design effort has gone into the production of devices that will send the largest number of bits per unit time through standard (voice-grade) channels. One result has been synchronous signaling.

Sending the Clock with the Data

Binary signals have two basic parameters: amplitude and duration. As the number of information bits sent per unit of time increases, the bit duration decreases.

Binary signals sent over a channel represent the quantization of data in two dimensions: amplitude (voltage of the electrical wave) and time (the duration of each signaling element). As the number of signaling elements per unit time (the "baud rate") increases, the duration of each element must decrease, as illustrated in Figure 5.1. If, as is the case with the asynchronous modems, the time base for the transmitter and receiver are independent, small differences between the two clocks become increasingly likely to cause errors due to the sampling of the data at the wrong time. This problem is overcome in synchronous modems by deriving the timing information from the received data.

FIGURE 5.1.

Baud rate versus element duration.

Duration decreases as baud rate increases.

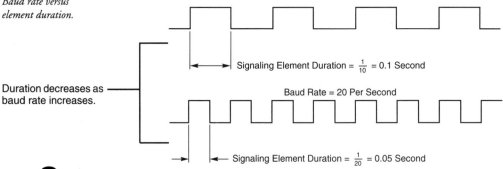

Baud Rate = 10 Per Second

Signaling Element Duration = $\frac{1}{10}$ = 0.1 Second

Baud Rate = 20 Per Second

Signaling Element Duration = $\frac{1}{20}$ = 0.05 Second

The data rate is limited by the bandwidth of the voice-baud channel to about 2400 baud. One way to increase the data is to pack two or more bits in a baud.

More Bits per Baud

Recall that in Chapter 3, "Messages and Transmission Channels," it was stated that for a channel of given bandwidth, the maximum signaling rate is fixed by the channel bandwidth and the signal-to-noise ratio (Shannon's formula). Because voice-grade channels have a fixed bandwidth (about 3000 Hz), they have a fixed maximum baud rate (about 2400 baud). The solution to this dilemma is to pack more than one bit into one signaling element—that is, two or more bits per baud.

Typical Synchronous Components

The greater complexity and cost of synchronous modems over asynchronous units is due to the circuitry necessary to derive the timing from the incoming data and pack more than one bit into one baud. Synchronous modems typically consist of four components, as shown in Figure 5.2: transmitter, receiver, terminal control, and power supply. We will look at the first three of these items in some detail.

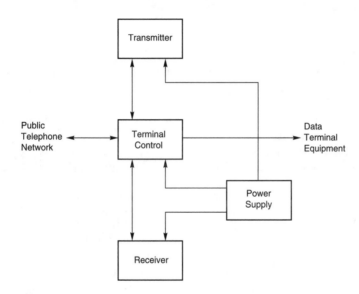

FIGURE 5.2.

A synchronous modem block diagram.

Transmitter

As shown in Figure 5.3, the transmitter section of a synchronous modem typically consists of timing (clock), scrambler, modulator, digital-to-analog converter, and equalizer circuits.

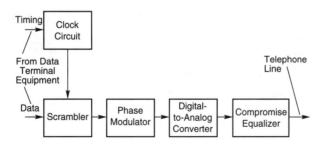

FIGURE 5.3.

A modem transmitter block diagram.

Timing Circuit

The timing circuit provides the basic clocking information for both the modem and the data terminal equipment (DTE) that is providing the data to be transmitted. Certain data circuit arrangements require that the clocking for the transmitted data be supplied by the DTE (which can be another modem). In these cases, an option is usually provided in the modem to phase-lock the internal clock to an external clock source, input through the DTE interface. The internal timing is usually controlled by a crystal oscillator to within about 0.05 percent of the nominal value.

Scrambler

Because the receiver clock is derived from the received data, those data must contain enough changes from 0 to 1 (and vice versa) to ensure that the timing recovery circuit will stay in synchronization. In principle, the data stream provided by the associated terminal or business machine can consist of any arbitrary bit pattern. If the pattern contains long strings of the same value, the data will not provide the receiver with enough transitions for synchronization. The transmitter must prevent this condition by changing the input bit stream in a controlled way. The part of the transmitter circuitry that does this is called the scrambler.

Scramblers are usually implemented as feedback shift registers, which can be cascaded (connected in series) as shown in Figure 5.4. Input bit 1 is modified by adding the state of selected bits of the seven-bit register to the incoming bit. Input bits 2, 3, and so forth are modified by the preceding bits, as indicated in the illustration. The scramblers are designed to ensure that each possible value of phase angle is equally likely to occur, to provide the receiver demodulator with enough phase shifts to recover the clocking signal. Although sampling is necessary for the reasons cited previously, it increases the error rate, because an error in one bit is likely (and in some cases is certain) to cause an error in subsequent bits. To counteract this problem, some modems encode the input to the scrambler into the Gray code so that the most likely error in demodulation (picking an adjacent phase state) will cause only a one-bit error when decoded at the receiver. As shown in Table 5.1, the Gray code has the property that between any two successive binary numbers (tribit numbers in this case), only one bit changes state.

Table 5.1. Binary and Gray code equivalence for three-bit code.

Decimal	Binary	Gray Code
0	000	000
1	001	001
2	010	011
3	011	010
4	100	110

Decimal	Binary	Gray Code
5	101	111
6	110	101
7	111	100

FIGURE 5.4.

A tribit scrambler.

Modulator

The modulator section of the transmitter converts the bit patterns produced by the scrambling process into an analog signal representing the desired phase and amplitude of the carrier signal. The carrier frequency, baud rate, and number of bits represented by each baud is different for modems of different data rates. The modulator collects the correct number of bits and translates them into a number giving the amplitude of the electrical signal that is correct for the carrier frequency and phase of the carrier at that instant. Modulation techniques differ for modems of different speed and from different manufacturers. Some of the more common ones are discussed later in this chapter.

Specific modulator characteristics such as the baud rate, number of bits per baud, and modulation techniques vary for modems of different rates and from different manufacturers.

Digital-to-Analog Converter

The digital-to-analog converter changes the binary encoded signal from the modulator into the required analog voltage.

The binary encoded signal from the modulator is fed to a digital-to-analog converter, which produces the actual analog voltage required. This in turn goes through a low-pass filter to remove frequencies outside of the voice baud, then through a circuit called an equalizer, which compensates for transmission impairments on the line.

Equalizer

The transmitter equalizer corrects amplitude distortion and group delay based on the average characteristics of the transmission medium.

The transmission equalizer is called a compromise or statistical equalizer because it is set to compensate for the nominal or average characteristics of the transmission medium. The equalizer compensates for amplitude distortion in the medium and for the problem called group delay. Group delay measures the amount by which a signal of one frequency travels faster in the transmission medium than a signal of a different frequency. Group delay usually is expressed in microseconds (µs) at a given frequency. Nominal values of delay variation versus frequency for some commonly available voice-grade channels are given in Table 5.2.

Table 5.2. Group delay variation versus frequency for conditioned transmission lines.

Conditioning Applied to Voice Grade Channel	Frequency Range (Hz)	Delay Variation (µs)
Basic (none)	800–2600	1750
C1	800–2600	1750
C2	600–2600	1500
C3	600–2600	260–300
C4	800–2800	500
C5	600–2600	300

Receiver

The receiving equalizer must deal with actual errors in the received signal. The errors are measured and corrected by adjusting specific circuit parameters.

As shown in Figure 5.5, the receiver section of a synchronous modem typically consists of an equalizer, timing (clock) recovery, a demodulator, a descrambler, and a DTE interface.

Equalizer

The equalizer section of the transmitter is relatively simple because it can compensate only for the average of expected errors on the output channel. The receiver equalizer, however, must compensate for the actual errors introduced in the transmission path. This is done via an adaptive equalizer, which measures errors observed in the received signal and adjusts some parameter of the circuit (usually the receiver clock frequency) to track slowly varying changes in the condition of the transmission line.

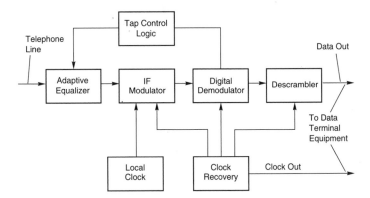

FIGURE 5.5.

A modem receiver block diagram.

Delay distortion has the greatest effect on the transmission of an analog signal. As mentioned previously, analog signals of different frequencies travel at different rates through a transmission medium. Because each signaling element contains many frequencies, the signaling elements arrive at the receiver over a period of time rather than all at once. The frequencies that travel faster (leading frequencies) arrive earlier, and those traveling slower (lagging frequencies) arrive later. The leading and lagging frequencies not only fail to make their proper contribution to the proper signaling element, but also cause interference with signaling elements behind and ahead of the proper element. The equalizer must get the parts of each element back together and cancel their effects on other elements.

The adaptive equalizer does this by use of a tapped delay line that stores the analog signal for a period. This time period includes the main signaling element to be corrected at the center, and several element times before and after the center, as shown in Figure 5.6. The taps in the delay line allow the analog voltage representing the signal to be picked off at specific time intervals before and after the element of interest. The time interval between each tap is the reciprocal of the baud rate. The voltage from each tap is amplified by a variable-gain amplifier whose gain is controlled by an amount determined by the correction calculator circuit.

In response to a phase error signal developed by the demodulator circuit, the correction calculator determines the amplitude and polarity of the signal needed from each tape amplifier. What makes the equalizer adaptive is that the error signal is continuously derived from the difference between the phase of the received signal and a nominal phase value determined by the demodulator.

●
The adaptive equalizer compensates for delay distortion by temporarily storing the analog signal in a tapped delay line. The signals from each tap, amplified by a different amount as determined by the amount of error detected, are summed to form the corrected signal.

FIGURE 5.6.

An adaptive equalizer.

The circuit adapts itself fairly slowly to changing line conditions because of all the delays. This can be a disadvantage for half-duplex operation, or at start-up on a one-way link, so a start-up or training sequence of bits usually is sent first to allow the receiver to adapt more rapidly than it would on random data. This process is called training. The amount of time required by the modem to retrain after changing the direction of transmission must be less than the turnaround time or request-to-send, clear-to-send (RTS-CTS) delay. This delay effectively reduces the data transmission rate on the circuit. Contemporary 4800 bps modems have RTS-CTS delays in the 10 to 20 millisecond (ms) range (about 50 to 100 bit times).

The equalizer section of some modern modems attempts to minimize the amount of line time lost in turnaround by a dual-speed or "gearshift" technique. This technique causes the modem pair to start at a lower data rate (say 2400 bps) at which training is very fast, and to transmit data at that rate while the adaptive equalizer goes through its training cycle. The modems then "shift gears" to run at the full data rate, as shown in Figure 5.7. Because for short messages the RTS-CTS delay is the controlling factor in throughput, and for long messages the transmission speed is dominant, the speed-changing technique minimizes the delay while still providing the higher speed.

FIGURE 5.7.
Dual-speed modem performance.

The incorporation of microprocessors into modems enabled their processing capability to be used to control numerous functions, including automatic equalization. When a pair of modems performs automatic equalization, each modem periodically transmits a training signal to the modem located at the opposite end of the circuit. The receiving modem knows the expected composition of the training signal and automatically adjusts its equalization to enable the best reception of the signal. In fact, you can probably think of automatic equalization as being similar to fine-tuning on your television. After it's set, it operates without requiring operator intervention. Today, almost all synchronous modems include an automatic equalization feature that compensates for both amplitude distortion and group delay.

To illustrate the operation of automatic equalization, consider Figure 5.8, which indicates how a modem compensates for the amplitude distortion of a signal by a technique referred to as attenuation equalization. Because high frequencies attenuate more rapidly than low frequencies, the modem measures circuit attenuation similar to the inverted U-shaped curve over the pass band of the channel. The modem then sets its equalization circuitry to generate a level of attenuation inverse to that occurring from the circuit as indicated by the upper U-shaped curve. The result of the attenuation equalization process is to produce a near-uniform or level amount of attenuation across the pass band of the circuit. In addition to simplifying procedures required for automatic equalization, the use of fast microprocessors has also reduced the training time required for equalization. Because no data can be transmitted during the training process, decreasing training time results in an increase in modem throughput.

FIGURE 5.8.

*Attenuation
equalization.*

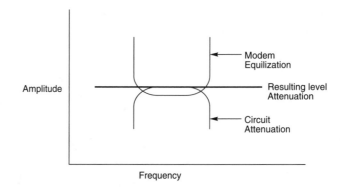

Timing Recovery

At the receiver, the incoming signal from the line is modulated or frequency translated using an internal clock. The resulting intermediate frequency is processed to produce a clock signal at the rate at which the data is actually being received. This signal is applied as the reference to a phase-locked loop oscillator. The output of this oscillator is a stable signal locked to the incoming line frequency in both phase and frequency.

Descrambler

The descrambler section of the receiver performs an operation that is the inverse of the scrambler described in the section on the transmitter. If the data have been Gray-coded by the transmitter before scrambling, they are converted back to straight binary, then applied to the DCE interface circuit.

Terminal Control Section

Each of the terminal control interface points requires different control and response signals.

The control section of synchronous modems must deal with two external interfaces: the telephone line at one end and the business machine at the other. If the modem is to be used on the public dial telephone network, it must be able to perform the following tasks:

- Sense the ringing signal.
- Provide line supervision (connecting and disconnecting the modem and the telephone line).
- In some cases, provide a busy indication to the incoming line without tying up telephone central office equipment.

At the other end, the control section must connect to the associated business machine or data terminal equipment. The DTE interface for most modems conforms to one of two standards: the Electronic Industries Association (EIA) RS-232 or the International Telephone and Telegraph Consultative Committee (CCITT) Recommendation V.24. These standards were covered in Chapter 4, "Asynchronous Modems and Interfaces."

Interface Circuits

Most synchronous modems support the set of interface circuits shown in Table 5.3. The backward-channel circuits (CCITT circuit numbers 118 through 122) are required only in modems that provide a reverse or backward channel for control information in the opposite direction to normal data flow. The Data Terminal Ready circuit (CCITT circuit No. 108.2) is required only for modems used on the dial-up connections.

Table 5.3. Synchronous modem DTE interface circuits.

Circuit Number		
EIA	*CCITT*	*Designation*
AA	101	Equipment Ground
AB	102	Signal Ground
BA	103	Transmitted Data
BB	104	Received Data
CA	105	Request to Send
CB	106	Clear to Send
CC	107	Modem Ready
CD	108.2	Data Terminal Ready
CE	125	Ring Indicator
CF	109	Received Line Signal Detector (Carrier)
CG	110	Signal Quality Detector
CH	111	Data Signal Rate Detector (DTE Source)
CI	112	Data Signal Rate Detector (DCE Source)
DA	113	Transmitted Signal Element Timing (DTE Source)
DB	114	Transmitted Signal Element Timing (DCE Source)
DD	115	Received Signal Element Timing (DCE Source)
SBA	118	Secondary (Backward Channel) Transmitted Data
SBB	119	Secondary Received Data
SCA	120	Secondary Request to Send
SCB	121	Secondary Clear to Send
SCF	122	Secondary Received Line Signal Detected (Carrier)

The Clear-to-Send signal is returned to the DTE in response to assertion of the Request-to-Send signal. It is delayed by the modem, however, by the amount of time necessary for the modem to "turn the line around"—that is, to send the required training pattern to the distant end.

External Timing

Systems that have terminals remote from the terminating modem on the main channel require that the remote modem be synchronized to the originating modem.

Many standard 9600 bps and higher-speed modems designed for leased-line operations usually contain internal time division multiplexers, which allow more than one terminal to operate simultaneously over a single channel. In many cases, one or more channels are carried to terminals remote from the first modem, terminating the circuit as shown in Figure 5.9. In such cases, which apply only to full-duplex operation, the clock signal for all the modems in the path must be synchronized to only one of the modems. The external clock input (EIA circuit DA) for the extension modem circuit is fed from the receive clock from the primary modem (EIA circuit DD), causing the clocks in all the modems to be slaved to the single modem at the originating end. Refer to Chapter 6, "Multiplexing Techniques," for information concerning the operation and utilization of time division multiplexers.

FIGURE 5.9.

A multiple-modem circuit requiring external clocking.

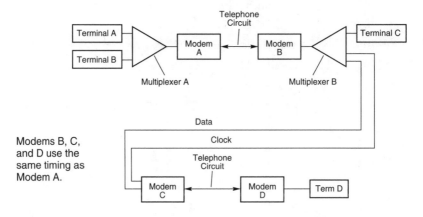

Modems B, C, and D use the same timing as Modem A.

Modem C must be supplied an external clock from multiplexer B, which must use the received data clock from Modem B.

Standard Modems

We'll now examine the implementation of some currently available modems, as well as evolving modems that can be expected to be readily available by the time you read this book. The types of modems that will be examined include these:

- 2400 bps half-duplex and full-duplex
- 4800 bps half-duplex and full-duplex
- 9600 bps half-duplex and full-duplex
- 9600 bps full-duplex modems that operate over two-wire dial-up circuits
- 14,400 bps full-duplex modems that operate over two-wire dial-up circuits
- 14,400 bps full-duplex modems that operate over four-wire leased lines
- 19,200 bps full-duplex modems that operate over two-wire dial-up circuits
- 24,400 bps full-duplex modems that operate over two-wire dial-up circuits

● 28,800 bps full-duplex modems that operate over two-wire dial-up circuits
● 33,600 bps full-duplex modems that operate over two-wire dial-up circuits

2400 bps Half-Duplex Two-Wire or Full-Duplex Four-Wire (DPSK)

Two common 2400 bps modems are the Western Electric 201 and the CCITT V.26.

Western Electric 201

A good example of the basic synchronous modem is the Western Electric (WE) 201 diagrammed in Figure 5.10. It operates at 1200 bauds with a carrier frequency of 1800 Hz. This modem uses a kind of phase shift modulation called the differential phase shift keying (DPSK) technique and encodes two bits (called a dibit) into one signaling element (two bits per baud). Phase shift keying encodes the binary values as changes of the phase of the carrier signal, as discussed in Chapter 4. Differential phase shift means that the reference point from which the phase angle is measured at any signaling interval is the phase angle of the immediately preceding interval. The WE 201 shifts the phase by multiples of 45 degrees according to Table 5.4.

> ●
> The Western Electric 201 is representative of standard 2400 bps synchronous modems. This modem encodes two bits per baud using differential phase shift keying (DPSK).

Table 5.4. WE 201 phase coding.

Dibit	Phase Change in Degrees
00	45
10	135
11	225
01	315

With this technique, the signal is self-referenced; that is, no separate absolute phase information needs to be transmitted, and the most likely error (picking an adjacent phase value) causes only a one-bit error. The WE 201 contains a local clock that is phase-locked to the detected phase of the incoming signal. Differences between the nominal phase values given in Table 5.4 and the detected phase of the incoming signal referenced to the phase of the local clock are used to measure the quality of the incoming line signal. Because the phase of the received signal changes for each signaling interval, there is always sufficient energy at the 1200-baud rate to recover the baud clock.

> ●
> DPSK requires no absolute phase information to be transmitted. It has its own clock that is phase-locked to the phase of the received signal.

FIGURE 5.10.

WE 201 modem block diagram.

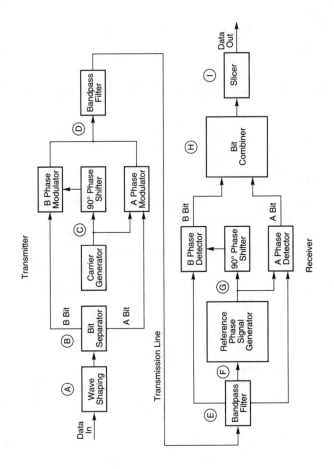

A. At the transmitter input, pulses are generated according to the data input, then filtered to shape them for modulation.
B. Alternate bits in the stream become A bits, and the others become B bits.
C. The two bit streams phase modulate a sine wave carrier. The carrier for the B bit stream is phase shifted by 90 degrees with respect to the A carrier.
D. The outputs of the modulators are combined, and the bandpass filter eliminates unwanted signals before transmission.
E. At the receiver, another bandpass filter removes noise and other unwanted signals.
F. The input signal is used to synchronize a sine wave reference phase signal.
G. The reference signal is applied directly to the A phase detector but is phase shifted 90 degrees before application to the B phase detector.
H. The A and B bit streams from the detectors are combined into a single bit stream.
I. The slicer output consists of clean rectangular pulses that convey the same data as the transmitter input.

ITU-T V.26

The ITU-T has published a recommendation for a standard 2400 bps modem with the designation "Recommendation V.26—2400 bits per second modem standardized for use on leased telephone-type circuits." It specifies a full-duplex, 1200-baud DPSK modem with a modulation rate of up to 75 baud in each direction on an optional "backward channel." In Europe, V.26 modems are commonly built into television receivers to provide a transmission capability for accessing Videotex systems. When the modem is used in this manner, pressing buttons on a TV remote control results in the transmission of "page" selection numbers to a Videotex system. The Videotex system in turn transmits the requested "page," which is displayed on the TV set. Because a small quantity of data flows from the TV set to the Videotex system in the form of page number requests, the use of the V.26 modem is reversed. That is, the 75-baud "backward channel" is used to transmit page number requests while Videotex information flows on the primary channel to the TV set.

The V.26 recommendations are generally similar to the specifications for the WE 201 (largely because the WE 201 had by 1968 become a de facto standard). One interesting difference is that the assignment of dibits to phase change values is allowed alternative sets of values. Alternative A is given in Table 5.5, and alternative B is the same as that given in Table 5.4 for the WE 201. Use of alternative A leads to the problem of no phase change at all for long strings of 00 dibits. Thus, the energy content in the transmitted stream at the 1200-baud rate is greatly reduced, making baud clock recovery uncertain.

●
The ITU-T V.26 2400 bps modem is similar to the WE 201, but one significant difference is the alternative set of phase codes.

Table 5.5. V.26 alternative A phase coding.

Dibit	Phase Change in Degrees
00	0
01	90
11	180
10	270

Recommendation V.26 specifies the form of the synchronizing signal between two modems to be continuous transmission of dibit 11 (giving continuous 180-degree phase shifts) during the RTS-CTS sequence. It also specifies incoming signal levels of −26 dBm or higher for the modem to assert the Carrier Detect (Circuit 109) and −31 dBm or lower for it to negate Carrier Detect. It is recommended that the modem be designed so that the operator cannot control the send level or receive sensitivity.

4800 bps Half-Duplex Two-Wire or Full-Duplex Four-Wire Modems (DPSK)

Modems representative of 4800 bps devices include the ITU-T V.27 and Western Electric 208 modems.

ITU-T V.27

The ITU-T Recommendation V.27 specifies a 4800 bps modem for use on leased telephone-type circuits. The modem has the following features:

- Can operate in either half- or full-duplex.
- Uses differential phase shift keying with eight phases.
- Provides an optional 75 bps backward channel in both directions for supervisory signaling.
- Has a manually adjustable equalizer.

Although the manual equalizers mentioned in ITU-T V.27 are no longer used, most of the standard is still used as the basis for many modems today, particularly in Europe.

This recommendation was promulgated in 1972, and the state of the modem art has progressed far beyond the manually adjustable equalizer. However, the remainder of the recommendation is the basis for many current modems, particularly for the European market. The carrier frequency is 1800 Hz, the modulation rate is 1600 baud, and the basic phase shift interval is 45 degrees. To signal at 4800 bps with 1600 baud requires that each baud represent three bits (tribits). The tribit to phase-change amount for V.27 is given in Table 5.6.

Table 5.6. V.27 phase coding.

Tribit Value	Phase Change in Degrees
001	0
000	45
010	90
011	135
111	180
110	225
100	270
101	315

The scrambler implements dividing the message polynomial by a generating polynomial by means of a feedback shift register.

The synchronization pattern for the V.27 modem is composed of continuous ones in tribits for at least 9 ms to train the demodulator, plus continuous ones at the input to the transmit scrambler until the CTS lead (circuit 106) is asserted by the transmitting modem to synchronize the scramblers. The general operation of a scrambler was described earlier in the chapter, but the details of the V.27 scrambler follow.

The transmitter scrambler divides the message polynomial, of which the input data bits are the coefficients in descending order, by a generating polynomial, which for V.27 is equal to $1 + X^{-6} + X^{-7}$. This division is continuously performed as each bit enters the scrambler, and the result is taken as the transmitted data pattern. The transmitted pattern is then searched continuously over 45 bits for repeating patterns of 1, 2, 3, 4, 6, 9, and 12 bits, which are eliminated. The result is sent as the scrambled data pattern. Figure 5.11 shows a feedback shift register that implements the polynomial division process.

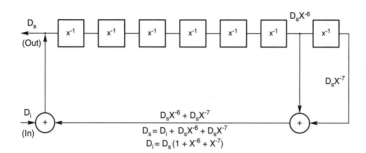

FIGURE 5.11.
ITU-T V.27 scrambler.

Western Electric 208

The WE 208 modem is another 4800 bps modem that at one time was widely used in the United States. It had been supplied by AT&T and the Bell Operating Companies when they were part of the Bell System. It is a DPSK unit, using eight phase angles to represent eight different groups of three bits. The coding pattern (after Gray-coding the binary input) for the WE 208 is given in Table 5.7.

Table 5.7. WE 208 phase coding.

Tribit Value	Relative Phase in Degrees
001	22.5
000	67.5
010	112.5
011	157.5
111	202.5
110	247.5
100	292.5
101	337.5

The carrier frequency for the WE 208 is 1800 Hz, and the baud rate is 1600 baud. The WE 208 is not equipped with an internal multiplexer because the 1600-baud rate of the modem is not a standard data rate for any other modem or business machine. The design of the WE 208 was covered in the previous section on typical synchronous modem components, including the scrambler implementation as four 7-bit feedback shift registers to randomize the first bit of each tribit.

> The WE 208 uses DPSK to encode tribits to transmit 4800 bps at 1600 bauds. Its design and operation are similar to the typical standard synchronous modem.

The demodulator in the WE 208 multiplies the carrier frequency by eight, then measures the interval between the 1600-baud clock transition and the first positive value of the current carrier cycle. This measurement is done digitally, and successive values of the count are compared to determine the phase shift that occurred during the preceding signaling interval. The measured phase shift, with any errors that might be present due to line noise, demodulator errors, baud clock errors, and such, is rounded to the nearest permitted value (22.5 degrees, 67.5 degrees, and so forth), and the transmitted tribit sequence is extracted and decoded from Gray code to binary. An error feedback signal is developed as the difference between the actual phase of the signal, as demodulated, and the nominal value. This error signal is monitored, and it causes the modem to retrain if it becomes too large.

The WE 208 modem normally operates with a basic retraining time of 50 ms, but it can be changed with internal strapping (jumper wires) to 150 ms for operation on long circuits (more than 2000 miles). Even this delay probably is still too short for operation on satellite links, due to the very long (about 650 ms) round-trip propagation delay.

9600 bps Half-Duplex Two-Wire or Half/Full-Duplex Four-Wire

Although the Western Electric 209 modem was one of the first devices to operate at 9600 bps, the ITU-T V.29 dominates the market for 9600 bps operations.

Modulation Types

> The data rate of the standard 9600 bps modem is increased by increasing its baud rate to 2400 bauds and increasing the number of bits per baud to four.

To increase the data rate of a synchronous modem over 4800 bps, it is necessary to either increase the baud rate or increase the number of bits per baud. Standard 9600 bps modems do both. The baud rate is increased to 2400 bauds, and the input data is taken four bits at a time (quadbits) for controlling the output of the modulator. Two modulation schemes are commonly used to read these extreme data rates: vestigial sideband modulation (VSB) and quaternary amplitude modulation (QAM).

The choice between modems using one of the two modulation schemes is less a matter of performance than of economics. Some VSB modems require little or no line conditioning, whereas a few QAM unit manufacturers generally recommend at least C2 conditioned circuits. The VSB units are less complex internally, which usually allows a price advantage over QAM units.

Vestigial Sideband Modulation

> The VSB transmitter modulator takes two bits at a time and constructs a four-level signal that modulates the carrier to transmit 9600 bps.

Because it is possible to transmit a double-sideband frequency-modulated (FM) signal (with a WE 202 type modem) at 1800 bps, one would think that it should be possible to send at 3600 bps using only one sideband because the entire bandwidth would be available for the one sideband. This is not possible, however, with an FM signal (the signal can't be recovered), but it is possible to use an amplitude-modulated (AM) single-sideband signal to transmit at 4800 bauds. Four different carrier amplitudes are used to represent the four different values of bits taken two at a time; thus, each baud represents two bits, which gives an effective rate of 9600 bps.

A VSB transmitter has a scrambler and Gray coder similar to those of 4800 bps modems. The modulator, however, takes the bits two at a time to form a four-level signal, which modulates a 2853 Hz carrier. The carrier and upper sideband are suppressed, and a 2853 Hz pilot signal is added back to what remains, but 90 degrees out of phase. A signal that is 90 degrees out of phase is called a *quadrature* signal because "in quadrature" means at right angles to the original carrier. The quadrature signal does not interfere with the modulated single-sideband signal, but it is necessary for the receiver to recover the exact frequency and phase of the original carrier so that it can recover the data.

The receiver's local 2853 Hz oscillator is locked to the phase and frequency of the pilot signal recovered from the received signal. This adjusted clock is used to demodulate the received single-sideband signal into the four-level 4800-baud baseband signal. The signal is processed by a 60-tap adaptive equalizer to remove intersymbol interference, then is put through a decision circuit to recover the dibits, which are then unscrambled.

Training a 60-tap equalizer is a lengthy process that reduces the cost effectiveness of using 9600 bps modems on half-duplex circuits. A four-segment training sequence must be sent to perform the following tasks:

● Set the automatic gain control circuits.

● Acquire the phase of the carrier tone.

● Set the equalizer tap coefficients.

● Synchronize the scrambler.

In the ITU-T Recommendation V.29 for a 9600 bps modem, the total four-segment sequence takes about 250 ms.

Quadrature Amplitude Modulation

QAM modems use some combination of differential phase shifts and amplitudes totaling 16 states of encoded four bits per baud. This combined with a baud rate of 2400 gives the desired 9600 bps. The ITU-T Recommendation V.29 specifies 8 phases, with two possible signal amplitudes at each phase change. The WE 209 modem uses 12 phases and three amplitudes, but some combinations of phase and amplitude are not allowed. Three common 9600 bps constellation patterns are shown in Figure 5.12. The choice of the number of phases and level spacing represents the modem manufacturer's best guess at the type and severity of various transmission-line errors the modem is likely to experience. It can be argued, however, that the V.29 recommendation resulted in a more optimal selection than the WE 209 due to the near-universal use of V.29 modems.

⬤

Modems using quadrature amplitude modulation achieve a data rate of 9600 bps by encoding four bits per baud and by using a baud rate of 2400.

FIGURE 5.12.

Common 9600 bps QAM modem constellation patterns.

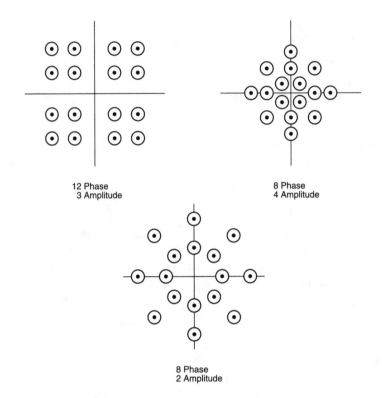

12 Phase
3 Amplitude

8 Phase
4 Amplitude

8 Phase
2 Amplitude

ITU-T Recommendation V.29—9600 bps Modem

The ITU-T V.29 modem's maximum data rate is 9600 bps, but it has automatic fallback to 7200 and 4800 bps if the error rate is too high.

The carrier frequency for the ITU-T V.29 modem is 1700 Hz, and it operates at 2400 bauds. This modem is specified to operate at 9600 bps with fallback rates of 7200 and 4800 bps. It has an automatic adaptive equalizer and can optionally contain a multiplexer for carrying up to four separate data streams whose aggregate (combined) rate does not exceed 9600 bps. The combined data stream to be transmitted is scrambled, then divided into sets of four bits (quadbits). The first bit (in time) of each quadbit determines the amplitude of the transmitted signal, as illustrated in Figure 5.13, and the remaining three bits determine the phase shift to be applied, as shown in Figure 5.14. The resultant "constellation pattern" resembles Figure 5.15.

FIGURE 5.13.

Bit Q1 determines amplitude.

Absolute Phase	Q1	Relative Signal Element Amplitude
0°, 90°, 180°, 270°	0	3
	1	5
45°, 135°, 225°, 315°	0	$\sqrt{2}$
	1	$3\sqrt{2}$

Q2	Q3	Q4	Phase Change*
0	0	1	0°
0	0	0	45°
0	1	0	90°
0	1	1	135°
1	1	1	180°
1	1	0	225°
1	0	0	270°
1	0	1	315°

*Note—The phase change is the actual online phase shift in the transition region from the center of one signaling element to the center of the following signaling element.

FIGURE 5.14.

Bits Q2, Q3, and Q4 determine phase shift.

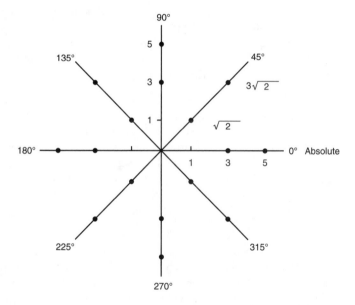

FIGURE 5.15.

Signal space diagram at 9600 bps.

At the fallback rate of 7200 bps, only three bits per baud are encoded, and there is no amplitude change. At the 4800 bps fallback rate, two bits per baud are encoded and they specify only four phase shifts.

Except for the WE 209-type modem, most 9.6 Kbps modems manufactured throughout the world adhere to the V.29 standard. This makes a V.29 modem popular for use on international leased lines because the selection of the modem to be placed on either end of the line might be restricted to one or a few models due to some countries' government restrictions. By using V.29, the modem's compatibility among different vendor products is ensured, which enables data transmission compatibility on international leased lines.

Although the V.29 modulation method provides compatibility with respect to modulation, many modems employing this standard are not compatible with one another. This lack of compatibility is attributable to the fact that several vendors designed proprietary modems to provide a pseudo full-duplex transmission capability over the two-wire public-switched telephone network. To accomplish this, modem designers added a microprocessor and memory to a V.29 data pump and developed several proprietary schemes to get a pseudo full-duplex transmission capability. One scheme involves adding a slow-speed reverse channel to a V.29 data pump to provide transmission at 300 bps in one direction and at 9600 bps in the other direction. Each modem monitors the flow of data in both directions and changes the assignment of the primary and reverse channels to correspond to the quantity of data flow in each direction.

Although data can flow in both directions simultaneously, each direction operates at a different speed. Thus, the modem is asymmetrical and provides users with the impression that it operates as a true full-duplex device. Asymmetrical transmission was incorporated by several modem manufacturers to support the communications requirements of personal computers. Included in an asymmetrical modem is an asynchronous-to-synchronous converter, which enables the asynchronous data flow of personal computers to be used with a modified V.29 pump that operates synchronously.

When asymmetrical modems reached the marketplace in the late 1980s, they were considered as potential successors to the V.22bis modem discussed in Chapter 4 due to the high price of V.32 modems. Unfortunately for asymmetrical modem manufacturers, the lack of standards governing the asymmetrical transmission technique, as well as a significant reduction in the cost of V.32 modems (discussed in the next section in this chapter), inhibited the asymmetrical modems' widespread acceptance. Today, most persons requiring high-speed data transmission on the PSTN use V.32, V.32bis, or V.34 modems. The one exception to this is the U.S. Robotics HST and HST Dual series of modems.

In the late 1980s, U.S. Robotics developed an asymmetrical 9600 bps modem that was marketed as the HST, an acronym for high-speed transmission. The company, among the first to recognize the growing popularity of bulletin board systems, provided bulletin board system operators with an attractive discount to enable them to purchase HST modems. This action resulted in a large number of individual personal computer users purchasing HST modems to get a high-speed transmission file transfer capability when accessing bulletin board systems.

Although reductions in the cost of V.32 modems have significantly increased their popularity, there is a large base of HST modems used with bulletin board systems. To provide compatibility with those modems, U.S. Robotics continues to manufacture HST modems as well as HST Dual modems, the latter a term used to indicate that the modem supports two major modulation methods. Today, U.S. Robotics offers HST Dual modems that support V.32 and HST, V.32bis and HST, and V.34 and HST, as well as HST.

ITU-T V.32

A ITU-T recommendation promulgated in the late 1980s and whose modulation technique forms the foundation for a series of higher speed modems used with personal computers is the V.32 standard. This standard is based on a modified quadrature amplitude modulation technique and is designed to permit full-duplex 9.6 Kbps transmission over the switched telephone network. The key to the operation of a V.32 modem is a built-in echo canceling technique that enables transmitted and received signals to occupy the same bandwidth.

When the V.32 modem connects to another V.32 modem, two high-speed channels in opposite directions are established, as illustrated in Figure 5.16. Each of these channels occupies roughly the same bandwidth as the other channel. Intelligence built into the receiver in each modem permits the modem to cancel the effects of its transmitted signal, which enables each device to distinguish its sending signal from the signal being received.

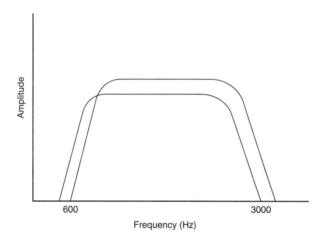

FIGURE 5.16.

ITU-T V.32 channel derivation.

Early V.32 modems required sophisticated circuitry to carry out echo canceling. The circuitry made the cost of V.32 modems two to three times the cost of V.29 modems, which provide the same data transmission rate on leased lines and was one of the contributing factors for the development of asymmetrical modems. Because firms manufacturing semiconductors developed chip sets to implement echo canceling, the cost of V.32 modems significantly decreased during 1990. By 1991, the cost of V.32 modems had declined to under $1000 per unit, and by early 1996, their cost had fallen below $100 per unit, resulting in their widespread use in both home and office.

The V.32 modem uses a carrier frequency of 1800 Hz and a modulation rate of 2400 baud. Under the V.32 standard, two methods of data coding are defined—nonredundant coding and Trellis coding. Under nonredundant coding, the data stream generated by the DTE is first divided into groups of four consecutive data bits. The first two bits in time, which are designated $Q1_n$ and $Q2_n$ in each four-bit sequence, are differentially encoded into $Y1_n$ and $Y2_n$, according to Table 5.8. Bits $Y1_n$, $Y2_n$, $Q3_n$, and $Q4_n$ are then mapped into the constellation pattern illustrated in Figure 5.17. This results in a 16-point signal constellation pattern when nonredundant coding is used at 9600 bps.

FIGURE 5.17.

V.32 nonredundant coding signal constellation pattern.

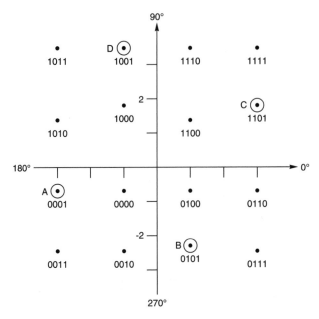

The binary numbers denote Y1$_n$ Y2$_n$ 03$_n$ 04$_n$

16-point signal structure with nonredundant coding for 9600 bps and subset A B C D of states used at 4800 bps for training.

Table 5.8. V.32 differential quadrant coding for 4800 bps and for nonredundant coding at 9600 bps.

Inputs		Previous Outputs		Phase Quadrant	Outputs		Signal State
Q1$_n$	Q2$_n$	Y1$_{n-1}$	Y2$_{n-1}$	Change	Y1$_n$	Y2$_n$	for 4800 bps
0	0	0	0	+90°	0	1	B
0	0	0	1		1	1	C
0	0	1	0		0	0	A
0	0	1	1		1	0	D
0	1	0	0	0°	0	0	A
0	1	0	1		0	1	B
0	1	1	0		1	0	D
0	1	1	1		1	1	C
1	0	0	0	+180°	1	1	C
1	0	0	1		1	0	D
1	0	1	0		0	1	B
1	0	1	1		0	0	A

Inputs		Previous Outputs		Phase Quadrant	Outputs		Signal State
$Q1_n$	$Q2_n$	$Y1_{n-1}$	$Y2_{n-1}$	Change	$Y1_n$	$Y2_n$	for 4800 bps
1	1	0	0	+270°	1	0	D
1	1	0	1		0	0	A
1	1	1	0		1	1	C
1	1	1	1		0	1	B

Similar to nonredundant coding, under Trellis coding, the data stream generated by the DTE is subdivided into groups of four consecutive data bits. The first two bits in time, $Q1_n$ and $Q2_n$ in each group, are first differentially encoded into the outputs $Y1_n$ and $Y2_n$ according to Table 5.9. The two differentially encoded bits, $Y1_n$ and $Y2_n$, are then used as input to a convolutional encoder that generates a redundant bit, $Y0_n$. That bit and the four information-carrying bits ($Y1_n$, $Y2_n$, $Q3_n$, and $Q4_n$) are then mapped into one of two sets of coordinates of the signal element to be transmitted. One set of coordinates is used with nonredundant coding, whereas the second set of coordinates is used with Trellis coding. Table 5.10 lists the two alternative V.32 signal state mappings for 9600 bps operations. When you plot each of the possible Trellis coding points listed in Table 5.10, you get a 32-point signal constellation. Figure 5.18 illustrates the 32-point signal constellation when Trellis coding is used by a V.32 modem, as well as the four states used at 4800 bps and for modem training.

Table 5.9. V.32 differential encoding for use with Trellis coded alternative at 9600 bps.

Inputs		Previous Outputs		Outputs		
$Q1_n$	$Q2_n$	$Y1_{n-1}$	$Y2_{n-1}$	$Y1_n$	$Y2_n$	
0	0	0	0	0	0	
0	0	0	1	0	1	
0	0	1	0	1	0	
0	0	1	1	1	1	
0	1	0	0	0	1	
0	1	0	1	0	0	
0	1	1	0	1	1	
0	1	1	1	1	0	
1	0	0	0	1	0	
1	0	0	1	1	1	

continues

Table 5.9. continued

Inputs		Previous Outputs		Outputs	
$Q1_n$	$Q2_n$	$Y1_n-1$	$Y2_n-1$	$Y1_n$	$Y2_n$
1	0	1	0	0	1
1	0	1	1	0	0
1	1	0	0	1	1
1	1	0	1	1	0
1	1	1	0	0	0
1	1	1	1	0	1

Table 5.10. Alternative signal-state mappings for 9600 bps operations.

	Coded Inputs				Nonredundant Coding		Trellis Coding	
(Y0)	Y1	Y2	Q3	Q4	Re	Im	Re	Im
0	0	0	0	0	-1	-1	-4	1
	0	0	0	1	-3	-1	0	-3
	0	0	1	0	-1	-3	0	1
	0	0	1	1	-3	-3	4	1
	0	1	0	0	1	-1	4	-1
	0	1	0	1	1	-3	0	3
	0	1	1	0	3	-1	0	-1
	0	1	1	1	3	-3	-4	-1
	1	0	0	0	-1	1	-2	3
	1	0	0	1	-1	3	-2	-1
	1	0	1	0	-3	1	2	3
	1	0	1	1	-3	3	2	-1
	1	1	0	0	1	1	2	-3
	1	1	0	1	3	1	2	1
	1	1	1	0	1	3	-2	-3
	1	1	1	1	3	3	-2	1
1	0	0	0	0			-3	-2
	0	0	0	1			1	-2

Coded Inputs				Nonredundant Coding		Trellis Coding	
(Y0) Y1	Y2	Q3	Q4	Re	Im	Re	Im
0 0	0	1	0			-3	2
0 0	0	1	1			1	2
0 0	1	0	0			3	2
0 0	1	0	1			-1	2
0 0	1	1	0			3	-2
0 0	1	1	1			-1	-2
0 1	0	0	0			1	4
0 1	0	0	1			-3	0
0 1	0	1	0			1	0
0 1	0	1	1			1	-4
0 1	1	0	0			-1	-4
0 1	1	0	1			3	0
0 1	1	1	0			-1	0
0 1	1	1	1			-1	4

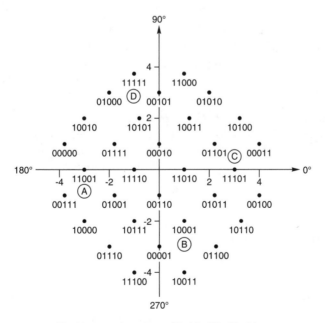

The binary numbers denote $Y0_n\ Y1_n\ Y2_n\ 03_n\ 04_n$

FIGURE 5.18.

32-point signal structure with trellis coding for 9600 bps (states A B C D used at 4800 bps and for training).

A Trellis coded modem has an error rate up to an order of magnitude less than another modem without this coding capability.

The extra bit generated by Trellis coding permits interdependencies between signal points to be noted, in effect permitting the receiving modem to recognize misplaced signal points in the signal constellation and to correct most errors. This results in a modem using Trellis coding having an error rate up to an order of magnitude less than another modem without this coding capability. Thus, almost all V.32 modems are operated using their Trellis coding capability rather than their nonredundant coding capability.

In addition to operating at 9600 and 4800 bps, a V.32 modem is V.22bis compatible. This compatibility enables the V.32 modem to communicate at 2400 bps with the large base of V.22bis modems that have been installed worldwide.

ITU-T V.32bis

The V.32bis standard was ratified by the ITU-T in February 1991. It provides a mechanism for achieving data rates up to 14,400 bps over the switched telephone network. Like the V.32 standard, V.32bis uses echo cancellation to get full-duplex transmission on the two-wire switched telephone network. It also uses Trellis coding to reduce the probability of errors occurring at the receiving modem due to the modem mistaking one constellation point for an adjacent point. The key difference between the V.32bis and V.32 modems concerns the former's method of getting a 14,400 bps operation. To do so, the V.32bis modem operates on six bits at a time and adds a redundant bit for Trellis coding. This method results in a signal constellation pattern of 127 or 128 points and an operating rate of 6 bits per baud times the 2400 (modem) baud rate, providing a data rate of 14,400 bps.

An additional difference between a V.32bis and a V.32 modem concerns their adaptive rate capability. Although a V.32 modem will adaptively fall back to a lower operating rate when line quality degrades, when operating at a lower speed it cannot fall forward if line quality improves. In comparison, a V.32bis modem supports both fall-back and fall-forward operations.

Most V.32bis modems support V.42 compression. This combination provides a potential throughput of 57.6 Kbps because that compression technique typically provides an average compression ratio of 4:1. In comparison, a V.32 modem with V.42 compression enabled provides a maximum throughput of 38.4 Kbps based on a compression ratio of 4:1.

In addition to a high-speed operating rate of 14,400 bps, a V.32bis modem supports an operating rate of 12,000 bps, as well as downward compatibility with the V.32 modem. Because the latter is compatible with the V.22bis modem, the V.32bis modem is compatible with both the V.32 and the V.22bis modems.

ITU-T V.33

The ITU-T V.33 modem standard was promulgated in 1988. It formed the basis for the V.32bis standard, which followed a few years later.

Developed to provide 14,400 bps full-duplex operations on leased lines, the V.33 modem does not use echo cancellation. This is because the four-wire leased line provides two signal paths, which removes the necessity for using that technique.

Similar to the V.32bis modem, which actually followed the V.33, the V.33 modem operates at 14,400 bps by packing six data bits into a baud and using a 2400-baud rate. At that data rate, the V.33 modem adds a redundant bit, which results in the generation of a 127- or 128-point signal constellation pattern. Like the V.32bis modem, the V.33 has a secondary signaling rate of 12,000 bps. However, the V.33 modem, unlike the V.32bis, has no additional downward compatibility because it was developed for use on leased lines.

One additional difference between the V.33 modem and its switched network V.32bis equivalent concerns a multiplexing option specified by the V.33 standard. Under the V.33 standard, a multiplexer option can be included that enables the combination of 2400, 4800, 7200, 9600, and 12,000 bps data sources to produce a single aggregate bit stream at either 12,000 or 14,400 bps for transmission. The multiplexer is a time division multiplexer (discussed in Chapter 6) that enables multiple data sources to share the use of a leased line. Because it is very difficult to get people to agree to access the same switched telephone number at the same time, multiplexers are not incorporated into dial modems. In comparison, leased lines are used to permanently provide a connection between two fixed locations. Leased lines provide an opportunity for economic savings by sharing the use of the line among two or more users.

ITU-T V.34

Previously referred to as V.fast, the V.34 standard represents several years of effort by modem manufacturers to develop a product that can support data rates up to 28.8 Kbps using multidimensional Trellis codes and an advanced equalization technique known as precoding. Under the V.34 standard, which was completed by the latter part of 1994, three-dimensional Trellis coding is employed to provide a significantly greater level of performance in comparison to V.32 and V.32bis modems. This increase in performance results not only from the higher data transfer rate of V.34 modems, but also from their lower error rate due to the use of three-dimensional Trellis coding. The lower error rate reduces the need for retransmission, which improves modem performance.

To achieve its top speed of 28,800 bps, a V.34 modem operates at 3200 baud, packing 9 bits into each signal change. In addition to supporting a 3200 baud rate, the V.34 standard specifies two additional mandatory baud rates and three optional rates. The two additional mandatory baud rates are 2400 and 3000; baud rates of 2743, 2800, and 3429 represent optional signaling rates.

In addition to an enhanced Trellis coding capability, the V.34 standard includes several features that can significantly boost the capability of this modem over its V.32bis predecessor. Those features include an asymmetrical transmission capability, an auxiliary channel, several baud rate options, and a nonlinear encoding and precoding capability. Unfortunately, although these features are mandatory for incorporation into the modem's transmitter section, they are optional with respect to their inclusion in the modem's receiver section. This means that the evaluation of V.34 modems must include determining the optional features supported in the modem's receiver.

Many V.34 modem features are optional with respect to their incorporation into the modem's receiver section.

The asymmetrical transmission capability of a V.34 modem enables the modem to send and receive at different data rates. This feature can be extremely useful if one modem user is located a relatively long distance from the telephone office serving the user. In such situations, the V.34 modem might be limited to an operating rate of 24.0 or 26.4 Kbps. If the other modem user is located a relatively short distance from the telephone office serving her location, she might be able to obtain a 28.8 Kbps operating rate. Without an asymmetrical transmission capability, transmission might be limited to 24.0 or 26.4 Kbps in both directions. The inclusion of an asymmetrical transmission capability in both modems would allow each modem to support the highest operating rate obtainable in each direction, without having to have a common data rate in each direction.

The auxiliary channel option enables a V.34 modem to support a low-speed management channel in addition to a high-speed data transfer capability. This optional channel would enable, for example, a network management system to control a distant router or multiplexer without requiring an additional circuit.

Figure 5.19 illustrates one possible use of a V.34 auxiliary channel. In this example, the V.34 modem is used on an analog leased line to connect a computer to a port on a multiplexer in a distant city. By connecting a port on a network management console to the local V.34 modem's auxiliary channel from the distant V.34 modem to the multiplexer's network management port, an operator at the local site can control the multiplexer at the remote site without requiring the use of a second line.

FIGURE 5.19.

Using an auxiliary channel.

The nonlinear coding capability of a V.34 modem increases its immunity to interference created by the Pulse Code Modulation of analog signals when they are converted into digital signals at a telephone company office. Through a nonlinear coding capability, constellation points are spaced unequally so that points in the constellation pattern that are most susceptible to noise are spaced farther apart. Through nonlinear encoding, the error rate when a V.34 modem operates at 28,800 bps can be reduced by as much as 50 percent.

The last major feature incorporated into V.34 modems is precoding, which represents a form of equalization. Through precoding, the amount of high-frequency noise on a channel is reduced, which decreases intersymbol interference.

Until early 1996, it was expected that the ITU-T would issue a new standard for 33,600 bps operations that many vendors referred to as V.34bis. Instead of issuing a new standard, however, the ITU-T completed the technical specification for a new version of V.34, which adds two new speed options. Those speed options include 33,600 bps and 31,200 bps, maintaining speed differences of 2400 bps between the different V.34 operating rates and the new speed options.

To provide compatibility with previously developed modems, the V.34 modem is downward compatible with V.32bis and V.32 modems. Because the V.32 modem provides compatibility with V.22bis and most modem vendors add V.23, V.21, and Bell System 212 compatibility, a V.34 modem can provide the capability to support seven distinct modulation methods.

One of the problems V.34 users can expect to encounter concerns the capability to use the modem effectively when it is set to perform compression and is communicating with another V.34 modem. The reason is that when compression is enabled, the modem becomes capable of receiving data from an attached DTE at 115.2 Kbps to support an operating rate of 28.8 Kbps and a compression ratio of 4:1. Unfortunately, the UART built into the serial port of many modern computers and almost all previously manufactured computers are 8250 or 16450. This nomenclature references part numbers of National Semiconductor chips, although the actual chips are available from many vendors.

The 8250 UART, which was used in all IBM PC, PC XT, and compatible computers, starts to lose characters at data rates beyond 19.2 Kbps. The 16450, which was originally used with the PC AT and compatible computers as well as most 80386 systems, can result in lost data at operating rates above 57.6 Kbps, limiting its use to V.32bis modems. To effectively support data transfer rates at 115.2 Kbps requires the use of the 16550 UART. This means that you might have to replace an existing UART to effectively use a V.34 modem. As an alternative to the replacement of a UART, several vendors anticipate marketing V.34 modems that can be cabled to the parallel port of a personal computer because that port can support a sustained data transfer rate of over 150 Kbps. Because most communications programs are limited to supporting the use of serial ports, users might be restricted to employing a modem-manufacturer-supplied program to use a V.34 modem connected to a parallel port.

Digital Transmission

In transmission systems that are not restricted by the bandwidth limitations of the voice-grade channel, it is advantageous to transmit the binary information from the source as binary data without conversion to analog form. The reasons for this were explained in Chapter 3. For end-user applications, the devices that connect between the business

●
It is advantageous to transmit data in binary form, rather than converting it to analog form. However, digital transmission must be restricted to channels with greater bandwidth than the voiceband.

machine (DTE) and the channel usually are called service units, digital modems, wireline modems, or channel interface units; most persons and organizations now use the term service unit. Although data is transmitted end-to-end in digital form, the line coding used on digital transmission facilities differs from the digital coding used by computers and at the familiar RS-232 interface between DTEs and DCEs.

When digital transmission facilities were first made available for commercial use, two types of service units were required by customers who used this service: Data Service Units (DSUs) and Channel Service Units (CSUs). Because a discussion of the operation and utilization of DSUs and CSUs requires basic knowledge of digital line coding and code violations, we will first discuss those topics before focusing on the two types of service units used with digital transmission facilities.

The most obvious difference between voiceband modems and direct digital transmission units is the increased bandwidth required by the latter. Recall from Chapter 3 that this increase is about a factor of eight. Thus, digital transmission is restricted to channels with bandwidths greater than the 3 KHz voiceband.

Line Coding

There are several techniques that can be used to code data. To help you understand the advantages and disadvantages of different methods, we'll examine the operation of several coding techniques.

Unipolar Code

The NRZ code works well for the shielded and short travel paths within a machine, but it is not suited for long-distance use because residual DC shifts the "zero" level.

The waveform of binary signals normally used in computers and terminals is called unipolar; that is, the voltage representing the bits varies between 0 V and +5 V, as shown in Figure 5.20a. (The code shown is called NRZ, Non-Return to Zero, because the voltage does not return to zero between adjacent 1 bits.) This representation works well inside machines where the transmission paths are short and well shielded, but it is unsuitable for long paths because of the presence of residual DC levels and the potential absence of enough signal transitions to allow reliable recovery of a clocking signal. Signal conditioning devices (the previously mentioned channel interface units) are used to convert the unipolar waveform to one of several different patterns that meet the goals of no long-term DC residual in the signal and strong timing content. Several of these signal patterns are shown in Figure 5.20b through 5.20e.

Polar NRZ Code

The simplest pattern that eliminates some of the residual DC problem is called a polar NRZ line code. It is shown in Figure 5.20b. This coding merely shifts the signal reference level to the midpoint of the signal amplitude. This shift has the effect of reducing the power required to transmit the signal by one-half compared with unipolar but has the disadvantage of having most of the energy in the signal concentrated around zero frequency, as illustrated in Figure 5.21.

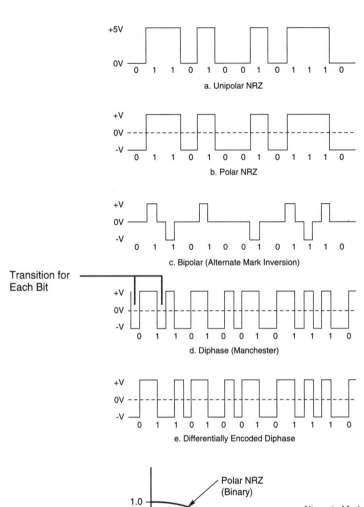

FIGURE 5.20.

Line coding of binary pulses.

a. Unipolar NRZ

b. Polar NRZ

c. Bipolar (Alternate Mark Inversion)

Transition for Each Bit

d. Diphase (Manchester)

e. Differentially Encoded Diphase

FIGURE 5.21.

Energy distribution of encoded pulses.

Polar NRZ (Binary)

Alternate Mark Inversion

Relative Energy*

Signaling Rate (Frequency)

*With equally likely 1's and 0's

A more satisfactory coding scheme is that used in the so-called T1 digital transmission system. This scheme, called bipolar or alternate mark inversion (AMI), is illustrated in Figure 5.20c. This format has no residual DC component and has zero power in the spectrum at zero frequency, as Figure 5.21 shows. It achieves these goals by transmitting pulses with a 50 percent duty cycle (only half as wide as the pulse interval allows) and by inverting the polarity of alternate 1 bits that are transmitted. Note that the bipolar format is really a three-state signal (+V, 0 V, –V). This increase in the code space of the signal adds redundancy without increasing the bandwidth of the signal and makes performance monitoring easier. Ensuring that long strings of zero bits do not occur (with an accompanying lack of timing information) is left to the transmitting terminal or channel interface.

The block diagram of a circuit to receive the bipolar signal and decode it into straight binary is shown in Figure 5.22. Note that the AMI pulse format is rectified into polar pulses inside the receiver, where suppressing the DC component of the signal is no longer critical.

FIGURE 5.22.

Bipolar decoder.

●

The bipolar (alternate mark inversion) coding scheme eliminates residual DC and has zero power in the spectrum at zero frequency. The polarity of every other 1 bit is inverted.

Diphase Code

●

In diphase, coding strong timing information is provided by having a transition for every bit, and residual DC is eliminated by having both polarities for every bit.

Another technique that has received considerable acceptance is called digital biphase, diphase, or Manchester coding. It is illustrated in Figure 5.20d. The diphase code provides strong timing information by supplying a transition for every bit, whether it be a one or a zero. If the diphase signal is differently encoded, as Figure 5.20e shows, it is even possible to determine the absolute phase of the signal because only a zero has a transition at the beginning of an interval. It also eliminates the residual DC problem by providing both a positive and a negative polarity for every bit.

All these desirable characteristics are gained, however, at the expense of requiring twice the bandwidth of a bipolar signal. Thus, diphase coding is not used by communications carriers, for whom bandwidth is a precious commodity. Instead, diphase coding has found considerable use in providing digital signaling on several types of local area networks because the bandwidth of the LAN cable does not have to be used to support the communications requirements of different organizations. The diphase scheme is used on the Ethernet local area network developed by the Xerox Corporation, Digital Equipment Corporation, and Intel Corporation. A modified diphase coding technique, referred to as differential Manchester coding, is used on the token-ring local area network.

Repeaters

Because it is not possible to separate the noise from an analog signal after the two are mixed on a transmission path, both the noise and the desired signal are amplified in repeaters. The signal-to-noise ratio gets progressively worse as the path length increases.

This effect does not occur when digital signals are used, because a different kind of repeater, called a regenerative repeater can be used (see Figure 5.23). This repeater doesn't just amplify the pulses; it regenerates them to restore the shape of the binary signal exactly as it was when it left the originating transmitter. This is a major advantage of the digital transmission technique because it is possible in principle, and to a large extent in practice, to reduce the error rate of the signal to as low a value as desired merely by putting the repeaters closer together.

> ●
> The regenerative repeater used in digital transmission doesn't just amplify the input signal; it actually regenerates the binary signal so that it is just like the original signal.

The regenerative repeater, like the sending line terminal circuit, has some of the same functions as a modem. For example, it does certain electrical transformations on the input waveform to make it suitable for the transmission path. Both the sending and the receiving ends of these operations can be studied by referring to Figure 5.23. On the input end, the line build-out (LBO) circuit matches the post-equalizer circuit with the length of the transmission cable on the input end. The post-equalizer circuit compensates for the frequency and phase nonlinearities of a standard length of input circuit, which is represented by the output of the LBO. The equalized input signal is amplified by an amplifier controlled by an automatic gain control (AGC) circuit; then the stabilized and normalized input goes to a clock-extraction circuit and a decision circuit/regenerator. The clock-extraction circuit, which is driven by the received data transitions, clocks the regenerator so that the original signal is regenerated exactly.

> ●
> The regenerative repeater has phase and frequency correction circuits to compensate for nonlinearities in the transmission path.

Bipolar Violations

Bipolar transmission requires that each data pulse representing a logical one is transmitted with alternating polarity. A violation of this rule is defined as two successive pulses that have the same polarity and are separated by a zero level.

FIGURE 5.23.

Regenerative repeater.

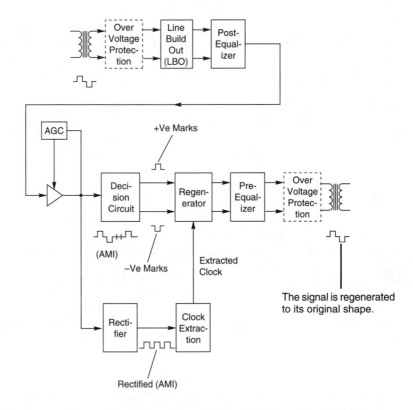

A bipolar violation indicates that a bit is missing or miscoded. Some bipolar violations are intentional and are included to replace a long string of zeros that could cause a loss of timing and receiver synchronization or to transmit control information. Figure 5.24 illustrates one example of a bipolar violation. The top of that figure shows the correct encoding to the bit sequence 01101010, using bipolar return-to-zero signaling. In the lower portion of Figure 5.24, the third one bit is encoded as a negative pulse. It represents a violation of the bipolar return-to-zero signaling technique, in which ones are alternately encoded as positive and negative voltages for defined periods.

On DDS transmission facilities, a maximum of five consecutive zeros is permitted. This means that a bipolar violation must be employed to maintain synchronization whenever a string of six or more zeros is encountered. Otherwise, repeaters on the line connecting the carrier office and the customer, as well as service units at the line interface, might not be able to get clocking as a result of an absence of ones from the signal. This could result in a loss of synchronization with the signal.

A. Bipolar Coding of Data

FIGURE 5.24.

Bipolar violations.

B. Bipolar Violation

Two successive negative or positive pulses
represent a bipolar violation of a bipolar return
to zero signaling technique.

To ensure a minimum ones density at 2.4, 4.8, 9.6, and 19.2 Kbps, any sequence of six consecutive zeros is encoded as 000X0V, in which

0   denotes zero voltage transmitted (binary zero),

X   denotes a zero or + or –A volts, with the polarity determined by conventional bipolar coding, and

V   denotes a + or –A volts, with the polarity in violation of bipolar rule.

Figure 5.25 illustrates the zero suppression sequence used to suppress a string of six consecutive zeros. For transmission at 56 Kbps, any sequence of seven consecutive zeros is encoded as 0000X0V.

Format: 000X0Y

Utilization

last binary one negative
000000 encoded as:

last binary one positive
000000 encoded as:

FIGURE 5.25.

DDS zero suppression sequence.

In addition to providing a mechanism to suppress a string of binary zeros, bipolar violations can also be used to transmit network codes that affect the operation of digital circuit terminating equipment, such as DSUs and CSUs. For example, when a DTE does not have data to transmit, the absence of a signal would result in the loss of clocking by repeaters on the line between the customer and the carrier's office. In this situation, the DSU/CSU transmits a bipolar violation sequence that enables repeaters to maintain clocking but that is recognized as an idle sequence and ignored by equipment at the carrier's office. Another example of the use of an intentional bipolar violation would be a sequence of bits that forms a loop-back code. The loop-back code would be recognized by the line-terminating equipment as a request to interconnect transmit and receive wire pairs on a four-wire circuit, enabling the circuit to be tested without human intervention.

For T1 circuits, AT&T publication G2411 sets the ones density requirement to be n ones in each window of $8x(n+1)$ bits, in which n varies from 1 to 23. This means that a T1 carrier cannot have more than 15 consecutive zeros ($n=1$) and that there must be approximately three ones in every 24 consecutive bits ($n=2$ to 23). Several methods are used to provide this minimum ones density on T1 circuits, including Binary 7 Zero Code Suppression and Binary 8 Zero Substitution (B8ZS). The latter, which represents the use of intentional bipolar violations, is discussed in Chapter 6, "Multiplexing Techniques."

Service Units

There are two distinct types of service units whose utilization can be categorized by the type of transmission facility they are used with. Those two digital transmission facilities are AT&T's Dataphone Digital Service (DDS) and equivalent offerings by other carriers, and T1 transmission lines.

Data Service Unit

Data Service Units are used at data rates from 2.4 Kbps through 56 Kbps for transmission on DDS. DSUs can also be used at 64 Kbps to get access to a fractional T1 line operating at that data rate. In actuality, transmission on DDS and on a 64 Kbps fractional T1 facility requires the use of a DSU and a Channel Service Unit. The CSU, which is located between the DSU and the digital line, physically terminates the line while providing signal amplification and initiating remote loop-back operations in response to special codes received over the line. The DSU is located between the user's terminal equipment and the CSU. The DSU converts unipolar digital signals from terminal devices into a bipolar digital format for transmission over the digital network. In addition, the DSU provides timing recovery, control signaling, and synchronous sampling.

Before deregulation, the CSU was provided by the communications carrier, whereas the DSU could be gotten from the carrier or from third-party sources. This resulted in an end-user connection to the DDS network similar to that illustrated in the top portion of Figure 5.26, in which the CSU terminated the carrier's four-wire loop and the DSU was cabled to the CSU. In this configuration, the CSU terminates the carrier's circuit. In addition, a separate CSU was designed to perform signal regeneration, monitor incoming signals to detect bipolar violations, and perform remote loop-back testing.

FIGURE 5.26.

The DSU/CSU connections.

Most manufacturers combine the functions of a DSU and CSU into a single device for use on low speed digital transmission facilities.

Since deregulation, most communications vendors have manufactured combined DSU/CSU devices, integrating the functions of both devices into a common housing that is powered by a common power supply. The lower portion of Figure 5.26 illustrates the connection of end-user terminal equipment to DDS using a combined DSU/CSU unit.

Channel Service Unit

Unlike transmission on DDS and equivalent carrier facilities in which the DSU originated as a separate device, these functions are built into most types of data terminal equipment (DTE) designed for operation on T1 lines. Thus, a CSU designed for 1.544 Mbps operation was developed as a separate entity to both interface a T1 line and provide a mechanism for the built-in DSU of most DTEs to be connected to the digital transmission facility.

In addition to performing a line termination function, a CSU used on a T1 facility provides signal amplification and initiates remote loopbacks similar to the functions performed by the CSU portion of a combined DSU/CSU used on DDS transmission facilities. Two additional functions performed by the CSUs connected to T1 transmission facilities include frame formatting and the computation of performance measurement statistics. Frame formatting is the process of encoding every 193rd bit to provide synchronization framing and, in some instances, to generate and store performance measurement data. Concerning the latter, industry standards require CSUs to both compute various performance statistics and store those statistics for transmission when predefined codes embedded in the T1 framing are received. Readers are referred to Chapter 6, "Multiplexing Techniques," for specific information concerning frame formatting and performance measurement statistics associated with T1 lines.

What Have You Learned?

1. The bandwidth of a channel sets a limit on the modulation or baud rate of the channel.

2. The data rate through a channel can be increased by sending more than one bit per baud.

3. Synchronous modems modulate a carrier wave in phase or amplitude, or both, to send more than one bit per baud.

4. Synchronous modems send the clock signal along with the data. They are more expensive than asynchronous modems because of the additional circuitry necessary to recover the clock from the data.

5. Usually, only phase modulation is used in 2400 bps modems, but both phase and amplitude modulation are used in 4800 and 9600 bps modems.

6. The most important transmission impairment that synchronous modems must deal with is differential delay distortion. Such modems have adaptive equalizers to correct for this distortion.

7. Accurate recovery of the signal in both synchronous modems and digital transmission of binary signals depends on having a sufficient number of one bits transmitted.

8. Asymmetrical transmission involves the assignment of different transmission operating rates for each direction.

9. The use of a high-speed modem with its data compression facility enabled might require the replacement of your computer's UART to support the modem's effective data transfer capability.

10. Digital transmission uses regenerative repeaters rather than amplifiers to correct the line signal.

11. Intentional bipolar violations can be used to maintain synchronization or to transmit control information on digital circuits.

Quiz for Chapter 5

1. What is one principal difference between synchronous and asynchronous transmission?

   a. The bandwidth required is different.

   b. The pulse heights are different.

   c. The clocking is mixed with the data in asynchronous transmission.

   d. The clocking is derived from the data in synchronous transmission.

2. Synchronous modems cost more than asynchronous modems because:

   a. They are larger.

   b. They must contain clock recovery circuits.

   c. The production volume is larger.

   d. They must operate on a larger bandwidth.

3. The scrambler in a synchronous modem is in the:

   a. Control section.

   b. Receiver section.

   c. Transmitter section.

   d. Terminal section.

4. Binary codes are sometimes transformed in modems into:

   a. Hexadecimal.

   b. Huffman codes.

   c. Gray code.

   d. Complementary codes.

5. The digital-to-analog converter in a synchronous modem sends signals to the:

   a. Modulator.

   b. Transmission line.

   c. Terminal.

   d. Equalizer.

6. The receive equalizer in a synchronous modem is called:

   a. A compromise equalizer.

   b. A statistical equalizer.

   c. An adaptive equalizer.

   d. An impairment equalizer.

7. The receive equalizer reduces delay distortion using a:

   a. Tapped delay line.

   b. Difference engine.

   c. Descrambler.

   d. "Gearshift."

8. A Western Electric 201 modem operates with a carrier frequency of:

   a. 1000 Hz.

   b. 1200 Hz.

   c. 1800 Hz.

   d. 600 bauds.

9. The CCITT V.26 modem has a modulation rate of:

   a. 1200 Hz.

   b. 1200 bauds.

   c. 1560 cps.

   d. None of the above.

10. The transmission signal coding method for a T1 carrier is called:

   a. Binary.

   b. NRZ.

   c. Bipolar.

   d. Manchester.

11. If a modem packs six bits into each signal change and operates at 2400 baud, its operating rate is:

   a. 2400 bps.

   b. 4800 bps.

   c. 9600 bps.

   d. 14,400 bps.

12. The use of V.42bis compression with a V.32bis modem operating at 14,400 bps can result in a maximum throughput of:

   a. 14,400 bps.

   b. 19,200 bps.

   c. 38,400 bps.

   d. 57,600 bps.

13. A key difference between a V.32bis modem and a V.32 modem is:

   a. A V.32bis modem supports fall-back operations.

   b. A V.32bis modem supports fall-forward operations.

   c. A V.32 modem supports V.22bis operations.

   d. A V.32 modem is more expensive.

14. A bipolar violation:

   a. Represents a zero bit followed by a one bit.

   b. Occurs when two successive pulses have the same polarity and are separated by a zero level.

   c. Occurs when two successive pulses have the same polarity and are separated by a one level.

   d. Represents a one bit followed by a zero bit.

15. On a digital circuit, the absence of a transmitted signal:

   a. Has no effect on equipment.

   b. Occurs when a DTE has no data to transmit.

   c. Is compensated for by the transmission of intentional bipolar violations to maintain equipment clocking.

   d. Occurs only after 9 p.m.

Multiplexing Techniques

About This Chapter

Until now, we have primarily focused on communications between individual devices, such as a personal-computer user transmitting information to a mainframe computer or an individual using a telephone to place a long-distance call. Whenever there is a requirement for the use of two or more transmission paths that are partially or completely routed in parallel, there also exists an opportunity to economize on transmission cost through multiplexing.

In this chapter, we will focus on the multiplexing techniques used by communications carriers and business organizations to share transmission facilities. After examining communications carrier multiplexing techniques, including frequency division multiplexing (FDM) and time division multiplexing (TDM), we will conclude with a discussion of the applicability of those techniques to business organizations, as well as the use of statistical time division multiplexers (STDM) by those organizations.

Multiplexing

Multiplexing provides a mechanism to share the use of a common channel or circuit by two or more users. As such, its original development was based on economics.

Sharing a Channel

Just as modulation can be explained with the idea of sending code with a flashlight, so multiplexing has a simple analogy. Imagine that you have several letters to take to the post office. You could get into the car and take one letter, mail it, come back home and get the second letter, take it to the post office and mail it, come back to get the third…silly, right? Why not take all the letters in the same trip, because they're all going to the post office?

This is what multiplexing amounts to: using a resource (in this case, the car going to the post office) to carry more than one message at a time. In the systems we are concerned with, a microwave system is a transmission facility (like the car), and a telephone call is the message (like the letter). The transmission facility is divided in either of two ways in order to share it: by frequency or by time.

Frequency Division Multiplexing

FDM translates the frequencies within each of several voiceband channels to different frequency channels that are combined and transmitted together.

Figure 6.1 shows the use of frequency division multiplexing to carry more than one telephone conversation over a transmission channel. In effect, the frequencies in each call are changed so that they can be placed side-by-side in a wideband channel and transmitted as a group. At the other end, the frequencies in each call are changed back to the original frequencies. FDM was the mainstay of telephone transmission for many years; it is more efficient in terms of bandwidth than digital systems. The problem is that noise is amplified along with the voice. This fact, and the great decrease in cost of digital electronics, has led to the widespread replacement of FDM systems with time division multiplexing systems.

FIGURE 6.1.

Frequency division multiplexing.

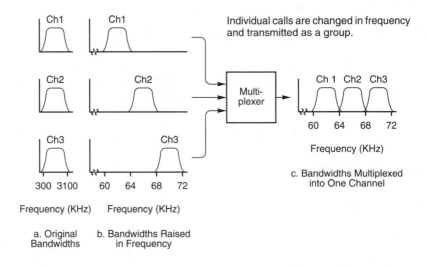

A second and perhaps more important reason for the tremendous reduction in the use of FDM during the past two decades was the conversion of most long-distance communications carrier transmission facilities from analog to digital. This conversion resulted in voice conversations being digitized at a carrier central office and carried in digital format to another central office. At the distant central office, the digitized conversation was converted back into its analog form and was routed to the destination telephone connected to that central office. By 1990, U.S. Sprint had converted all of its long-distance circuits to digital, and AT&T and MCI had converted more than 90 percent of their long-distance transmission facilities. A few years later, all long-distance communications in the United States were being transported over digital circuits, and most European communications carriers were well along on similar conversion efforts. To get an appreciation for the method by which analog voice is converted into a digital format, we'll examine digital modulation, which forms the basis for the use of TDMs by communications carriers.

Digital Modulation

Sine waves are all we have to work with in transmitting over the analog telephone channel because it doesn't transmit pulses. Digital transmission systems will transmit pulses, and with them we can encode either analog or digital information by modulating pulses.

Figure 6.2 shows three ways to modulate a series of pulses to carry data. When the amplitude of the pulses is varied to represent analog information, the method is called pulse amplitude modulation (PAM). This method is very susceptible to electrical noise interference. In the second method, called pulse width modulation (PWM), the information is represented by varying the width of the pulses. Both of these techniques are used in telephone switching equipment, such as a private branch exchange (PBX). The third technique, which varies the position of pulses within a group of pulses (called the frame) to represent information, is called pulse position modulation (PPM).

●
Digital modulation methods include PAM, PWM, PPM, and PCM.

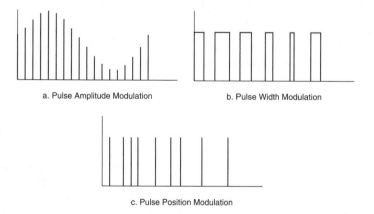

a. Pulse Amplitude Modulation

b. Pulse Width Modulation

c. Pulse Position Modulation

FIGURE 6.2.
Pulse modulation.

Figure 6.3 shows the process of sampling an analog signal as in PAM, but the amplitudes of the samples are encoded into binary numbers represented by constant amplitude pulses that are transmitted. This process, called pulse code modulation (PCM), overcomes the noise interference problem of PAM. Most long-distance telephone calls are transmitted by PCM.

FIGURE 6.3.

Pulse code modulation.

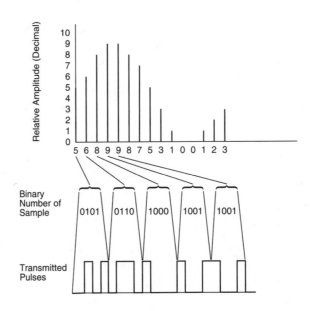

PCM

●

PCM involves a three-step process: sampling, quantization, and coding.

The PCM system used by communications carriers employs a three-step process: sampling, quantization, and coding. During the sampling process, the analog signal is sampled 8000 times per second. This sampling rate is based on the Nyquist theorem, which states that to faithfully reconstruct an analog signal, the number of sample points must equal twice the maximum frequency of the signal. Because each voice channel has a bandwidth of 4 kilohertz (KHz), the sampling rate becomes 8000 samples per second.

The resulting samples, which are illustrated in the top portion of Figure 6.3, represent an infinite number of voltages. Thus, the second step in the PCM process, which is called quantization, reduces the PAM signal to a limited number of discrete amplitudes. The third step in the PCM process, which is known as coding, reduces the number of unique values of the PAM signal so that they can be coded through the use of an eight-bit byte. For simplicity, the lower portion of Figure 6.3 uses four bits to represent each PAM signal sample; in actuality, however, eight bits are used.

●

Early PCM systems were used to relieve cable congestion in urban areas.

One of the earliest uses of PCM systems was to relieve cable congestion in urban areas during the 1960s. At that time, communications carriers installed equipment called channel banks in their central offices. Each channel bank contained a codec, time division multiplexer, and line driver. The codec (coder-decoder) accepts and samples 24 analog voice signals. It produces a series of PAM signals that are quantized and coded into eight-bit bytes. The TDM combines the digitized bit stream from each of the 24 inputs into one high-speed serial bit stream, and the line driver converts the electrical characteristics of the bit stream for transmission on the circuit linking channel banks. Figure 6.4 illustrates a channel bank system that was the forerunner of what is now commonly known as a T-carrier transmission system.

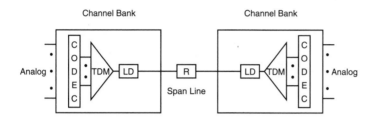

FIGURE 6.4.

Channel bank system.

Legend
CODEC - Coder - Decoder
R   - Repeater
LD   - Line Driver

The repeater illustrated in Figure 6.4 actually represents a series of devices installed approximately 6000 feet from one another on the span line. Each repeater examines the digital pulses transmitted on the span line connecting a pair of channel banks and regenerates each pulse. Because the repeater "throws away" the old pulse and generates a new pulse, it removes any prior distortion. In comparison, amplifiers used with analog transmission boost the strength of an analog signal, including increasing any prior distortion to the signal. This explains why, in general, digital transmission provides a higher level of signal quality and lower error rate than analog transmission.

● Repeaters on a span line regenerate the digital pulses, removing any prior distortion to the pulses.

Framing

To provide a method of synchronization of transmission, a framing format was developed for use with channel banks. Currently, the most popular framing format is called D4; however, a new framing format called ESF is gaining in use.

Under the D4 framing format, which is illustrated in Figure 6.5a, a frame bit is used to prefix each group of 24 eight-bit bytes, with each byte representing a digitized voice sample for each of 24 voice channels. Thus, a D4 frame contains $1 + 24 \times 8$, or 193 bits. The framing bits of 12 frames are used to develop a framing pattern that enables a receiving channel bank to synchronize itself to the transmission of data from a channel bank at the opposite end of a span line.

● Under D4 framing, the frame bit of 12 frames is used to provide a synchronization pattern.

FIGURE 6.5.

The D4 framing structure and framing pattern.

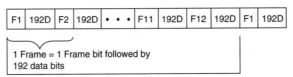

F1	192D	F2	192D	• • •	F11	192D	F12	192D	F1	192D

1 Frame = 1 Frame bit followed by
192 data bits

Superframe = Frames F1 through F12

a. D4 Framing Structure

F1	F2	F3	F4	F5	F6	F7	F8	F9	F10	F11	F12
1	0	0	0	1	1	0	1	1	1	0	0

Terminal Framing FT 101010
Signal Framing FS 001110

b. D4 Framing Pattern

The framing bits in a D4 superframe are alternately designated as terminal framing bits (Ft) or signal framing bits (Fs). The terminal framing bits consist of the odd framing bits, as illustrated in the lower portion of Figure 6.5. Under D4 framing, the Ft bits form an alternating pattern of ones and zeros, enabling one frame to be distinguished from another. Thus, the sequence of terminal framing bits is also referred to as a Frame Alignment Signal.

The signal framing bits that represent the repeating pattern "001110" are the even frame bits. These bits are used to define multiframe boundaries and enable the extraction of signaling bits from frames. Signaling bits are used to carry such mechanical signaling information as on-hook, off-hook, dialed digits, and call progress information. The method used to provide signaling bits, called bit robbing, is beyond the scope of this book. Readers are referred to the book *Digital Networking and T-Carrier Multiplexing,* written by Gilbert Held and published by John Wiley & Sons, Inc., of New York, for detailed information concerning digital transmission systems, including the bit-robbing process.

ESF extends D4 framing to 24 consecutive frames, enabling synchronization patterns as well as performance measurement information to be transmitted.

A second framing format, known as extended superframe, or ESF, extends D4 framing to 24 consecutive frames. Unlike D4 framing, which contains a specific repeating pattern, ESF framing contains both fixed and variable patterns. Out of the 24 frame bits in an extended superframe, only 6 are used for a framing pattern for synchronization.

The remaining frame bits are used to transmit error performance and network monitoring information. Although only 30 percent of channel banks currently support ESF framing, this percentage is expected to increase due to the performance measurement data it provides.

The T-Carrier

The span line illustrated in Figure 6.4 is now commonly referred to as a T-carrier. This circuit originally provided communications carriers with the capability to multiplex 24 voice conversations on one high-speed digital circuit.

● The T-carrier provides a transmission path for multiplexing up to 24 voice conversations.

Because each voice conversation is sampled 8000 times per second and each sample is encoded into 8 bits, the digitization rate per channel is 8000 samples/second × 8 bits/sample, or 64 Kbps. The aggregate of 24 channels represents a data rate of 64 Kbps × 24, or 1.536 Mbps. Because the framing rate is 8000 bits per second, the operating rate of the T-carrier is 1.536 Mbps + 8 Kbps, or 1.544 Mbps.

Until the early 1980s, the use of T-carrier transmission facilities was limited to communications carriers. Since then, the use of the T-carrier has been made available to commercial organizations. In the digital transmission hierarchy of carrier facilities, the 1.544 Mbps transmission rate represents the first level in the hierarchy and is commonly referred to as a T1 transmission facility. As a result of the commercial availability of this transmission facility, a large number of independent companies began to manufacture T1 multiplexers. Through the use of this type of multiplexer, companies could integrate the transmission of voice, data, and video between locations, routing this mixture of data onto a common high-speed transmission line operating at 1.544 Mbps.

● Through the use of a T1 multiplexer, organizations can transmit voice, data, and video information on a common circuit operating at 1.544 Mbps.

Figure 6.6 illustrates one example of an organization's use of a T1 multiplexer that enables the integration of voice, data, and video transmission. In the example shown, the T1 multiplexer contains PCM cards that enable analog voice conversations routed from a private branch exchange to be digitized before being multiplexed. If a digital PBX was installed, data could be directly multiplexed without the use of PCM cards.

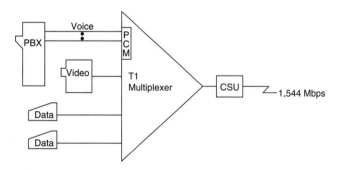

FIGURE 6.6.

A typical T1 multiplexer application.

Legend:

PCM - Pulse Code Modulation cards that sample, quantize, and encode each
analog voice signal into a 64 Kbps digital data stream.
CSU - Channel Service Unit

Digital data is manipulated within a T1 multiplexer in a unipolar NRZ format, as previously indicated in Figure 5.19a. Although this data representation format is commonly used by the computer systems, electronic equipment, and the data terminal equipment (DTE) to data communications equipment (DCE) interface, it is unsuitable for transmission on a T1 transmission facility.

●

Bipolar coding enables a signal and power to be carried on a common line and separated by the use of a transformer.

When span lines were first routed between channel banks, communications carriers desired a method that would enable them to transmit both a digital signal and power on the same circuit, separating the signal from the power through the use of a transformer at each channel bank location. To get this capability, a signaling method that resulted in no residual DC voltage was required, which would enable the use of transformers to separate the signal from the power carried on the line. The resulting line coding method that provided this capability is the bipolar alternate mark inversion (AMI) coding format previously illustrated in Figure 5.19c.

Most T1 multiplexers convert unipolar RTZ signals into bipolar AMI signals for transmission. Before actual transmission on the T1 line, however, the digital signal must be framed according to the line code supported by the communications carrier—D4 or ESF. The framing function is but one of several operations performed by the channel service unit (CSU). Other functions performed by CSUs include storing performance data when an ESF framing format is used, recognizing and responding to network codes transmitted by the communications carrier and equipment connected to the T1 line, and transmitting a minimum number of binary ones, referred to as "ones density."

Ones Density

●

A minimum number of marks, referred to as "ones density," must flow on a digital transmission facility to enable repeaters to get timing from the data.

The requirement for a ones density level on T1 circuits resulted from the need of repeaters to maintain timing. If a long string of binary zeros was transmitted, the repeaters on a span line could conceivably lose timing. Thus, the CSU must be capable of ensuring that a binary one or mark pulse occurs every so often, which enables repeaters to get timing from the pulse.

Specifically, carrier requirements are such that the number of consecutive zeros must be less than 15, and each eight-bit byte must include at least one "1" bit. To support carrier ones density requirements, several techniques are used, including binary 7 (B7) zero code suppression and binary 8 zero substitution.

Under B7 zero code suppression, a 1 bit is substituted in bit position 7 of an all-zero byte. Although this technique ensures that the carrier's ones density requirements are met, it also restricts data to seven usable bits rather than eight. This means that each 64 Kbps voice channel multiplexed on a T1 line is restricted to 64 Kbps × 7/8, or 56 Kbps, when used for data transmission.

To understand why bit position 7 was selected for substitution, consider a worst-case scenario, as illustrated in Figure 6.7. In this example, the 8-bit byte representing the 24th channel contains a mark in bit position 1 followed by the remainder of the byte's bit positions set to zero. If the framing bit following the 24th channel has a value of zero and is followed by an all-zero byte, 16 bit positions would be between marks if bit position 8 had its value altered to 1. Normally, this would be more desirable because it represents the least significant position in a byte and would minimize its effect on a digitized voice signal. Selecting bit position 8, however, would then violate the carrier's ones density requirements, which resulted in the selection of bit position 7 for substitution.

FIGURE 6.7.

A B7 zero code suppression worst-case scenario.

Binary 8 Zero Substitution (B8ZS), developed by Bell Laboratories, represents a considerable improvement over B7 Zero Suppression because it enables data to be transmitted at 64 Kbps on a voice channel. This capability, in which a minimum ones density is gotten without corrupting data, provides what is known as a clear channel. Under B8ZS coding, each byte of eight consecutive zeros is replaced by a code that includes an intentional bipolar violation. Figure 6.8 illustrates the B8ZS coding process.

●
B8ZS provides a clear channel capability, enabling data transmission to occur at 64 Kbps on a voice channel.

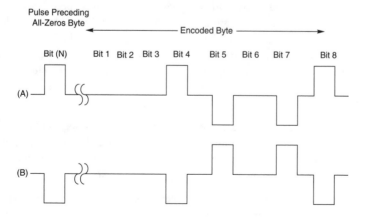

FIGURE 6.8.

B8ZS coding.

B8ZS coding uses intentional bipolar violations to maintain a minimum ones density.

On examination of Figure 6.8, the coding used becomes more meaningful if we review how bipolar coding normally functions. That is, under bipolar coding, marks or binary ones are encoded using alternating polarities, and spaces are encoded as a zero voltage level. Thus, the encoded byte, when the pulse preceding an all-zeros byte was positive, commences with bit position 4 high, which represents a bipolar violation. This is illustrated at A in Figure 6.8. Next, bit positions 5 and 7 are both encoded as negative marks, which represents another bipolar violation. Because bits 4 and 8 are positive pulses while bits 5 and 7 are negative pulses, the encoded byte does not result in any DC voltage buildup, although it violates bipolar coding rules. At the receiving CSU, the encoded byte is recognized as defining the occurrence of an all-zeros byte, and the CSU then replaces the B8ZS code with eight binary zeros. Similarly, if the pulse preceding an all-zeros byte was negative, the all-zeros byte is encoded in the opposite manner, as illustrated at B in Figure 6.8.

Note that the state of bit position 4 represents a bipolar violation with respect to the pulse preceding the all-zeros byte, whereas bit positions 5 and 7 represent a bipolar violation with respect to each bit position's polarity. Also note that there are an equal number of positive and negative pulses to prevent DC voltage buildup.

The bipolar violations contained in the B8ZS coding represent intentional bipolar violations. Other examples of intentional bipolar violations are loopback codes that when recognized by a CSU bring about a loopback mode of operation. Intentional bipolar violations do not represent coding errors. In comparison, unintentional bipolar violations do represent coding errors resulting from line impairments whose measurement over a period of time provides an indication of the quality of a digital circuit.

Time Division Multiplexing

The T1 multiplexer that evolved from channel banks represents one of the earliest types of TDMs. Until T1 lines were made available for use by commercial organizations, most TDMs were manufactured for use with analog leased lines or low-speed Dataphone Digital Service (DDS) digital transmission facilities. When a TDM is used with analog leased lines, the aggregate data rate of the TDM is normally limited to 19.2 Kbps, whereas its use with DDS limits its aggregate data rate to 56 Kbps. The 19.2 Kbps operating-rate limitation on analog leased lines is a constraint resulting from the operating rate of leased-line modems. In comparison, the 56 Kbps DDS operating-rate limitation is a service offering constraint.

When multiplexing is used by commercial organizations, the rationale for multiplexing is the same as for communications carriers—economics.

Most communications networks used by organizations include several TDM systems that are used primarily because of economics. When one circuit and a pair of multiplexers replace two or more data circuits, the savings that accrue from the elimination of data lines usually can pay for the required equipment in less than a year.

To understand the rationale for using multiplexers, consider an example in which eight terminals located in San Francisco must communicate with a mainframe computer located in Chicago. If each terminal requires four hours of computer access per day and the cost of one hour of communications on the switched telephone network is $30, conventional dialing by each terminal operator to Chicago costs the organization $960 per day. If a month has 22 business days, the monthly cost for accessing the Chicago computer would slightly exceed $21,000, exclusive of the cost of the modems.

When terminal devices at one location require access to a computer at a second location, multiplexing should be considered. Figure 6.9 illustrates a network configuration that could be used to satisfy the San Francisco-to-Chicago communications requirements of the organization.

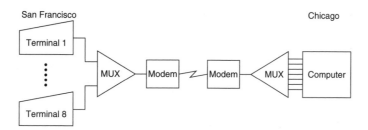

FIGURE 6.9.

Using multiplexers to reduce communications costs.

Assuming that the cost of each multiplexer is $3,000 and the leased line costs $1,000 monthly, during the first year, the multiplexing method would cost $18,000, exclusive of modems. In the second year of operation, the cost of multiplexing would be reduced to $12,000 because we assume that the equipment was purchased the first year. Thus, in this example, the two-year cost of multiplexing is $30,000. Because dialing without multiplexing would cost over $500,000 during the two-year period, multiplexing results in substantial savings.

A second reason for the use of multiplexers is the relative fixed cost associated with their use. Multiplexer systems are connected to one another by leased lines with rates that can increase slightly from year to year because of tariff changes. The cost of the multiplexer system is rather stable and predictable because the cost of the line is billed monthly based on the distance between locations and is not dependent on usage. In comparison, the cost of using the switched telephone network depends on many factors, including the duration of the call, the distance between calling and called parties, the day and time the call was originated, and whether operator assistance was required. If only a few terminal users increase their connect time 15 minutes per day, the monthly cost of communications could substantially increase.

Operation

A TDM, as its name implies, uses time as a reference for multiplexing data. To understand the operation of a TDM as well as the limitations associated with this technology, we'll examine how data from a few terminals or personal computers are multiplexed and demultiplexed. Figure 6.10 illustrates the multiplexing of data from three terminal devices at a remote location to a mainframe computer at another location. For simplicity of illustration, it was assumed that terminal 1 transmitted the character sequence "BA," terminal 2 transmitted "DC," and terminal 3 transmitted "FE." The TDM at the remote location scans each port connected to a terminal for data, recognizing "A," "C," and "E" as input to ports 1, 2, and 3 of the multiplexer during the first scan. The TDM accepts data from each port and builds a multiplexing frame that represents the data from each port during the scan. Thus, frame 1 contains the character sequence "ECA," and frame 2 contains "FDB." In actuality, each TDM frame will also contain synchronization characters prefixing data as well as data from one or more scans.

FIGURE 6.10.

The multiplexing process.

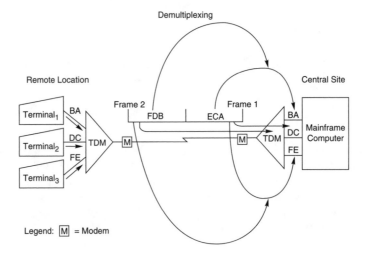

At the receiving TDM, the position of data in each frame is used to ensure the correct demultiplexing of data. As indicated in Figure 6.10, "A" is the first position of frame 1, which tells the TDM that that byte of information should be output onto port 1 of the multiplexer. Similarly, in frame 1 the character "C," which is located in the second position, and "E," which is located in the third position, inform the multiplexer at the central site to output those characters onto ports 2 and 3, respectively. Next, the data in frame 2 is examined by the central site multiplexer. Because "B" is in position 1, it is output onto port 1. Next, "D" and "F," which are located in positions 2 and 3 of frame 2, are output onto ports 2 and 3. Thus, the TDM demultiplexing process depends on the position of data within each frame.

> The position of data within a TDM frame is used to ensure that data is demultiplexed correctly.

To understand the limitation of the TDM process, consider the actual operation of terminal devices. Some terminal operators might be reading a manual, attempting to determine how to correct a programming error or how to respond to a message requesting a specific type of data entry. Other terminal operators might be diligently entering data or receiving information, while some operators might be on a coffee break or simply thinking about the response they should enter to an application program they are accessing. Thus, at any instant, it is highly probable that there is no data transmission activity from

> Null characters are inserted into TDM frames to enable demultiplexing to occur based on the position of data within a frame.

or destined to one or more terminal devices. Because a TDM demultiplexes by the position of data in each frame, the absence of activity could result in the misinterpretation of data. To prevent this problem from happening, a TDM inserts null characters in each frame whenever there is no activity when input from a port is sampled by the TDM scanning process.

At the receiving multiplexer, the null characters maintain the positioning within the frame required for demultiplexing to occur correctly. They are "stripped," however, by the receiving multiplexer and are not output to devices attached to the TDM.

Although the use of null characters ensures that demultiplexing occurs correctly, it also indicates that the multiplexing process is not as efficient as it could be. For example, when several terminal users are on a break, thinking, or even entering data at a normal typing rate, most frames flowing between multiplexers contain a large percentage of null characters. Thus, for most periods, data transmission between TDMs is highly inefficient. Although a T1 multiplexer has the same inefficiency, its 1.544 Mbps operating rate enables the transmission of up to hundreds of devices to be carried on one very high-speed line. In comparison, TDMs connected to analog or DDS circuits operating at much lower data rates are limited to supporting a much smaller population of devices. Thus, the inefficiency of TDMs is much more pronounced when used with analog or DDS transmission facilities. This inefficiency resulted in the development of a different type of multiplexer for use on those transmission facilities. This type of multiplexer, referred to as a statistical time division multiplexer (STDM), provides a much higher level of line utilization efficiency than TDMs and has essentially replaced the use of TDMs by many organizations.

STDMs

In comparison to TDMs, which use fixed frames with data positioned in each frame, STDMs use variable-length frames. To understand the operation of STDMs, we'll examine how variable frames are created. In doing so, we will discuss one of several methods used to create variable positional information within a multiplexing frame.

●
STDMs create
variable-length
frames.

To understand the operation of STDMs, assume that eight terminal devices are connected to a multiplexer as illustrated in Figure 6.11a. Further assume that during one scan operation, terminals 1, 2, 3, and 6 were active and transmitted the characters X, Y, Z, and Q, respectively. If the STDM employs a bit map character to denote the activity of each port during a scan, the multiplexer sets the bit position that corresponds to a port to a 1 if there is activity. Otherwise, a bit map position setting of 0 indicates that no activity occurred on a port during the scan.

FIGURE 6.11.

STDM operation.

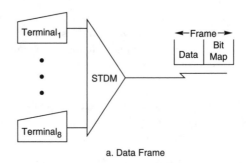

a. Data Frame

Terminal	Terminal Activity	Frame	
1	X	00100111	Bit Map
2	Y	X	Frame
3	Z	Y	Data
4	No Activity	Z	
5	No Activity	Q	
6	Q		
7	No Activity		
8	No Activity		

b. Frame Construction

The frame construction example illustrated in Figure 6.11b indicates how the use of a bit map can reduce the size of a frame when some ports connected to the STDM are inactive. In this example, terminals 1, 2, 3, and 6 were active; hence, bit map positions 1, 2, 3, and 6 were set to ones. Therefore, the character from each terminal can be added after the bit map to form a variable-length frame without requiring the use of null characters, because the bit map indicates the actual position of each character in the frame.

In general, an STDM can double to quadruple the number of asynchronous data sources serviced by a conventional TDM. This additional servicing capability is known as the multiplexer's service ratio. In addition to taking advantage of idle times, the STDM strips start, stop, and parity bits from each asynchronous character before transmission and "rebuilds" the character when it is demultiplexed. Some STDMs add data compression to a list of functions they perform, further increasing their service ratio.

Service Ratio

To understand the concept of an STDM's service ratio, first consider Figure 6.12a, which illustrates the use of a conventional TDM connected to a modem operating at 9600 bps. When a conventional TDM is used to multiplex data, the aggregate input data rate cannot exceed the output data rate. Hence, up to eight terminals operating at 1200 bps could be serviced by the TDM, resulting in a total input of 8 × 1200, or 9600 bps, being equal to the line operating rate.

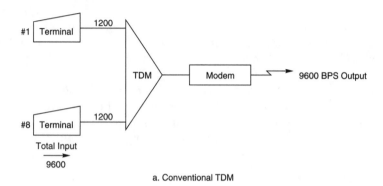

FIGURE 6.12.

STDM service ratio.

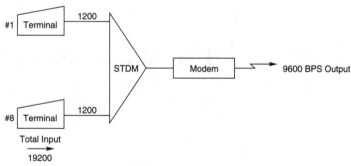

A service ratio of a multiplexer indicates the average data input to an STDM based on its line operating rate.

If the STDM's service ratio is 2, on the average it can service an aggregate input twice the line operating rate, or 19,200 bps. The term "on the average" is used because during a long period, some terminals are powered off and unused, some terminal operators are thinking about what to do next, and other terminal operators are entering data or receiving responses to their queries. Due to the previously explained STDM functions, over a prolonged period, the multiplexer can accept an input data rate of twice its output rate.

Consider a worst-case scenario, however, in which each terminal is a personal computer and every terminal operator attempts to transmit a large file at the same time. In this situation, the total input to the STDM becomes 19,200 bps, and the multiplexer cannot take advantage of idle times because each terminal is transmitting a continuous sequence of data. Even after stripping start, stop, and parity bits, the aggregate input data rate will exceed the line operating rate. Although the STDM contains a buffer area, as each terminal continues to transmit data, the buffer area would eventually fill and overflow, resulting in a loss of data. To prevent the loss of data, the STDM initiates flow control to turn off one or more devices whenever its buffer reaches a certain level of occupancy. Then, as data from its buffer is transmitted onto the line and the level of buffer occupancy decreases to a certain level, the STDM turns off flow control, allowing devices connected to the multiplexer to resume transmission.

The capability of STDMs to service, on average, two to four times the aggregate data rate of the line connecting multiplexers resulted in their wide acceptance by most organizations. By 1990, almost 80 percent of all TDMs incorporated a statistical multiplexing process. Today, conventional TDMs are primarily used in which delays from the use of flow control cannot be tolerated—such as in T1 multiplexers, in which a delay in voice would be most annoying.

Low-Speed Voice/Data Multiplexers

Combining the operational capability of TDM and statistical time division multiplexers resulted in a new type of multiplexer for use by organizations requiring the transport of both voice and data. Known as a low-speed voice/data multiplexer, this device was developed for organizations that required the use of a few voice and data circuits between two locations. As such, this device fills a rapidly expanding market for organizations with small branch offices that require both voice and data communications capability to a regional office of company headquarters. Because the key to the operation of this multiplexer is its capability to digitize voice at data rates significantly below the PCM operating rate of 64 Kbps, we will first focus on a few of the methods used by this class of communications equipment to digitize voice conversations through voice compression.

Adaptive Differential Pulse-Code Modulation

Adaptive Differential Pulse-Code Modulation (ADPCM) is a voice digitization and compression technique that reduces PCM eight-bit samples to four-bit words, with each four-bit word representing 16 quantization levels. Those levels, which represent sample amplitudes under PCM, now represent the difference between successive samples under ADPCM. They permit a digitization data rate of 32 Kbps rather than the 64 Kbps operating rate required by PCM.

The key to the operation of ADPCM is the fact that the amplitude of voice does not rapidly change when sampled 8000 times per second. This fact enabled engineers to design adaptive predictor circuitry into ADPCM equipment that anticipates the value of the next sample based on the level of the previously sampled signal. A feedback loop used by the predictor minimizes the possibility of deviations between samples. Because this technique results in a very accurate prediction value, the difference between the predicted and the actual signal is relatively small, enabling it to be encoded through the use of four bits. If successive samples increase in their value difference, the adaptive predictor adapts to this change by increasing the range represented by the four bits. This adaption process decreases the signal-to-noise ratio, however, and reduces the accuracy of the decoded signal.

For normal voice conversations, ADPCM provides a voice quality that is most difficult to differentiate from a PCM digitized voice conversation.

The key difference between ADPCM and PCM is in the area of modem transmission support. PCM can support modems operating at data rates up to 24 Kbps. In comparison, due to the use of an adaptive predictor, ADPCM is limited to supporting modem rates up to 4.8 Kbps. At higher operating rates, the modem signal changes too fast to be accurately predicted by ADPCM, resulting in an increase in transmission errors as the modem operating rate increases. Thus, ADPCM is primarily used in private networks that can restrict the use of voice channels to ADPCM digitized voice and other channels to data. In comparison, communications carriers normally cannot restrict the use of the switched telephone network to modems that operate at or below 4.8 Kbps, which explains why most carriers use PCM equipment to digitize voice communications for transportation over the switched telephone network.

Continuously Variable Slope Data Modulation

Continuously Variable Slope Data Modulation (CVSD) is a voice digitization technique originally developed for military use. This digitization technique has gained acceptance in the commercial market as a mechanism to digitize voice at a low data rate.

The key to the operation of CVSD is the fact that the higher the rate at which an analog signal is sampled, the smaller the resulting difference between sampled amplitudes. This means that at a high enough sampling rate, the difference between sampled amplitudes can be represented by a single bit. That bit represents the change in the slope of the analog voice conversation. The bit is set to 1 to represent an increase in the slope between two samples, 0 to represent a decrease in the slope. Figure 6.13 illustrates the operation of CVSD.

●
ADPCM predicts the next voice sample based on the level of the previously sampled signal. This method halves the digitization rate to 32 Kbps.

●
The key limitation of ADPCM is in its incapability to reliably pass modem signals at data rates above 4800 bps.

●
By sampling at a high rate, CVSD encodes the difference between sampled amplitudes in 1-bit, which represents the change in the slope of the voice amplitude from the previous sample.

FIGURE 6.13.

CVSD operation.

Under CVSD, an increase in the slope of the sampled
conversation is represented by a '1', and a decrease
in the slope is represented by a '0'.

●
Because each
CVSD-encoded bit
represents a change
in the slope of an
analog signal, this
technique is ill-suited
for carrying modem
modulated data.

CVSD commonly operates at 32K and 16K samples per second, resulting in digitization rates of 32 Kbps and 16 Kbps. At 16 Kbps, CVSD is four times as efficient with respect to its data rate than PCM and twice as efficient as ADPCM. However, due to its use of a single bit to represent a change in slope, CVSD is not recommended for use by modems transmitting data.

Although CVSD is not to be used for transporting modulated data, its capability to represent a voice conversation at a low data rate resulted in the use of this technique as well as ADPCM as a mechanism to transport digitized voice by low-speed voice/data multiplexers.

As previously noted, a low-speed voice/data multiplexer can be considered as a combination TDM and statistical time division multiplexer. The TDM portion of the device is used exclusively for multiplexing two or more digitized voice conversations onto a fixed portion of the operating rate of the high-speed line that the multiplexer is connected to. Although the term *high-speed line* is used, the operating rate of the composite channel of the voice/data multiplexer is typically 56 or 64 Kbps—relatively low in comparison to a T1 multiplexer. This explains why this voice/data multiplexer is commonly referred to as a low-speed voice/data multiplexer. For example, a low-speed voice/data multiplexer connected to a 64 Kbps digital leased line might multiplex three voice conversations using CVSD onto 48 Kbps of the 64 Kbps leased line. The statistical time division multiplexer would then contend with one or more data sources for the remaining 16 Kbps operating rate of the leased line.

Figure 6.14 illustrates the bandwidth allocation of a 64 Kbps digital leased line based on the previously mentioned scenario. In this example, each voice conversation is digitized and is always placed into a fixed slot of 16 Kbps. In comparison, data sources contend for the remaining 16 Kbps. This technique ensures that each voice digitized signal is always carried by the multiplexer and eliminates potential delays from the statistical multiplexing process that could cause havoc to a reconstructed voice conversation.

FIGURE 6.14.

Potential voice/data multiplexer bandwidth allocation.

To illustrate the potential use of low-speed voice/data multiplexers in an organizational environment, assume that a branch office and a regional office each have a PBX. Also assume that branch office employees regularly converse with persons at a regional office and have between one and three simultaneous calls between offices during normal business hours. Also assume that 10 low-speed (2400 bps) terminals in the regional office require access to a computer located in the regional office.

Figure 6.15 illustrates as a network diagram schematic the use of a pair of low-speed voice/data multiplexers between branch and regional offices to consolidate both voice and data communications requirements between the two locations onto one 64 Kbps digital circuit. In this example, each PBX has three lines routed into a data/voice multiplexer installed at each office. Through the use of CVSD adapter cards installed in both multiplexers, each voice conversation will be digitized into a fixed 16 Kbps time slot, as previously illustrated in Figure 6.14. The ten 2400 bps terminals illustrated in the lower-left portion of Figure 6.15 would be statistically multiplexed into a fixed 16 Kbps time slot, as previously illustrated in Figure 6.14. If all ten terminals were transmitting files to the computer in the regional office, the aggregate terminal data rate of 24 Kbps would exceed the capacity of the fixed 16 Kbps time slot. If this situation occurs or another situation occurs in which enough terminals become active that their aggregate transmission exceeds the fixed 16 Kbps time slot, the multiplexer issues flow control to inhibit one or more data sources from transmitting.

FIGURE 6.15.

Using low-speed voice/data multiplexers.

● A voice/data multiplexer uses flow control only to inhibit data traffic.

Although flow control affects only the throughput of data, its use on voice traffic would result in random voice delays that would be entirely unacceptable for conducting a conversation. Thus, a voice/data multiplexer uses TDM for multiplexing voice conversations and STDM onto a fixed time slot for multiplexing data.

From an economic perspective, a voice/data multiplexer can pay for itself in as little time as one or two months. Of course, the actual payback period depends on the distance between locations, current and anticipated switched-telephone-network usage, the number of voice and data sources to be multiplexed, and the cost of voice/data multiplexers.

What Have You Learned?

1. Multiplexing is the process of sharing the use of a transmission facility by time or by frequency.

2. The conversion of most long-distance communications carrier transmission facilities from analog to digital resulted in a large replacement of FDM by TDM systems.

3. To faithfully reproduce an analog signal, it must be sampled at a rate equal to twice the bandwidth it occupies.

4. Repeaters regenerate digital pulses, removing any prior distortion. In comparison, amplifiers boost the strength of analog signals, including increasing any prior distortion.

5. Framing is used to provide a method of synchronization between channel banks.

6. D4 framing is restricted to providing synchronization data, whereas ESF framing enables the flow of performance measurement information as well as synchronization data.

7. Bipolar transmission allows a digital signal and power to be carried on the same line and separated from one another by the use of transformers.

8. A minimum number of binary ones, known as "ones density," must occur on a digital transmission line to enable repeaters to get timing from data.

9. Intentional bipolar violations, which occur when two successive marks have the same polarity, can be used to convey information or maintain a minimum ones density on a digital transmission facility.

10. When no activity occurs on a TDM input port, the multiplexer inserts a null character into the frame it builds. This character maintains the correct positioning of data from all ports, enabling demultiplexing to occur by position of data within a frame.

11. ADPCM and CVSD enable voice conversations to be digitized at data rates one-half to one-fourth that of PCM.

12. A voice/data multiplexer uses time division multiplexing to support multiple voice conversations and uses statistical time division multiplexing to support multiple data sources.

Quiz for Chapter 6

1. Multiplexing is:
   a. The process of increasing bandwidth on a channel.
   b. A technique that enables more than one data source to share the use of a common line.
   c. Mailing letters at the Post Office.
   d. The capability to share frequency by time.

2. One of the reasons frequency division multiplexing has essentially been replaced by time division multiplexing is because:
   a. There is more time than frequency.
   b. It is difficult to place channels side by side.
   c. Noise is amplified with voice when an FDM system is used.
   d. Most available frequencies have been used.

3. When the amplitude of pulses is varied to represent analog information, the method is called:
   a. PCM.
   b. PWM.
   c. PAM.
   d. PPM.

4. The PCM sampling rate is 8000 samples per second because:
   a. That represents the maximum rate that technology supports.
   b. This rate allows unique values.
   c. This rate allows the faithful reconstruction of an analog signal.
   d. This rate is easily produced by a sampling chip.

5. In general, digital transmission provides a higher level of signal quality than analog transmission because:
   a. Repeaters regenerate digital pulses and remove distortion, whereas amplifiers increase an analog signal, including any prior distortion to the signal.
   b. Digital signals are smaller than analog signals and cannot be easily distorted.
   c. Analog signals are continuous and are not easily distorted.
   d. Digital signals are easier to sample than analog signals.

6. The D4 framing pattern contains a sequence of:
   a. 24 bits.
   b. 4 terminal and 8 framing bits.
   c. 8 terminal and 4 framing bits.
   d. 12 bits.

7. Bipolar signaling is used in place of unipolar signaling on T1 lines because:

    a. Bipolar signaling produces twice as many marks as a unipolar signal.

    b. It allows transmission at polar locations.

    c. Bipolar signaling reduces residual DC voltage buildup, allowing a digital signal to be separated from power through the use of a transformer.

    d. It allows transformers to be spaced far from one another, which reduces the cost of transmission.

8. B7 Zero Code Suppression is a technique that:

    a. Allows data to flow on a digital line.

    b. Ensures that each byte has at least one mark bit.

    c. Is the latest clear channel encoding technique developed by Bell Laboratories.

    d. Provides a clear channel transmission capability, allowing 64 Kbps data transmission on a voice channel.

9. Intentional bipolar violations:

    a. Represent coding errors caused by line impairments.

    b. Are used to convey information or maintain a minimum number of ones on a digital line.

    c. Result in successive marks having opposite polarities.

    d. Occur only in the laboratory.

10. Demultiplexing by a time division multiplexer occurs based on:

    a. The position of data within a frame.

    b. The position of a frame within a group of frames.

    c. The activity of a connected device.

    d. The priority assigned to a connected device.

11. The key to the operation of ADPCM is:

    a. Fast sampling.

    b. High amplitude.

    c. Adaptive predictor.

    d. Digitization.

12. The maximum modem operating rate that can be transported by ADPCM is:

    a. 300 bps.

    b. 1200 bps.

    c. 4800 bps.

    d. 9600 bps.

13. The higher the rate an analog signal is sampled:

    a. The smaller the difference between sampled amplitudes.

    b. The larger the difference between sampled amplitudes.

    c. The greater the noise level.

    d. The more bits required to represent the sample.

14. Common CVSD digitization rates are:

    a. 8 and 64 Kbps.

    b. 64 and 128 Kbps.

    c. 4 and 8 Kbps.

    d. 32 and 16 Kbps.

15. A voice/data multiplexer will not flow control:

    a. Voice.

    b. Data.

    c. Time slots.

    d. Odd channels.

Fiber-Optic and Satellite Communications

About This Chapter

This chapter is about transmission of data using light as a carrier. This chapter details some of the history of the development of this form of communications and explains why the technique has generated so much excitement in the communications world. We will discuss why fiber-optic systems work and will cover some of the terms used in describing their operation. Some current terrestrial and undersea fiber-optic systems will be described. We will discuss the application of fiber optics to local area data networks. Finally, we will look at some of the techniques and considerations in transmitting data via geostationary satellites.

Introduction and Historical Perspective

Alexander Graham Bell was a very curious and inventive man. In 1880, four years after the invention of the telephone, he patented an "apparatus for signaling and communicating, called Photophone." This device, illustrated in Figure 7.1, transmitted a voice signal over a distance of 2000 meters using a beam of sunlight as the carrier. As the speech into the speaking trumpet vibrated the mirror, the light energy that reflected onto the photovoltaic cell was varied. The electric current produced by the cell varied in accordance with the varying light energy.

FIGURE 7.1.

Alexander Graham Bell's Photophone.

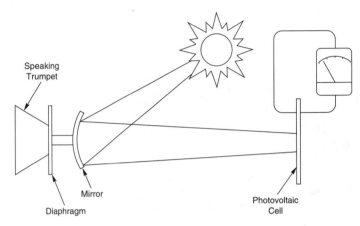

Demonstrates basic principles of optical transmission.

The device demonstrated the basic principle of optical communications as it is practiced today. The two requirements for commercial success, however, were almost a hundred years away. These requirements were a powerful and reliable light source and a reliable and low-cost medium for transmission.

The use of light as a commercially feasible communications system had to wait until the development of the laser as a powerful, reliable light source, and the clad glass fiber as an inexpensive, reliable medium.

In 1960, the laser was recognized as the long-sought light source, and systems were tried using both the atmosphere and beam waveguides as the transmission medium. The application of a glass fiber with a cladding was proposed in 1966, and by 1970, fibers with losses of only 20 decibels per kilometer (dB/km) were demonstrated. Since then, progress in the invention and application of fiber optics has been startling. Fibers with losses of less than 0.2 dB/km have been demonstrated in the laboratory (in 1979), as have systems that can transmit at data rates in excess of 400 million bits per second (Mbps) for distances in excess of 100 km without repeaters or amplifiers. Advances in fiber optics began to threaten to make satellite systems obsolete for some kinds of communications (point-to-point where large bandwidths are required, such as transoceanic telephone systems) only 15 years after the satellite systems were commercially employed as the communications systems of the future.

Optical-fiber transmission has come of age as a major innovation in telecommunications. Such systems offer extremely high bandwidth, freedom from external interference, immunity from interception by external means, and cheap raw materials (silicon, the most abundant material on earth).

Light rays are guided within the optical fiber by the phenomenon of light refraction. Refraction is the change in direction of light rays caused by the change in speed of propagation when they pass from one medium to another.

Fundamentals of Fiber-Optic Systems

Optical fibers guide light rays within the fiber material. They can do this because light rays bend or change direction when they pass from one medium to another. They bend because the speed of propagation of light in each medium is different. This phenomenon is called refraction. One common example of refraction occurs when you stand at the edge of a pool and look at an object at the bottom of the pool. Unless you are directly over the object, as shown in Figure 7.2a, it appears to be farther away than it really is, as indicated in Figure 7.2b. This effect occurs because the speed of the light rays from the object increases as the light rays pass from the water to the air. This causes them to bend, changing the angle at which you perceive the object.

FIGURE 7.2.

Bending of light rays.

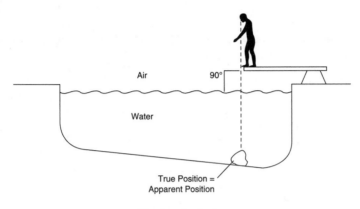

a. View from directly above

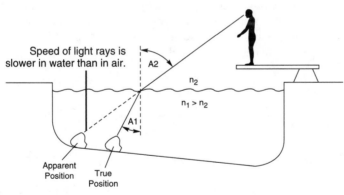

b. View from an angle

Snell's Law

How optical fibers work can be explained by Snell's Law, which states that the ratio of the sine of the angle of incidence to the sine of the angle of refraction is equal to the ratio of the propagation velocities of the wave in the two respective media. This is equal to a constant that is the ratio of the refractive index of the second medium to that of the first. Written as an equation, Snell's Law looks like this:

$$\frac{\sin A_1}{\sin A_2} = \frac{V_1}{V_2} = K = \frac{n_2}{n_1}$$

In this equation,

> A_1 and A_2 are the angles of incidence and refraction, respectively,
>
> V_1 and V_2 are the velocities of propagation of the wave in the two media, and
>
> n_1 and n_2 are the indices of refraction of the two media.

The parameters are demonstrated graphically in Figure 7.3. In each case, A_1 is the angle of incidence, and A_2 is the angle of refraction. The index of refraction of material 1, n_1, is greater than the index of refraction of material 2, n_2. This means that the velocity of propagation of light is greater in material 2 than in material 1.

FIGURE 7.3.

The index of refraction.

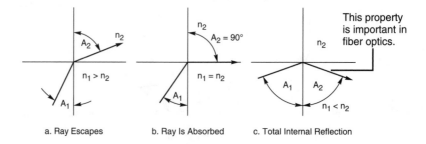

a. Ray Escapes   b. Ray Is Absorbed   c. Total Internal Reflection

●

Using Snell's Law, the light rays are totally contained within the fiber-optic material when the angle of incidence is greater than the critical angle.

Figure 7.3a demonstrates how a light ray passing from material 1 to material 2 is refracted in material 2 when A_1 is less than the critical angle. Figure 7.3b demonstrates the condition that exists when A_1 is at the critical angle and the angle A_2 is at 90 degrees. The light ray is directed along the boundary between the two materials.

As shown in Figure 7.3c, any light rays that are incident at angles greater than A_1 of Figure 7.3b will be reflected back into material 1 with angle A_2 equal to angle A_1. The condition in Figure 7.3c is the one of particular interest for optical fibers, and it is discussed further in later sections.

Fiber Composition

●

Optical fibers are constructed with three separate regions: the fiber core, the cladding around the core, and the protective outer sheath.

An optical fiber is a dielectric (nonconductor of electricity) waveguide made of glass or plastic. As shown in Figure 7.4, it consists of three distinct regions: a core, the cladding, and a sheath or jacket. The index of refraction of the assembly varies across the radius of the cable, with the core having a constant or smoothly varying index of refraction called n_c, and the cladding region having another constant index of refraction called n. The core possesses a high refractive index, whereas the cladding is constructed to have a lower refractive index. The result of the difference in the refractive indexes is to keep light flowing through the core after it gets into the core, even if the fiber is bent or tied into a knot. For a fiber designed to carry light in several modes of propagation (called a multimode fiber), the diameter of the core is several times the wavelength of the light to be carried. Wavelength is a measure of the distance between two cycles of the same wave measured in nanometers (nm) or billionths of a meter, and the cladding thickness will be greater than the radius of the core. Following are some typical values for a multimode fiber:

- An operating light wavelength of 0.8 micrometers (μm).
- A core index of refraction n_c of 1.5.
- A cladding index of refraction n of 1.485 (=0.99 × n_c).
- A core diameter of 50 μm.
- A cladding thickness of 37.5 μm.

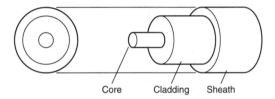

FIGURE 7.4.
Optical-fiber construction.

Core   Cladding   Sheath

The clad fiber would have a diameter of 125 μm, and light would propagate as shown in Figure 7.5.

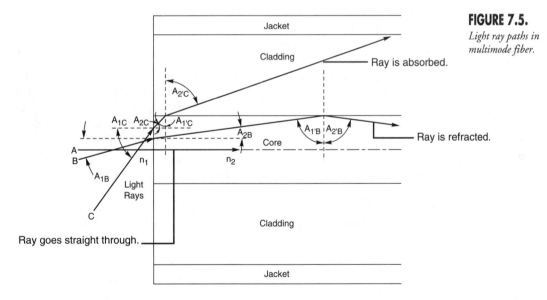

FIGURE 7.5.
Light ray paths in multimode fiber.

A light source emits light at many angles relative to the center of the fiber. In Figure 7.5, light ray A enters the fiber perpendicular to the face of the core and parallel to the axis. Its angle of incidence A_1 is zero; therefore, it is not refracted, and it travels parallel to the axis. Light ray B enters the fiber core from air (n_1 = 1) at an angle of incidence of A_{1B} and is refracted at an angle A_{2B} because n_2 is greater than n_1. When light ray B strikes the boundary between the core and the cladding, its angle of incidence, $A_{1'B}$, is greater than the critical angle. Therefore, the angle of refraction, $A_{2'B}$, is equal to $A_{1'B}$, and the light ray is refracted back into the core. The ray propagates in this zigzag fashion down the core until it reaches the other end.

The angle at which light rays enter an optical fiber determines how the rays will propagate in the fiber—parallel to the fiber axis, in a zigzag path, or not at all.

If the angle of incidence, A_{1C}, is too large, as it is for light ray C, the light ray strikes the boundary between the core and the cladding with an angle of incidence, $A_{1'C}$, less than the critical angle. The ray enters into the cladding and propagates in, or is absorbed in, the cladding and jacket (which is opaque to light).

Multimode and Single-Mode Propagation

• The angle at which light enters an optical fiber is called its mode of propagation. When a fiber carries more than one mode, it is a multimode fiber.

For optical fibers in which the diameter of the core is many times the wavelength of the light transmitted, the light beam travels along the fiber by bouncing back and forth at the interface between the core and the cladding. Rays entering the fiber at differing angles are refracted varying numbers of times as they move from one end to the other and consequently do not arrive at the distant end with the same phase relationship as when they started. The differing angles of entry are called modes of propagation (or just modes), and a fiber carrying several modes is called a multimode fiber. Multimode propagation causes the rays leaving the fiber to interfere both constructively and destructively as they leave the end of the fiber. This effect is called modal delay spreading.

Because most optical communications systems transmit information in digital form consisting of pulses of light, the effect of modal delay spreading limits the capability of the fiber to transport recognizable pulses. This is because modal delay spreading broadens the pulses in the time domain, as illustrated in Figure 7.6. The effect of pulse spreading is to make it difficult or impossible for an optical receiver to differentiate one pulse from another after a given transmission distance. Thus, after a predefined transmission distance, a multimode fiber either causes a very high error rate or precludes the capability of the pulse to be recognized and terminates the capability of the cable to be used for communications.

FIGURE 7.6.

Pulse spreading.

• Much of the power in a single-mode fiber, which does not have a core diameter large enough to transmit more than one mode, is propagated in the cladding.

If the diameter of the fiber core is only a few times the wavelength of the transmitted light (say a factor of 3), only one ray or mode will be propagated, and no destructive interference between rays will occur. These fibers, called single-mode fibers, are the media that are used in most transmission systems. Figures 7.7a and 7.7b show the distribution of the index of refraction across, and typical diameters of, multimode and single-mode fibers.

One of the principal differences between single-mode and multimode fibers is that most of the power in the multimode fiber travels in the core, whereas in single-mode fibers, a large fraction of the power is propagated in the cladding near the core. At the point where the light wavelength becomes long enough to cause single-mode propagation, about 20 percent of the power is carried in the cladding, but if the light wavelength is doubled, more than 50 percent of the power travels in the cladding.

a. Step Index, Multimode Fiber

FIGURE 7.7.

Refractive index profiles.

b. Step Index, Single-Mode Fiber

c. Graded Index, Multimode Fiber

Figure 7.7c shows the distribution of another kind of multimode fiber, called a graded-index fiber. The index of refraction varies smoothly across the diameter of the core but remains constant in the cladding. This treatment reduces the inter-modal dispersion by the fiber, because rays traveling along a graded-index fiber have nearly equal delays. Other refractive-index profiles have been devised to solve various problems, such as reduction of chromatic dispersion. Some of these profiles are shown in Figure 7.8; the step and graded profiles are repeated for comparison.

●
Graded-index multimode fibers have fairly equal propagation delays due to a reduction in inter-modal dispersion.

FIGURE 7.8.

Different refractive index profiles for optical fibers.

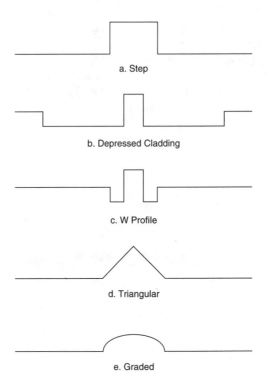

a. Step

b. Depressed Cladding

c. W Profile

d. Triangular

e. Graded

Bandwidth

Material dispersion is the spreading of pulses that occurs when the light source sends light through the optical fiber at more than one wavelength.

The limitations on bandwidth in fiber-optic systems arise from two main sources: modal delay spreading and material dispersion. Modal delay spreading, which was previously described, is evident primarily in multimode fibers. Material dispersion arises from the variation in the velocity of light through the fiber with the wavelength of the light.

If the light source, such as a light-emitting diode (LED), emits pulses of light at more than one wavelength, the different wavelengths travel at different velocities through the fiber. This causes spreading of the pulses. At a typical LED wavelength of 0.8 μm, the delay variation is about 100 picoseconds (ps) per nanometer (nm) per km. If the width of the spectrum emitted by the LED is 50 nm, pulses from the source are spread by 5 nanoseconds (ns) per km. This limits the modulation bandwidth product to about 50 to 100 MHz/km. Fortunately, at certain wavelengths (near 1.3 and 1.5 μm for some types of fibers), there is a null in the material dispersion curve, giving much better modulation bandwidth performance. Figure 7.9 shows the relationship of loss in doped silicon glass fibers versus light wavelength. Most current development work is aimed at making fibers, light sources, and detectors that work well at the loss nulls at 1.3 and 1.5 μm.

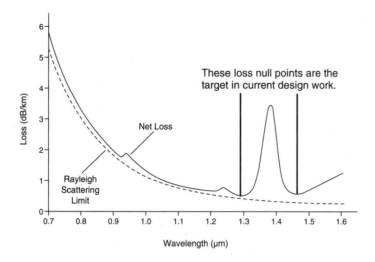

FIGURE 7.9.

The net spectral loss curve for a glass core.

Attenuation

The loss in signal power as the light travels down the fiber is called attenuation. Attenuation in the fibers is controlled mainly by four factors: radiation of the propagated light, called scattering; conversion of the light energy to heat, called absorption; connection losses at splices and joints in the fiber; and losses at bends in the fiber.

Scattering Losses

Scattering arises due to microscopic imperfections in the fiber, such as the inclusion of water in the glass. The effect of impurities in the transmission medium is evident when we look up at the sky and see a blue color. In fact, deep space has no color (appears as black), but due to the scattering of sunlight by the dust in the atmosphere, the sky appears bright blue.

● Signal power loss (attenuation) is a function of four factors: scattering, absorption, connections, and fiber bending.

● Scattering occurs because of microscopic imperfections in the fiber.

There is a limit below which scattering cannot be reduced, no matter how perfectly the glass fiber is made, because of irregularities in the molecular structure of glass. This limit, called the Rayleigh scattering limit, has a strong wavelength dependence ($1/\lambda^4$). Thus, as the wavelength of the light source increases, the effect of Rayleigh scattering on optical loss is reduced. This effect is shown graphically in Figure 7.9. For light with a wavelength of 0.8 µm, it is about 2.9 dB/km. At a wavelength of 1.3 µm, the value is about 0.3 dB/km, and at 1.55 µm wavelength, the limit is about 0.15 dB/km. Commercially available glass fibers exhibit losses of about 3.5 dB/km at 0.8 µm, and 0.7 to 1.5 dB/km at 1.3 and 1.5 µm. There is less attenuation through 6 meters (about 20 feet) of good quality optical-fiber glass than through an ordinary clean windowpane.

Absorption Losses

Opaque imperfections also cause signal power loss because when a light beam strikes them, some of the light's energy is converted into heat.

Absorption refers to the conversion of the power in the light beam to heat in some material or imperfection that is partially or completely opaque. This property is useful, as in the jacket of the fiber, to keep the light from escaping the cable, but it is a problem when it occurs as inclusions or imperfections in the fiber. Current fiber-optic systems are designed to minimize intrinsic absorption by transmitting at 0.8, 1.3, and 1.5 μm, where there are reductions in the absorption curve for light.

Connection Losses

A relatively large amount of signal power is lost at every connection point, particularly at repair splices.

Connection losses are inevitable. They represent a large source of loss in commercial fiber-optic systems. In addition to the installation connections, repair connections will be required because experience has shown that a typical line will be broken accidentally two or three times per kilometer over a 30-year period. The alignment of optical fibers required at each connection is a considerable mechanical feat. The full effect of the connection is not achieved unless the parts are aligned correctly. The ends of the fibers must be parallel to within one degree or less, and the core must be concentric with the cladding to within 0.5 μm. Production techniques have been developed to splice single-mode fibers whose total diameter is less than 10 μm by using a mounting fixture and small electric heater.

The heater is usually an electric arc that softens two butted fiber ends and allows the fibers to be fused together. Due to the cost of an electric arc and the time required to let the heated ends cool, other methods to connect broken fibers, such as mechanical splices and couplers, are more commonly used. Mechanical splicing is based on the use of a mechanical clamp to permanently splice together two fibers. This task is accomplished through the use of a portable workstation that is used to prepare each fiber end. That preparation includes stripping a thin layer of plastic coating from the fiber core before its splicing. The typical mechanical splice loss is approximately .15dB. In comparison, the use of a connector enables fibers to be glued to the device through a special epoxy after each fiber is stripped to its proper dimension. The connector provides a splice that joins the two fibers to enable light to pass from one fiber to the other. Although connector loss can range from .25 to 1.5dB, use of connectors is preferred for many labor-intensive applications because the process is relatively quick and can usually be accomplished in 30 minutes or less with a minimal amount of equipment.

Bending Losses

Bending the fibers also can cause signal loss because the light rays on the outside of a sharp bend cannot travel fast enough to keep up with the other rays, and they are lost.

Bending an optical fiber is akin to playing crack-the-whip with the light rays. As light travels around the bend, the light on the outside of the bend must travel faster to maintain a constant phase across the wave. As the radius of the bend is decreased, a point is reached where part of the wave would have to travel faster than the local speed of light—an obvious impossibility. At that point, the light is lost from the waveguide. For commercial single-mode fiber-optic cables operating at 1.3 and 1.5 μm, the bending occurring in fabrication (the cables are made with the fibers wound spirally around a center) and installation does not cause a noticeable increase in attenuation.

Numerical Aperture and Acceptance Angle

The numerical aperture of the optical fiber is a measure of its light-gathering capability (much like the maximum f-stop of a camera lens). The numerical aperture is defined as the maximum angle of incidence of a ray that is totally reflected at the core/cladding interface. Mathematically, the numerical aperture, NA, is expressed in this way:

$$NA = \sqrt{n^2_{core} - n^2_{cladding}}$$

The optical power accepted by the fiber varies as the square of the numerical aperture, but unlike the camera lens f-stop, the numerical aperture does not depend on any physical dimension of the optical fiber.

The acceptance angle is the maximum angle that an entering light ray can have relative to the axis of the fiber and still propagate down the fiber. A large acceptance angle makes the end alignment less critical when fibers are being spliced and connected.

> The numerical aperture is the measure of a fiber's capability to gather light. The acceptance angle is the largest angle at which a light ray can enter and still propagate down the fiber.

Fiber-Optic Subsystems and Components

Several components provide the foundation for the construction of fiber-optic systems and subsystems. Those components are discussed in the following five sections of this chapter.

Fiber Production

Optical fibers are fabricated in several ways, depending on the vendor and the purpose of the system. The core and cladding regions of the fiber are doped to alter their refractive indices. This doping is carried out by heating vapors of various substances such as germanium, phosphorus, and fluorine, and depositing the particles of resulting oxidized vapor or "soot" on high-quality fused-silica glass mandrels, called preforms. The preforms are a large-scale version of the core and cladding that is then heated to a taffy-like consistency and drawn down into the actual fiber. The core and cladding dimensions have essentially the same relationship in the final fiber as in the preform. Deposition of the dopants is done in one of three standard ways: outside, inside, and axial vapor deposition.

Light Sources

Light sources for fiber-optic systems must convert electrical energy from the computer or terminal circuits feeding them to optical energy (photons) in a way that allows the light to be coupled effectively to the fiber. Two such sources currently in production are the surface light-emitting diode (LED) and the injection laser diode (ILD).

Light-Emitting Diodes

To convert the electrical energy of a computer or terminal to light energy for use by an optical-fiber system, LEDs or ILDs are used.

FIGURE 7.10.

Construction of a light-emitting diode of 1.3 µm operation.

A cross section of a surface LED is shown in Figure 7.10. It emits light over a relatively broad spectrum, and it disperses the emitted light over a rather large angle. This causes the LED to couple much less power into a fiber with a given acceptance angle than does the ILD. Currently, LEDs are able to couple about 100 microwatts (µW) of power into a fiber with a numerical aperture of 0.2 or more with a coupling efficiency of about 2 percent. The principal advantages of LEDs are low cost and high reliability.

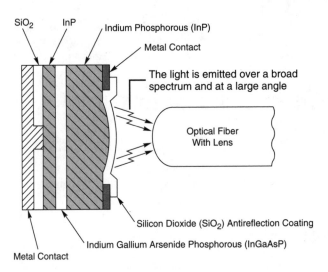

Injection Laser Diodes

A cross section of a typical ILD is shown in Figure 7.11. Because of its narrow spectrum of emission and its capability to couple output efficiently into the fiber lightguide, the ILD supplies power levels of 5 to 7 milliwatts (mW). At present, ILDs are considerably more expensive than LEDs, and their service life is generally less by a factor of about 10. Other disadvantages of laser diodes are that they must be supplied with automatic level control circuits, the laser power output must be controlled, and the device must be protected from power supply transients.

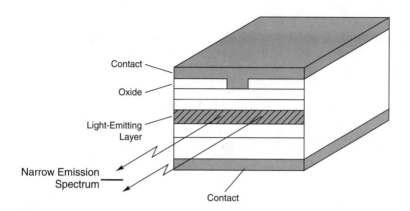

FIGURE 7.11.

Construction of an injection laser diode.

Light Detectors

At the receiving end of the optical communications system, the receiver must have very high sensitivity and low noise. To meet these requirements, there is a choice of two types of devices to detect the light beam, amplify it, and convert it back into an electrical signal: the integrated p-i-n field-effect transistor (FET) assembly and the avalanche photodiode (APD).

In the p-i-n FET device, a photodiode with unity gain (the p-i-n device) is coupled with a high-impedance front-end amplifier. This device combines operation at low voltage with low sensitivity to operating temperature, high reliability, and ease of manufacture.

The avalanche photodiode produces a gain of 100 or more; however, it also produces noise that might limit the receiver sensitivity. The APD devices require high voltage bias that varies with temperature. Receivers using APDs are so sensitive that they require as few as 200 phototons to be detected at the receiver per bit transmitted at data rates of 200 to 400 Mbps.

● Light detectors are used at the receiving end of the optical fiber to detect, amplify, and convert the light signal back into its original electrical form.

Wavelength Multiplexing

A combination of single-mode fiber (low dispersion by the transmission medium), narrow output spectrum (power concentration at a single frequency), and narrow dispersion angle (good power coupling) from ILDs makes possible the extreme bandwidth-distance characteristics given for systems at the beginning of this chapter. The narrow ILD emission spectrum also makes it possible to send several signals from different sources down the same fiber by a technique called wavelength multiplexing. The capability to multiplex several analog signals in the frequency domain has been described in detail in Chapter 6, "Multiplexing Techniques." As illustrated in Figure 7.12, wavelength multiplexing at optical frequencies is the equivalent of FDM at lower frequencies. Light at two or more

● Wavelength multiplexing, a technique similar to frequency division multiplexing, is used to send light signals from several sources down the same fiber.

discrete wavelengths is coupled into the fiber with each wavelength carrying a channel at whatever modulation rate is used by the transmission equipment driving the light source. Thus, the information capacity of each fiber is doubled or tripled.

FIGURE 7.12.

Wavelength multiplexing.

a. Frequency Division Multiplexing

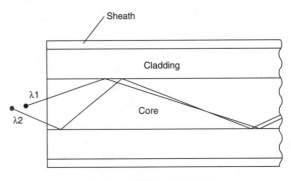

b. Wavelength Division Multiplexing

Transmission Systems

During the past decade, most carrier transmission systems have moved from the use of copper wire to optical fiber. In fact, by mid-1994, almost 100 percent of long-distance communications was carried over optical transmission systems.

Local and Intercity Systems—The FT3C System

Studies by AT&T of a digital lightwave transmission system indicated that it would cost less than traditional systems because of differences in terminal multiplexing equipment requirements and cost.

An AT&T study in 1978 noted a striking advantage of installing a digital transmission system over comparable analog systems: $900 per circuit termination when interconnecting multiple digital switching machines. The savings came from the difference in requirement for terminal multiplexing equipment. The AT&T FT3C lightwave system was devised to provide the most economical digital transmission system possible with the current state of the fiber-optic art. It used wavelength multiplexing techniques to send three 90 Mbps signals over the same fiber, giving more than 240,000 digital channels at 64,000 bps in a cable containing 144 optical fibers. The first application of the system was in the Northeast Corridor project by AT&T, between Boston and Washington, and in the North/South Lightwave Project on the West Coast of the United States by Pacific Telesis, between San Francisco and San Diego. Figure 7.13a is a map of the Northeast Corridor system, which contains 78,000 fiber-kilometers of lightwave circuits. Figure 7.13b is a map of the North/South Lightwave Project. The two systems were placed in service in 1983 and have been expanded considerably since then.

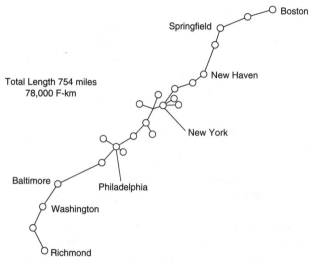

a. Fiber-Optic Network for Northeast Corridor

FIGURE 7.13.

Fiber-optic networks.

b. Pacific Telephone North/South Lightwave Project

The significant advantages associated with the use of fiber-optic transmission systems resulted in tens of thousands of miles of fiber being installed during the 1980s. By early 1991, U.S. Sprint had converted 100 percent of its intercity transmission facilities from microwave to fiber. A few years later, AT&T and MCI Communications completed the conversion of their systems to fiber.

SONET

● SONET is an optical standard that enables the fiber-optic transmission systems of interexchange carriers and telephone companies to be interoperable.

Advances in the use of fiber-optic transmission systems resulted in a requirement for standards to enable interoperability between interexchange carriers and telephone companies. In addition, a considerable growth in communications from companies and government agencies resulted in a requirement to define the interface of commercial communications equipment to an evolving optical network. The resulting standard, known as the Synchronous Optical Network (SONET), represents a transport vehicle capable of supporting data rates in the gigabit range, optical interfaces, network management, and diagnostic testing methods.

Until SONET standards were developed, there was a void in compatibility between fiber terminal equipment operating at rates above the DS3 transmission rate of 44.736 Mbps. That operating rate is formed by a communications carrier using a device known as an M13 multiplexer to combine 28 DS1 channels into a DS3 signal. The resulting DS3 signal is asynchronous because each DS1 signal is independently timed. Although each DS1 signal includes 8000 bits per second for framing, the resulting multiplexed DS3 signal includes three intermixed framing signals, which makes it almost impossible to locate an individual DS0 signal within the DS3 signal. Thus, to remove one PCM digitized voice signal in a carrier's DS3 transmission hierarchy typically required the carrier to first demultiplex the DS3 signal, requiring additional equipment and adding to the cost of the carrier's infrastructure. Recognizing this problem, the developers of the SONET standard developed a frame structure that enables lower-speed channels within a higher-speed signal to be easily removed from or added to the signal. This process is known as drop (removal of the signal on a channel) and insert (addition of a signal on a channel).

Figure 7.14 illustrates the SONET frame structure. As indicated, the basic SONET frame consists of nine rows of bytes with 90 bytes per row, with 8000 of these frames transmitted each second. This arrangement results in a composite data rate of 51.84 Mbps. Because 27 bytes of each 810-byte frame represent overhead, the payload of the basic SONET frame is limited to 50.112 Mbps, with 2.3 Mbps representing overhead. That overhead includes positioning information that enables a single DS0 channel to be identified and data easily extracted or inserted into the channel position.

This also means that a DS3 signal representing 28 DS1 signals can be carried within the basic SONET frame, and each of the 672 DS0 channels within the 28 DS1 signals can have data easily removed (dropped) or added (inserted).

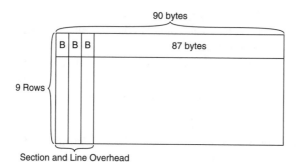

FIGURE 7.14.
The SONET frame structure.

The basic SONET frame illustrated in Figure 7.14 that occurs 8000 times per second is referred to as a Synchronous Transport Signal-Level 1, or STS-1. SONET is called synchronous because the frame is synchronized with respect to each input DS0 channel through the use of pointers in the 27 bytes of overhead per frame, which results in a synchronous multiplexing format. In addition to pointers, a significant portion of the overhead bytes in the STS-1 frame are reserved for management data, enabling network management functions to include loopback, bit error rate testing, and collection and reporting of performance statistics to be carried within the SONET frame.

The Optical Interface

One of the major elements included in the SONET standard is its set of defined optical interfaces. Until the development of SONET, each manufacturer designed its fiber terminal device to its own optical signal interface. This "do it yourself" approach precluded terminal devices from different vendors from being able to be interconnected to a common fiber backbone. Under SONET, 256 OC (optical carrier) optical interfaces are defined, although the current standard explicitly calls for the use of 8 interfaces. Those interfaces, listed in Table 7.1, define the SONET digital signal hierarchy. Note that the OC-1 level represents an STS-1 signal, whereas higher levels represent multiplexed STS-1 signals.

Table 7.1. The SONET signal hierarchy.

Level	Line Rate	DS3 Channels
OC-1	51.84 Mbps	1
OC-3	155.52 Mbps	3
OC-9	466.56 Mbps	9
OC-12	622.08 Mbps	12
OC-18	933.12 Mbps	18
OC-24	1.244 Gbps	24
OC-36	1.866 Gbps	36
OC-48	2.488 Gbps	48

Although SONET primarily represents a standard for optical interoperability among public network transmission providers, it also provides the capability for large organizations and government agencies to provide an STS-1 signal to the central office of a public network provider through the use of an optical multiplexer connected to a fiber routed from the customer premise to the carrier's central office. Figure 7.15 illustrates the use of an STS-1 signal to the public network. Note that due to the pointers imbedded into the SONET frame, the carrier can easily break out previously multiplexed signals originating at the customer's optical multiplexer without having to demultiplex and remultiplex the data stream as would be required when a DS3 signal is used. Eventually, SONET should reduce the cost of transmission for large network users as well as increase network reliability due to the use of fiber directly to the customer premises.

> The pointers within a SONET frame enable data to be directly added or removed from individual DS0 channels without first requiring the demultiplexing of the composite signal.

FIGURE 7.15.

Using SONET to connect public and private networks.

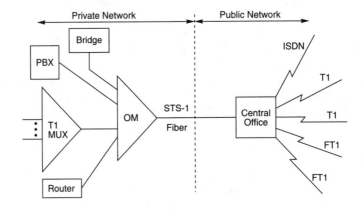

Legend OM optical multiplexer
PBX private branch exchange

International Systems—The SL Underwater Cable

> Undersea optical-fiber cables can provide a data communications channel with a carrying capacity equal to that of satellite systems, but with greater security, less interference, less noise, and lower cost.

The advent of optical-fiber technology for undersea cables provides point-to-point channel capacity equal to satellite systems at reduced cost and without long transmission delays, unstable environmental interference, induced noise, and broadcast of potentially sensitive information to half the world.

Undersea cable systems have some understandably difficult environmental requirements. The environment includes pressures of 10,000 pounds per square inch (psi) at depths of 7300 meters, salt water, and the possibility of mechanical damage from anchors and earth movement in shallow waters. An important requirement for these systems is that the regenerator spacing be as wide as possible to cut down on the system failure probability and the power requirements, because power must be fed from the ends of the cable.

A schematic of the SL Undersea Lightguide System is shown in Figure 7.16. It is composed of a high-voltage power supply, a supervisory terminal, a multiplexer with inputs for several types of information, the cable light source, the cable itself, and the repeaters. The cable is made of a central core and a surrounding support, as shown in Figure 7.17. The core has an outside diameter of 2.6 mm and consists of 12 optical fibers wound helically around a central copper-clad steel wire called a kingwire, all embedded in an elastomeric substance and covered with a nylon sheath. This assembly is in turn covered with steel strands, a continuously welded copper tube, and an insulation of low-density polyethylene for electrical insulation and abrasion resistance. The outside diameter of the completed cable is 21 mm (about 0.8 in.).

FIGURE 7.16.

The SL Undersea Lightguide System.

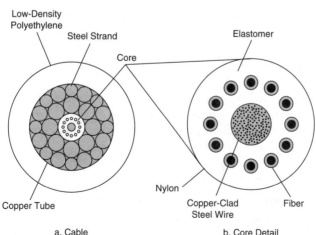

FIGURE 7.17.

Embedded fiber core cable.

The fibers are single-mode optical lightguides operating at 1.312 μm. The data rate on each fiber pair is 280 Mbps, and repeaters are spaced every 35 km. The total capacity of the system is more than 35,000 two-way voice channels. Inputs from binary data sources are multiplexed directly into the stream. Analog channels are first converted to binary by the adaptive delta modulation technique, then processed by a type of digital circuit (Digital TASI) that interleaves inputs from a number of input speech channels onto a smaller number of output channels. The light sources for the systems are ILDs operating near 1.3 μm with an average output power of 1 mW (0 dBm). Light detectors are indium-gallium-arsenide (InGaAs) p-i-n diode receivers followed by silicon bipolar transimpedance amplifiers. Three spare laser diodes, which can be switched in remotely if a failure occurs, are provided per circuit.

By the late 1980s, several fiber-optic undersea cables were laid across the Atlantic, linking New York to England, France, and Spain via light transmission. The successful operation of those systems resulted in communications carriers expanding their plans for fiber-optic undersea cables. During the early 1990s, several trans-Pacific and trans-Mediterranean fiber-optic cables were in the process of being installed. By the mid-1990s, most voice, data, and video transmissions between the United States and Europe, Japan, and Australia were routed via fiber-optic cable between continents.

As the use of fiber-optic cable has increased, a corresponding decrease has resulted in the use of satellites for voice transmission. The primary reason for the wide acceptance of fiber-optic cable over satellites is the immunity of the fiber-optic cable to electromagnetic interference as well as the elimination of one-half second or longer delays associated with the use of satellites due to the signal having to traverse a distance of more than 50,000 miles during transmission. Today, most satellites are used for television and data transmissions that are insensitive to transmission delays. However, a new series of low earth-orbiting satellites expected to be deployed during the late 1990s (described in the next section in this chapter) can be expected to significantly increase the use of satellites for voice communications. Those satellites are being designed to support a new class of mobile communications referred to as Personal Communications Service (PCS), which is also described later in this chapter.

Fiber to the Home

One of the most publicized terms in the field of communications is the so-called "digital highway." First promoted by Vice President Gore as a term to represent the interconnections of computer research centers via high-speed optical transmission, the term has been applied to all types of high-capacity communications to include fiber cables routed to the home.

By early 1994, several field tests of fiber to the home were being conducted in California and Florida. Each test was similar in that the large bandwidth capacity of an optical fiber enabled the simultaneous transmission of up to hundreds of television signals along with voice conversations and interactive data channels. Where each test differed was in the scope of interactivity offered to the home consumer and the ability of the consumer to request different functions interactively. Some tests enabled the consumer to order films to be displayed at a predefined time, a feature known as video-on-demand. Other tests primarily focused on providing consumers with online banking, grocery ordering, and catalog shopping. A new term used to define the provider of integrated voice, data, and video is multimedia, although the range of services offered by different multimedia vendors currently varies considerably from vendor to vendor.

HFC and Cable Modems

In addition to fiber-to-the-home trials being performed by both telephone and cable TV (CATV) operators, the cable TV industry has been busy upgrading a good portion of its infrastructure using a hybrid fiber coax (HFC) cable combination. Through the use of HFC between 500 and 3000, cable TV subscribers can be supported by one fiber main trunk node being connected to coax feeder and drop cables. In addition, the large bandwidth of the fiber trunk cable enables the CATV operator to support transmission in the return direction from subscribers in a large service area via the fiber trunk. Thus, an HFC infrastructure provides the opportunity for cable TV operators to provide telephone service, Internet access, and other services that require bidirectional transmission in an economical manner.

Figure 7.18 illustrates in schematic form a hybrid fiber coax network. Note that each main trunk consists of a fiber cable, and feeder and drop cables routed to the subscriber continue the use of coax. This method of cabling enables the CATV operator to increase considerably the capacity of the system in an economical manner, because the existing coaxial cable previously routed to subscribers remains in place.

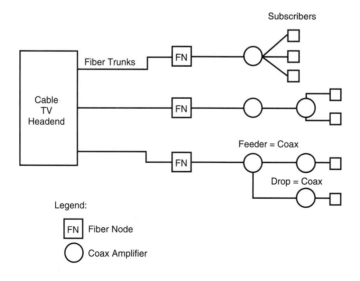

FIGURE 7.18.
A CATV hybrid fiber coax network.

To provide two-way services, existing unidirectional amplifiers in a cable TV system must be replaced by bidirectional amplifiers.

In examining Figure 7.18, note that to provide two-way services, CATV operators must upgrade their amplifiers to support bidirectional transmission. In addition, note that the cable TV headend represents the broadcast area where satellite video feeds are received and broadcast to subscribers. Although Figure 7.18 illustrates a hybrid fiber coax network bidirectional transmission necessary to support telephone service, note that interactive TV, Internet applications, and similar applications can be supported on conventional coaxial TV systems that were upgraded to support bidirectional transmission. The key difference between the two is that the use of fiber trunks significantly reduces the number of trunks that must be routed into neighborhoods, as well as provides immunity to noise and other transmission impairments resulting from electrical disturbances.

Evolving Application

The most prominent application evolving from the use of an HFC cabling infrastructure is high-speed Internet access via the use of a cable modem installed at the subscriber's premises. Although standards were in the process of being developed when this book revision was prepared, most modem vendors that announced cable modem products were basing their products on similar technology. That technology involves the use of 6 MHz cable TV channels for transmission and reception of data. Understanding how a cable modem works requires a short digression to obtain an overview of the bandwidth used in North American cable TV systems.

The forward and reverse channels standardized for use in North America differ in terms of both frequency bandwidth and data bandwidth. In North America the forward bandwidth, which references transmission from the headend to the subscriber, ranges from 50 to 550 MHz, with 6 MHz used for TV channels for "legacy" analog cable TV broadcasts. Most new plant upgrades now support an upper forward bandwidth of 750 MHz, permitting more than 110 TV channels. The reverse bandwidth from the subscriber to the headend ranges from 5 to 42 MHz. Unlike the forward bandwidth that is well-defined for 6 MHz subdivisions, the reverse bandwidth was not used until recently, and its subdivision has yet to be standardized.

The key difference between modems designed for use on the public switched telephone network and cable modems is in their use of bandwidth. A conventional modem designed for use on the switched telephone network is limited to using the bandwidth between 300 and 3300 Hz. In comparison, a cable modem must be tunable to operate on any available TV channels a CATV operator designates for its use. Those channels provide for forward and reverse transmission, and each provides considerably more bandwidth than the switched network, enabling data rates several orders of magnitude beyond those obtainable on the PSTN.

Most cable modems have a receiver tunable to the 50 to 750 MHz range in 6 MHz increments, enabling the modem to use a full TV channel for data reception. Through the use of 64- or 256-point Quadrature Amplitude Modulation (QAM) using a majority of the bandwidth of the TV channel, a data rate up to 43 Mbps can be supported. In the return direction, there is a considerable difference in the operation of cable modems, with some modem transmitters using a 2 MHz bandwidth in the 5 to 42 MHz spectrum to provide a 3 Mbps data rate, whereas other modems use a fraction of a MHz to a full 6 MHz of that spectrum to provide return rates from 600 Kbps to 10 Mbps.

Figure 7.19 illustrates the Hewlett-Packard QuickBurst cable modem. This modem's receiver uses 64 QAM to provide a forward data rate of 30 Mbps on a 6 MHz TV channel between the 88 and 806 MHz frequency spectrum. In the reverse direction, the modem uses Quadrature Phase Shift Keying (QPSK) modulation to provide a 3 Mbps data rate using a 2 MHz channel in the 10 to 32 MHz frequency spectrum.

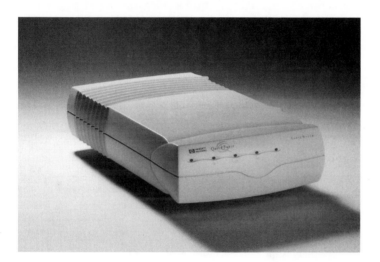

FIGURE 7.19.

The Hewlett-Packard QuickBurst cable modem. (Courtesy of Hewlett-Packard)

Today, the home multimedia effort is in its infancy, probably equivalent to where the personal computer industry was during the 1970s. Although it's difficult to predict the outcome of current field trials as well as the range of services that will be offered to consumers, one thing is certain: Regardless of the resulting suite of services offered to the consumer under the labels "video-on-demand," "multimedia," or another term, those services will be transported through the use of fiber-optic cable to the home, either directly or via the use of hybrid fiber coax systems.

Satellite Transmission Systems

Satellite transmission systems provide users with the ability to bypass conventional communications carrier offices, as well as to broadcast information to multiple locations for a nominal cost.

Basic Satellite Technology

Broad focus of the downlink signal and propagation delay caused by the great distance between earth and satellite can present problems in two-way satellite communications.

Satellite communications systems are basically line-of-sight microwave systems with a single repeater. As stated in Chapter 3, "Messages and Transmission Channels," the satellite is said to be in geostationary orbit. It is called a geostationary satellite because the speed of the satellite is matched to the rotation of the earth at the equator. Because of the great distance of the satellite from the earth (about 22,300 miles) and antenna size limitations that limit focusing capability, the cone of coverage for a single satellite transmitter can be as large as the entire continental United States.

For those transmission services that originate at a single point and flow to many points in one direction, such as television and radio signals, the large area of coverage is ideal. The relatively long delay between the instant a signal is sent and when it returns to earth (about 240 milliseconds [ms]) has no undesirable effect when the signal is going only one way. However, for signals such as data communications sessions and telephone conversations, which go in both directions and are intended to be received at only one other point, the large area of coverage and the delay can cause problems.

Data and telephone conversations usually proceed as a series of messages in one direction that are answered or acknowledged by messages in the other direction. When the delay between the message being sent and the reply or acknowledgment is long, the transmission rate of information slows down. In the case of voice messages, long delays between utterance and reply make the speaker think he or she has not been heard or understood. This leads to requests for repeating (the equivalent of negative acknowledgment in the data world) and increased frustration. There is also a serious privacy issue with communications that are intended for only one destination but are broadcast so that an entire continent can receive them. One of the factors causing the rush to all-digital transmission is the ease of encrypting information in digital form so that when the inevitable interception of broadcast signals occurs, the information intercepted is at least somewhat difficult to decipher.

The main components of a satellite system are the earth sending and receiving stations and a geosynchronous satellite equipped with transponders.

A satellite transmission system consists of one or more earth stations and a geostationary satellite that can be seen by the stations. Figure 7.20 illustrates the Americatel "teleport" consisting of three large-diameter satellite dishes located in Miami, Florida, that represent earthstations. Americatel is a regional telecommunications carrier that provides voice, data, and facsimile services via a gateway and switching center in Miami to common carriers and private organizations throughout Central and South America. In Central and South America, many subscribers to Americatel use Very Small Aperture Terminals (VSATs) to communicate with North America, bypassing the necessity to use terrestrial lines. Through the use of VSAT facilities in remote areas, such as mining locations, users can receive a modern communications capability that was previously restricted to major metropolitan locations. To facilitate satellite communications, as well as to eliminate interference between transmission and reception, standards govern the use of satellite frequencies. Separate frequencies are assigned for sending to the satellite (the uplink) and receiving from the satellite (the downlink). The current frequency assignments for satellite systems are shown in Table 7.2.

FIGURE 7.20.

Americatel's U.S. teleport consists of three large-diameter satellite dishes. (Courtesy of Americatel Corporation)

Table 7.2. Frequency assignments for satellite systems.

Uplink Frequencies	Downlink Frequencies
5.925–6.425 GHz	3.700–4.200 GHz
7.900–8.400 GHz	7.250–7.750 GHz
14.00–14.50 GHz	11.70–12.20 GHz
27.50–30.00 GHz	17.70–20.20 GHz

Satellites are equipped with multiple repeater units called transponders. Many systems have 10 or 12 transponders, but a new series of international satellites, called INTELSAT VI, has 46 transponders. Transponders are assigned different uses, but in the case of those used for voice or voice-equivalent data communications channels (nominal 4 KHz bandwidth), the transponder capacity can be as large as 3000 channels.

The INTELSAT VI satellite provides a total bandwidth, using frequency reuse techniques, of 3460 MHz.

Multiple Access Systems

Telephone switching systems and data multiplexers are designed based on the fact that not every telephone or terminal that can send information will do so at the same time; or alternatively, the telephone or terminal user does not need or want to pay for the entire capacity of a channel. These conditions are also true for the users of satellite systems. Several methods have been devised to allow sharing of the satellite and earth station resources among several users so that it appears that the transmission channel is dedicated to each user.

Frequency Division Multiple Access

Frequency Division Multiple Access (FDMA) is simply another example of the familiar data and voice transmission technique called frequency division multiplexing (FDM). This technique is used to allocate small portions of a large bandwidth (500 MHz for satellite transponders) to individual users. For instance, a telecommunications common carrier in a particular country, say Brazil, might want 132 voice-grade channels for sending voice- and analog-coded data to various other countries. The bandwidth required on the current international satellite systems for this many channels is 10 MHz. Because one transponder has a bandwidth of 500 MHz, it could accommodate 50 users, each requiring 132 channels. The Brazilian user might be allocated the frequency band between 5990 and 6000 MHz for the uplink to the satellite, and the corresponding downlink frequencies would be 3765 to 3775 MHz. Other users might be assigned similar portions of the bandwidth in the same transponder. For example, a Portuguese user might be allocated the 6220 to 6230 MHz uplink band and the 3995 to 4005 MHz downlink band. A Canadian user might operate on the 5930 to 5940 MHz uplink band and the 3705 to 3715 MHz downlink band. Figure 7.21 illustrates how the three users each have one uplink, all into a single transponder, but all users can receive all three downlinks. This arrangement makes possible simultaneous two-way transmissions between any of the three sites using only a part of one satellite transponder.

FIGURE 7.21.

Multiuser satellite system.

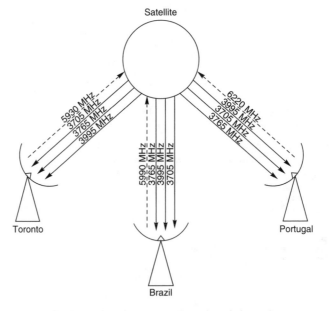

Each user has a permanently assigned channel.

Time Division Multiple Access

Time Division Multiple Access (TDMA) is the equivalent of FDMA, but in the time domain rather than the frequency domain. TDMA works just like time division multiplexing (TDM) for land-based data and voice transmissions, with each satellite transponder having a data rate capacity of between 10 and 100 Mbps. While a station is sending on the uplink, it has available the entire data rate capacity of the transponder, but then it must stop sending for a short time to allow another station access to the transponder. The information flows to the satellite in frames, each frame containing one burst of information from each earth station allowed access to the single transponder. A typical format for a frame is shown in Figure 7.22. The sum of the durations of the individual bursts do not quite equal the frame time in order to give some guard time between bursts.

●
In TDMA, access to a satellite transponder is divided into discrete time frames.

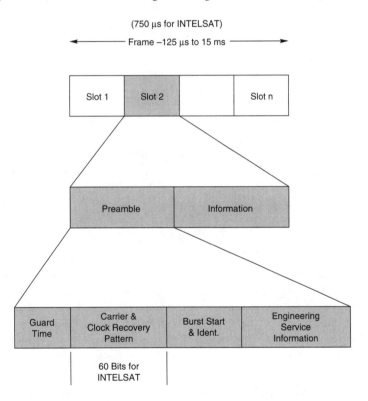

FIGURE 7.22.

TDMA transmission frames.

Timing for keeping the station bursts apart is a major problem, and it is complicated by two facts. First, the satellites are not perfectly stationary in orbit (each appears to travel in a small figure-eight pattern). Also, the times of travel of the signal between different earth stations and the same satellite are different because of different slant range distances. TDMA techniques allow the satellite transmitter to be operated at higher power levels than FDMA. This method is permissible because only one carrier at a time occupies the transponder, reducing the amount of intermodulation distortion generated.

Demand Assignment Multiple Access

DAMA is similar to FDMA except that channels are not assigned permanently.

Using the Demand Assignment Multiple Access (DAMA) technique, each satellite transponder is used much like a telephone switch; that is, a subchannel is assigned only when traffic is available to be carried on it. This is in contrast to the FDMA and TDMA techniques described previously, in which channels are assigned to users permanently, even if there is no traffic demand. DAMA is a variant of FDMA in that a part or all of the transponder is divided into individual channels that can be accessed by all DAMA terminals on the ground that are serviced by the DAMA transponder. A central computer system, or a system of distributed and cooperating computers, on the ground keeps tracks of who gets which channel when. DAMA is particularly useful for loading transponders efficiently when each of several ground sites needs only a few channels.

Personal Communication Services

During the 1970s and 1980s, satellite communications were often thought of as the data communications technology of the future. In fact, many authors wrote about the use of satellite technology eventually replacing the use of most terrestrial communications. This conversion did not occur primarily due to the delays associated with transmitting a signal more than 25,000 miles into the atmosphere and then having that signal retransmitted back to earth. The delay time associated with the use of satellites significantly affects their use for data transfer when data blocks have to be periodically acknowledged. Due to the minimal effect on voice conversations, the use of satellites has taken on a new role as a mechanism for personal communication services.

The key difference between the evolving personal communications system and existing cellular telephones is in their method of communications. A cellular telephone user communicates with a cell site connected via terrestrial lines to the public switched telephone network. In comparison, although initial PCS offerings provide cellular-like voice services using different frequencies to transmit to cell stations, ground users will within a few years be able to communicate directly to and through low earth-orbiting satellites.

Within the next few years, several companies are expected to develop satellite systems consisting of 12 to 60 or more non-geostationary low and middle earth-orbiting satellites that will provide either continental or near-global communications coverage. Such systems are being developed to support a new type of wireless telephone service that will transmit in the L and Ka-band frequency spectrums and support high-quality voice service as well as facsimile and paging signal transmission.

One of the first satellite-based personal communications services scheduled for operation is the Iridium system from Iridium, Inc. This firm represents a consortium of telecommunication operators and industrial companies originally sponsored by Motorola, Inc., which still has a minority interest in this venture. The first Iridium satellite is scheduled for launch in 1996, and initial service is anticipated to commence in 1998.

The Iridium satellite network is planned to consist of 66 satellites in six orbital planes approximately 480 miles above the earth. Communications to Iridium satellites will be via special Iridium mobile telephones and via conventional telephone systems through the use of satellite earth station gateways that will convert terrestrial signals to the Ka-band for transmission to an Iridium satellite. In addition to Iridium, other major communications firms have announced potentially competitive satellite-based personal communications services. Services announced during 1993 and 1994 for operation later in the decade include TRW's Odyssey and the Loral and Qualcomm's Globalstar satellite-based systems.

What Have You Learned?

1. Light traveling in an optical fiber obeys Snell's Law.
2. Light can travel in a multimode optical fiber along several paths, or in a single-mode fiber along only one path.
3. The index of refraction of the glass making up an optical fiber varies across the diameter of the fiber, with the highest index in the middle of the fiber.
4. Fiber-optic system bandwidth is limited by modal delay spreading and material dispersion.
5. Fiber-optic system transmission distance is limited by scattering, absorption, losses at connections, and losses at bends in the cable.
6. Fibers with varying indices of refraction across the fiber are made by heating a preform that has been doped with metal salts such as germanium and phosphorus and drawing it down to a small diameter.
7. Transmitters for fiber-optic systems are light-emitting diodes or semi-conductor injection lasers.
8. Receivers in fiber-optic systems are avalanche photodiodes or integrated p-i-n field-effect transistors.
9. SONET provides a set of standards that enables the fiber-optic transmission systems of interexchange carriers and telephone companies to be interoperable.
10. New services to the home consumer under such terms as video-on-demand and multimedia can be expected to be based on the use of fiber to the home.
11. Satellite transmissions have four uplink bands and four downlink bands.
12. TDMA techniques allow the satellite transmitter to be operated at higher power levels than FDMA.

Quiz for Chapter 7

1. The requirements for a successful transmission system using light are:

    a. Powerful, reliable light source.

    b. Strong glass.

    c. Reliable, low-cost transmission medium.

    d. Powerful amplifiers.

2. The core of an optical fiber has:

    a. A lower index of refraction than air.

    b. A lower index of refraction than the cladding.

    c. A higher index of refraction than the cladding.

    d. None of the above.

3. For single-mode fibers, the core diameter is about:

    a. 10 times the fiber radius.

    b. 3 times the wavelength of the light carried in the fiber.

    c. 15 micrometers.

    d. 10 times the wavelength of the light carried in the fiber.

4. Over a period of 30 years, a kilometer of fiber-optic cable is likely to be broken:

    a. Not at all.

    b. Once.

    c. 10 times.

    d. 2 or 3 times.

5. Deposition of dopants on fiber preforms is done by:

    a. Outside vapor deposition.

    b. Axial vapor deposition.

    c. Inside vapor deposition.

    d. All the above.

6. A light-emitting diode can couple how much power into an optical fiber?

    a. 10 watts.

    b. 10 milliwatts.

    c. 100 microwatts.

    d. 1 picowatt.

7. Avalanche photodiode receivers can detect bits of transmitted data by receiving:

    a. 1 photon.

    b. 10 photons.

    c. 100 photons.

    d. 200 photons.

8. One unsolved problem with satellite systems is:

    a. Coverage.

    b. Privacy.

    c. Bandwidth.

    d. Access.

9. The AT&T FT3C fiber-optic transmission system is designed to use how many light wavelengths?

    a. 1.

    b. 2.

    c. 3.

    d. 10.

10. The SL Undersea Lightguide system can carry how many two-way voice channels?

    a. 10,000.

    b. 100,000.

    c. 35,000.

    d. 760.

11. When the index of refraction is greater in Material 1 than it is in Material 2, the velocity of propagation in Material 1 compared to Material 2 is:

    a. Equal or greater.

    b. Greater.

    c. Lesser.

    d. Equal.

12. The different angles of entry of light into an optical fiber in which the diameter of the core is many times the wavelength of the light transmitted are called:

    a. Emitters.

    b. Modes.

    c. Sensors.

    d. Refractors.

13. In single-mode fibers, a large fraction of the power is propagated in the:

    a. Sheath.

    b. Core.

    c. Cladding.

    d. Air.

14. The loss in signal power as light travels down a fiber is called:

    a. Propagation.

    b. Scattering.

    c. Absorption.

    d. Attenuation.

15. The coupling efficiency of an LED light source to an optical fiber with a numerical aperture of 0.2 or more is:

    a. 60 percent.

    b. 10 percent.

    c. 2 percent.

    d. 0.1 percent.

16. The FT3C lightwave system contains the following number of fibers:

    a. 12.

    b. 144.

    c. 128.

    d. 64.

17. A key advantage of SONET is its capability to enable:

    a. Data to be carried at high operating rates.

    b. The interoperability of optical transmission between interexchange carriers and telephone companies.

    c. Routing of data to the home.

    d. Interconnection of private networks.

18. The number of bytes of overhead in a SONET frame is:

    a. 90.

    b. 9.

    c. 27.

    d. 87.

19. The number of OC-1 signals within a SONET OC-3 signal is:

    a. 3.

    b. 6.

    c. 9.

    d. 12.

20. The key difference between modems designed for use on the public switched telephone network and cable modems is in their use of:

    a. Wires.

    b. Cable.

    c. Bandwidth.

    d. Modulation.

21. A geostationary satellite used for communications systems:

    a. Is stationary in the sky.

    b. Rotates with the earth.

    c. Is positioned over the equator.

    d. Remains stationary relative to the earth's surface.

    e. a and c.

    f. b, c, and d.

22. Multiple repeaters in communications satellites are known as:

    a. Transponders.

    b. Detectors.

    c. Modulators.

    d. Stations.

23. In the current frequency assignments, how many frequency bands are there for the uplink frequencies?

    a. 16.

    b. 8.

    c. 4.

    d. 2.

24. The bandwidth required to send 132 voice-grade channels by FDM on an international satellite system is:

    a. 500 MHz.

    b. 10 MHz.

    c. 1320 MHz.

    d. 50 MHz.

25. The capability to provide consumers with video-on-demand:

    a. Will occur by the year 2000.

    b. Depends on the results of field trials.

    c. Is based on fiber to the home.

    d. Is based on the use of satellites.

Protocols and Error Control

About This Chapter

This chapter is about the rules that data communications systems use when communicating with each other, the ways in which systems discover that an error has been made in transmission, and some methods used in correcting those errors. Because there are many data transmission schemes in use (for example, asynchronous and synchronous, half- and full-duplex), many sets of rules, called protocols, and many error detection and correction schemes have been devised. The most common of these techniques are explained in this chapter.

Protocols and Interfaces

Protocols are agreements between people or processes (usually nowadays the processors are computer programs) about which of them can do what to whom, and when. A protocol is different from an interface. An interface is a set of rules, often embodied in pieces of hardware, controlling the interaction of two different machines or processes, such as a computer and a modem. A protocol, on the other hand, is a set of rules defining the interactions between two machines or processes that are alike or that have similar functions. The difference is illustrated in Figure 8.1. House A and House B look alike but are occupied by a curious set of people. The British engineer on the top floor of house A needs to communicate with another engineer, also British, on the top floor of B. The only telephone, however, is guarded by a Swedish businessman on the bottom floor of each house. The engineer speaks no Swedish, and the businessman no English.

FIGURE 8.1.

Protocols and interfaces.

● A protocol is a set of rules defining the interactions between two machines or processes that are alike or that have similar functions. An interface is a set of rules controlling the interaction of two different machines or processes.

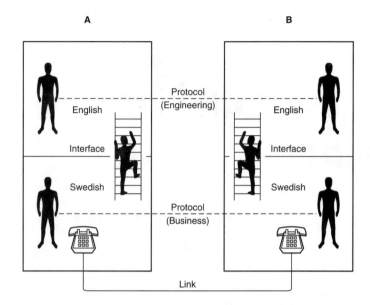

● Protocols for machine communication function much like the formats and rules for human conversations, and they are used for the same reasons.

The two engineers, like most people who talk on the telephone, have a routine, worked out over many years, for communicating. The one answering says, "Hullo." The one calling says, "Hullo, this is Reggie." Then the first says, "Oh, hullo, Reggie. How are you, old boy?" This is called a preamble. The men then begin discussing Wimbledon, the weather, and even some business. At the end of most sentences, the one being questioned makes a reply, even if it is only a sound rather than a word or sentence. If one party does not hear some sort of reply from the other at fairly short intervals, he might say, "I say, are you still there?" If he still receives no reply, he might terminate the conversation and begin the whole process over. If one party does not understand the other, he says, "What?" and the second party repeats the last sentence. When the conversation is over, the person terminating the call says, "Well, good-bye for now." The called party replies, "Good-bye," and both hang up. The Swedish businessman has a similar technique for conversing with his counterpart. All of these conventional conversational actions make up a protocol. As we will see in the remainder of this chapter, protocols developed for communicating between processes in computers have all the same mechanisms as those used between humans, for exactly the same reasons.

Even though our two engineers can communicate reliably with each other because they have a communications protocol, they still have the problem of having no direct access to the communications channel, which is jealously guarded by the large Swedish businessman. The solution is an interface. The engineers engage a person who stands midway up the stairs and who speaks both engineering English and business Swedish. The engineer in house A speaks in English to the person halfway up the stairs, who relays the conversation in Swedish to the businessman, who relays it over the telephone to his Swedish counterpart in house B, who relays it in Swedish to another person on the stairs, who finally conveys the messages in English to the called party.

This seems like a clumsy and inefficient procedure, and in many respects it is. But it is the same procedure used in millions of data communications systems to enable an applications program, communicating in one set of symbols (perhaps ASCII) and at one rate of symbol production, to communicate through a teleprocessing monitor, using another set of symbols (perhaps EBCDIC) at a vastly different rate, to a line interface program dealing with yet a third set of symbols (bits). The story of standard interfaces is told in Chapter 4, "Asynchronous Modems and Interfaces." The story in this chapter is about protocols.

Elements of a Protocol

The basic elements of a communications protocol are a set of symbols, called a character set, a set of rules for the sequence and timing of messages constructed from the character set, and procedures for determining when an error has occurred in the transmission and how to correct the error. The character set consists of a subset that is meaningful to people (usually called printing characters) and another subset that conveys control information (usually called control characters). There is a correspondence between each character and a group of symbols on the transmission channel. For instance, the printing character A might correspond to the binary code 1000001. Several standard codes with equivalent sets of ones and zeros (bits), such as the ASCII discussed in previous chapters, have been defined over the years. The set of rules to be followed by the sender and receiver gives the meaning, permissible sequences, and time relationships of the control characters and messages formed from the symbols. The error detection and correction procedure allows for the detection of and orderly recovery from errors caused by factors outside the control of the terminal at either end.

● A protocol has three main elements: a character set, a set of rules for message timing and sequence, and error determination and correction procedures.

Teletypewriter and XMODEM Protocols

The simplest protocols in general use are those associated with the transmission of start-stop or asynchronous data that were originally developed for communications between teleprinter machines. For a long period after the development of the teleprinter, the machines were electromechanically controlled, and protocols had to be appropriate to a very simple mechanical controller in each machine. One of the first teletypewriter (TTY) protocols used a character set containing 58 symbols: 50 printing characters, a space, and seven control characters, as shown in Figure 8.2. These symbols were encoded into a five-bit binary code as shown (the octal representation is shown only for readers familiar with octal).

● TTY protocols are the simplest ones in general use. The 58 characters in the character set of one TTY protocol were encoded by a five-bit binary code.

FIGURE 8.2.

CCITT alphabet No. 2.

Binary	Octal	LTRS	FIGS
0 0 0 0 0	00	BLANK	BLANK
0 0 0 0 1	01	E	3
0 0 0 1 0	02	LF	LF
0 0 0 1 1	03	A	–
0 0 1 0 0	04	Space	Space
0 0 1 0 1	05	S	'
0 0 1 1 0	06	I	8
0 0 1 1 1	07	U	7
0 1 0 0 0	10	CR	CR
0 1 0 0 1	11	D	WRU
0 1 0 1 0	12	R	4
0 1 0 1 1	13	J	BELL
0 1 1 0 0	14	N	,
0 1 1 0 1	15	F	
0 1 1 1 0	16	C	:
0 1 1 1 1	17	K	(
1 0 0 0 0	20	T	5
1 0 0 0 1	21	Z	+
1 0 0 1 0	22	L	)
1 0 0 1 1	23	W	2
1 0 1 0 0	24	H	
1 0 1 0 1	25	Y	6
1 0 1 1 0	26	P	0
1 0 1 1 1	27	Q	1
1 1 0 0 0	30	O	9
1 1 0 0 1	31	B	?
1 1 0 1 0	32	G	
1 1 0 1 1	33	FIGS	FIGS
1 1 1 0 0	34	M	.
1 1 1 0 1	35	X	/
1 1 1 1 0	36	V	=
1 1 1 1 1	37	LTRS	LTRS

The printing characters are the uppercase letters, the numbers, and 14 punctuation marks. Three control characters allow for carriage return (CR), line feed (LF), and ringing the terminal bell (BELL) to announce a message. Also provided are a NULL (or blank) character (which is not the same as a space) and a WRU character. WRU, which stands for "Who Are You," causes a mechanical device in the teleprinter to send a character sequence identifying that particular terminal. The other two control characters are the FIGS character, which causes the machine to print numbers and punctuation, and the LTRS character, which causes the machine to print the uppercase alphabet. As mentioned in Chapter 1, "An Overview of Data Communications," this character set and associated binary code is commonly referred to as the Baudot code, after Emile Baudot, who invented the first code with symbols of a fixed length.

The protocol for operation of a message system using the Baudot code goes something like this (the procedure varies somewhat according to the operator of the system):

1. A communications channel is connected between the two machines. This might be a temporary dialed connection or a permanent private line.

2. The sending machine sends a WRU, to verify that the receiving machine is the proper one for the message to be sent.

3. The sending machine sends a "Here is…," which is normally the same sequence of characters that is sent when it receives a WRU, to identify the sender.

4. The sending machine sends a preamble or message header that identifies the name and address of the intended message recipient, the date and time entry of the message into the system, the date and time of transmission, and the message sequence number assigned by the sender. In some systems, the sender uses two sequence numbers: one to count the number of messages sent by the sender that day, and the other to count the number of messages sent to the receiver's terminal that day.

5. At the end of the message, the sending machine sends another "Here is…" and another WRU. The second WRU is to determine whether the receiving machine is still connected to the line. If the message is being sent manually, the operator of the sending machine sometimes sends several BELL characters to alert a person at the receiving end that a message is ready for delivery.

This protocol has developed over many years of sending messages manually between individual terminals operated by people. You will note that it has all the elements described in the opening paragraphs: a previously defined set of symbols and corresponding codes suitable for electronic transmission, a preamble, a message, and even a rudimentary error detection procedure (the invocation of the WRU at the beginning and end of the session).

The simple teletypewriter protocol described does not work very well in the presence of even fairly low error rates on the path between the machines. Individual characters can be mutilated in such a way as to cause the receiving machine to begin printing gibberish, and the transmitter will never know. The WRU check at the end of a message ensures only that the receiving machine received the WRU correctly and that the circuit is still good in the backward direction. The WRU check says nothing about whether the message got through. To provide better assurance of correct transmission, two more techniques are sometimes used for simple protocols: character parity and echoplex.

> ●
> Because the simple TTY protocol does not check for errors in the message, even low error rates cause the received message to be gibberish, and the sender does not know of the problem.

Parity

This is the Communicator's Creed: "Now abideth faith, hope, and parity, but the greatest of these is parity."

The addition by the transmitter of another bit to the bits that encode a symbol for the purpose of error detection is called parity. The bit is always transmitted, and it is usually set to the value that will cause the coded symbol to have an even number of 1 bits; thus, the scheme is called even parity. The parity bit is recomputed by the receiver. If the newly computed value gives the correct parity, all is well. If not, some indication is given to the receiving terminal, usually by substituting a special error character for the one received.

For an example of parity checking, consider the ASCII character *M*, which has a bit composition of 1001101. Because the character has four 1 bits, a 1 bit is added if odd parity checking is used, whereas a 0 bit is used if even parity checking is employed. Figure 8.3 illustrates the formation of the parity bit for odd and even parity checking for the ASCII character *M*.

Parity is the technique in which a bit is added to every symbol for the purpose of error detection. It can be either even or odd parity.

FIGURE 8.3.

Parity bit formation for the ASCII character M.

```
            P
            A
 | Data  |  R
 |← Bits→|  I
 1001101   T
            Y

            B
            I
            T

 1001101  1   Odd Parity Check
 1001101  0   Even Parity Check
```

The parity scheme detects single-bit errors in the transmitted symbols, but it might not detect multiple bit errors. The capability of the scheme to detect multiple bit errors is dependent on the location in the character where the bit errors occur and the composition of bit settings in the character. For example, assume that noise on the transmission line causes the values of the first two bits of the ASCII character *M* to be inverted, resulting in the bit composition of the character becoming 0101101. In this situation, the number of set bits remains the same, which precludes parity being used to detect the transmission error. Now assume that transmission noise adversely affects the second through fourth bits, changing the composition of the character *M* to 110101. Note that five bits are now set, which enables parity to detect the error. Thus, parity might or might not be able to detect multiple bit errors. Error correction can occur by the receiver sending a message back that requests retransmission.

Echoplex is an error detection technique in which each character of a message is retransmitted by the receiver to the originator as it is received.

Echoplex

Echoplex is perhaps not properly classed as an element of protocols, but I will discuss it here anyway. It is the technique of sending back (or echoing) each character by the receiver as the characters are received. The sender can then see by the copy printed locally whether the characters are making the round trip without being mutilated. When an echoed character is received in error by the original sender, it is not possible to tell whether the data was received correctly at the destination and scrambled on the return path, or whether it was erroneous when received at the original destination. But at least some error indication is immediately available to the sender.

Checksums

In the preceding discussion on parity, the bit required to make the number of 1-bits in an individual character was added to the end of the character and sent along with it. This scheme is sometimes called vertical redundancy checking (VRC), or vertical parity, because if one holds a punched paper tape with its length in the horizontal, each character appears as a vertical column of holes across the tape. It is possible, and is common in some systems, to include a horizontal check character, which performs the parity function for each row of holes in the tape.

Figure 8.4 shows a set of characters represented as holes punched in a tape, with the vertical or character parity bit at the top of each character, and the horizontal or block parity character at the right. The block parity character is usually called a checksum, because it is formed by performing a binary addition without carry of each successive character. It also is sometimes referred to as a longitudinal redundancy check (LRC) character. It is sent as an extra character at the end of each message block. A system that uses both vertical parity and a checksum usually can detect all single-bit errors in a single character and some multiple-bit errors within a single character. In fact, this method of error detection is one of the three types supported by the BiSync protocol described later in this chapter.

●
In addition to character (or vertical) parity, in which a parity bit is added to each character, a block parity character can be added at the end of each message block.

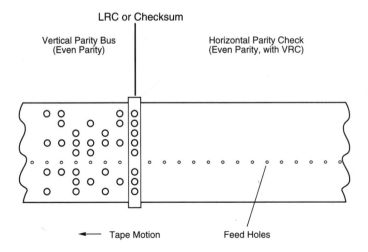

FIGURE 8.4.

Vertical and horizontal parity.

XMODEM Protocol

XMODEM protocol has an error-checking technique that can be used between microcomputers. Messages are sent in blocks of 128 characters surrounded by control characters.

The XMODEM protocol was devised by Ward Christensen as a simple error checking scheme suitable for file transfer operations between microcomputers. It requires that one terminal or computer be set up (by an operator or a computer program) as the sender and that the other be set up as the receiver. After the protocol is started, the transmitter waits for the receiver to send a Negative Acknowledge (NAK) character. The receiver meanwhile is set to send NAKs every 10 seconds. When the transmitter detects the first NAK, it begins sending messages as blocks of 128 data characters, surrounded by some protocol control characters. The beginning of each block is signaled by a Start Of Header (SOH) character. This is followed by a block number character in ASCII, followed by the same block number with each bit inverted. The bit inversion, known as the 1's complement, results in the block number being followed by the 1's complement of the block number. A 128-character piece of the file is sent, followed by a checksum that is the remainder of the sum of all the 128 bytes in the message divided by 255. Mathematically, the XMODEM checksum can be represented as

$$CHECKSUM = R \left[\frac{\sum_{1}^{128} ASCII\ Value\ of\ Character}{255} \right]$$

in which R is the remainder of the division process.

Figure 8.5 shows the XMODEM protocol block format.

FIGURE 8.5.

The XMODEM protocol block format.

Start of Header	Block Number	1's Complement of Block Number	128 Data Characters	Checksum

The receiver checks each part of the received block:

- Was the first character an SOH?
- Was the block number exactly one more than the previous block received?
- Were exactly 128 characters of data received?
- Was the locally computed checksum identical to the last character received in the block?

If the receiver is satisfied, it sends an Acknowledge (ACK) back to the transmitter, and the transmitter sends the next block. If not, a NAK is sent, and the transmitter resends the block found in error. This process is continued, block by block, until the entire file is sent and verified. At the end of the data, the transmitter sends an End Of Text character. The receiver replies with an ACK, and the session is terminated.

There are several points to be made about the XMODEM protocol. First, it is easy to implement with a small computer, but it does require a computer at each end. Second, it requires manual setup for each file to be transferred. Third, the error detection technique (ordinary sum of the data characters) is unsophisticated and unable to detect reliably the most common type of transmission error, which is a noise burst that can last on the order of 10 milliseconds (the duration of about 12 bits at 1200 bps). Fourth, it is a half-duplex protocol; that is, information is sent, and then the sender waits for a reply before sending the next message. Because operation of the XMODEM protocol generally assumes a full-duplex line, it is inefficient in use of the transmission facility.

In spite of the previously mentioned limitations, the XMODEM protocol and several derivatives are supported by most asynchronous communications programs designed for operation on personal computers. The rationale for the widespread support of those protocols is related to the initial placement of the XMODEM protocol into the public domain. This action enabled software developers to use the protocol without cost. In addition, it provided communications compatibility between programs developed by different vendors, which was extremely important in the 1970s when many software developers preferred to introduce proprietary protocols that worked only when two computer systems used the same software program.

Most of the asynchronous communications programs developed during the early 1980s eventually included XMODEM support. In the late 1980s, several derivatives of the XMODEM protocol gained acceptance due to the increased level of functionality they provided. Some new versions of the XMODEM protocol added CRC error checking, a process described later in this chapter. Other versions provided a full-duplex transmission capability with CRC error detection, further increasing the efficiency of the protocol. Today, almost all communications programs designed for use on personal computers support XMODEM and several of its derivatives.

XMODEM Derivatives

If you use an external modem and transfer a file under the XMODEM protocol, you can visually observe two deficiencies of the protocol: its small block size and the half-duplex method of transmission. If you are receiving a file, you will note that your modem's Receive Data (RD) indicator light illuminates for a short time, after which your modem's Send Data (SD) light momentarily illuminates as a flash. This process of RD being on for a second and SD flashing on and off continues until the file transfer is completed or until it aborts if 10 retransmissions occur due to a poor-quality line.

In observing the illumination of SD and RD, you will note that one always follows the other because transmission is half duplex. Thus, after receiving a block of data, your computer stops receiving data and then transmits an ACK or a NAK. By turning off the modem's receiver and turning on its transmitter, the computer creates a small delay. This

●
Even though the XMODEM protocol is simple and easy to operate, it requires a computer at each end, and every file to be transferred must be set up manually.

delay is further increased by the distant computer having to wait for an ACK or a NAK response to the previously transmitted block before being able to resume transmission. In comparison, a few file transfer protocols that support full-duplex transmission enable the simultaneous transmission and reception of data, which increases the effective throughput of the file transfer operation.

When XMODEM was developed during the 1970s, a data block the size of 128 bytes was probably a reasonable size with respect to line quality, because increasing the block size would result in more characters being retransmitted when an error was detected. Beginning in the late 1970s, tens of thousands of miles of fiber-optic cable were installed by communications carriers. Because fiber-optic cable is immune to electromagnetic interference, the probability of transmission errors occurring has substantially decreased. This in turn made the 128-byte block size used by the XMODEM protocol inefficient for modern communications. Although the XMODEM protocol is still very popular, you might want to consider using such derivatives as XMODEM/CRC, YMODEM, and ZMODEM, among others, which provide an enhanced file transfer capability.

XMODEM/CRC

This protocol is the same as the previously described XMODEM protocol with the exception that the checksum is replaced by a polynomial-generated CRC whose formation is described later in this chapter. Because the use of a CRC provides a higher level of error detection than the use of a checksum, the use of this protocol reduces the probability of an undetected error in comparison to using the XMODEM protocol.

XMODEM-1K

XMODEM-1K is essentially an XMODEM/CRC protocol that uses 1024-byte (1K) data blocks. For most transmissions, the use of this protocol reduces transmission time in comparison to the use of XMODEM or XMODEM/CRC. The transmission time is reduced because the large block size reduces both the number of line turnarounds and the number of times the transmitting device must wait for a response before sending the next block or retransmitting the previously sent block.

XMODEM-G

The XMODEM-G protocol is a variation of XMODEM-1K developed in recognition of error detection and correction capability being incorporated into many types of modems. The transmission of a file using error detection and correction via modems that have an error detection and correction feature would be inefficient and would introduce additional delays that would adversely affect the efficiency of the file transfer process.

XMODEM-G is the same as XMODEM-1K, with the exception of an error detection and correction capability that is omitted. This results in XMODEM-G becoming a "streaming" protocol in which 1K blocks are sent one after another. Although the protocol computes a CRC similar to XMODEM-1K, it is ignored by the protocol. Because this protocol does not provide any error detection capability, it should be used only with modems which have that capability enabled. Otherwise, the transfer of a file occurs without error protection.

YMODEM

Unlike XMODEM and its variations that are limited to transferring a single file, YMODEM supports the transmission of multiple files. Because the protocol enables you to batch a group of files for transmission, many software programs refer to YMODEM as YMODEM BATCH. To provide a multiple file transmission capability, YMODEM uses a header block that carries the filename of each file being transferred, its date of creation or last modification, and the file length.

Figure 8.6 illustrates the basic YMODEM block format. Although this block format is similar to XMODEM's, it has some distinct differences. First, YMODEM replaces the SOH character used by XMODEM with the Start of Text (STX) character. That character informs the receiver that the block contains 1024 data characters. YMODEM can switch to a 128-data-character block by replacing the STX character with the SOH character. It automatically does so under certain conditions, such as concluding the transfer of a file when the use of one or more 128-data-character blocks is more efficient than the use of one 1024-data-character block.

STX	Block Number	1's Complement of Block Number	1024 Data Characters	CRC High Byte	CRC Low Byte

FIGURE 8.6.
YMODEM block format.

A second difference between the XMODEM and YMODEM block formats concerns the block number field. Unlike XMODEM, which commences block numbering at one, YMODEM supports a block number zero, a special block used to transport the filename, its date of creation or last modification, and its length. In addition to the previously discussed capability to transport 1024 data characters per block, another difference between the YMODEM and XMODEM block formats concerns the error detection data contained in the block. As indicated in Figure 8.6, YMODEM contains two bytes of CRC data, resulting in this file transfer protocol having the capability to transport a 16-bit polynomial in place of XMODEM's 8-bit checksum.

Like XMODEM-1K, YMODEM uses 1024-byte (1K) data blocks and is a half-duplex protocol. Some implementations of YMODEM enable you to specify filenames using global characters, such as the asterisk (*) and question mark (?), within the filename and filename extension. Other implementations of YMODEM require you to enter each filename to be batched for transmission. Regardless of the method of specifying filenames, the use of YMODEM enables you to eliminate the delays between one file transfer ending and specifying the name of the next file to be transferred. Before you use YMODEM, however, it is a good idea to check your available disk storage against the storage requirements of the files you want to transfer. Otherwise, you could initiate the transfer of several files and go to the coffee machine only to return and find that the file transfer operation was only partially completed. Unfortunately, YMODEM does not tell you it aborted due to a lack of storage capacity, and you must take a directory listing to determine that there is no available storage left and that the lack of storage caused the file transfer to abort.

YMODEM-G

YMODEM-G can be considered as a batch transfer version of XMODEM-G. That is, YMODEM-G transmits data from one file after another file in 1024-byte (1K) data blocks without providing an error detection or correction capability. Like XMODEM-G, YMODEM-G should be used only with error-correcting modems.

WXMODEM

The WXMODEM protocol is a full-duplex "sliding window" protocol that allows the transmission of up to four XMODEM 128-byte data blocks before requiring an acknowledgment. This protocol uses a CRC for error checking. It was developed for use on packet-switching networks in which the flow of data in small packets that require acknowledgments could adversely affect throughput. By enabling multiple data blocks to be transmitted before requiring an acknowledgment from the receiving device, transmission efficiency is increased. Unfortunately, WXMODEM does not support multiple file transfers.

ZMODEM

The ZMODEM protocol is a full-duplex protocol that supports both 128 and 1024 data block transfers. Unlike the file transfer protocols previously discussed, ZMODEM varies the block size based on the quality of the line determined by the number of retransmission requests received. That is, a poor-quality line indicated by a large number of retransmission requests results in ZMODEM using a 128-byte data block because the small block size requires fewer characters to be retransmitted when an error occurs. Conversely, a good-quality line indicated by a small number of retransmission requests results in ZMODEM using a 1024-byte data block size. Although additional characters will be retransmitted while ZMODEM is using a 1024-byte data block when an error is detected, the low error rate results in a higher level of throughput because most 1024-byte data blocks are received correctly.

In addition to alternating the block size to correspond to the line error rate, ZMODEM enables an interrupted file transfer to be restarted from the point of failure. This can be especially useful because the other protocols require you to restart the file transfer process from the beginning. Two additional features of ZMODEM are its support of multiple file transfers and its support of conventional and extended CRC error checking. Extended CRC checking results in the generation of a four-byte CRC using 32 bits and reduces the probability of an undetected error to less than one in many millions of characters.

Similar to YMODEM, ZMODEM transfers the filename of the file transmitted as well as the file length and creation date at the beginning of the transmission. Through the use of this information, a communications program can be developed to provide a status report of the progress of a file transfer operation or a series of file transfers.

Figure 8.7 illustrates the file progress dialog box generated by the ProcommPlus for Windows communications program for a ZMODEM file transfer. Note that at the time the file transfer screen was captured, 40,960 bytes had been received. By using the file length of 145,263 bytes and keeping track of the transfer rate in bytes per second (916), the communications program can provide a real-time display of the time remaining for the file transfer. As indicated in Figure 8.7, at the time the screen was displayed, 1 minute and 53 seconds remained for completing the file transfer operation. Also note that the file progress bar at the top of the display indicates that 28 percent of the file transfer was completed when the screen was captured.

FIGURE 8.7.

ProcommPlus for Windows ZMODEM file progress dialog box.

If you transfer multiple files using ProcommPlus for Windows, the program uses ZMODEM information sent at the beginning of the transmission about each of the files to provide batch progress information. Thus, if multiple files were being transferred rather than a single file, the batch progress bar would indicate the percentage of the batch transfer completed, and the batch remaining display field would indicate the time remaining for the batch transfer.

KERMIT

The KERMIT protocol, developed at Columbia University, was named after Kermit the frog, one of Jim Henson's popular muppets. This protocol differs from the XMODEM series of file transfer protocols primarily due to the characteristics of the operating system used on some mini- and mainframe computers. The XMODEM series and its derivatives were developed for eight-data-bit transfers. Some computer operating systems are limited to seven-bit characters, however, and might not be able to work with ASCII control characters (ASCII 0 through 31) and the delete character (ASCII 127). To provide a file transfer mechanism for such computers, KERMIT was developed.

KERMIT was originally developed as a half-duplex protocol. It uses seven or eight data bits per character. The protocol is designed to convert the eighth bit by stripping it and prefixing the resulting character with another character. Doing so enables operating systems that cannot support eight-bit data characters or certain ASCII control characters to support file transfers in which those characters are disguised.

Since KERMIT was originally developed, many enhancements have been added to the protocol. This protocol now supports multiple file transfers, can operate in a full-duplex sliding window mode, and supports variable block sizes up to 1024 characters per block. Although this protocol is a necessity for accessing computers that cannot handle eight-bit characters or ASCII control characters, it should not be used otherwise. This is because the prefixing of characters significantly adds to the overhead of the protocol and makes the protocol approximately 10 to 20 percent less efficient than the XMODEM protocol, which is the least efficient of all protocols in that series.

SEALINK

The SEALINK protocol was developed by System Enhancement Associates of New Jersey to minimize the effect of delays when data is being transmitted through a packet network. This protocol is a full-duplex sliding window variation of XMODEM. It uses 128-byte data blocks that are error-protected through the use of a CRC. Up to six blocks can be transmitted before an acknowledgment from the receiver is required, which makes this protocol more suitable for use on packet networks that use WXMODEM.

Protocol Selection

The selection of an appropriate file transfer protocol first depends on the protocols supported by your computer and the computer you want to communicate with. Although this limitation might narrow your choice, you might still be faced with a half dozen or more protocols commonly supported from which to make your selection. In doing so, you might want to narrow your choice by considering whether the modem you use and the distant modem you will communicate with support a common error detection scheme, such as MNP Class 5 or the CCITT V.42bis protocol, both of which were described in Chapter 4, "Asynchronous Modems and Interfaces." If so, you might then consider using XMODEM-G if you have a single file to transfer or YMODEM-G if you have multiple files to transfer. Both protocols are "streaming" protocols that do not implement error detection, and their effective use is dependent on enabling error detection in your modem to match the distant modem's method of error detection.

If you previously experienced poor-quality transmission due to communications via an antiquated switchboard in a rundown hotel, an in-progress thunderstorm, or another cause, you might want to consider using ZMODEM. Although many people prefer to use ZMODEM as their first choice because of its full-duplex transmission mode, in actuality, a streaming protocol provides an equivalent to slightly better level of throughput. Where ZMODEM excels is in its capability to restart a transmission at its previous point of failure, alleviating the necessity to retransmit the entire file when transmission impairments result in a break in a transmission session.

If you are using a packet network to access another computer system, consider ZMODEM, SEALINK, and WXMODEM. Each of these three protocols allows many blocks to be unacknowledged, and they are designed to increase throughput when transmission is via a packet network. Because ZMODEM uses a larger data block than either SEALINK or WXMODEM, consider using ZMODEM, if it is available, before using SEALINK or WXMODEM.

If your available file transfer protocols are limited to XMODEM, XMODEM/CRC, and XMODEM-1K, consider XMODEM-1K before XMODEM/CRC, and XMODEM/CRC before the original XMODEM protocol. XMODEM-1K uses 1024-byte data blocks as well as a CRC for error detection and provides a higher throughput than XMODEM/CRC. Although XMODEM/CRC and XMODEM both use 128-byte data blocks, the use of the CRC by the XMODEM/CRC protocol provides a higher probability of data integrity than is gotten from the use of a checksum in the XMODEM protocol.

If you have multiple files to transfer and are considering the use of YMODEM or YMODEM-G, use the latter only if your modem can communicate with the distant modem using a modem error correction protocol. Otherwise, use the YMODEM protocol because it includes an error detection capability based on the use of a CRC.

Three remaining protocols whose uses have not yet been summarized are SEALINK, KERMIT, and ASCII. Because SEALINK uses a CRC for error detection and supports full-duplex transmission, its use provides a higher level of throughput than XMODEM. Unfortunately, its 128-byte data block size negates its performance in comparison to 1024-byte data block protocols. Another limiting factor is its availability, because it does not have a high level of use on many bulletin board systems. Concerning KERMIT, its primary use is for communicating with computer systems whose operating system cannot support the extended ASCII code and ASCII control characters. Because KERMIT strips the eighth bit and prefixes the resulting character with another character, the conversion degrades throughput. Thus, you should use the KERMIT protocol only when absolutely necessary for access to a computer that requires its use.

Because the ASCII protocol has no error detection capability, you might wonder why you should consider its use. The answer to this question is that most electronic mail systems require ASCII input. Thus, if you compose a message offline using a word processor, you should save the file in its ASCII format and then transmit the file when online to the electronic mail system using the ASCII protocol.

To assist readers in comparing the file transfer protocols previously discussed, Table 8.1 compares their key features.

Table 8.1. File transfer protocol comparison.

Protocol	Support Batch	Block Size	Error Detection	Transmission Mode	Data Characters
ASCII	no	n/a	none	n/a	7
XMODEM	no	128	CS	H	8
XMODEM/CRC	no	128	CRC	H	8
XMODEM-1K	no	128/1024	CRC	H	8
XMODEM-G	no	128/1024	none	H	8
YMODEM	yes	128/1024	CRC	H	8
YMODEM-G	yes	128/1024	none	H	8
WXMODEM	no	128	CRC	F	8
ZMODEM	yes	128/1024	CRC	F	8
KERMIT	yes	1024 Max	CRC/CS	H/F	8
SEALINK	yes	128	CRC	F	8

Note: CS = checksum, H = half-duplex, F = full-duplex

Convolutional Coding—Cyclic Redundancy Checks

Convolutional coding attaches a BCC to the end of each message block. The receiver recomputes the BCC and compares it to the one transmitted to determine whether the message was correctly received.

Several schemes have been devised to detect errors in binary communications systems using feedback or convolutional coding. These methods all append information computed at the transmitter to the end of each message transmitted to enable the receiver to determine whether a transmission error has occurred. The added information is mathematically related to the messages and is therefore redundant. The receiver recomputes the value and compares the recomputed number with the number received. If the two are the same, all is well. If not, the receiver notifies the transmitter that an error has occurred, and the message is re-sent. These methods go by the name of Cyclic Redundancy Checking (CRC), and the values appended to the messages are called CRCs or Block Check Characters (BCCs). A CRC is calculated by dividing the entire numeric binary value of the block of data by a constant, called a generator polynomial. The quotient is discarded, and the remainder is appended to the block and transmitted along with the data.

CRCs can be computed in hardware using multiple section feedback shift registers with Exclusive-OR (XOR) logic elements between each section and at the end. A typical arrangement is shown in Figure 8.8. This register implements the CCITT/ISO High-Level Data Link Control (HDLC) CRC, which is known as the ITU-T-CRC. The circles with a + in the middle represent XOR logic elements. For B = 0 or B = 1, these are the two rules for XOR:

B XOR 1 = 0
B XOR 0 = B

● The check character is determined by dividing the total binary value of the entire block by a constant called a generator polynomial.

FIGURE 8.8.

Shift register implementation of ITU-T-CRC.

The shift register is initialized to all ones at the beginning of the CRC calculation for a message. As each bit of the transmitted characters is applied to the transmission facility, it is also applied at point A of Figure 8.8, and then the entire register is shifted right one bit. As the bits are transmitted and shifted, each 1 bit that appears at A also affects the state of the other XOR elements, and that effect is propagated throughout the register for several bit times after the bit initially appears. Thus, any bit continues to have an effect on the transmitted data for a considerable time after that bit is sent. When the last data bit has been sent, the bits in the CRC shift register are complemented and transmitted.

At the receiver, the identical process is performed, and when the end of the message including the CRC is detected, the CRC is tested for the unique value 0001110100001111. If this value is found, all is well and the CRC register is reset to all ones for the next message. If the special value is not found, the program is notified that a transmission error has occurred, and a negative acknowledgment is returned to the sender.

The CRC process has the advantage that the current state of the shift register is the result of considerable past history. It is therefore unlikely that a burst of errors, such as normally occurs in serial data transmission, will produce a calculated CRC at the receiver that is the same as that which was originally sent. In fact, the 16-bit CRC calculation procedures, CRC-16 and CRC-ITU-T, detect all error bursts of 16 bits or less in length. They also detect over 99.9 percent of error bursts of greater than 16 bits. Another advantage of CRC is that it does not require the addition of another bit per character sent as do the VRC and LRC schemes. It does, however, require the sending of one of two (two for CRC-16 and CRC-ITU-T) extra characters at the end of each transmitted block.

CRC algorithms were initially implemented in hardware, and integrated circuits were developed to do the entire process for more than one method (for example, CRC-12, CRC-16, and CRC-ITU-T). It is also possible to do the calculations in software, with table lookup techniques providing reasonable performance.

> The CRC error detection process has a very high rate of success in accurately detecting error bursts of up to 16 bits because of the history held in the shift registers.

Half-Duplex Protocols

A half-duplex protocol is also commonly referred to as a stop and wait protocol. This is because transmission in one direction must stop before transmission in the opposite direction occurs.

Links

> Data links, either point-to-point or multipoint, are the data communications equipment and circuits that allow two or more terminals to communicate.

The basic notion in link protocols is that of the data link. A data link is an arrangement of modems or other interface equipment and communications circuits connecting two or more terminals so that they can communicate. Probably the most widely used link protocol through the mid-1980s was represented by the Binary Synchronous Communications procedures defined by IBM (usually abbreviated as BiSync or BSC). These procedures allow for operation on a data link in one direction at one time. BiSync can be operated on full-duplex circuits, but information still flows in only one direction at a time, so in many cases the advantage of the full-duplex circuit is minimized.

For the purpose of discussion of protocols, the physical form of the link is important in that the procedures for connecting and disconnecting the link might be different depending on whether the link is permanently connected or a dial-up, and also depending on the delay between when a data bit is sent and when it is received. This latter factor is of particular concern on satellite links due to the large difference in round-trip propagation delay between satellite links and terrestrial links. Regardless of the physical form of the link, however, the data is sent over it as a serial stream of symbols encoded as bits, and the control procedures between the ends of the link are effected using the transmission and recognition of the line-control characters or control codes.

Point-to-Point Links

A point-to-point link is one that connects only two stations at one time, as Figure 8.9a shows. Point-to-point links can be established on dedicated or dial-up circuits, and they can be half-duplex or full-duplex.

a. Point-to-point

FIGURE 8.9.

Point-to-point and multipoint links.

b. Multipoint

Multipoint Links

Multipoint links connect more than two stations at a time, as Figure 8.9b shows. Obviously, some control procedure must be in place to designate which stations can use the link at any one time. For this purpose, one station on the multidrop lines is designated as the control or master station, and all other stations are designated as tributaries or slaves. The control station is the traffic director, designating which stations are to use the link by a polling and selection process. At any instant, transmission on a multipoint link will be between only two stations, with all other stations on the link in a passive receive mode.

Transmission Codes—Character Sets

BiSync is defined by IBM to accommodate three character sets and their associated binary codes. Each set consists of a set of graphics (letters, numbers, and punctuation), a set of terminal control and format control codes (BELL, Form Feed, WRU, and so forth), and a set of data link control codes (Start of Text, End of Transmission, and so on). The three sets are the Six-Bit Transcode (SBT), Extended Binary Coded Decimal Interchange Code (EBCDIC), and United States of America Standard Code for Information Interchange (USASCII, or more commonly, just ASCII).

The codes differ in number of bits per symbol encoded (six for SBT, seven for ASCII, and eight for EBCDIC), and the different numbers of characters in the character set (64 for SBT, 128 for ASCII, and 144 for EBCDIC). There are significant differences between the sets in properties such as the sorting order between letters and numbers.

Link Control Codes

Link control is affected by the proper recognition of control characters and the taking of appropriate actions. The control codes used in BiSync are defined as listed here:

Synchronous Idle (Syn)—Establishes and maintains synchronization between DCEs. Is used as a filler between data blocks.

Start of Header (SOH)—Identifies the beginning of a block of heading information. Headers are control information (such as addresses, priority, and message numbers) used by the system to process the text part of the message.

Start of Text (STX)—Identifies the end of a header and the beginning of a block of text. Text is the part of the message from an applications program that is destined for another applications program and that must pass through the communications system unchanged.

End of Transmission Block (ETB)—Identifies the end of a block started with an SOH or STX. A BCC is sent immediately following an ETB. Receipt of an ETB requires a status reply (ACK0, ACK1, NAK, WACK, or RVI).

End of Text (ETX)—Terminates a block of data started by an STX or SOH that was transmitted as an entity. A BCC is sent immediately following an ETX. ETX also requires a status reply.

End of Transmission (EOT)—Indicates the end of message transmission by this station; the message might have contained one or more blocks. Receipt of an EOT causes all receiving stations to reset. The EOT is also used as a response to a poll when the polled station has nothing to send, and as an abort signal when the sender cannot continue transmission.

Enquiry (ENQ)—Requests a repeat transmission of a response to a message block if the original response is garbled or is not received. ENQ can also indicate the end of a polling or selection sequence, and it is used to bid for the line when the line is a point-to-point connection.

Affirmative Acknowledgment (ACK0 or ACK1)—Indicates correct receipt of the previous block and that the receiver is ready to accept the next block. ACK0 and ACK1 are used alternately, and receipt of the wrong one is an indication of an error in the protocol. ACK0 is the correct response to a station selection (on a multipoint circuit) or a line bid (on a point-to-point circuit).

Wait-Before-Transmit Affirmative Acknowledgment (WACK)—Indicates a temporary not-ready-to-receive condition to the sending station and affirmative acknowledgment of the previously received data block. The normal response to WACK by the sending station is ENQ, but EOT and DLE EOT are also valid. If ENQ is received after sending WACK, the sending station continues to send WACK until it is ready to continue sending data.

Negative Acknowledgment (NAK)—Indicates that the previously received block was received in error and that the receiver is ready to receive another block. NAK is also used as a station-not-ready reply to a station selection or line bid.

Data Link Escape (DLE)—Indicates to the receiver that the character following the DLE is to be interpreted as a control character.

Reverse Interrupt (RVI)—Indicates a request by a receiving station that the current transmission be terminated so that a high-priority message can be sent (such as a shutdown notice). RVI is also an affirmative acknowledgment to the previous block received. In a multipoint circuit, RVI sent from the control station means the control station wants to select a different station. When a sending station receives an RVI, it responds by sending all data that would prevent it from becoming a receiving station.

Temporary Text Delay (TTD)—Indicates that the sending station is not ready to send immediately but wants to keep the line. The receiving terminal reply to TTD is NAK. TTD normally is sent after two seconds if the sender cannot transmit the next block; this control code holds off the normal three-second abort timer at the receiving terminal. The response to TTD is NAK, and TTD can be repeated several times. TTD also is used as a forward abort, by sending EOT in response to the NAK reply.

Switched Line Disconnect (DLE EOT)—Indicates to a receiver that the transmitter is going to hang up on a switched line connection.

Code Sequences

Reference to the ASCII and EBCDIC code charts will reveal no code assigned to several of the control characters mentioned in the preceding listing. Such control codes are represented by two-character sequences of the characters that are defined in the charts. Table 8.2 gives the correspondence between these control characters and sequences of standard characters.

●

Some control characters require a two-character sequence of standard characters.

Table 8.2. Character sequences for BiSync control characters.

| BiSync Data Link Character | Character Sequences for Various Code Sets | | |
	ASCII	EBCDIC	SBT
ACK 0	DLE 0	DLE 70	DLE -
ACK 1	DLE 1	DLE /	DLE T
WACK	DLE ;	DLE ,	DLE W
RVI	DLE	DLE @	DLE 2
TTD	STX ENQ	STX ENQ	STX ENQ

Polling and Selection

● In a BiSync link, the control station determines which tributary station is active on the link, as well as the direction of transmission.

The active participants on a BiSync link are managed by a control station that issues either a Poll or a Select message addressed to the desired tributary. The Poll is an invitation-to-send from the control to the tributary. This allows the tributary to send any messages desired to the control station. The Select is a request-to-receive notice from the control station, telling the tributary that the control station has something to send to it. The control station thus controls which station has the link, and the direction of transmission.

Stations on the data link are assigned unique addresses that can consist of one to seven characters. The first character defines the station, and succeeding characters define some part of the station, such as a printer, as required. Some BiSync implementations repeat the station address for reliability purposes.

Message Blocks

Messages consist of one or more blocks of text, called the body of the message, surrounded by synchronization, header, and error control characters. The beginning of each block is identified by the STX control character, and all blocks except the last in a message are ended by either an ETB or an ITB character. The last block of the message is ended by an ETX character.

Error Checking

● Three types of error detection modes are used by BiSync: an odd parity check of each character including VRC/LRC, a BCC comparison using CRC-12, and a BCC comparison using CRC-16.

BiSync uses three types of error detection: VRC/LRC, CRC-12, and CRC-16. Table 8.3 shows under what conditions each is used. Transparency mode is described later in this section. The VRC is an odd-parity check performed on each character transmitted, including the LRC character at the end of the block. Each bit in the LRC character provides odd parity for the corresponding bit position of all characters sent in the block. Figure 8.10 illustrates the formation of the VRC and LRC for an eight-character data block. Note that the LRC is formed in the same manner as the VRC; however, the LRC covers all characters in the data block, whereas the VRC covers individual characters.

Table 8.3. Type of redundancy check.

Code Set	No Transparency	Transparency Installed and Operating	Transparency Installed but Not Operating
EBCDIC	CRC-16	CRC-16	CRC-16
ASCII	VRC/LRC	CRC-16	VRC/CRC-16
SBT	CRC-12	CRC-12	CRC-12

```
Character        |←— Data Bits —→|  Character
                 |               |  Parity Bit
                 |               |  (VRC)
    1             1 0 1 0 1 1 0 1 0
    2             0 1 1 0 1 0 1 0 1
    3             0 1 1 1 0 1 0 1 0
    4             1 0 1 0 0 1 0 1 1
    5             1 0 0 1 0 0 1 0 0
    6             0 1 0 0 1 0 0 1 0
    7             1 0 0 1 0 0 1 0 0
    8             0 1 1 0 1 0 0 1 1
Block Parity
Character (LRC)   1 1 0 0 1 0 0 1 0
```

FIGURE 8.10.
VRC/LRC parity check.

In BiSync, the LRC character is called the Block Check Character (BCC). It is sent as the next character following an ETB, ITB, or ETX character. The BCC sent with the data is compared at the receiver with the one accumulated by the receiver, and if the two are equal, all is well. The BCC calculation is restarted by the first STX or SOH character received after the direction of transmission is reversed (called a line turnaround). All characters except SYN characters received from that point until the next line turnaround are included in the calculation. If the message is sent in blocks with no line turnaround, each block is followed by an ITB, then the BCC. The BCC calculation is then restarted with the next STX or SOH character received.

The Cyclic Redundancy Check codes are used for error checking in the same fashion as the LRC code. If the transmission code set is SBT, the CRC-12 method is used, because each transmitted character is only six bits. For EBCDIC, the CRC-16 scheme is always used. For the ASCII code set, IBM specified that the VRC/LRC scheme be used in the nontransparency (standard) mode, and that CRC-16 be used in transparency mode. Transparency mode is described in detail in the following discussion.

Message Formats

Information is carried in BiSync as messages. Each message can have several parts: a synchronization sequence, a header, some text, and a block check sequence. Each part is identified by one or more control characters. In the case of messages used only for control, some parts such as the header, the text, or the BCC might be missing.

Synchronization

Unless the transmitter and receiver agree on the exact (to the bit) starting point of a message, they cannot communicate. Achieving this synchronization requires three steps:

1. The modems or other data communications devices at both ends of the circuit must acquire bit synchronization. The methods for doing this were discussed in Chapter 5, "Synchronous Modems, Digital Transmission, and Service Units."

2. The link interface equipment in the DTE must acquire character synchronization. This is done by searching the bit stream for a specific pattern of bits called a Synchronization Character (SYN). In ASCII, the bit pattern for SYN is 0010110. To help insure against recognition of a false SYN, most systems including BiSync require transmission and detection of two successive SYNs before the next step in the synchronization process is taken. The two SYN characters taken as a control set are called a Sync Sequence and are shown in most diagrams as a 0. To ensure that the first and last characters of a transmission are correctly sent, some BiSync stations add a PAD character before the first SYN and after every BCC, EOT, and ACK. This stratagem was devised primarily to overcome hardware limitations in some early hard-wired BiSync terminals.

3. The program operating the protocol must acquire message synchronization. In other words, the program must be able to find the beginning of each message or control character sequence. This is achieved by a program search of the characters received after the sync sequence for a control character that is defined to begin a block of data or control sequence. Such characters are SOH, STX, ACK0/1, NAK, WACK, RVI, and EOT.

Heading

A heading is a sequence of characters beginning with the SOH character that is used for message type identification, message numbering, priority specification, and routing. Receipt of the SOH initiates accumulation of the BCC (but the SOH is not included in the BCC). The heading can be of fixed or variable length, and it is ended by an STX.

Text

The text part of the message contains the information to be sent between applications programs. The text begins with an STX and ends with ETX. Text can be broken into blocks for better error control. Each block begins with an STX and ends with an ETB, except for the last block, which ends with an ETX. The normal end of a transmission is signaled by sending an EOT following the ETX. Control characters are not allowed within the body of a text block. If a control character is detected, the receiving station terminates reception and looks for a BCC as the next two characters.

Timeouts

Timeouts must be provided by the communications program or terminal to prevent indefinite delays caused by data errors or missing line turnaround signals. Four functions are specified in BiSync for timeouts: transmit, receive, disconnect, and continue.

Transmit timeout is normally set for one second. It defines the rate of insertion of synchronous idle (SYN SYN or DLE SYN) sequences in the data to help maintain bit and character synchronization.

Receive timeout is normally set for three seconds. It carries out a few actions:

● It limits the time a transmitting station will wait for a reply.

● It signals a receiving station to check the line for synchronous idle characters, which indicate that transmission is continuing. The receive timeout is reset each time a sync sequence is received.

● It sets a limit on the time a tributary station in a multipoint circuit can remain in control mode. The timer is reset each time an end signal such as an ENQ or ACK is received as long as the station stays in control mode.

Disconnect timeout causes a station on a switched network to disconnect from the circuit after 20 seconds of inactivity.

Continue timeout causes a transmitting station sending a TTD to send another if it is still unable to send text. A receiving station must transmit a WACK if it becomes temporarily unable to receive within a two-second interval.

Four BiSync timeout functions prevent indefinite delays due to data errors or missing line turnaround signals.

Transparent-Text Mode

It is often necessary in communicating between machines to send data that does not represent characters but instead represents some purely arbitrary quantity or object. An example is the binary representation of a computer program. In such a case, it is likely that some of the data will have the same bit pattern as a BiSync control character. Transparent-text mode, sometimes called transparency, allows such data to be sent without being misinterpreted by the communications program. The basic technique in transparency is to precede each true control character with the DLE character, as Figure 8.11a shows. If a DLE bit pattern appears in the text of the message, it also is preceded by a DLE. Thus, a bit pattern is interpreted as a control character only if preceded by a DLE. The resulting message after processing by the link interface program to remove the DLE is shown in Figure 8.11b. Note that any DLE DLE sequence in the text has the first DLE suppressed and the second sent along as part of the data.

Data communications often requires the sending of information that is in binary rather than in a character code. A transparent-text mode is used for this purpose.

FIGURE 8.11.

BiSync transparency mode.

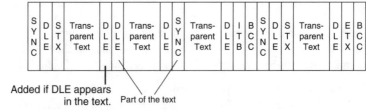

Added if DLE appears in the text.

Part of the text

a. Block As Transmitted

Part of the text

b. Block After Stripping Transparency Control Characters

Full-Duplex Protocols

Online applications using CRT terminals required a protocol for full-duplex operations that contained a powerful error detection and correction system that prevented aliasing.

The Binary Synchronous Communications procedures were devised at a time when most data communications circuits were operated at 2400 bits per second, and were two-wire half-duplex circuits connecting remote job entry card reader/printer terminals to mainframes. As online applications using remote CRT terminals became more cost-effective, and as four-wire private line circuits became available, the demand for a communications protocol that could handle full-duplex operations arose. These were the requirements for such a protocol:

- Messages must flow in both directions simultaneously.
- It must be possible to have more than one message in the channel at one time (BiSync allows only one).
- Transparency must be designed in, not tacked on as an afterthought.
- The protocol must allow switched-network, half-duplex, and multipoint operation, as well as full-duplex point-to-point.
- The error-detection and correction scheme must be powerful and must prohibit the problem of aliasing.

The last condition is a particularly difficult one. Aliasing occurs when a message fragment caused by a transmission error is interpreted as a good message at the receiver; that is, when a bad or broken message "looks like" a good message. This can be a serious problem, especially in critical applications such as funds transfer and military command and control. Much design effort in the international standards organizations and in private companies was devoted to the development of protocols that prevented the aliasing problem. This led to the development of three widely used schemes. Two of them were alike in principle and operation and in requiring special hardware but were promulgated by different organizations. The third, developed at Digital Equipment Corporation, uses a different technique but can operate with standard character-oriented line interface equipment.

High-Level Data Link Control Procedures

The critical issue in preventing aliasing is the determination of where a legal message block begins and ends, and exactly what part of the information taken in by the receiver is to be included in the CRC. As a result of work done at IBM by J. Ray Kersey and others in the early 1970s, a protocol was proposed and later adopted as an international standard by the International Standards Organization in 1979. It is called the High-level Data Link Control (HDLC) procedures. In HDLC, the message synchronization indicator (called a Flag) was originally generated by a hardware circuit, and other hardware circuits were used to prevent any data being transmitted from having the same pattern as the Flag. The Flag then becomes a kind of out-of-band framing signal, much like the break signal in the teletypewriter protocol. Today, HDLC operations can be performed via software due to the enhanced processing capabilities of modern microprocessors.

●
Protocols to prevent aliasing must determine where a true message block begins and ends and what part of the message is to be included in the CRC. HDLC is one of these.

Because the data being transmitted is examined bit by bit to screen out possible aliases of the Flag, HDLC and other similar protocols, such as IBM's Synchronous Data Link Control (SDLC), are referred to as bit-oriented protocols, or BOPs. Unlike BiSync and DDCMP (which will be described later), the text part of messages sent using the HDLC protocol can, in principle, be any arbitrary number of bits long, and HDLC is defined to allow this. In practice, as with BiSync and DDCMP, most implementations of BOPs restrict the text (and in fact all the message including the Flag) to be an integral multiple of the number of bits in a character (almost always eight).

●
Data is examined bit by bit in HDLC; thus, it is called a bit-oriented protocol.

In HDLC, all information is carried by frames that can be of three types: information frames (I-frames), supervisory control sequences (S-frames), or unnumbered command/responses (U-frames). Figure 8.12 shows one information frame as a rectangular block divided into its six fields: a beginning Flag (F1) field, an Address (A) field, a Control (C) field, an Information (I) field, a Frame Check Sequence (FCS) field, and a final flag (F2) field. S-frames and U-frames have the same fields except that the I field is left out.

FIGURE 8.12.

HDLC format.

F1 - Flag to Indicate Beginning
     of Frame (01111110)
A - Address
C - Control

I - Information
FCS - Frame Check Sequence
F2 - Flag to Indicate End
      of Frame (01111110)

I-frames perform information transfer and independently carry message acknowledgments, and Poll or Final bits. S-frames perform link supervisory control such as message acknowledgments, retransmit requests, and requests for temporary holds on I-frame transmissions (like a WACK in BiSync). U-frames provide a flexible format for additional link control data by omitting the frame sequence numbers and thus providing a place for an additional 32 command and 32 response functions. The fields in the HDLC frame are used as detailed here:

Flag field—Every frame begins and ends with a Flag, which is the bit patter 01111110. The same Flag can end one frame and begin the next. Every station connected to a link must continuously search the received data for the Flag.

Address field—In command frames, the address identifies the destination station for the command. In response frames, the address identifies the station sending the response.

Control field—The control field carries commands and responses, according to Figure 8.13.

FIGURE 8.13.

Control field contents.

HDLC Frame Format	Bits in Control Field							
	1	2	3	4	5	6	7	8
I-frame (Information transfer commands/responses)	0	$N(S)$[1]			P/F[2]	$N(R)$[3]		
S-frame (Supervisory commands/responses)	1	0	S[4]		P/F	N(R)		
U-frame (Unnumbered commands/responses)	1	1	M[5]		P/F	M		

Notes:
[1]N(S) is the transmitting station send sequence number, bit 2 is the low order bit.
[2]P/F is the Poll bit for primary station transmissions, and the final bit for secondary station transmissions.
[3]N(R) is the transmitting station receive sequence number. Bit 6 is the low-order bit.
[4]S are supervisory function bits.
[5]M are modifier function bits.

Information field—The information field can contain any sequence of bits, which in principle need not be related to a particular character set or data structure. In practice, the information field is almost always an integral multiple of one character in length, which is usually eight bits.

Frame Check Sequence field—The FCS (or CRC) for HDLC is the ITU-T-CRC, as previously discussed.

To ensure that the Flag is unique, the transmitting hardware must monitor the bit stream continually between the beginning and ending Flags for the presence of strings of five one-bits in a row. If such a string occurs, a zero-bit is inserted (called bit stuffing) by the hardware after the fifth one-bit so that the string will not look like a Flag. The added zero-bit is removed at the receiver. This procedure makes any appearance of strings of one-bits greater than five in number a Flag, an error on the transmission line, or a deliberately sent fill pattern between frames of all one-bits. One method of aborting transmission of a frame is to begin transmitting continuous ones.

Specification in the protocol of a unique, hardware-generated Flag pattern and the length of the Address, Control, and FCS fields provides complete transparency for the Information field. The hardware prevents any bit pattern sent by the applications program from having more than five continuous ones, and the hardware-added zeros are stripped from the data stream as it passes through the receiver. Also, the position of the FCS is defined by the receipt of the ending Flag so that the residual pattern in the CRC register can be immediately compared with the fixed value (0001110100001111).

The order of bit transmission is defined for addresses, commands, responses, and sequence numbers to be low-order bit first, but the order of bit transmission for the information field is not specified. The FCS is transmitted beginning with the coefficient of the highest order term (x^{15}). An invalid frame is defined as one that is not properly bounded by Flags or is shorter than 32 bits between Flags. Invalid frames are ignored (in contrast with frames that have a bad FCS, which require a NAK).

HDLC Semantics

The preceding discussion dealt with what is called the syntax of HDLC. The syntax is the definition of the bit patterns and order of sending bits that will make correctly formed messages—that is, those that are legal in the protocol. For you to understand what happens when HDLC is used, however, it is necessary to define the semantic content of messages, or the meanings that should be assigned to correctly formed messages.

The normal sequence of messages in HDLC consists of the transfer of one or more frames containing I-fields from a data source (the transmitting station) to a data sink (the receiving station). The receipt is acknowledged by the sink by sending a frame in the backward direction. The source must retain all transmitted messages until they are explicitly acknowledged by the sink. The value of N(R) indicates that the station transmitting the N(R) has

In HDLC, there are six fields in an information frame but only five fields in other frames, which are supervisory control sequences or unnumbered command/responses.

A normal message sequence involves sending frames from a transmitting station to a receiving station and having the receiving station acknowledge receipt by sending a frame back to the sender.

correctly received all I-frames numbered up to N(R)–1. I-frames and S-frames (see Figure 8.13) are numbered, the numbers going from 0 to 7 (for unextended control fields). An independent numbering sequence is carried for each data source/data sink combination. The response from a sink can acknowledge several (but not more than seven) received messages at one time and can be contained in an I-frame being sent from the sink to the source.

A data link consists of two or more communicating stations, so for control purposes it is necessary to designate one station as the primary station, with responsibility for managing data flow and link error recovery procedures. Primary stations send command frames. Other stations on the link are called secondary stations, and they communicate using response frames. Primary stations can send to secondaries using the Select bit in the control field of an I-frame, or a primary can allow a secondary to send by sending a Poll bit.

Secondary stations can operate in one of two modes: a Normal Response Mode (NRM) or an Asynchronous Response Mode (ARM). In NRM, the secondary can send only in response to a specific request or permission by the primary station. The secondary station explicitly indicates the last frame to be sent by setting the final bit in the control field. In ARM, the secondary can independently initiate transmission without receiving an explicit permission or Poll from the primary.

Space does not permit covering HDLC in greater detail. The interested reader is referred to International Standards ISO 3309-1979 (E), ISO 4335-1979 (E), and ISO 6256-1981 for the complete definition of the HDLC protocol. There is a data link control procedure standard promulgated by the American National Standards Institute (ANSI) in the United States called Advanced Data Communications Control Procedures (ADCCP), which is functionally equivalent to HDLC.

Synchronous Data Link Control

SDLC, developed by IBM, has the same frame format and is similar in function to HDLC.

The standard full-duplex synchronous data link control protocol used by the IBM Corporation in products conforming to its System Network Architecture is called Synchronous Data Link Control (SDLC). It is functionally equivalent to HDLC, but with these exceptions:

- SDLC information fields must be an integral multiple of eight bits long.
- Current IBM products support only the Unbalanced Normal operation with Normal Disconnected mode class or procedures as defined in ISO DIS 6159 and DIS 4335/DAD1.
- SDLC contains additional commands and responses not defined in the ISO Elements of Procedure, for example, a TEST command and response. Figure 8.14 shows the frame structure of SDLC (which is the same as HDLC), along with the common modes, commands, and responses. A close examination of this illustration will help you understand the SDLC format and the differences between HDLC and SDLC.

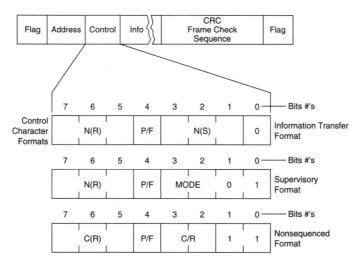

FIGURE 8.14.
SDLC format.

Flag is always 01111110 (If a sequence of 5 "1" bits occurs in the middle of a
   transmission, the transmitter "stuffs" a "0" bit and the receiver removes it.)
Address is the Station Address on a particular line
N(S) is Sending Sequence Number = 000 through 111 and then repeats
P/F is Primary Station Poll when = 1 from Primary Station
   Secondary Station Final when = 1 from Station on the line
N(R) is Receiving Sequence Number = 000 through 111 and then repeats
Mode is Receive Ready (RR) when 00
   Receive Not Ready (RNR) when 10
   Reject (REJ) when 01
C/R is Command from Primary Station or Response from Secondary Station
   Nonsequenced Information (NSI) = 000-00 ⎫
   Set Normal Response Mode (SNRM) = 001-00 ⎪
   Disconnect (DISC) = 010-00 ⎬ Commands
   Optional Response Poll (ORP) = 100-00 ⎪
   Set Initialization Mode (SIM) = 000-10 ⎭

   Nonsequenced Information (UI) = 000-00 ⎫
   Nonsequenced Acknowledgment (UA) = 110-00 ⎪
   Request for Initialization (RIM) = 000-10 ⎬ Responses
   Command Reject (FRMR) = 001-10 ⎪
   Request Online (DM) = 000-11 ⎭
Info is Information = Variable Length for Information Transfer
                Prohibited for Supervisory Format
                Variable Length for Nonsequenced Format with NSI
                Fixed Format with CMDR
CRC = Cyclic Redundancy Check Remainder

Digital Data Communications Message Protocol

At about the same time SDLC was being developed at IBM, George Friend, Steven Russell, and Stuart Wecker were given the task of developing a synchronous protocol at Digital Equipment Corporation. The requirements were similar to those given before full-duplex protocols, but with one important additional item: the protocol must run on existing data communications hardware, and preferably on asynchronous as well as synchronous links. The result was the Digital Data Communications Message Protocol, or DDCMP.

●
DDCMP is
character-oriented
rather than bit-
oriented.

DDCMP is a character-oriented protocol rather than a bit-oriented protocol, as is SDLC. Therefore, DDCMP requires no special bit stuffing and destuffing hardware and can be used with various types of line interfaces, including asynchronous units. The method of specifying the length of a message in order to look for the BCC at the right time is inclusion of a 14-bit count field in the header. This is a count of the number of characters in the information field of the message. Because error-free transmission depends on the count field being detected correctly, the header of DDCMP messages is a constant length and has its own BCC, which is checked before setting up to receive the information part of the message. The format of DDCMP messages is shown in Figure 8.15. A detailed study of this figure reveals the bit pattern of the various fields in the frame for different types of messages.

FIGURE 8.15.

*DDCMP message
format in detail.*

Data Messages	1000001	Character Count	QS	Resp #	Message#	Address
Acknowledgment	0000101	00000001000000	QS	Resp #	00000000	Address
Negative Acknowledge	0000101	00000010Reason	QS	Resp #	00000000	Address

Reason

BCC Header Error	000001
BCC Data Error	000010
Rep Response	000011
Buffer Unavailable	001000
Receiver Overrun	001001
Message Too Long	010000
Header Format Error	010001

Reply Message	00000101	000000011000000	QS	00000000	LstMess#	Address
Start Message	00000101	00000110000000	11	00000000	00000000	Address
Start Acknowledgment	00000101	00000111000000	11	00000000	00000000	Address
Maintenance Message	10010000	Character Count	11	00000000	00000000	Address

Notes

1. Only the Data Message and the Maintenance Message have character counts, so only these messages have the information and CRC2 fields shown in the message format diagram above.

2. "Resp #" refers to Response Number. This is the number of the last message received correctly. When used in a negative acknowledge message, it is assumed that the next higher numbered message was not received, was received with errors, or was unaccepted for some other reason. See "Reasons."

3. "Message#" is the sequentially assigned number of this message. Numbers are assigned by the transmitting station modulo 256; i.e., message 000 follows 255.

4. "LstMess#" is the number of the last message transmitted by the station.

5. "Address" is the address of the tributary station in multipoint systems and is used in messages both to and from the tributary. In point-to-point operation, a station sends the address "1" but ignores the address field on reception.

6. "Q" and "S" refer to the quick sync flag bit and the select bit.

DDCMP has two principal advantages and some disadvantages. One advantage is that it is usable without special hardware on asynchronous, synchronous, or even parallel data channels. Another advantage is that the sequence number field allows for up to 255 messages to be outstanding on the channel at one time, a requirement when operating full-duplex channels over satellite links. On the other hand, it does not support a go-back-N or selective reject mode of operation, and it is, in principle, more vulnerable to the aliasing problem than bit-oriented protocols. It also has been mistakenly criticized for inefficiency because of the inclusion of a BCC after the header on the equivalent of I-frames. In fact, for messages of average length, DDCMP is somewhat more efficient than bit-stuffing protocols because of the extra bits added by the hardware in the bit-oriented schemes. In practice, aliasing has not caused noticeable problems with DDCMP.

●
The DDCMP does not require any special hardware to perform successfully on synchronous, asynchronous, or parallel data channels.

What Have You Learned?

1. Protocols are rules for communications between processes that are alike. Interfaces are rules for communicating between processes that are different.

2. Data communications protocols are made up of symbols to be communicated, a code set translating those symbols to a binary code, and rules for the correct sequencing of the symbols.

3. Parity is a method of adding redundancy to coded symbols to help detect errors in transmission.

4. XMODEM is a simple protocol used in asynchronous transmission between microcomputers.

5. YMODEM permits multiple files to be transferred between computers.

6. ZMODEM supports the resumption of a file transfer at its point of interruption as well as the dynamic adjustment of the size of data blocks based on the error rate on the line.

7. A Cyclic Redundancy Check is a number calculated from the data transmitted by the sender and recalculated by the receiver that allows the data to be checked for errors in transmission.

8. The most widely used code sets in the United States are ASCII and EBCDIC.

9. Protocols must be suitable for use on dial and private line connections, and for point-to-point and multipoint network arrangements.

10. The most widely used protocols in the United States are TTY, XMODEM, BiSync, SDLC, and DDCMP.

Quiz for Chapter 8

1. Communications protocols always have a:
   a. Set of symbols.
   b. Start of header.
   c. Special Flag symbol.
   d. BCC.

2. The Baudot code uses how many bits per symbol?
   a. 9.
   b. 7.
   c. 5.
   d. 8.

3. When transmitting odd-parity coded symbols, the number of bits that are zeros in each symbol is:
   a. Odd.
   b. Even.
   c. Unknown.
   d. None of the above.

4. In the XMODEM protocol, the sender waits for what character from the receiver before beginning transmission?
   a. WACK.
   b. ACK.
   c. RVI.
   d. NAK.

5. If each character in an XMODEM block has an ASCII value of 50, what would be the value of the checksum added to the block?
   a. 50.
   b. 23.
   c 41.
   d 25.

6. Under the YMODEM protocol, block 0 is used to transport:
   a. Error-recovery information.
   b. Two checksums.
   c. Information about the file to be transferred.
   d. A 1024 data character block.

7. The second YMODEM block used to transport a 1100 byte file would use a data field of:
   a. 1024 characters.
   b. 100 characters.
   c. 128 characters.
   d. 64 characters.

8. A streaming protocol:
   a. Provides error detection.
   b. Does not provide error detection.
   c. Uses 64 byte blocks.
   d. Requires a manual setup.

9. An example of a sliding window protocol is:
   a. XMODEM.
   b. YMODEM.
   c. YMODEM-G.
   d. WXMODEM.

10. A protocol that adjusts its block size based on the line error rate is:
    a. XMODEM.
    b. YMODEM.
    c. ZMODEM.
    d. WXMODEM.

11. Which of the following is not a valid rule for XOR?

    a. 0 XOR 0 = 0

    b. 1 XOR 1 = 1

    c. 1 XOR 0 = 1

    d. B XOR B = 0

12. Which of the following BiSync control codes is not defined in the EBCDIC character set?

    a. STX.

    b. ACK0.

    c. ENQ.

    d. TTD.

13. How many messages can be outstanding (unacknowledged) on a BiSync link?

    a. 1.

    b. 2.

    c. 4.

    d. 8.

14. Which code set is used in BiSync when using VRC/LRC but not operating in transparency mode?

    a. EBCDIC.

    b. ASCII.

    c. SBT.

    d. Fieldata.

15. The escape character that identifies control characters in BiSync Transparency mode is:

    a. ESC.

    b. SYN.

    c. DLE.

    d. RVI.

16. One primary difference between DDCMP and SDLC is:

    a. DDCMP does not have a transparent mode.

    b. SDLC does not use a CRC.

    c. DDCMP has a message header.

    d. DDCMP does not require special hardware to find the beginning of a message.

Personal Computer Communications Software

UNDERSTANDING

About This Chapter

In this chapter, we turn our attention to software that enables personal computers to communicate via the switched telephone network. In doing so, I will discuss some important communications software features that enable you to control the operation of a modem, emulate a specific type of terminal, transfer binary and ASCII files, and perform other communications functions. Because the best way to become acquainted with personal computer communications software is through the use of representative programs, this chapter uses the popular ProcommPlus and ProcommPlus for Windows communications programs from Datastorm Technologies, Inc., for illustrative purposes. Through a series of personal computer screen images, readers are walked through the use of each program to establish a communications session, change dialing directory entries, and perform a file transfer operation.

Communications Program Features

You can gain an appreciation for the features built into many personal computer communications programs by learning about their general operation and utilization. First and foremost, the program must be written to operate on the PC platform you use.

Operating System and Operating Environment Support

When considering the potential use of a communications program, you should evaluate both the operating system and the operating environment supported by the program.

Until the late 1980s, there was essentially one operating system for each type of personal computer, which simplified the selection of a communications program. The Macintosh operating system was later significantly revised with the introduction of System 7. In the IBM PC and compatible computer world, DOS was supplemented by several versions of Windows and OS/2 operating environments. This means that you now must consider whether the communications program was written to work under a specific operating environment as well as a specific operating system.

Although both Windows and OS/2 provide facilities to operate DOS programs, when run in that mode, the program will not support such operating environment features as cursor support, cutting and pasting of information between applications, and the familiar graphical user interface (GUI) of the previously mentioned operating environments.

Modem Support

After you select a communications program that satisfies your operating environment and computer platform requirements, you must also consider another important hardware device, the modem you anticipate using. Although most modems support the Hayes Microcomputer Products modem command set, that support primarily references a core set of commands that govern the operation of basic modem functions. As discussed in Chapter 4, "Asynchronous Modems and Interfaces," when such features as data compression, flow control, and error detection and correction were added to intelligent modems, vendors incorporated the control of those features in different ways. Some vendors used AT commands, and others used different S Register settings to control new features. This situation resulted in most vendors using proprietary methods to control the operation of modem features beyond the basic modem control functions supported by the standard Hayes modem command set.

Due to differences in the design of advanced features in modern modems, their support normally requires the communications program to explicitly support the command set of the modem.

Whereas a few years ago the support of the standard Hayes command set was sufficient to operate most modems, today a communications program might include the support of a dozen to fifty or more modems. As an alternative to supporting the command sets used by a large number of modems, some programs enable users to configure the program to operate with any intelligent modem. In doing so, such programs provide users with a menu of modem functions and enable the entry of the appropriate AT command or S Register setting for each function. Although this requires program users to spend a considerable amount of time looking through a modem manual to locate the command or register setting for each function and then manually entering the function, it also allows the program to support any modem.

Now that you've read about the relationship of software to the computer platform and modem, we'll turn our attention to the interface between the two devices and the communications program features you might want to consider to control the transfer of data between the devices.

Controlling the Interface

Communications software must provide control over the movement of data between a computer and a modem. To help you understand the control features you should consider when examining communications software, I'll examine the flow of data between the two devices and how that flow must be controlled if such modem features as data compression and error detection and correction are enabled.

Figure 9.1 illustrates in schematic diagram format the relationship of the flow of data between a computer and a modem. Note that the computer's data transfer rate does not necessarily have to equal the modem's operating rate. In fact, when you use a compression-performing modem, you will normally use the communications program to set the computer's serial port to a data rate two to four times the operating rate of the modem. For correct operation during data compression, the data rate into the modem must exceed its operating rate. For example, if a modem has an average compression ratio of 4:1 and an operating rate of 9600 bps, the computer's serial port should be set to transfer data to the modem at four times the modem's operating rate, or 38,400 bps. However, because the compression ratio varies based on the compressibility of data, what happens when the modem cannot compress data or compresses data at a lower compression ratio?

> For a modem to operate effectively when compressing data, the computer serial port's operating rate must exceed the modem's operating rate.

FIGURE 9.1.

Data flow between a computer and a modem.

If data is flowing into the modem at 38,400 bps but the modem compresses data at a rate less than a 4:1 compression ratio, its output is less than its input. This means that within a very short period, the modem's limited buffer storage will overflow and data will be lost. Obviously, modem users do not want this to happen; they can prevent this situation from occurring by enabling flow control.

Flow Control

Flow control can be defined as the orderly regulation of the transfer of data. You can turn on or enable modem flow control via an appropriate command or S Register setting. When turned on, the modem signals the attached computer whenever its buffer fills to a pre-defined level. That signal tells the computer to suspend transmission. When the modem's buffer is emptied to a certain level, it sends another signal to the computer, which disables flow control.

> Flow control is the orderly regulation of data transfer. To prevent the loss of data, the communications program must be configured to support the method of flow control used by the modem.

Three types of flow control are supported by most modems: inband signaling, outband signaling, and ENQ/ACK. Inband signaling references the transmission of XON and XOFF control characters. Outband signaling references the modem raising and lowering the Clear to Send (CTS) signal on the RS-232 interface, whereas ENQ/ACK references a signaling method similar to XON and XOFF used primarily by Hewlett-Packard terminal devices. Thus, your communications software that turns your computer into a terminal must support one or more modem flow control techniques to prevent the loss of data when the modem operates in its compressed mode. In addition, flow control becomes a necessity when a modem performs error detection and correction, and transmission errors occur.

This is because the modem must retain blocks of data in memory until they are positively acknowledged. If line errors occur, the modem's buffer rapidly fills as additional data is transferred from the computer to the modem, and the modem cannot purge previously transmitted data from memory. Again the modem will transmit a flow control signal to the computer that the communications program operating on the computer must recognize. Now that you have an understanding of flow control and the relationship between the computer data transfer rate and the modem operating rate, we'll discuss the range of rates supported by communications programs and how those rates are set up.

Operating Rates

The computer data transfer rates supported by most communications programs range from 300 to 115,200 bps. Typically, a 115,200-bps rate is set when a modem operating at 28,800 bps has its compression feature enabled. Other high-speed computer data transfer rates supported by some communications programs include 57,600 bps and 76,800 bps, which are normally used to support compression-performing modems operating at 14,400 and 19,200 bps, respectively.

Before setting the computer data transfer operating rate, you should ensure that the modem's serial port is set to auto-baud detect, or you should set it to the computer data transfer rate you want to use. Otherwise, the modem will not be able to recognize the data being transferred to it from the computer due to an interface data rate mismatch.

The dialing directory is the key to the functionality of most communications programs because it provides users with the ability to assign, view, and modify different communications parameter settings associated with each telephone number in the directory.

You set both the modem serial port and the modem operating rate via command codes or S register settings. Both settings are independent of the capability of the communications program because they are dependent on the operating capability built into the modem. Thus, the method by which the communications program enables you to set those operating rates should not be evaluated because the actual settings depend on the modem used.

Dialing Directory

One of the more important features of a communications program is its dialing directory. The basic function of the dialing directory is to enable a user to enter telephone numbers to be dialed as well as to provide a description of each number. Most communications programs expand the functionality of the dialing directory by building into the directory the ability of the user to assign, view, and modify different communications settings. Some of the more common communications settings that are changed through the use of a dialing directory include the operating rate of the computer's serial port, the parity, the number of data bits and stop bits per character, the file transfer protocol to be used as a default for file transfers, the type of terminal the communications software emulates, and whether a script file is associated with the dialing directory. Of those previously mentioned settings, the ones most persons will want to evaluate are the range of serial port operating rates supported, the types of file transfer protocols and terminal emulations included with the program, and the inclusion of a script programming language, as well as the commands supported by the programming language and its ease of use.

The file transfer protocols supported govern your ability to upload and download files from bulletin board systems, other personal computers, and information utilities. Although almost all communications programs support a core set of file transfer protocols, some programs include WXMODEM, ZMODEM, and other protocols that were developed to satisfy one or more communications requirements lacking in other protocols. For example, ZMODEM uses a 32-bit CRC, which reduces the probability of an undetected error to an order of magnitude below other file transfer protocols, and WXMODEM facilitates the transfer of files through packet networks.

The types of terminal emulations supported by the communications program govern its capability to communicate with different types of computer systems. This can be extremely important when the program is accessing mainframes and minicomputers designed to support certain types of full-screen terminal devices. Those computers transmit special control codes to perform such functions as clearing the screen, moving the cursor to a specific location, displaying different colors, establishing protected fields, and highlighting information. Without the correct terminal emulator, your personal computer will more than likely fail to correctly display information received from a distant computer. In addition, certain keystrokes from your computer will more than likely be received incorrectly at the mainframe or minicomputer when you do not use a correct terminal emulator. This problem occurs because terminal emulators use different key combinations to represent certain control keys, such as IBM program function (PF) keys that are not included on conventional personal computer keyboards.

●

The terminal emulations supported by a communications program govern its capability to communicate with different types of mainframe and minicomputer systems.

With a script programming language, you can automate communications functions, such as logging onto an electronic mail system, checking for new mail, and, if any is found, downloading the messages in your mailbox. Some communications programs include a script-learning capability. This feature enables you to perform the required operation once while the program constructs the appropriate script language commands that duplicate the functions manually performed. Thereafter, you can invoke the script to automatically perform the series of manual operations you previously conducted.

The following list shows the communications program features you might want to consider. This list can be used to evaluate the suitability of two or more programs you are considering purchasing or as a mechanism to compare the functionality of a program against your communications requirements.

Operating system compatibility
Operating environment compatibility
Modem support
Flow control support
Serial port operating rates supported
Number of dialing directory entries allowed
File transfer protocols supported
Terminal emulations supported
Script programming language support

Now that we have reviewed the major features of personal computer communications programs, we'll focus on the use of those features by performing a communications session with a bulletin board system using ProcommPlus. We'll then use ProcommPlus for Windows to gain an appreciation for how the use of a graphical user interface can facilitate communications operations.

Using ProcommPlus

ProcommPlus is a comprehensive communications program that is easy to use when you understand the use of a few Alt key combinations. After you install the program on your computer and invoke its operation, the program displays its name on-screen as it loads, then displays a screen in which only the top and bottom lines display information. This initial program screen is shown in Figure 9.2. Although the top line is self-explanatory, the bottom line warrants an explanation for persons not familiar with this program.

FIGURE 9.2.

The initial ProcommPlus program screen with status information displayed on the bottom line of the display.

```
PROCOMM PLUS Ready!




















Alt-Z FOR HELP| ANSI     | FDX |  1200 E71 | LOG CLOSED | PRINT OFF | OFF-LINE
```

The bottom line on the ProcommPlus display can be considered as a status line that indicates the state of key program functions and provides users with a prompt concerning the use of the program. That prompt is the message Alt-Z FOR HELP, which indicates the key combination to press for assistance. Other information displayed on the status line in Figure 9.2 includes the current terminal emulation (ANSI), the transmission mode (FDX), the operating rate, the parity, data and stop bit settings (1200 E71), whether the program's log facility was enabled or disabled (LOG CLOSED), whether each line of information displayed is printed (PRINT OFF), and the status of communications (OFF-LINE). Later in this chapter when we use the program to establish a communications session, I will point out how several entries on the status line automatically change.

ProcommPlus Command Menu

To see the ProcommPlus help facility, press the Alt+Z key combination. Doing so results in the display of the program's command menu, which is shown in Figure 9.3. In examining the command menu displayed in Figure 9.3, note that most program functions are invoked by pressing two keys. Because this menu is easy to invoke, it provides a rapid mechanism to "look up" keystrokes required to perform different communications functions without requiring the use of the program's manual. As we examine the use of the program, I will mention how several communications functions are easily invoked by pressing a multikey combination.

FIGURE 9.3.

The ProcommPlus command menu screen display indicates the key and key combinations required to invoke different program functions.

As noted in Figure 9.3, the first key combination listed is Alt+D, which invokes the dialing directory. That key combination is listed first in the command menu because the use of the dialing directory enables users to set communications parameters as well as establish communications sessions using previously specified communications parameter settings.

Dialing Directory

Figure 9.4 illustrates the ProcommPlus dialing directory in which I entered directory information for all entries except the first, which is the default entry that enables you to dial the bulletin board system of the program developer. After you move the highlight bar over an entry in the dialing directory and press Enter, the program transmits the telephone number stored in the entry to the modem for automatic dialing. Because the highlight bar is over the first entry, we'll communicate with the program developer by pressing Enter.

FIGURE 9.4.

The ProcommPlus dialing directory screen.

```
DIALING DIRECTORY: PCPLUS.DIR

      NAME                        NUMBER        BAUD PDS D P   SCRIPT
    1 datastorm                 8,3148750503    2400 N81 F D
    2 tymnet                    9,929-0804      2400 E71 F D
    3 mci                       9,,18002346245  2400 071 F D
    4 frederick engineering     8,301-290-6944  2400 N81 F D
    5 delphi                    9,1,800-3654636 2400 N81 F D
    6 network world             8,508,620-1160  2400 N81 F D
    7 tymnet                    9,923-7590      1200 071 F D
    8 Telenet                   9,743-8844      2400 E71 F D
    9 the corner  gh            8,206-242-8574  2400 N81 F D
   10 boyan                     8,410-730-2917  2400 N81 H D

 PgUp Scroll Up      Space Mark Entry      C Clear Marked     L Print Directory
 PgDn Scroll Dn      Enter Dial Selected   E Erase Entry(s)   P Dialing Codes
 Home First Page     D Dial Entry(s)       F Find Entry       X Exchange Dir
 End Last Page       M Manual Dial         N Find Next        T Toggle Display
 ↑/↓ Select Entry    A Add Entry           G Goto Entry       S Sort Directory
 Esc Exit            R Revise Entry        J Jot Notes

 Choice:

 Alt-Z FOR HELP| ANSI    | FDX |  1200 E71 | LOG CLOSED | PRINT OFF | OFF-LINE
```

Figure 9.5 illustrates the establishment of a communications session using ProcommPlus. Note that certain entries in the status line changed to correspond to the settings in the dialing directory entry invoked. Thus, 2400 N81 indicates that the serial port of the computer is transmitting data at 2400 bps using eight data bits per character, no parity bit, and one stop bit per character. Also note that because a communications session was established, the extreme right of the status line now contains the entry ON-LINE.

FIGURE 9.5.

Establishing a communications session.

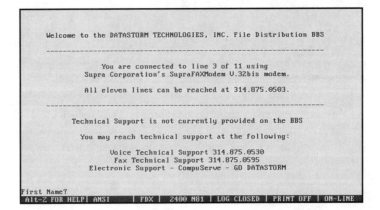

```
Welcome to the DATASTORM TECHNOLOGIES, INC. File Distribution BBS

-----------------------------------------------------------------

          You are connected to line 3 of 11 using
     Supra Corporation's SupraFAXModem V.32bis modem.

        All eleven lines can be reached at 314.875.0503.

-----------------------------------------------------------------

     Technical Support is not currently provided on the BBS

     You may reach technical support at the following:

          Voice Technical Support 314.875.0530
          Fax Technical Support 314.875.0595
     Electronic Support - CompuServe - GO DATASTORM

First Name?
 Alt-Z FOR HELP| ANSI    | FDX |  2400 N81 | LOG CLOSED | PRINT OFF | ON-LINE
```

In the event one or more dialing directory entries do not satisfy your communications requirements, you can use the dialing directory screen to change various communications settings. Figure 9.6 shows the previously displayed dialing directory screen in which the R key was pressed to revise the selected entry. This results in the display of a window labeled "Revise Entry 1," which lists the communications-related features, functions, and settings you can revise. As you move the highlight bar down the second column in that window, certain entries cause other windows to be displayed. When the highlight bar is positioned over the protocol entry, the program displays a window listing the file transfer protocols supported, which enables you to move the highlight bar over a file transfer protocol and press Enter to assign a new protocol to the selected entry in the dialing directory.

●
The ProcommPlus dialing directory provides users with the ability to store telephone numbers for automated dialing as well as to assign various communications parameter settings to each entry.

FIGURE 9.6.

Using the dialing directory to change the file transfer protocol assigned to a directory entry.

Figure 9.7 illustrates how you can use ProcommPlus to select or change a file transfer protocol when you are online. Pressing the Page Down key causes the program to display a window labeled "Download Protocols." That window enables you to change a previously established default protocol or press the Enter key to retain the default file transfer protocol.

```
T - TYPE file to your screen
C -  ┌─ Download Protocols - 227139584 bytes free ─┐
A -  │                                              │
X -  │   X) XMODEM              A) ASCII            │
O -  │   Z) ZMODEM              R) RAW ASCII        │
Y -  │   Y) YMODEM (Batch)      T) TELINK           │
G -  │   G) YMODEM-G (Batch)    M) MODEM7           │
S -  │   O) 1K-XMODEM           W) WXMODEM          │
K -  │   E) 1K-XMODEM-G         I) IMODEM           │
W -  │   C) COMPUSERVE B+       1) [EXT 1]          │
Z -  │   K) KERMIT             2) [EXT 2]          │
     │   S) SEALINK            3) [EXT 3]          │
Choo │                                              │
     │   Your Selection:    (press ENTER for ZMODEM)│
File └──────────────────────────────────────────────┘
File Size: 52 Records
 Protocol: XMODEM
Est. Time: 0 mins, 39 secs at 2400 bps

Awaiting Start Signal
(Ctrl-X to abort)

Alt-Z FOR HELP| ANSI    | FDX | 2400 N81 | LOG CLOSED | PRINT OFF | ON-LINE
```

FIGURE 9.7.

You can change the download file transfer protocol while online by pressing the Page Down key and selecting the desired protocol.

After you initiate a file transfer, ProcommPlus automatically provides you with a visual indication of the status of the transfer by displaying a window indicating the progress of the transfer. Figure 9.8 shows the progress of a file transfer when the ZMODEM protocol is used. The window in the right portion of Figure 9.8, which shows information about the file transfer, varies with respect to information content based on the file transfer protocol used. Some protocols, such as XMODEM, do not transfer information concerning the file size or its date of creation or last modification. For those protocols, ProcommPlus cannot compute the percentage of the file transmitted nor display the progress of the file transfer visually as a horizontal bar, as shown in the lower portion of the window displayed in Figure 9.8. In examining the file transfer window, note that one entry is Average CPS. By transferring the same file using different file transfer protocols, you can determine which protocol provides you with a higher throughput based on a specific communications environment.

FIGURE 9.8.

The ProcommPlus file transfer window indicating the status of a file transfer using the ZMODEM protocol.

```
T - TYPE file to your screen
C - ASCII with DC2/DC4 Capture
A - ASCII only, no Control Codes
X - XMODEM
O - XMODEM-1k                                  PROTOCOL: ZMODEM
Y - YMODEM (Batch)                            FILE NAME: mnp-9.exe
G - YMODEM-g (Batch)                          FILE SIZE: 6581
S - SEAlink                                  BLOCK CHECK: CRC-32
K - KERMIT                                   TOTAL BLOCKS:
W - SuperKERMIT (Sliding Windows)           TIME ESTIMATE: 00:27
Z - ZMODEM-90(Tm)                             TRANSMITTED: 31%
                                              BYTE COUNT: 2048
Choose one (Q to Quit): Z                     BLOCK COUNT:
                                              CORRECTIONS: 0
File Name: MNP-9.EXE                          AVERAGE CPS: 228
File Size: 6581 Bytes                         LAST MESSAGE:
 Protocol: ZMODEM-90(Tm)                         PROGRESS: ████████████
Est. Time: 0 mins, 28 secs at 2400 bps

Awaiting Start Signal
(Ctrl-X to abort)

          File transfer in progress...  Press ESC to abort
```

Using ProcommPlus for Windows

The beginning of the 1990s was accompanied by the acceptance of graphical user interface–based operating environments, resulting in most software developers focusing their efforts on application programs that work under one or more graphical user interface (GUI) environments. By the mid-1990s, many DOS-based communications programs were redesigned from the ground up to take advantage of the point-and-click operational capability afforded by different GUI environments. Datastorm Technologies, the developer of ProcommPlus, was no exception to this redesign effort. The company followed its DOS communications program with its ProcommPlus for Windows program, which could run under several GUI environments to include the original Microsoft Windows, its updated Windows 95 operating system, and Windows NT. For readers perhaps a bit confused about the different flavors of GUIs, let's digress a bit to explain their basic differences.

Versions of Windows

The term *Windows* commonly references a series of Microsoft operating environments through version 3.1 that overlayed DOS to provide a point-and-click GUI interface. Because Windows overlayed DOS, point-and-click operations referencing functions performed by DOS commands were translated so that they could be executed by DOS, slightly degrading computer performance. In addition, Windows was developed as a 16-bit operating environment, which did not tap the full capability of Intel 486 and Pentium-based PCs, whose processors are capable of executing instructions in 32-bit chunks. Recognizing the desirability to overcome those constraints, as well as a few more that are beyond the scope of this book, Microsoft developed Windows 95, which can be considered as an operating system rather than an operating environment because it does away with the necessity to overlay DOS.

Before introducing Windows 95, Microsoft developed an "industrial strength" version of Windows known as Windows NT, with NT being a mnemonic for *new technology*. Windows NT can be considered a sophisticated version of Windows that adds such features as multiple user accounts, security, and performance monitoring. Thus, it provides what many persons consider a mini-mainframe capability on a PC. ProcommPlus for Windows can operate under each of the three flavors of Windows. Although the method used to execute a program under each version of Windows can differ slightly, when the program is executed, the resulting screen display is very similar in appearance under each version of Windows. Because our goal is to gain an appreciation of the benefits resulting from the use of a GUI-based communications program, in the remainder of this section we will focus on several screen displays resulting from the execution of ProcommPlus for Windows that illustrate many of the advantages associated with using a GUI-based communications program.

Viewing the Main Program Screen

The adage "You be the judge" is applicable when comparing many DOS and Windows programs. Figure 9.9 shows the ProcommPlus for Windows main screen. The cursor is shown positioned over the second icon from the left, resembling a book, with the label, Dialing Directory, displayed.

If you compare Figure 9.2 with Figure 9.9, you will note a considerable difference between the main program screens used by the DOS and Windows versions of ProcommPlus. When working with the DOS version of ProcommPlus, you had to either remember command key combination sequences or press Alt+Z to get a command menu. In comparison, you can simply click an icon to perform most of the operations that require the use of a command key or multikey sequence when using the Windows version of the program.

FIGURE 9.9.

The main screen of ProcommPlus for Windows.

Because no standards define the functions associated with different icons, it can be a bit confusing if a person switches between two Windows-based programs that incorporate a series of icons or infrequently uses a program containing a series of icons. To facilitate the recognition of the meanings associated with different icons, ProcommPlus for Windows uses two methods to display the meanings associated with icons. First, as you move the cursor over an icon, a short label that defines its function is displayed. The label associated with the dialing directory icon is shown slightly under and to the right of the icon when the cursor was placed on the icon. The second method involves the display of text information on the program screen's status line. If you look at the lower-left corner of the display shown in Figure 9.9, you will note the text message `Show the current Dialing Directory`. As you move the cursor over different icons, the program provides an extended description of the function of the icon on the screen's status line.

Dialing Directory

An advantage associated with the use of GUI-based application programs is the capability to rapidly perform operations by pointing and clicking the cursor instead of having to enter commands by hand.

Because the cursor in Figure 9.9 is shown placed on the Dialing Directory, let's click that icon. Doing so results in the display of the program's dialing directory, which is shown in Figure 9.10. That dialing directory should be compared to the DOS version's dialing directory previously shown in Figure 9.4.

If you compare the DOS and Windows program dialing directories, you will note that the Windows version has numerous buttons. When those buttons are clicked, they initiate predefined operations that perform functions associated with one or more key sequences. In addition to eliminating the necessity to know and enter key sequences, many times a point-and-click operation can be considerably faster to perform, enhancing user productivity.

FIGURE 9.10.

The ProcommPlus for Windows Dialing Directory.

Multiple Choices

Another advantage associated with many GUI-based communications programs is the fact that they normally support multiple methods for accomplishing the same task. Typically, many commands selected from a menu are also capable of being invoked by an icon selection. This enables users to employ whichever method they are most comfortable with, further enhancing user productivity.

Figure 9.11 illustrates the display of the ProcommPlus for Windows Online menu. Note the first two entries in the menu, Send File and Receive File. You can also initiate those functions by clicking the folder icons with the upward (Send) and downward (Receive) pointing arrows. In addition, you can initiate other functions, such as Clear Screen, by selecting a menu entry, clicking an icon, or, as a leftover from the DOS version, entering a multikey combination. Specifically, to clear the screen, you could enter Alt+C, select that function from the Online menu, or click the fourth icon from the right. As an old politician would say, a GUI interface gives you a choice, not an echo!

Operation

To illustrate the use of ProcommPlus for Windows, let's access CompuServe and download a file from that information utility. Because I previously set up the program's dialing directory to include an entry for CompuServe, I could select that entry either from the program's dialing directory or from the program's Rapid Dial-Data drop-down menu previously shown in the upper-left corner of Figure 9.9. Selecting the CompuServe entry results in the program displaying a dialog box labeled Dialing using..., which also indicates the modem being used to dial the selected entry. Figure 9.12 illustrates the dialing dialog box that displays information about the call in progress and enables you to cancel the call.

FIGURE 9.11.

The ProcommPlus for Windows Online menu.

FIGURE 9.12.

Dialing CompuServe.

After I was connected to CompuServe and located in the appropriate library, I initiated a file transfer operation. The beginning of this file transfer operation is illustrated in Figure 9.13.

In examining the left portion of the background of Figure 9.13, you will note a series of numbers from 1 to 7 followed by the names of seven file transfer protocols supported by CompuServe. Although CompuServe supports XMODEM and YMODEM, it does not support ZMODEM, which was the default file transfer protocol I previously set for use by the program. To change the program's file transfer protocol, I simply clicked the button labeled ZMODEM, resulting in a pop-up display of protocols supported by the program. From that pop-up menu, I selected CIS-B+, which represents a file transfer protocol developed by CompuServe and which is commonly used with file transfers to or from that information utility. Thus, the dialog box labeled CIS-B+, shown in Figure 9.13, indicates that the CompuServe B+ file transfer protocol is being used to transfer the files THMPLS.EXE.

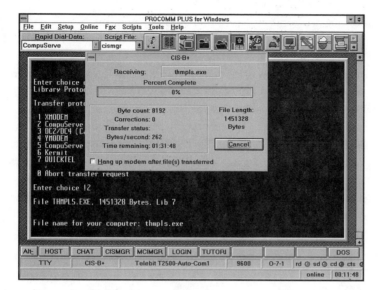

FIGURE 9.13.

Initiating a file transfer operation using ProcommPlus for Windows.

As indicated by the use of a series of program screen displays shown in this section, a GUI-based application program can significantly enhance user productivity. Programs supporting point-and-click operations, enabling users to select from several methods to perform the same function, and providing a mechanism to view the functions associated with icons make it easier for persons to use a computer. By removing the necessity to enter commands and use multikey sequences to invoke predefined functions, a GUI-based application program has been found to be easier to use. This in turn has increased the number of persons using PCs from the technical literate to encompass the occasional user as well as students starting with grade school.

What Have You Learned?

1. Both the support of a specific operating system and the operating environment govern the capability of a communications program to operate on a specific computer platform with a graphical user interface.

2. Support of the Hayes modem command set normally references the operation of basic modem functions. For the control of advanced modem functions, the communications program must support the modem you want to use.

3. For a modem to operate effectively when compressing data requires the computer's serial port operating rate to exceed the modem's operating rate.

4. Flow control is the orderly regulation of data transfer. To prevent the loss of data between a computer and modem requires the communications program to be configured to support the method of flow control used by the modem.

5. The dialing directories of most communications programs provide both a facility to select and dial different telephone numbers and the capability to assign specific communications parameter settings to each entry.

6. The terminal emulations supported by a communications program govern its capability to be used to communicate as a full-screen terminal device with minicomputers and mainframe computers.

7. A script programming language permits predefined communications functions to be automated.

8. The capability of a program to display different information concerning the status of a file transfer depends on the protocol used to transfer the file.

9. The use of a graphical user interface–based application program can enhance user productivity.

Quiz for Chapter 9

1. Hayes Microcomputer Products modem command set compatibility refers to:
   a. The control of basic modem functions.
   b. The control of advanced modem functions.
   c. Flow control.
   d. Data compression.

2. XON/XOFF is:
   a. Seldom used.
   b. Always enabled.
   c. A method of flow control.
   d. A data compression function.

3. To effectively use a compression performing modem:
   a. Set the serial port rate equal to the modem operating rate.
   b. Set the serial port rate higher than the modem operating rate.
   c. Set the serial port rate lower than the modem operating rate.
   d. Set the serial port rate to automatic speed detect.

4. A compression-performing modem operating at 14,400 bps that has a 4:1 average compression ratio requires which computer serial port operating rate to effectively operate?
   a. 14,400 bps.
   b. 28,800 bps.
   c. 55,400 bps.
   d. 57,600 bps.

5. An example of outband signaling is:
   a. XON/XOFF.
   b. ENQ/ACK.
   c. RS-232.
   d. CTS.

6. The basic function of a dialing directory is to:

    a. Store address information.

    b. Enable a user to enter telephone numbers to be dialed.

    c. Store communications parameters.

    d. Enable flow control.

7. An example of a file transfer protocol that uses a 32-bit cyclic redundancy check (CRC) is:

    a. YMODEM.

    b. XMODEM.

    c. XYMODEM.

    d. ZMODEM.

8. Information concerning communications parameter settings is displayed on the ProcommPlus:

    a. Main menu.

    b. Status line.

    c. Protocol window.

    d. Log facility.

9. The key or key combination required to be pressed to invoke the ProcommPlus line hang-up function is:

    a. Alt+X.

    b. Page Down.

    c. Alt+Q.

    d. Alt+H.

10. Information concerning the progress of a line transfer displayed by ProcommPlus varies based on:

    a. The file transfer protocol used.

    b. The average CPS.

    c. The date the file was created.

    d. The size of the file.

11. One difference between Windows 95 and Windows 3.1 is that:

    a. Windows 3.1 operates on Pentium computers.

    b. Windows 95 operates on Pentium computers.

    c. Windows 3.1 moves data in 32-bit chunks.

    d. Windows 95 moves data in 32-bit chunks.

12. You can initiate a file transfer using ProcommPlus for Windows by:

    a. Clicking the icon with an arrow flowing into a folder.

    b. Selecting the Receive File entry from the Online menu.

    c. Clicking on the Rapid Dial entry.

    d. Either clicking the icon with an arrow flowing into a folder or selecting the Receive File entry from the Online menu.

Alternatives in Local Area Networks

About This Chapter

This chapter begins by describing the characteristics of an ideal local area network (LAN) and the major obstacles to achieving the ideal. The most common types of existing LAN architectures—contention-access-based coaxial cable systems, token-passing systems, polled-access-based coaxial cable systems, and frequency-division broadband systems—are discussed through examples of existing LANs. LANs examined in this chapter include the different types of Ethernet networks defined by the Intel, Digital Equipment, and Xerox specification and the IEEE 802.3 standards, Datapoint's ARCnet, and IBM's 4 and 16 Mbps token-ring networks. After basic information concerning the operation of the most common types of LANs is presented, this chapter focuses on network devices used to expand local area networks. Networking devices covered include bridges, routers, gateways, and LAN switches.

What Is a LAN?

A LAN is a data communications facility located within a single building or campus that provides all high-speed switched connections to its terminal processors and peripheral devices.

In its most basic form, a LAN is a data communications facility providing high-speed switched connections between processors, peripherals, and terminals within a single building or campus. Historically, LANs have evolved from the data processing or office processing industry, in which economics suggest that relatively expensive storage devices and printers should be shared by multiple computers. Thus, LANs have evolved partly in response to the emergence of low-cost computing and its need for high-cost peripherals. Indeed, the first-generation LANs were actually one form of distributed computer systems using proprietary high-speed data links between processing nodes and peripheral equipment. A second rationale for the growth in the use of LANs is related to the need of modern organizations for distributed computing. A LAN allows computing power to be directly distributed to the desktop yet enables the desktop user to tap into other computer resources connected to the LAN. This distribution of computer power enables users to be more productive and in many organizations also allows conventional data centers to be eliminated or reduced in size, a process commonly referred to as downsizing.

LAN Versus Other Techniques

Each of the three data communications technologies has its own particular strengths and weaknesses regarding bandwidth versus distance trade-offs.

A perspective of a local area network as a digital communications facility is shown in Figure 10.1. This illustration depicts the bandwidth versus distance capabilities of three data communications technologies: computer buses, voiceband data links, and LANs. The computer buses are internal to a computer mainframe. They achieve very high data transfers by using high clock rates (for example, a few MHz) and parallel transmission (for example, 32 or 64 bits per clock cycle). Such systems are economical and practical only at distances up to a few meters. Voiceband data transmission uses readily available telephone wire pairs with modems. These systems are virtually unlimited in distance, but the standard analog telephone channel usually restricts voiceband data rates to 28,800 bps. From a cost-effectiveness point of view, 19,200 bps is very popular for dial-up data communications.

As you can see in Figure 10.1, the capabilities of a typical LAN represent a compromise between long distances and wide bandwidths. Some computer architectures have moved in on the region occupied by LANs by moving away from high-speed parallel buses to more loosely coupled distributed systems. Thus, the LAN region is overlapped on the left edge by distributed computer systems. Similarly, digital telephone systems are overlapping the LAN region on the bottom by providing moderate data rates (up to a few hundred kilobits per second) as a low-cost addition to basic telephone service.

The distance versus data-rate aspect of a local area network depicted in Figure 10.1 actually represents only one level of definition of a LAN. As the market and technology have grown, so has the recognition that a LAN should solve or alleviate more problems pertaining to data communications than merely the data transmission problem. The data communications manager or service organization responsible for a particular building or campus is typically concerned with various applications and associated types of equipment. If these different applications can be supported by one transmission facility, one type of hardware and software interface, and one set of maintenance procedures, total systems costs are reduced and overall administration is greatly simplified. For example, Figure 10.2 illustrates a local area network serving several independent applications.

FIGURE 10.1.

Distance versus data rate comparison.

FIGURE 10.2.

Local area network supporting multiple independent applications.

The next section presents the attributes of an ideal local area network—one that is supportive of all applications. In the sections that follow, present-day LANs are described and compared to the ideal as a means of contrasting one type of LAN with another.

The Ideal LAN

The ideal LAN would be an information distribution system that is as easy to use as the conventional AC power distribution system in a building. Thus, adding a data terminal, processor, or peripheral to a local area network should require nothing more than plugging it into a conveniently located access port. When plugged in, it should communicate intelligently with any other device on the network. This ideal system is summarized by the features that make the AC power system so easy to use:

- One-time installation
- Widespread access
- Application independence
- Excess capacity
- Easy maintenance and administration

> The ideal LAN should provide the same ease of access and equipment utilization that is found in a building's AC circuit.

The features identified in this list have been developed over the years to minimize life-cycle costs for supplying AC power within a building. Although the costs of a typical installation can be reduced by wiring only to locations with immediate electrical needs, the costs of only small amounts of rewiring to supply additional locations later would more than offset the initial savings. To achieve a one-time installation, it is necessary to provide widespread access—that is, an electrical outlet virtually everywhere one might be needed. Furthermore, the capacity at every outlet is generally greater than the needs of the electrical appliances that connect to it. Adding wiring or rewiring becomes necessary only for particularly high-power consuming devices (for example, those needing 240 volts or dedicated, high-current circuits).

If an information distribution system were available with all the desirable properties listed previously, it would mean that telephones, data terminals, printers, and storage devices could be moved as easily as unplugging and plugging in a lamp. Moreover, the equipment could be supplied by various vendors. Although such an ideal system does not now exist, local area networks of several forms represent some of the first steps in the development of such a system.

Major Obstacles to the Ideal LAN

The major obstacles to overcome in the development of the ideal system are summarized in the following sections.

> In the development of the ideal LAN, four major obstacles must be overcome.

No Single Standard

Due to the continually changing status of LANs and the competitive nature of the vendors, various local area network standards exist—both official and de facto. The situation is improving, however, because even the dominant suppliers who have been protecting their proprietary interfaces are being pressured by a maturing market to release interface specifications.

Diverse Requirements

The communications needs of a modern office building include voice, video, high-speed data, low-speed data, energy management, fire alarm, security, electronic mail, and so forth. These systems present transmission requirements that vary greatly in terms of data rates, acceptable delivery delays, reliability requirements, and error rate tolerance.

Costly Transmission Media

Being able to deliver tens of megabits per second to one device and only a few thousand bits per second to another implies that the lower rate devices are burdened with a costly transmission media. The best economic solution must involve a hierarchical network design (one with stepped levels of capacity) that allows twisted-pair connections for low and medium data rate devices (a low step) feeding into a backbone high bandwidth transmission system (a higher step such as coaxial cable or optical fibers).

Sophisticated Functional Requirements

Providing a network with the desired data rates and distances is only one item that must be considered in the data communications problem. Before one data device can communicate intelligently with another, numerous higher-level communications functions must be compatible. These include codes, formats, error control, addressing, routing, flow control, configuration management, and cost allocations.

The ISO Model

A formal hierarchical identification of all data communications network functions has been established by the International Standards Organization (ISO) and referred to as the ISO Model for Open Systems Interconnection (OSI). This model, shown in Figure 10.3, identifies seven distinct levels of functional requirements pertaining to data communications networks. The lower three levels of this model were originally proposed by the ITU-T to encourage vendor commonality in interfacing to public packet switching networks. This standard, designated as the ITU-T recommendation X.25, is described in detail in Chapter 11, "Architectures and Packet Networks," along with the ISO model.

●
A formal data communications hierarchy model containing seven levels of functional requirements has been established by the International Standards Organization.

FIGURE 10.3.

The ISO Model for
Open Systems
Interconnection.

Realization of the ideal LAN would require all levels of functions included in the OSI standard. However, not all levels of the OSI standard need to be implemented to provide effective communications in a LAN. If only the lower levels of the standard exist, a LAN can usefully support the multiple applications shown in Figure 10.2. In essence, the transmission media and lower-level interfaces are common so that data can be exchanged within virtual subnetworks—for example, the financial management group indicated in Figure 10.2.

LAN Standards

Local area network standards (as with other communications standards) get established by two groups: dominant manufacturers who attract plug-compatible competitors, and official standards organizations. The leading official standards organization for LANs in the United States is the IEEE 802 Standards Committee. This committee has several working groups responsible for establishing these LAN standards:

- 802.1—Coordinating the interface between OSI Levels 1 and 2 with the five higher-level layers
- 802.2—Logical data link standard similar to HDLC and ADCCP
- 802.3—CSMA/CS standard similar to Ethernet
- 802.3μ—Fast Ethernet
- 802.4—Token-bus standard
- 802.5—Token-ring standard
- 802.9a—IsoENET
- 802.12—100VG-AnyLAN

Logical Link Control—IEEE 802.2

To accommodate multiple LAN access methods, the IEEE 802 standards committee separated the OSI Data Link Layer into two sublayers: a logical link control (LLC) sublayer and a media access control (MAC) sublayer, as shown in Figure 10.4. Under working group 802.2, the LLC control procedures have been defined to be basically the same as the ITU-T X.25 Link Access Procedure HDLC in a balanced mode (LAPB). The balanced mode is used for peer structured networks wherein any station can originate communications directly with any other station.

●

The IEEE 802 Standards Committee separated the OSI data link layer into LLC and MAC layers.

●

LLC control procedures are similar to the ITU-T X.25 Link Access Procedure HDLC in a balanced mode.

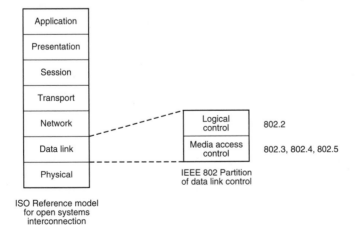

FIGURE 10.4.

The relationship of the IEEE 802 partition to the ISO reference model.

Two basic types of services are provided within 802.2 LLC. The type 1 service involves unacknowledged "connectionless" operation wherein the source station sends a message to another station (or stations) without having established a logical connection for sequencing and acknowledging messages. This mode of operation is intended for transmission of messages that are not essential and for systems in which higher levels provide error recovery and sequencing functions (as in Ethernet).

The type 2 service is the more conventional balanced data communications service that establishes logical connections between two LLCs. Each LLC can send and receive both messages and responses. Each LLC also has the responsibility of ensuring complete and accurate deliveries of its outgoing messages.

CSMA/CD—IEEE 802.3

The IEEE 802.3 standard defines the MAC sublayer for Carrier Sense Multiple Access/Collision Detection and a corresponding physical layer for connection to baseband coaxial cable and twisted-pair wiring. The standard is basically patterned after the Ethernet specification.

Variations in the physical layer allow signaling rates of 1, 5, 10, and 100 Mbps. A multidrop coaxial cable segment is limited to 500 meters (with 100 stations) rather than 1500 meters in Ethernet, but there can be as many as five coaxial segments in an IEEE 802.3 system. Later in this chapter, we will examine in detail the original Ethernet and the IEEE 802.3 standards, including network architecture and frame formats.

Token Passing Ring Access—IEEE 802.5

The IEEE 802.5 standard defines a token passing ring method in which access to a shared medium is obtained by the passing of a token. The token, which is a predefined sequence of bits, provides a receiving workstation on a token-ring LAN with the right to transmit a frame or a sequence of frames onto the ring.

When a workstation receives a free token, it builds a frame that includes the destination address of its transmission, its source address, and an information field, as well as a frame check sequence. The frame check sequence is used for frame verification similar to the manner in which a CRC or BCC is used. As the frame circulates around the ring, each workstation examines the destination address. If the destination address matches the address of the workstation, the workstation receives data from the information field and sets a field in the frame to indicate the successful receipt of the frame. As the frame continues around the ring, it returns to the originator, which notes the successful transfer of information in the frame. The originator now generates a new token, which provides other workstations with the capability to gain access to the transmission medium.

Ethernet (CSMA/CD)

Although Ethernet was not the first data communications network to technically qualify as a local area network, it is the most important because it represents the first major product offering with nonproprietary communications interfaces and protocols. Using an experimental design developed in a Xerox Corporation research laboratory, Xerox, Digital Equipment, and Intel teamed to define some commercial products based on jointly published communications standards. This action has invited other manufacturers to develop compatible products. The marketing strategy has been successful enough to establish the Ethernet interface as a standard even on systems utilizing transmission media different from the baseband coaxial cable originally specified for use in Ethernet.

The Ethernet architecture is based in concept on the Aloha satellite communications network developed at the University of Hawaii. The Aloha system allows multiple distributed devices to communicate with each other over a single radio channel using a satellite as a transponder. One station communicates with another by waiting until the radio channel is idle (determined by carrier sensing) and then sending a packet of data with a destination address, a source address, and redundant check bits to detect transmission errors. All idle stations continuously monitor incoming data and accept those packets with their address and valid checksums. Whenever a station receives a new packet, the receiving station returns an acknowledgment to the source. If an originating station receives no acknowledgment within a specified time interval, it retransmits the packet under the assumption that the previous packet was interfered with by noise or by a transmission from another station at the same time. (The latter situation is referred to as a collision.) Ethernet employs the same basic system concept, originally using coaxial cable for distribution throughout a building or campus.

●
Ethernet, which uses baseband coaxial cable as its carrier medium, was a joint effort by Xerox, Digital Equipment, and Intel. Ethernet was the first commercially available LAN.

Physical Layer

The transmission media of Ethernet was originally restricted to the use of conventional "thick" coaxial cable using baseband transmission at 10 Mbps. Other media now used for Ethernet transmission include "thin" coaxial cable and different types of twisted-pair wire. Both types of coaxial cable media support the use of a bus technology, and the use of twisted-pair wire requires the use of a star topology for an Ethernet LAN.

Baseband transmission implies that data is transmitted without the use of a carrier and with only one channel defined in the system. In comparison, broadband signaling results in the bandwidth of the media subdivided by frequency into multiple channels that can support the concurrent transmission of different types of signals, such as voice, data, and video. Figure 10.5 illustrates the operation of baseband and broadband signaling. Under the IEEE 802.3 set of LAN network standards, a broadband Ethernet referred to as 10BASE-36 was standardized. Later in this chapter, we will compare Ethernet to the IEEE 802.3 series of standards.

●
Baseband signaling results in one signal on a cable, whereas broadband signaling supports multiple simultaneous signaling on a cable.

FIGURE 10.5.

Baseband versus broadband signaling.

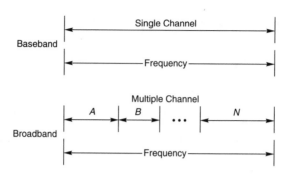

In a 10 Mbps Ethernet environment, when a station is transmitting, it uses the entire capacity of the system. Data is encoded using a Manchester code as shown in Figure 10.6. On 100 Mbps versions of Ethernet, different coding methods are used; those are described later in this chapter. The use of a Manchester code provides a strong timing component for clock recovery because a timing transition always occurs in the middle of every bit. In this type of coding, each bit period is divided into two complementary halves. A negative-to-positive voltage transition in the middle of the bit period designates a binary 1, whereas a positive-to-negative transition represents a binary 0. The Manchester line code has the additional property of always maintaining equal amounts of positive and negative voltages. This method prevents the build-up of a DC component, which simplifies the implementation of decision thresholds in the data detectors.

FIGURE 10.6.

Manchester line code.

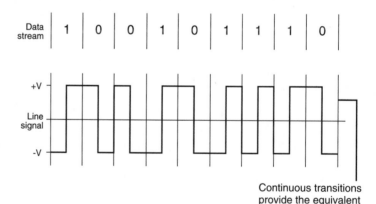

The Manchester code provides a form of carrier in its continuous transition. Multiple stations can enter or leave the line without causing traffic interruptions by using passive taps.

Although the data are not transmitted with a carrier per se, the continuous transitions of the Manchester code provide the equivalent of a carrier, so the channel is easily monitored for activity (for example, by a carrier sense technique). Multiple access to a coaxial cable–based network is provided by passive taps, thereby allowing station connections (called drops) to be added or removed without disrupting traffic in the system.

Another requirement of the transmission link and its associated access electronics is that while transmitting, a transceiver must be capable of detecting the existence of another active transmitter. This is referred to as collision detection. Thus, the three basic steps for accessing an Ethernet are denoted CSMA/CD (Carrier Sense, Multiple Access with Collision Detection).

The capability to detect collisions allows colliding stations to release the channel after using it for only a short period. A conventional Aloha system (one without collision detection), on the other hand, transmits entire messages without knowing whether a collision has occurred. Because an Ethernet station checks for carrier presence before transmitting, collisions occur only if two stations begin transmitting within a time interval equal to the propagation delay between the stations. By restricting the maximum distance between transceivers on a bus-based coaxial cable LAN to 2500 meters, the collision window is limited to 23 microseconds (μs), including amplifier delays.

When a station begins transmitting, it can be sure that no collision will occur if none is detected within a round-trip propagation of 46.4 μs. Because one bit time is 0.1 μs at 10 Mbps, the collision-detection decision is made within 464 bit times. The maximum length of a frame is 12,144 bits; thus, the collision-detection feature detects a collision very early in the frame to save significant transmission time that would be wasted if the entire frame were transmitted before detection.

Whenever a collision occurs, all colliding stations detect the condition and wait individually random amounts of time before retrying the transmission. Thus, the stations do not wait for acknowledgment timeouts to trigger a retransmission. (Acknowledgments are unnecessary at this level of the protocol but might be used at a higher level to ensure that the message was received at the final destination.) The method of waiting random amounts of time before transmitting reduces the probability of repeated collisions. In heavy traffic conditions, the average delay before retransmission begins to increase after 10 unsuccessful attempts. After 16 collisions, no further attempts are made to transmit that message, and the station is notified of the error by the transceiver.

In preparation for transmitting a data frame, the physical layer must insert a 64-bit preamble so that all receivers on the network can synchronize with the data stream before the desired data frame begins. The preamble consists of alternating ones and zeros, ending in two ones to signify the start of a frame.

> A transceiver must be able to detect any other active transmitters on the line while it is transmitting. This is called collision detection.

Physical Layer Interface

Standard Ethernet transceiver cable connectors: are 15-pin D-shell connectors (MIL-C-24308 or equivalent). The transceiver has a male connector, and the station apparatus has a female connector. Thus, the interconnecting cable must have one connector of each type.

These are the pin assignments:

1. Shield
2. Collision Presence +
3. Transmit +
4. Reserved
5. Receive +
6. Power return
7. Reserved
8. Reserved
9. Collision Presence –
10. Transmit –
11. Reserved
12. Receive –
13. Power
14. Reserved
15. Reserved

Figure 10.7 illustrates the relationship of the Ethernet hardware components required to connect a workstation to a bus-based coaxial cable. The interface board or adapter card is normally installed in a system expansion slot within the system unit of a personal computer. That board or card is also known as a controller and is often referred to as an Ethernet controller.

FIGURE 10.7.

The relationship of Ethernet hardware components.

The Ethernet controller formats data from the computer into frames for transmission via the transceiver cable to the transceiver. The transceiver converts unipolar digital signals generated by the computer into Manchester encoded digital signals. In addition, the transceiver is responsible for detecting collisions by examining the voltage level on the cable. That is, when the voltage level rises beyond its normal nominal height, it indicates the occurrence of a collision.

Data Link Layer

The data link is concerned with message frame format, message addressing, and error checking, and as such, it is largely independent of the medium-dependent physical channel.

The data link layer is primarily concerned with message packaging and link management. It is largely independent of the medium-dependent physical channel. The message packaging function includes the following items:

● Framing: Identification of the beginning and end of a message.

● Addressing: Specified fields for source and destination addresses.

● Error checking: Redundant codes for detecting channel errors.

The format of an Ethernet frame is shown in Figure 10.8. The preamble, which consists of the repeating sequence 101010... for 8 bytes or 64 bits, announces the occurrence of the frame. The preamble's generation and removal are functions of the physical layer. Similarly, the end of a frame is provided by the removal of the carrier sense signal detected by the absence of a bit transition following the last bit of the frame check sequence. Notice that frame sizes must be an integral number of bytes, ranging from 72 to 1526 bytes. (At 8 bits per byte, that's 572 to 12,208 bits.) The Type field is reserved to indicate which of several possible higher-level protocols might be in use.

8 Bytes	6 Bytes	6 Bytes	2 Bytes	46-1500 Bytes	4 Bytes
Preamble	Destination Address	Source Address	Type	Data	Frame Check Sequence

FIGURE 10.8.

The Ethernet data link frame format.

System Configurations

Besides the single cable system indicated in Figure 10.7, other Ethernet configurations are possible in which several multidrop segments (possibly one in each of several buildings) are interconnected with point-to-point cables and repeaters. Figure 10.9 shows a typical configuration of a multisegment system. The following specifications apply:

●

By use of point-to-point cables and repeaters, several multidrop segments can be connected to add flexibility to Ethernet systems.

Maximum Lengths:

1500 meters of multidrop cable

1000 additional meters of point-to-point cable between cable segments

300 additional meters in six transceiver cables

50 meters in a single transceiver cable

Maximum Number of Stations: 1024

FIGURE 10.9.

A typical large-scale Ethernet configuration.

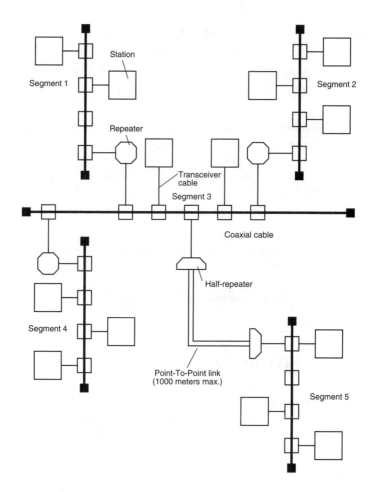

Other Ethernet Networks

In actuality, when referring to Ethernet, we reference a group of networks based on the CSMA/CD access protocol. The original Ethernet standard defined by Xerox, Digital Equipment, and Intel operated at 10 Mbps over a bus-based thick 50 ohm coaxial cable. When Ethernet was standardized by the IEEE 802.3 committee, five additional "Ethernet" standards were promulgated that provided support for operating rates up to 10 Mbps. Since then, several new high-speed "Ethernet" standards have been promulgated. The IEEE 802.3μ Fast Ethernet standard actually references a series of three 100 Mbps physical layer LAN specifications that use the CSMA/CD access protocol. Although some persons refer to the IEEE 802.12 standard known as 100VG-AnyLAN as an Ethernet LAN, that standard actually represents a demand priority access scheme that can be used to support Ethernet or another type of local area network; however, such support is restricted to one type of LAN. After giving you an appreciation for the operational characteristics of what is now considered low-speed Ethernet, I will focus on Fast Ethernet.

Table 10.1 compares the operational characteristics of each low-speed IEEE 802.3 network standard with the characteristics of the original Ethernet standard.

Table 10.1. Ethernet and IEEE 802.3 network characteristics.

Operational Characteristics	Ethernet	10BASE-5	10BASE-2	1BASE-5	10BASE-T	10BROAD-36
Operating rate Mbps	10	10	10	1	10	10
Access protocol	CSMA/CD	CSMA/CD	CSMA/CD	CSMA/CD	CSMA/CD	CSMA/CD
Type of signaling	baseband	baseband	baseband	baseband	baseband	broadband
Data encoding	Manchester	Manchester	Manchester	Manchester	Manchester	Manchester
Maximum segment length (meters)	500	500	185	250	100	1800
Stations/ segment	100	100	30	12/hub	12/hub	100
Media	50 ohm coaxial (thick)	50 ohm coaxial (thick)	50 ohm coaxial (thin)	unshielded twisted pair	unshielded twisted pair	75 ohm coaxial
Topology	bus	bus	bus	star	star	bus

The IEEE uses the general format *s type l* to develop the name of each CSMA/CD network. Here, *s* references the speed in Mbps; *type* indicates the type of signaling, either BASE for baseband or BROAD for broadband; and *l* generally indicates the maximum segment length in hundreds of meters. For example, 10BASE-5 denotes the standard for a 10 Mbps baseband LAN that has a maximum segment length of 500 meters and uses the CSMA/CD access protocol. Readers should note that *l* does not always indicate the maximum segment length or an accurate maximum segment length. For example, 10BASE-2 has a maximum segment length of 185 meters, and 10BASE-T, in which T indicates the use of twisted-pair wiring, has a maximum segment length of 100 meters.

Under the IEEE 802.3 standard, changes occurred to the Ethernet frame illustrated in Figure 10.8. A few minor changes resulted in the incompatibility of equipment designed for use in computers based on the original Ethernet specification and the IEEE 802.3 frame format.

The IEEE 802.3 committee defined five additional types of CSMA/CD networks.

Figure 10.10 illustrates the IEEE 802.3 data link frame format. In comparing that format to the Ethernet data link frame format illustrated in Figure 10.8, note that the Preamble field was reduced to 7 bytes, and a Start of Frame Delimiter field was added under the IEEE 802.3 frame format. The Start of Frame Delimiter field is actually a continuation of the preamble, with the sequence 10101011. However, the ending two bits are 11 rather than the 10 contained in the Ethernet Preamble field.

FIGURE 10.10.

The IEEE 802.3 data link frame format.

IEEE 802.3

Preamble	Start of Frame Delimiter	Destination Address	Source Address	Length	Data	Frame Check Sequence
7 bytes	1 byte	2/6 bytes	2/6 bytes	2 bytes	46-1500 bytes	4 bytes

●

Under the IEEE 802.3 frame format, the Ethernet Type field was replaced by a Length field.

Another difference between the two frame formats is the replacement of the Type field by a Length field in the IEEE 802.3 frame. Here the length field specifies the number of bytes that follow that field as data.

●

The IEEE 10BASE-5 network standard resulted in changes in terminology of hardware used in the original Ethernet network.

10BASE-5

Although a 10BASE-5 network follows the same configuration rules as the original Ethernet network, certain changes in terminology cause some confusion to many persons. To alleviate that potential confusion, Figure 10.11 illustrates the changes in terminology between the original Ethernet 50 ohm coaxial cable bus-based network and the IEEE 802.3 10BASE-5 bus-based network.

FIGURE 10.11.

Terminology changes between Ethernet and IEEE 10BASE-5.

Legend:
AUI = Attachment Unit Interface
MAU = Media Attachment Unit
NIC = Network Interface Card

As indicated in Figure 10.11, the controller under 10BASE-5 is now referred to as a NIC (pronounced "nick"), or network interface card. The transceiver cable is now known as an AUI, or attachment unit interface, and the transceiver is called a MAU (pronounced to rhyme with "cow"), or media attachment unit.

Most 10BASE-5 NICs include both a DB-15 and a BNC connector. The DB-15 provides a connection to the AUI, whereas the BNC permits the use of the NIC on a 10BASE-2 network. Thus, the dual connectors permit the use of the NIC on two types of 802.3 standards.

10BASE-2

A 10BASE-2 network is based on the use of thin coaxial cable that provides a degree of cabling flexibility not obtainable with the thick coaxial cable used with a 10BASE-5 network. In addition, the use of thin coaxial cable makes cabling more economical. A 10BASE-2 workstation is connected to the thin coaxial cable by BNC connectors, which are also referred to as barrel connectors.

Figure 10.12 illustrates the cabling of stations to a 10BASE-2 network. This type of Ethernet network permits a maximum of 30 stations per cable segment. You can extend a 10BASE-2 network through the use of inter-repeater cable segments (IRCS), or you can combine 10BASE-2 and 10BASE-5 networks, although when doing so you must ensure that you do not violate any cabling rules. Refer to the book *Ethernet Networks, Second Edition,* written by Gilbert Held and published by John Wiley & Sons, for specific information concerning Ethernet IEEE 802.3 cabling restrictions and the interconnection of different types of IEEE 802.3 networks.

● A 10BASE-2 network is limited to 30 stations per segment and uses thin coaxial cable for the transmission media.

Station 1   Station 2   Station 3   Station 30

FIGURE 10.12.
Cabling a 10BASE-2 network.

10BASE-T

Another series of configurations is obtainable through the use of 10BASE-T, which is a more modern standard that allows the construction of 10 Mbps Ethernet LANs over unshielded twisted-pair wire. Under the 10BASE-T standard, which is also referred to as the IEEE 802.3i standard, workstations are cabled using twisted-pair wire to medium access units (MAUs). Each MAU normally has a built-in attachment interface unit (AIU) that can be cabled to a coaxial transceiver attached to a coaxial cable. Thus, workstations can be configured in a star topology and cabled to a bus structured backbone cable that serves to interconnect MAUs. Figure 10.13 illustrates a hybrid Ethernet media configuration in which personal computer workstations are cabled to MAUs via the use of twisted-pair wire. The MAUs in turn are connected to a coaxial cable that not only links MAUs, but also provides access to a mainframe computer.

FIGURE 10.13.

A hybrid Ethernet media configuration.

Legend

PCW = Personal Computer Workstation

AIU = Attachment Interface Unit

CT = Coaxial Transceiver

Fast Ethernet

As briefly noted earlier in this chapter, Fast Ethernet is a term used to reference a series of three 100 Mbps physical LAN specifications described in the IEEE 802.3μ addendum to the 802.3 standard. Those specifications include 100BASE-TX, 100BASE-FX, and 100BASE-T4. Each specification maintains the use of the CSMA/CD access control protocol, and dual functioning 10/100 Mbps network adapter cards are available that allow an investment in 10 Mbps technology today to be upgraded to a 100 Mbps LAN tomorrow.

Physical Layer Subdivision

For each version of Fast Ethernet, the physical layer was subdivided to permit the use of different types of media for 100 Mbps operations.

Similar to the manner in which the data link layer was subdivided, under the IEEE 802.3μ specification, the physical layer was also subdivided. Here the subdivision of the physical layer was performed to facilitate the support of three types of media by the standard: unshielded twisted pair (UTP), shielded twisted pair (STP), and fiber optic.

Figure 10.14 illustrates the physical layer subdivision associated with Fast Ethernet. Because different coding schemes are required to support 100 Mbps operations on different types of media, a physical coding sublayer was required to perform the necessary coding for each media. Under the physical coding layer is a physical media dependent (PMD) sublayer. The PMD sublayer transfers the physical coding onto the media by providing an appropriate interface to the media.

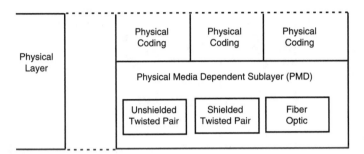

FIGURE 10.14.

The Fast Ethernet physical layer subdivision.

100BASE-T4

100BASE-T4 represents a 100 Mbps CSMA/CD network that operates over four pairs of category 3, 4, or 5 unshielded twisted-pair or shielded twisted-pair cable. Although 100BASE-T4 is similar to 10BASE-T in that it is a hub-based network, to ensure proper collision detection, the span of the network was reduced to 250 meters, with a maximum of 100 meters permitted between a workstation and a hub port.

To obtain a 100 Mbps operating rate required three changes at the physical layer. First, three pairs of wires are used for transmission (the fourth is used for collision detection), which provides a threefold increase over 100BASE-T. Next, 8 BGT coding, in which 8 input bits are transformed into a unique code group of 6 ternary symbols, is used to replace Manchester coding, boosting throughput by 265 times that of 10BASE-T. The third change was an increase in clock signaling speed from the 10BASE-T 20 MHz to 25 MHz, boosting throughput by 1.25 times that of 10BASE-T. When all three changes are considered, 100BASE-T can operate at 10 times 10BASE-T, or 100 Mbps.

Figure 10.15 illustrates a typical 100BASE-T4 network structure, including cabling constraints and a breakout of pin assignments. Note that the connectors used for 100BASE-T4 are RJ-45, which simplifies connecting cable to workstations and hub ports to the insertion of a jack into a plug receptacle.

●

100BASE-T4 requires four pairs of cable but is capable of operating on category 3, 4, or 5 shielded or unshielded twisted-pair wire.

FIGURE 10.15.

A typical 100BASE-T4 network structure.

100BASE-TX

●

Although 100BASE-TX is designed to use two pairs of wire, that wire is restricted to category 5 cable.

100BASE-TX represents a second type of 100 Mbps Fast Ethernet. This standard is based on the use of two pairs of category 5 unshielded twisted-pair cable. One pair of wires is used for collision detection and reception of data.

The use of two wire pairs rather than the four used by 100BASE-T4 required a change to both the clock rate and the coding method used. 100BASE-TX uses a 125 MHz frequency and a 4B5B coding stream in which every 4 data bits are mapped into a 5-bit code. Because this coding method requires only 16 symbols to represent data, the remaining symbols are available for control use. Due to the higher line frequency used by 100BASE-TX, it can be implemented only through the use of category 5 UTP. In comparison, the 25 MHz clock rate of 100BASE-T4 permits the use of four pairs of category 3, 4, and 5 UTP or STP cable. Similar to 100BASE-T4, however, a 100BASE-TX network is limited to a maximum network diameter of 250 meters, and the maximum cable run is 100 meters from a hub port to a network station.

100BASE-FX

The third wiring scheme supported by Fast Ethernet is two-strand 62.5/125 micron multimode fiber media. This media is used by the 100BASE-FX version of Fast Ethernet, and the coding scheme is identical to that of 100BASE-TX. Although 100BASE-FX standards were in the process of being developed when this book was written, the use of fiber optics can be expected to result in longer cabling runs than are permissible with 100BASE-T4 or 100BASE-TX. This should enable 100BASE-FX to be used for connections between bridges, routers, and switches.

Token-Passing Networks

Because access to a CSMA network involves a certain amount of contention (competition) between stations trying to send a message at the same time, the behavior of the network must be analyzed and controlled statistically. Token passing networks, on the other hand, provide a different access procedure. Access is determined by which station has the token; that is, only one station at a time, the one with the token, is given the opportunity to seize the channel. The token is passed from one idle station to another until a station with a pending message receives it. After the message is sent, the token is passed to the next station. In essence, a token passing network is a distributed polling network.

Two basic topologies (configurations or arrangements) exist for token-passing networks: token-passing rings and token-passing buses. In a token-passing ring, shown in Figure 10.16, the closed loop topology defines the logical topology (that is, the order in which the token is circulated). A token-passing bus, shown in Figure 10.17, has more operational flexibility because the token-passing order is defined by tables in each station. If a station (for example, a printer) never originates communications, it will be a terminate-only station, and it need not be in the polling sequence. If a station needs a high priority, it can appear more than once in the polling sequence.

●
Token passing networks provide access to the network by only one station at a time— the one with the token that is ready to send a message.

●
Token topologies can be either a token-passing ring or a token-passing bus; each has its own strengths and weaknesses.

FIGURE 10.16.
A token-passing ring.

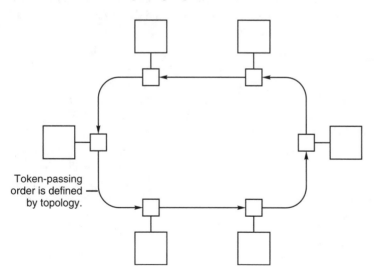

Token-passing order is defined by topology.

FIGURE 10.17.

A representative access sequence in a token-passing bus.

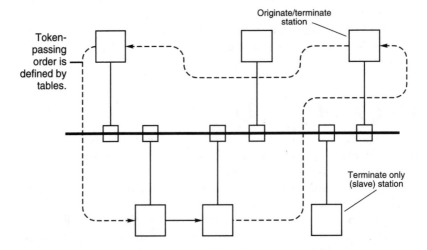

Besides the operational differences between bus and ring topologies, other major contrasts exist, as listed here:

- A ring requires an active interface module in series with the transmission link. A bus uses a passive tap like a CSMA system.

- The point-to-point nature of a ring's transmission links implies that the signal quality is easily controlled. Multiple taps in a linear bus system, on the other hand, each contribute to signal distortions.

- A ring has no inherent (built-in) distance limitation (as does the bus) because there is no delay dependence in its operation, and the access taps at each station serve as regenerative repeaters to the digital signals.

- A bus allocates the entire channel to an active device. The channel of a ring can be subdivided into time division multiplexed subchannels for time-continuous, lower-data-rate applications. Figure 10.18 shows a ring with time division multiplexed subchannels. Such a system, also referred to as a loop, typically requires a unique control node to define framing for the subchannels. Access to the TDM channels is distributed by passing tokens.

- The ring topology is ideally suited to the particular capabilities of fiber-optic transmission. As discussed in Chapter 7, "Fiber-Optic and Satellite Communications," optical fibers provide very wide bandwidth and complete elimination of electrical interference, but they are presently practical only as point-to-point transmission links.

FIGURE 10.18.

A time division multiplex loop.

ARCnet

The forerunner of token-passing networks in the United States is the Attached Resource Computer Network, ARCnet, developed by Datapoint Corporation. Initially, the network and protocol were kept proprietary, but the data link protocol, interface specs, and even integrated circuits were made publicly available in 1982. Functionally, the ARCnet is a token-passing bus, but the physical topology, shown in Figure 10.19, is a hybrid bus/star. Instead of distributing taps along a linear bus as suggested in Figure 10.17, the ARCnet uses hubs with individual ports to connect Resource Interface Modules (RIMs) to the transmission media.

The hub-based architecture is an effective means of controlling the signal quality because the hub isolates each RIM port from the main coaxial cable. Unidirectional (one-way) amplifiers in the hubs provide zero insertion loss and suppress reflections because only one direction of transmission is enabled at a time. Amplifier switching is possible because a token-passing network transmits in only one direction at a time.

●
ARCnet is a type of token-passing bus. Its topology is a hybrid bus/star.

FIGURE 10.19.
*The physical topology
of the ARCnet.*

Physical Layer

●

RG62 coaxial cables
with a baseband
transmission rate of
2.5 Mbps are used
to connect the hubs
and RIMs in an
ARCnet.

The ARCnet interconnects the hubs and RIMs with RG62 coaxial cable using baseband transmission at 2.5 Mbps. Although 2.5 Mbps is a relatively low data rate, ARCnet uses inexpensive coax and can be configured (laid out) with as much as four miles between stations. The cable length between a hub and a RIM is limited to 2000 feet, but a four-mile span can have up to a maximum of 10 hubs in a series path.

Link Protocol

●

There are five basic
message formats
used in link
protocol—four
control messages
and one data
carrier. Eight bits
are used in all
address fields.

The ARCnet employs five basic message formats, as shown in Figure 10.20. The first four formats are used for control messages; the fifth carries data between stations. All address fields consist of eight bits, which restricts the number of stations to 255 (address 0 is reserved as a broadcast address to all stations). As indicated in Figure 10.20, the destination address (DID) is duplicated with every message for error protection.

A logical flow diagram of the token-passing procedure implemented in every RIM is shown in Figure 10.21. On receiving a token (message type 1) with the proper address, a RIM chooses one of two paths, depending on whether it has transmit data pending. If data is pending, the RIM sends a free-buffer request (message type 2) to the desired destination RIM inquiring whether it is ready to receive. The destination RIM responds with an ACK (message type 3) if it has buffer space available, or a NAK (message type 4) if it does not have buffer space available.

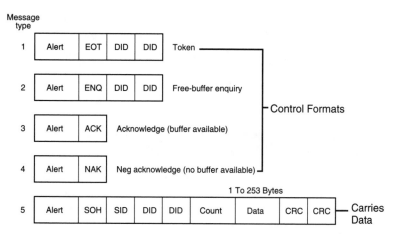

FIGURE 10.20.

Message formats in ARCnet.

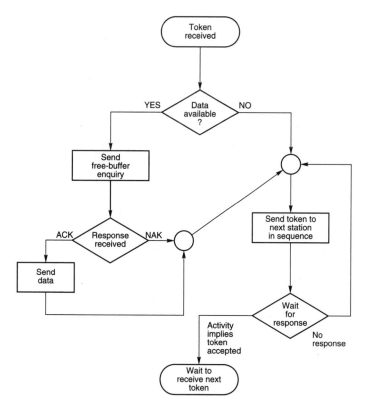

FIGURE 10.21.

Flow diagram of token-passing procedure in ARCnet.

After a RIM has transmitted its data or determined that it cannot, it passes the token to the station with the next higher address. After sending the token, the RIM monitors the channel to see whether it is accepted. The occurrence of a message type 1, 2, or 5 indicates the token is accepted. No response on the channel within 74 μs implies that the intended station is offline, and the token should be passed to the station with the next highest address.

IBM Token-Ring Network

In the mid-1980s, IBM introduced its token-ring network based on the use of token passing. This token-ring network uses a logical ring topology that is physically wired as a star, with workstations connected to a wiring concentrator known as a multistation access unit (MAU, sometimes also known as MSAU). MAUs are cabled to each other to form a ring, in effect resulting in a star-ring topology for the token-ring network.

Figure 10.22 illustrates the wiring of workstations to each MAU. Each workstation uses a twisted-pair connection for "ring-in" and a second twisted pair for "ring-out," with the data flowing from station to station in one direction to represent a logical ring. In addition to functioning as a central wiring point, the MAU also controls access of each workstation to the LAN. This is accomplished by the use of relays in each MAU port, enabling the MAU to simply short the relay to bypass a workstation. To get access to the LAN, a workstation raises a 5-volt signal that causes the MAU to open the relay on the port and add the workstation to the ring. This technique enables all inactive stations on a ring to be automatically bypassed, which serves to maximize LAN performance.

FIGURE 10.22.

Wiring workstations to a MAU.

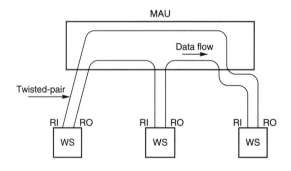

Legend:

MAU = Multistation Access Unit

WS = Workstation

RI = Ring-In

RO = Ring-Out

Although three workstations are shown connected to one MAU in Figure 10.22, in actuality, up to eight workstations can be connected. A token-ring network is expanded to support additional workstations through the use of additional MAUs, with the MAUs interconnected to form a ring.

IBM, as well as several third-party manufacturers, produces token-ring adapter cards that can be installed in personal computers to allow PCs to be cabled to MAUs. The original IBM token-ring network operated at 4 Mbps and supported a maximum of 72 device connections, which is the equivalent of interconnecting nine MAUs. This network, for which 4 Mbps token-ring adapter cards are used in PCs, can use shielded or unshielded twisted-pair wiring. A second IBM token-ring network operates at 16 Mbps and extends the support of devices to 250 but requires the use of shielded cable. The 16 Mbps network requires the use of 16 Mbps token-ring adapter cards. Although IBM and third-party manufacturers market 4/16 Mbps token-ring adapters that can operate at either data rate, all devices on a LAN must be set to operate at either 4 or 16 Mbps. This means that users migrating from a 4 Mbps token-ring network to 16 Mbps must change all adapters for the LAN to operate at the higher rate.

Network Expansion

As previously mentioned, you can expand a token-ring network by adding one or more MAUs and connecting the ring-out (RO) port of one MAU to the ring-in (RI) port of another MAU. The original IBM MAU, known as the 8228, contained 10 ports, of which 8 provided connections to workstations because one was the ring-in port and another was the ring-out port used for network expansion. When an organization had many workstations to be connected to a token-ring network, it would have to get a number of 8228s and cable the RI and RO ports of each device together. In addition, one or more racks might be required to install the 8228s to facilitate cabling of workstations to ports on each 8228. Recognizing the problems associated with the cabling and rack mounting of individual 8228s, both IBM and third-party hardware vendors developed different types of products that essentially represent multiple 8228 MAUs. One such product is the IBM 8230 control access unit.

The control access unit (CAU) can be considered an expandable MAU. The basic unit consists of a control unit and one lobe attachment module where the latter device provides the capability to cable individual workstations to the 8230. The 8230 is expanded by the addition of one or more lobe attachment modules. Figure 10.23 illustrates the expansion of a token-ring network through the use of a MAU and CAU. Here it was assumed that many workstations were clustered in one portion of a floor in a building and that eight workstations were clustered at another location on the same floor. Note that only two long-distance cables are required to connect the MAU and CAU. In comparison, if one CAU were used, you would require the installation of eight long-distance cables

●

A control access unit is expanded by the use of lobe attachment modules to support additional workstations on a token-ring network.

to connect the workstations located in the upper-right portion of Figure 10.23 to the CAU. Thus, the appropriate use of MAUs and CAUs can reduce cabling requirements, which can be an important consideration when conduits do not have room for the installations of a large number of additional cables.

FIGURE 10.23.

Ring construction using a MAU and CAU.

Fiber Distributed Data Interface

Fiber Distributed Data Interface (FDDI) represents an evolving local area network technology that provides a 100 Mbps operating rate over fiber cable. The FDDI standard was developed by the American National Standards Institute (ANSI) X3T9.5 Task Group because it was originally developed as a mechanism for connecting storage systems and loosely coupled microprocessors in a data center. Although FDDI was standardized as an "I/O standard" by ANSI rather than the IEEE 802 committee, which primarily focuses on local area networks, the evolution of the standard during the 1980s resulted in the first widely implemented and multivendor LAN technology capable of supporting 100 Mbps operations.

Network Topology

FDDI is based on the use of two rings for backbone network transmission. One ring is known as the primary; the second is known as the secondary. The secondary ring provides a "self-healing" mechanism designed to negate the effect of a cable failure for the backbone ring. When a ring network failure occurs on an FDDI LAN, data flow on the secondary ring is initiated counter to the flow of data that occurred on the primary ring. Thus, many persons refer to FDDI as a counter-rotating ring topology.

An FDDI includes a self-healing capability that automatically negates the effect of a single cable failure on the backbone ring.

Network Access

Similar to a token-ring, a rotating token is used on an FDDI network to provide stations with permission to transmit data. Three types of stations are supported by FDDI: a single attached station (SAS) and two types of dual attached stations (DAS). Computers and other networking devices, such as bridges and routers, obtain access to an FDDI network via a connection to an SAS, which is then connected to a concentrator DAS.

Dual attached stations are used to form the backbone of an FDDI ring, as illustrated in Figure 10.24. In this example, the effect of a cable failure between a pair of dual attached stations is shown. Each DAS contains two optical connection pairs referred to as A and B interfaces or ports. The A interface or port contains one primary ring input and the secondary ring input, whereas the B interface or port contains the primary ring input. Through the use of two optical transceivers, each DAS can transmit and receive data on each ring.

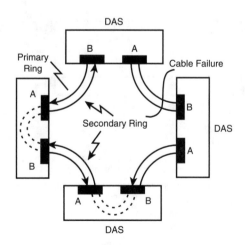

FIGURE 10.24.

Dual attached stations form the backbone of an FDDI network.

Legend:

A Interface containing primary ring input and secondary ring output

B Interface containing primary ring output and secondary ring input

DAS Dual attached station

By monitoring the light levels received, each dual attached station can recognize a cable failure. When a failure is noted, two adjacent dual attached stations wrap away from the detected cable failure, restoring connectivity by converting the dual ring into a single ring. After the failure condition is corrected, the restoration of an appropriate light level causes each DAS to remove the previously implemented wrap, which restores the network to its dual ring operation.

A second type of DAS functions as a concentrator, containing a series of extra ports as well as the previously described A and B interfaces. Those extra ports, referred to as M or master ports, are used to provide connectivity to single attached stations, a DAS, or another DAS concentrator. Thus, a DAS concentrator provides additional ports that extend the capability to access the primary ring to other stations.

Figure 10.25 illustrates the connection of several single attached stations to a multiple M port, dual-attached station. The M (master) port on the DAS concentrator and S (slave) port on the SAS reference the connector receptacles on each device and not their operation. FDDI was designed with different connectors on SAS and DAS concentrators to facilitate the correct connection of cable between S and M ports.

FIGURE 10.25.

FDDI SAS-DAS transmission.

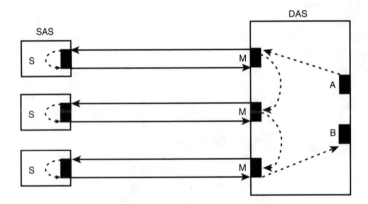

Legend

A	Interface containing primary ring input and secondary ring output
B	Interface containing primary ring output and secondary ring input
M	Master port
S	Slave port
DAS	Dual attached station
SAS	Single attached station

Note that the connection of an SAS's port to a DAS M port can resemble a star topology, even though the interconnection of DAS and DAS concentrators forms a ring. Also note that the connection of an SAS to a DAS port is via the cabling of a single cable sheath containing two fiber-optic cables, one for transmission and one for reception of data. This restricts the SAS-to-DAS connection to a single ring. Thus, the self-healing feature of an FDDI network is restricted to the backbone ring formed by interconnecting DASs.

A common use for FDDI networks during the mid-1990s was as a backbone for connecting lower-speed LANs via bridges or routers to an FDDI network. Another popular use for FDDI was as a high-speed port on a switching hub to provide a 100 Mbps connection from the switching hub to a file server. Due to the relatively high cost of optical components, work was proceeding on a copper-based version of FDDI. However, due to the advent of low-cost 100 Mbps versions of Ethernet, CDDI technology might not result in a competitive economically viable product.

Bridges

Bridges are devices that connect LANs at the ISO data-link level. In a token-ring network, a local bridge can be used to connect two adjacent token-ring LANs into one LAN. One example of a local bridge is an IBM PS/2 Model 55 personal computer containing two token-ring adapter cards, with each card cabled to the MAU of a local token-ring network. Figure 10.26 illustrates the use of a local bridge to connect two token-ring networks.

FIGURE 10.26.
Using a local bridge.

A second type of bridge is a remote bridge. This type of bridge is used to connect token-ring networks located at a distance from one another that require interconnection via the use of a communications carrier transmission facility. When two LANs are connected by remote bridging, a remote bridge must be installed on each LAN. In place of a second token-ring adapter, each remote bridge would contain a serial communications port, allowing the device to be connected to a modem or a DSU/CSU, which, in turn, would be connected to an analog or a digital transmission facility. The remote bridge examines addressing information in each token-ring frame, and on recognition of an address on the distant LAN, routes the frame via the serial port of the device onto the communications carrier transmission facility linking the remote LANs together. Figure 10.27 illustrates the use of remote bridges to interconnect two LANs located remotely from one another.

●
Local and remote bridges can be used to interconnect LANs.

FIGURE 10.27.

Using remote bridges.

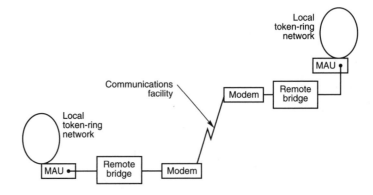

Routers

Routers operate at the network layer of the ISO Reference Model and permit support of several functions that bridges are not capable of providing due to their operation at the data link layer. Two additional functions that routers can perform include dynamic path assignment and frame fragmentation.

The capability to dynamically assign different paths permits routers to use alternative paths in the event a communications circuit becomes inoperative. In addition, this capability enables routers to perform a dynamic load balance of communications traffic when alternative routes are available between networks. This capability can reduce or eliminate the potential effect of congestion when too much traffic from one network destined to another exceeds the transmission capability of a single communications circuit.

Frame fragmentation permits routers to interconnect dissimilar LANs easily. For example, a 4 Mbps token-ring network has a maximum frame length of 4500 data bytes, whereas a 16 Mbps token-ring network has a maximum frame length of 18,000 data bytes. When connecting the two networks through the use of bridges, you would have to set software configuration parameters on each workstation on the 16 Mbps token-ring LAN to limit the maximum frame length to 4500 data characters to permit interoperability between networks. In comparison, if routers are used, they can fragment frames exceeding 4500 data characters originating on the 16 Mbps token-ring network into multiple frames for transmission on the 4 Mbps token-ring network. Because it's easier to configure one router than to configure numerous workstations connected via bridges, the use of routers can simplify network interoperability.

Gateways

To provide an interconnection capability for accessing mainframe computers, IBM markets several products that can be equipped with token-ring adapters and function as gateway devices. Two examples of such products are the IBM 3174 control unit with token-ring adapter (TRA) and the IBM 3745 token-ring interface coupler (TIC). The 3174 control unit can be located locally or remotely from a mainframe computer and allows up to 32 terminal devices to share access to the mainframe over a common cable or transmission facility. When equipped with a TRA, the 3174 can serve as a local or remote LAN gateway for accessing an IBM mainframe.

Because the maximum data rate of a 3174 is 56 Kbps, the use of a TRA on that device can result in degraded performance if too many LAN users attempt to access the mainframe simultaneously. To provide an increased level of gateway access, the IBM 3745 front-end processor (FEP) can be equipped with a TIC, which allows the FEP to be directly connected to a 4 or 16 Mbps token-ring network. Figure 10.28 illustrates several methods by which the IBM 3174 control unit and the IBM 3745 front-end processor can provide token-ring network users with access to an IBM mainframe computer.

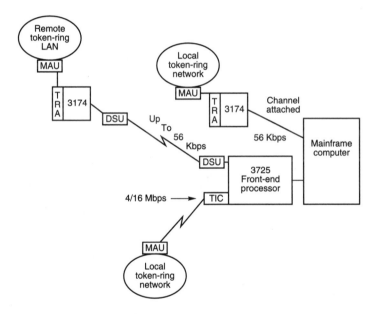

FIGURE 10.28.

Gateway access to an IBM mainframe.

LAN Switches

A key problem associated with LANs is the fact that the bandwidth of the cable is shared among all workstations connected to the local area network. For example, a 100-station 10BASE-T network results in each workstation on the average obtaining 10 Mbps/100, or an average bandwidth of 100 Kbps. With the development of multimedia applications that can incorporate audio, video, and still images with text, conventional LANs become severely taxed.

To illustrate the effect of images on the transmission capability of a LAN, consider the storage of a 3×5 color image versus a screen of text. If the image is scanned using a resolution of 300 dots per inch, each of the 15 square inches represents 90,000 dots on pixels.

If a color scan capable of representing 256 colors is used, each pixel must have 8 bits ($2^8 =$ 256) associated with it to represent the color of the pixel. Thus, the 3×5 color image requires 1.35MB of storage. If a workstation obtains an average LAN bandwidth of 100 Kbps, the transmission of the image can be expected to average 108 seconds. In comparison, an 80-row by 25-line screen consists of 2,000 characters or 16,000 bits. At an average LAN bandwidth of 100 Kbps, the transmission of the screen of text can be expected to require .16 seconds.

A LAN switch enables multiple simultaneous connections to occur between two or more networking devices, boosting network throughput.

The effect of multimedia applications was one of several factors governing the development of switching hubs. Other factors included the capability of switching hubs to enhance the operation of an existing network, as well as to provide an expansion capability to support traffic growth.

Figure 10.29 illustrates the use of a switching hub to interconnect two Ethernet LAN segments. Note that by connecting two file servers to individual ports, up to two simultaneous connections between workstations and file servers can occur, increasing the maximum bandwidth from 10 Mbps on an Ethernet 10BASE-T LAN to 20 Mbps via the use of the switch shown in Figure 10.29.

FIGURE 10.29.

Through the use of a LAN switch, multiple simultaneous connections between networking devices are supported.

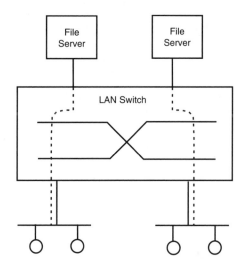

Legend: ◯ workstations

To boost bandwidth even higher, many switches provide several high-speed ports, typically supporting a 100BASE-T4 or FDDI connection. This enables access between the switch and highly used devices, such as file servers, to occur at 100 Mbps, and it further enhances the throughput through a switch.

Operation

Internally, a switch functions as a bridge, keeping track of the source address of frames on each port and examining the destination address of frames as a mechanism for their routing. The number of addresses per port a switch can store determines the capability of the switch to support individual stations or LAN segments that can contain multiple workstations. If only one address per port is supported, the switch functions as a port switching device. If the switch supports multiple addresses per port, it functions as a segment switching device.

In addition to the switching method, switches can be classified by their switching technique. Two switching techniques are cut-through, which is also known as "on the fly," and store-and-forward. A cut-through switch immediately affects a cross-connection between source and destination port after it reads the destination address in a frame. This type of switch has a minimal delay or latency time. In comparison, a store-and-forward switch stores the entire frame in memory and performs an error check on the frame, discarding it if the CRC computation performed does not match the CRC in the frame.

Store-and-forward switching is required whenever a frame must be moved from a low-speed LAN to a high-speed LAN. Due to the requirement to store the entire frame, a small degree of latency is associated with this switching method.

Broadband Networks

Broadband local area networks use wide bandwidth coaxial cables with frequency division multiplexing (FDM) to establish multiple channels within a system. The FDM channels are typically 6 MHz wide following the standards and technology developed by the CATV (cable TV) industry. Because the usable bandwidth of a CATV cable is 500 to 750 MHz, there can be from as many as 80 to 120 or more separate channels. Often separate FDM channels are used for separate applications.

The power and attraction of a broadband network is evident in Figure 10.30. Notice that the transmission system supports not only a data network, but also closed-circuit TV distribution, point-to-point voice telephone circuits, and point-to-point data circuits.

Use of a broadband system for data transmission requires modems in the physical interface equipment. If the modems are assigned to a fixed frequency (channel), the associated station can communicate only with other stations assigned to the same frequency. If frequency agile modems (modems that have a tuner to allow changing channels) are used, the stations can switch between the FDM channels to gain access to much larger networks.

Physical Layer

Broadband LAN systems utilize either one or two cables routed to every station. Single-cable systems are patterned after customary CATV systems where the FDM channels are separated into two groups as shown in Figure 10.31. One group of frequencies carries

> Frequency division multiplexing over wide bandwidth coaxial cables is used by broadband local area networks to transmit on multiple channels. This technique was developed by the cable TV industry.

> Single-cable systems use a dual-frequency architecture: one frequency for sending, one for receiving on the same cable.

signals from the transmitter of all station interfaces to a frequency translation module referred to as the head end. The head end amplifies the received signals and shifts them to the second group of frequencies, and then they travel back along the cable to the receivers of every station interface. Thus, a single channel in a functional sense requires a pair of FDM channels in a physical sense. The dual-frequency architecture permits the use of unidirectional amplifiers as shown in Figure 10.31.

FIGURE 10.30.

Broadband LAN supporting multiple services.

FIGURE 10.31.

Dual-frequency single-cable broadband network.

An alternative to the dual-frequency approach is the dual-cable architecture shown in Figure 10.32. Each station interface transmits on a particular channel in one cable and receives on the same channel in the second cable. The head end no longer provides FDM group translation; in fact, it might be nothing more than a passive cable-to-cable connection.

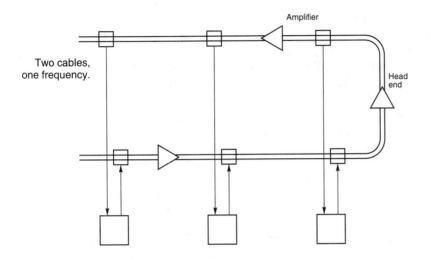

FIGURE 10.32.
Dual-cable/single-frequency broadband network.

Whichever physical architecture is used, the advantage of unidirectional amplification appears in the maximum distance specifications of broadbent networks. Distance limits of 5 to 30 miles are typical except in cases where access protocols like CSMA/CD restrict the allowable propagation times.

Data Link Layer

Due to the flexibility and multiple services supported by broadband networks, no one standard configuration or agreement on operation has come about or is likely to come about that explicitly defines the entire use of the bandwidth on the cable. For example, under 10BROAD-36, the CSMA/CD protocol is specified for use on defined channels with the use of radio frequency (rf) modems to modulate data at assigned frequencies. However, this standard does not define other signals that can be carried on the same cable. The only thing that appears to be a standard is the assignment of FDM channels, which must be standardized to interface with CATV systems. Suppliers of data communications services on broadband cables generally have decided to use the data link protocols of the baseband systems. In particular, both Ethernet and ARCnet access protocols are available for rf channels on a broadband network. Thus, the OSI goal of separating the physical layer from the higher layers has proven to be useful by allowing data communications suppliers these options.

There is no single standard for broadband networks. Only the FDM channels have been given specific frequency assignments to allow interface with CATV systems.

Voice and/or Data PBX

The local area networks described in the preceding sections have evolved primarily from the data processing or office equipment industry; therefore, they are strongly influenced by data communications applications. At the same time that LAN technology has been developing, voice telephone systems called private branch exchanges (PBXs) have been incorporating more and more digital electronics as a means of providing switched voice

As LAN technology has been developing, PBXs have been evolving and using more digital electronics in voice-switched services.

service. As shown in Figure 10.33, the conventional PBX architecture utilizes dedicated twisted-pair wires from every station to the central node (switch). Connection requests are signaled by an off-hook signal and dialed digits or "hot line" addresses stored in the memory of the switch controller. After a connection is established, the associated transmission channels are dedicated to that connection for its duration.

FIGURE 10.33.

A representative application of a data PBX.

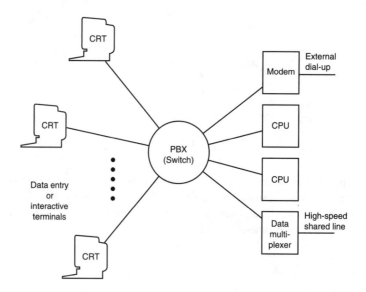

The data PBX depicted in Figure 10.33 provides an economical solution to several data communications problems:

- A terminal can be switched to different computers (CPUs) for different applications, to modems for external dial-up connections, or to data multiplexers for efficient use of external leased lines.

- The distance between the computer ports and the data terminals is extended to as much as several thousand feet. The standard EIA specification for the RS-232 interface is limited to 50 feet (although RS-232 interfaces are often used over longer distances).

- The switch acts as a port concentrator; that is, many external device ports can be handled by a few computer ports. The switch accomplishes this by connecting only active terminals to the computer ports. This greatly reduces the number of ports required in each computer.

PBXs are not capable of effectively handling high-speed processor-to-processor communications because of the 50 Kbps to 1 Mbps transmission rate range.

Although twisted-pair wires are relatively inexpensive and easy to install, they restrict the capacity of the data channels to a range of 50 Kbps to 1 Mbps, depending on distance. Thus, the data PBX is a viable solution for data entry and medium rate interactive terminal communications, but not for high-speed processor-to-processor communications.

Integrated Voice/Data PBXs

Beginning in the mid-1970s, PBXs began utilizing digital technology in their switching matrices because, despite the cost of voice digitization at line interfaces, the total switch cost is lower due to economics in the matrix. More recently, the point of digitization has begun to move from within the central equipment to the voice stations themselves. These are the main motivations for digitizing in the instruments:

● To easily multiplex control information (which is inherently digital) onto the same pair or pairs of wires that carry the voice signals (typically 64 Kbps). This allows sophisticated multiline telephones to operate over one or two pairs of wires. Conventional analog telephone systems use expensive 25-pair cables for multiline key sets.

● To multiplex data channels on the same pairs of wires used for voice so that one installation can simultaneously provide voice and data communications.

Initially, the digital instruments could be cost-justified only in sophisticated applications. As the cost of digital instruments decreased, however, it became possible to cost-justify an all-digital system, thus providing 64 Kbps digital channels at every location of a telephone. The widespread presence of 64 Kbps digital channels makes it easier to add other digital transmission services, as shown in Figure 10.34.

●
Digitization of PBX systems will enable control information to be multiplexed onto the voice signal wires, allowing only one or two wires to handle multiple lines rather than the normal 25 pairs.

It is now easier and more cost effective to provide all digital networks.

FIGURE 10.34.

Integrated voice/data PBX with digital instruments.

LAN Comparisons and Trends

Each of the LAN system architectures presented in the previous sections has unique technical and operational advantages and disadvantages. The following paragraphs contrast the systems in terms of the properties of an ideal LAN.

One-Time Installations

The overall goal of a one-time installation is not satisfied in practice by any of the LAN architectures. Even a telephone system, which is a necessity in every building, typically requires significant rewiring as people move, if only from one side of an office to another.

Widespread Access

Before widespread access becomes a reality for an information distribution network, the cost of significant numbers of unused ports must be reduced. Even though telephone twisted pairs are relatively inexpensive, unused telephone ports typically represent a significant hidden cost in terms of the electronics interfaces that the wires are connected to in the central equipment. Distributed access architectures such as CSMA or token passing do not produce hidden costs for unused ports as long as the maximum number of ports is not exceeded.

Application Independence

A major prerequisite for an information network to support multiple applications is the support of higher level data communications functions. The suppliers of coaxial-cable-based LANs are generally most advanced in this regard, although it is more a matter of market orientation than a technology difference. The CSMA and token-passing systems also provide a high data rate for those applications that need it.

Excess Capacity

In one sense, the CSMA or token-passing architectures are ideal because the entire capacity of the system is available at every port. A port can use as much bandwidth as it needs. On the other hand, this feature limits the system capacity. If the total bandwidth requirements of the stations exceed the system bandwidth, the needed expansion is either very costly or impossible.

In contrast, circuit switched (PBX) architectures can be expanded almost without limit. The bandwidth delivered to every port remains unchanged as more stations are added.

Easy Maintenance and Administration

The most difficult systems to maintain are the broadband systems because of the tight gain requirements of the amplifiers and equalizers. From a data communications point of view, the integrated voice/data PBX is the easiest to maintain because well-established procedures already exist for the voice services. Furthermore, PBX suppliers are accustomed to providing turnkey system support for the life of the installation. However, due to product background, they typically do not support higher level communication requirements.

No presently available single LAN system architecture can economically satisfy the needs of all communications within a building or campus. Nor is it likely that one system will ever evolve to economically fulfill these needs. Thus, there will always be a need for either separate systems tailored to specific applications or possibly hybrid systems employing the best features of selected individual architectures. One such hybrid architecture that is beginning to evolve is shown in Figure 10.35. This illustration depicts an integrated voice/data PBX that collects terminal traffic and switches it onto high-speed multiplexed computer to PBX interfaces (CPIs). Communications between processors (CPU) and their shared high-speed peripherals is best accomplished with a high-speed coaxial cable or fiber-optic LAN. The advantage of the configuration in Figure 10.35 is that low-speed, short messages to and from the terminals are not contending for the high-speed facility optimized for file transfers.

●
No single LAN system architecture has sufficient capabilities to fulfill all possible needs. Each has its own special qualities and technical advantages and disadvantages.

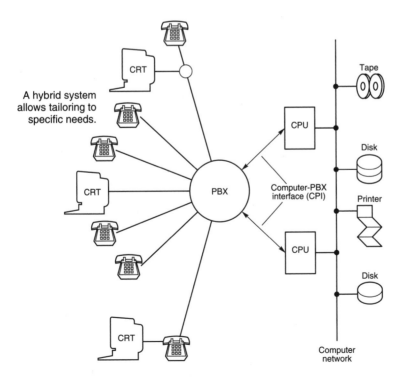

FIGURE 10.35.
Hybrid PBX/LAN network.

A hybrid system allows tailoring to specific needs.

Voice/Computer access network

What Have You Learned?

1. LANs provide high-speed switched connections between such data equipment as computers, storage devices, printers, word processors, and display terminals at distances up to a few thousand meters.

2. The usefulness of a LAN is maximized if it provides higher level data communications support in addition to basic transmission and switching functions.

3. Communications functions within a network should be partitioned in a hierarchical manner to isolate the implementation of major functional components from each other.

4. Myriad LAN architectures are possible, but these are the most prevalent:

   a. Contention-access-based coaxial cable systems (for example, Ethernet).

   b. Token passing systems (for example, IBM token-ring network).

   c. Polled-access-based coaxial cable systems (for example, ARCnet).

   d. Frequency division broadband systems based on cable television technology and practice.

5. Some of the incompatibilities that traditionally arise in LAN equipment supplied by different vendors are being resolved by IEEE standards committee 802.

6. The IEEE 802.3 standard is really a set of standards that defines several types of CSMA/CD LANs.

7. Digital PBXs for telephone switching are being designed to carry data in addition to basic telephone service. Although these systems do not provide the very high rates of a conventional LAN, they represent a very economical alternative to a LAN for moderate data rate switched connections.

Quiz for Chapter 10

1. Which of the following transmission systems provides the highest data rate to an individual device?

   a. Voiceband modem.

   b. Local area network.

   c. Computer bus.

   d. Digital PBX.

2. Which of the following systems provides the longest digital transmission distances?

   a. Voiceband modem.

   b. Local area network.

   c. Computer bus.

   d. Digital PBX.

3. Which of the following options is a characteristic of a LAN?

    a. Parallel transmission.

    b. Unlimited expansion.

    c. Low cost access for low bandwidth channels.

    d. Application-independent interfaces.

4. Which of the following transmission media is not readily suitable to CSMA operation?

    a. Radio.

    b. Optical fibers.

    c. Coaxial cable.

    d. Twisted pair.

5. Which of the following functions is not provided as part of the basic Ethernet design?

    a. Access control.

    b. Addressing.

    c. Automatic retransmission of a message.

    d. Multiple virtual networks.

6. Which of the following options is not a useful property of a Manchester line code for an Ethernet?

    a. Continuous energy.

    b. Continuous clock transitions.

    c. No DC component.

    d. No signal change at a 1 to 0 transition.

7. Which of the following data communications functions is generally provided for in a LAN?

    a. Data link control.

    b. Applications processing.

    c. Flow control.

    d. Routing.

8. The purpose of the preamble in an Ethernet is:

    a. Clock synchronization.

    b. Error checking.

    c. Collision avoidance.

    d. Broadcast.

9. The difference between the Ethernet frame preamble field and the IEEE 802.3 Preamble and Start of Frame Delimiter fields is:

    a. 1 byte.

    b. 1 bit.

    c. 8 bits.

    d. 16 bits.

10. A 10BASE-2 network is limited to:

    a. 20 bytes per data field.

    b. 30 stations per segment.

    c. 40 segments.

    d. 50 feet of cable.

11. Each version of Fast Ethernet subdivides the physical layer to support:

    a. Different operating rates.

    b. Different media.

    c. Different data.

    d. Different people.

12. A key difference between a 100BASE-T4 and a 100BASE-TX network is in their:

    a. Operating rates.

    b. Support of Ethernet frames.

    c. Network span.

    d. Use of cable pairs.

13. A key characteristic of an FDDI network is its:

    a. Self-healing capability.

    b. 10 Mbps operating rate.

    c. Ring enable capability.

    d. IEEE standardization.

14. A common use for FDDI networks is for:

    a. Extending fiber.

    b. Serving as a backbone for connecting lower-speed LANs.

    c. Rotating rings.

    d. Transporting decision data.

15. Which of the following features is possible in a token-passing bus network?

    a. Unlimited number of stations.

    b. Unlimited distances.

    c. Multiple time division channels.

    d. In-service expansion.

16. Which of the following features is not possible in a token-passing loop network?

    a. Unlimited number of stations.

    b. Unlimited distances.

    c. Multiple time division channels.

    d. In-service expansion.

17. Which of the following LAN architectures can be expanded to the greatest total system bandwidth?

    a. Digital PBX.

    b. CSMA/CD baseband system.

    c. Token-passing network.

    d. Broadband cable system.

18. Which of the following systems is the most capable of servicing a wide range of applications?

    a. Digital PBX.

    b. CSMA/CD baseband system.

    c. Token-passing network.

    d. Broadband cable system.

19. Which of the following options is a characteristic of a token-passing ring as opposed to a token-passing bus?

    a. Signal quality control.

    b. Passive interface (tap).

    c. Flexible polling sequence.

    d. Priority access capabilities.

20. Which of the following options is not a characteristic of the hub architecture of ARCnet?

    a. Directionalized transmission.

    b. RIM port isolation.

    c. Zero insertion loss amplifiers.

    d. Alternate routing.

21. A router operates at:

    a. The data link layer.

    b. The application layer.

    c. The network layer.

    d. The segmentation layer.

22. A major advantage associated with the use of a LAN switch is its capability to:

    a. Convert frames.

    b. Support multiple simultaneous connections.

    c. Enable cut-through storage.

    d. Connect file servers.

23. Which of the following items cannot be provided in a broadband LAN?

    a. Frequency agile modems.

    b. Closed-circuit TV.

    c. Voice circuits.

    d. Fiber-optic transmission.

24. Which of the following features is not possible in a digital (data) PBX using twisted-pair transmission?

    a. Computer port concentration.

    b. 64 Kbps data circuits.

    c. High-speed file transfers.

    d. Transmission up to several thousand feet.

25. Which of the following options is not a motivation for digitizing a voice signal in the telephones of a digital PBX?

    a. Simplified control signaling.

    b. Lower cost telephones.

    c. Fewer wire pairs.

    d. Multiplexed voice and data channels.

Architectures and Packet Networks

About This Chapter

This chapter deals with several data networking architecture concepts—that is, the way data networks are arranged or structured. These include the concept of architectural levels or layers. Without emphasizing architectural structure or terminology, previous chapters have actually described data networking and switching on two different levels: the physical level and the link level. Packet networks, which involve a third architectural level, are discussed in this chapter. The ITU-T (formerly known as the CCITT) X.25 standard packet switching architecture is described; then the Open Systems Interconnection (OSI) Reference Model is explained along with its relationship to X.25 and other systems.

Protocol Layering

A protocol is a set of rules governing a time sequence of events that take place between peer entities—that is, between equipment or layers on the same level.

Physical Layer

In Chapter 4, "Asynchronous Modems and Interfaces," I discussed the mechanical, physical, electrical, logical, and functional relationships between the various wires and signals in a serial interface and how the bits of data are passed through them between Data Terminal Equipment (DTE) and Data Circuit-terminating

Equipment (DCE). We saw, for example, that bits passing through the transmit data wire from a source DTE should eventually pass through a receive data wire to a sink DTE. These are called physical layer or level one protocols.

Level one protocols deal with the physical layer of data communication, or the passing of the bits through the wires to and from DTEs. Link protocols cover a higher level of architecture; they are concerned with all aspects of maintaining order within the link.

Link Layer

In Chapter 8, "Protocols and Error Control," I discussed means by which various fields, such as address, text, and error checking, can be present within the same bit stream. Several specific link protocols were discussed, showing techniques that are used to define (without any possibility of confusion) the boundaries of the fields within a bit stream, send information to a specific terminal on a multipoint link, check for and correct transmission errors, and generally maintain order within the line.

Architecturally speaking, link protocols are at a higher level (a more "intelligent" level) than physical protocols, yet all the information used in the link protocol is actually contained in the bit stream transmitted through the serial interface. Conceptually, we speak of the link protocol fields as embedded (contained within) or layered within the physical protocol bits.

Network Layer

The highest level of protocol architecture is the network layer. This layer is used to route data link-to-link through a network.

At the third architectural level is the network layer. Protocols at this layer can be used to route data from link to link through a network containing intelligent nodes called packet switches. The method by which this routing and associated administration takes place is called the network layer protocol. The network layer protocol information, called the packet header, is embedded in the information field of a link-level frame. The packet switch uses part of this information to route the data to the next link, and so on. The packet header, together with the user data, is called a packet.

Packet Networks

Packet networks function with the help of special intelligent switching nodes.

A packet network is a special kind of data network containing intelligent switching nodes. Packet networks have the following general characteristics:

- Before transmission, each data message is segmented into short blocks of specified maximum length, and each block is provided with a header containing addressing and sequencing information. Each packet becomes the information field of a transmission at the link protocol level, which usually contains error control capabilities.

● The packets are passed very quickly from node to node, arriving in a fraction of a second at their final destination.

● The node computers do not archive (store) the data. Messages are "forgotten" by the sending node as soon as the next node checks for an error (if required) and acknowledges receipt.

The terms DTE and DCE have been discussed previously. In packet networks, an additional term is introduced: the Data Switching Exchange (DSE). A DSE is a network node joining three or more links. Figure 11.1 shows the relationship between DTEs, DCEs, and DSEs in a packet network. The point where the serial interface cable connects to the DCE is sometimes referred to as the network gateway.

FIGURE 11.1.
A two-node packet network.

The DSE is an intelligent switching node joining three or more links.

Unlike in level one switching, in which a specific link is dedicated to a particular message or group of messages, data packets are forwarded from DSE to DSE in such a way that packets from many sources and to many sinks can pass through the same internode link at different moments during the same short period.

Advantages of Packet Switching

Depending on the situation, packet switching can offer several possible advantages over other data communications techniques:

● For data applications in which the amount of traffic between terminals cannot justify a dedicated circuit, packet switching might be more economical than transmission over private lines.

● For applications in which data communication sessions are shorter than a minimum chargeable time unit for a telephone call, packet switching might be more economical than dialed data.

●
Packet switching can offer significant advantages over other data communications techniques.

- Because destination address information is inherently a part of the packet, a large number of messages can be sent to many different destinations as fast as the source DTE can turn them out. Depending on the type of packet service being used, there might not be any connection time delay before transmission of packets containing actual data.

- Because of the intelligence built into the network (that is, computers at each node), dynamic routing of data is possible. Each packet travels over the route established by the network as the best available path for that packet at that time. This characteristic can be used to maximize efficiency and minimize congestion.

- Built-in intelligence also facilitates a "graceful degradation" property of the packet network, because whenever there is a failure of a link or node, packets can be automatically rerouted around the defective portion of the network.

- Because of the intelligence within the network, a rich array of basic communications services is possible. Examples include error detection and correction, message delivery verification, group addressing, reverse billing, message sequence checking, and diagnostics.

X.25 Packet Systems

The ITU-T X.25 standard for packet switching systems is one of the most significant networking architectures affecting data communications for the present and the foreseeable future. The X.25 standard is actually only a part of a much larger collection of ITU-T recommendations on public data networks. To fully understand the subject, one must study the entire "X" series.

The X.25 standard itself describes the physical, link, and network protocols in the interface between the DTE and DCE at the gateway to a packet switching network. At first glance, the concept of describing a packet network in terms of gateway parameters might seem peculiar, but from the user's point of view, it's all that's needed. In voice telephone network terms, if we were to collect all the standards relating to the physical, electrical, logical, and functional properties of local loops and their signals into one document, we would have the telephone network equivalent of X.25. As shown in Figure 11.2, X.25 relates a data terminal to the gateway of a packet network in precisely the same way that local loop signaling standards relate a telephone to the central office of a telephone network.

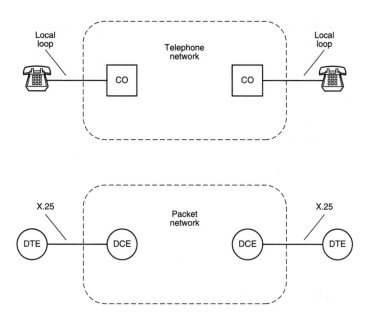

FIGURE 11.2.

An analogy between X.25 and the total specifications for a local loop.

If we had never seen a telephone or placed a telephone call, our knowing all there is to know about a local loop and its signaling wouldn't teach us much about the design of the telephone or of the network—but we would know how to use them. Similarly, the X.25 standard describes neither the data terminal nor the packet data network, but it reveals a great deal about what the terminal and the network must be able to do. It is for this reason that the X.25 has taken on so much importance.

As already mentioned, the X.25 standard specifies three separate protocol layers at the serial interface gateway. The physical-layer characteristics of X.21 (or X.21bis) are specified as the physical layer protocol ("bis" is the Swiss/French equivalent of "alternate form"). X.21 uses a 15-pin synchronous interface, which has not enjoyed enthusiastic acceptance in the United States because of the popularity of RS-232 and V.35, which existed before X.21. In recognition of this fact, the ITU-T has endorsed X.21bis as a suitable alternative. X.21bis specifies V.24/V.28 (essentially the equivalent of RS-232), X.26/IS-4902 (essentially the equivalent of RS-449), and V.35 at their appropriate respective bit rates. Because U.S. vendors generally provide RS-232 or V.35, no change is required.

> ●
> The primary emphasis of the X.25 standard is to describe what a terminal and its associated network must be able to do, not to describe the terminal and network themselves.

Link Level

At the link level, the protocol specified is a subset of HDLC, referred to in X.25 terminology as LAPB (Link Access Procedure Balanced). (An older version of X.25 used a link protocol called LAP, which has been essentially phased out.) LAPB provides for two-way simultaneous communication between the DTE and DCE at the network gateway. LAPB

> ●
> The protocol at the link level, LAPB, provides for two-way simultaneous communications between the DTE and DCE at the network gateway.

frame structure is identical to that of SDLC, which was explained in Chapter 8, "Protocols and Error Control." The delimiter (flag), abort, idle channel, transparency (zero insertion), frame sequencing, flow control, and error control mechanisms are identical to those of SDLC. The differences between the LAPB procedures and the SDLC procedures are mainly in the areas of line control and addressing; these topics are covered later.

Network Level

The packet level of X.25 is the network level, and it is transmitted as an information field in the command frame. At least three octets are used in the header.

The network level of X.25 is referred to in the standard as the packet level. All X.25 packets are transmitted as information fields in LAPB information command frames. A packet contains at least a header of three or more octets. (An octet is a group of eight bits.) Most packets also contain user data, but some packets are only for control, status indication, or diagnostics. (The preceding terms will be explained in later text and illustrations.) The maximum amount of user data that can be included in a data packet is determined by the network vendor but is usually 128 octets.

Capabilities of X.25

The X.25 standard, together with its references, specifies two essential services that must be offered by carriers to be in full compliance with the standard. These services are Virtual Call Service and Permanent Virtual Circuit Service.

Virtual Call Service

Virtual connections are made and disconnected by use of special, non-data-carrying packets that have a unique bit stream. In a virtual connection, no fixed physical path actually exists in the network.

In Virtual Call Service (VC), a virtual "connection" normally must be established first between a logical channel from the calling DTE and a logical channel to the called DTE before any data packets can be sent. Establishment of a virtual connection is the functional equivalent of placing a telephone call before beginning a telephone conversation. The virtual connection is established and disestablished by use of special packets that have unique bit streams but usually contain no data. After the connection has been established, the two DTEs can carry on a two-way dialog until a "clear request packet" (disconnect) is sent.

The VC connection is referred to as "virtual" because a fixed physical path through the network does not exist. The intelligence in the network simply relays a specified logical channel number at one DTE to that at the other DTE.

A given DTE can have many logical channel numbers active in the same X.25 interface at the same time. (That statement was important. Read it again.) After a virtual connection has been established, say, between logical channel #319 on one DTE and #14 on another DTE, the actual data packet headers need refer only to logical channel numbers. The intelligent network keeps up with their conversational relationship; that is, a data packet from logical channel #319 at the one DTE will appear on logical channel #14 at the other, with the network performing the conversion. Further details on this subject are given later.

Permanent Virtual Circuit Service

Permanent Virtual Circuit (PVC) service is the functional equivalent of a private line service. As in VC, no end-to-end physical pathway exists; the intelligent network relates the respective logical channels of the two DTEs involved. No special packets are sent by the DTE to establish or disestablish connections. A PVC is established by requesting it in writing from the carrier providing the packet network service, and it remains in effect until disestablished by written request. Terminals between which a PVC has been established need send only data packets on the carrier-assigned logical channels as required. Because a DTE can have many logical channels active at the same time within the X.25 interface, some can be assigned as PVCs and others can be used for setting up VCs as required—all in the same X.25 interface!

● After a PVC has been established, only data packets are sent between the terminals on the carrier-assigned logical channels.

For both VC and PVC, the network is obligated to deliver packets in the order submitted, even if the physical path changes due to circuit loading, failure, or whatever. Costwise, the relationship between VC and PVC is similar to that between long-distance telephone and private-line services. Other standard packet network features, such as error control and diagnostics, are equivalent for VC and PVC.

Facilities

In ITU-T terminology, a facility is an optional feature offered with a service, sometimes at extra cost. X.25 specifies a rich array of facilities for VC and PVC services. In any case, the final choice of services and facilities is up to the customer.

● Facilities are optional features customers can use to customize VC service.

Examples of facilities for VC service are fast select, incoming calls barred, outgoing calls barred, closed user group, and reverse billing. Fast select gives the user the ability to send and receive data to and from a number of different remote stations very quickly and efficiently without actually establishing regular virtual connections. Such a capability has many potential uses for distribution of electronic mail, polling of inventories, and so on.

LAPB Procedures

Space does not allow for a complete discussion of the link layer protocol of X.25; the following information, however, provides general knowledge of the LAPB procedures. A thorough treatment is included in the X.25 standard, and examples of operation are included in ISO 4335 Addendum 2.

LAPB provides for two-way simultaneous transmission on a point-to-point link between a DTE and a DCE at the packet network gateway (see Figure 11.1). Because the link is point-to-point, only the address of the DTE or the address of the DCE can appear in the A (address) field of an LAPB frame. These addresses are shown in Figure 11.3. The A field refers to a link address, not to a network address. The network address of the destination terminal is embedded in the packet header (PH), which is part of the I field.

FIGURE 11.3.

Commands versus responses in LAPB.

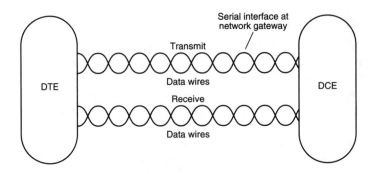

Frames in transmit data wires contain
A = 10000000 for commands and
A = 11000000 for responses.

Frames in receive data wires contain
A = 11000000 for commands and
A = 10000000 for responses.

Commands and responses can be made by both the DTE and the DCE. The function of a frame depends on the direction in which it is moving and the value of A.

Both stations (the DTE and the DCE) can issue commands and responses to each other, as shown in Figure 11.3. Whether a frame is a command or a response depends on a combination of two factors:

- Which direction it is moving in—that is, whether it's on the transmit data wires from the DTE or the receive data wires toward the DTE.
- What the value of A is.

Because of the addressing scheme, there can be no uncertainty even if frames are moving in opposite directions at the same time between DTE and DCE.

Table 11.1 and Table 11.2 show the legitimate commands and responses in the LAPB frame, along with their respective control octet values. Explanations of the abbreviations and terms are given in the following paragraphs.

Table 11.1. The LAPB commands.

| Command Name | *Content of Control Octet Bit Number* | | | |
	876	*5*	*432*	*1*
I (Information)	N(R)	P	N(S)	0
RR (Receiver Ready)	N(R)	P	000	1
RNR (Receiver Not Ready)	N(R)	P	010	1
REJ (Reject)	N(R)	P	100	1
SABM (Set Asynchronous Balanced Mode)	001	P	111	1
DISC (Disconnect)	010	P	001	1

Table 11.2. The LAPB responses.

| Response Name | Content of Control Octet Bit Number | | | |
	876	5	432	1
RR (Receiver Ready)	N(R)	F	000	1
RNR (Receiver Not Ready)	N(R)	F	010	1
REJ (Reject)	N(R)	F	100	1
UA (Unnumbered Acknowledgment)	011	F	001	1
DM (Disconnect Mode)	000	F	111	1
FRMR (Frame Rejected)	100	F	011	1

Explanation of LAPB Commands and Responses

During LAPB operation, most frames are commands. A response frame is compelled when a command frame is received containing P = 1; such a response contains F = 1. All other frames contain P = 0 or F = 0.

SABM/UA is a command/response pair used to initialize all counters and timers at the beginning of a session. Similarly, DISC/DM is a command/response pair used at the end of a session. FRMR is a response to any illegal command for which there is no indication of transmission errors according to the frame check sequence (FCS) field.

I commands are used to transmit packets—that is, in the I field. Packets are never sent as responses. N(S) is a three-bit packet counter capable of counting from 0 through 7 (000 through 111 in binary). After seven packets have been sent, the counter simply rolls over to 000 again for the next value of N(S).

While N(S) counts packets sent from one end of the link, the value of N(R) indicates the next value of N(S) expected to be returned from the other end of the link. By updating the value of N(R), a station acknowledges correctly received packets in the same way as SDLC frames are acknowledged. For example, if a DTE sends an I command (a packet) for which N(S) = 5 and P = 1, and the DCE returns an RR response with N(R) = 6 and F = 1, the DTE knows that the packet was received correctly. If N(R) = 5 and F = 1, the packet was received incorrectly. No more than seven unacknowledged packets can be outstanding, because an ambiguity would result.

RR is what a station sends when it needs to send something but has no packets to send. For example, a compelled response to an I command might be an RR with F = 1. This procedure is called checkpointing. Checkpointing is one of the techniques LAPB makes available for error detection.

REJ is another way of requesting transmission of frames. RNR is used for flow control to indicate a busy condition. It prevents further transmissions until cleared by an RR.

Most frames in LAPB operations are commands. Response frames are issued only when a command frame with P = 1 is received.

In checkpointing, a type of LAPB error detection, RR is the response by a station that has no packets to send but must answer a compelled response.

Packet-Level Procedures

The most interesting feature of X.25 is the network (packet) layer protocol. Remember that the packets are contained in the I command frames at the link (frame) level and that each packet has a header of at least three octets. Most, but not all, packets contain user data; other packets are used for control, status indication, or diagnostics. Figure 11.4 illustrates the general layout of X.25 packet headers.

FIGURE 11.4.

The general layout of X.25 packet headers.

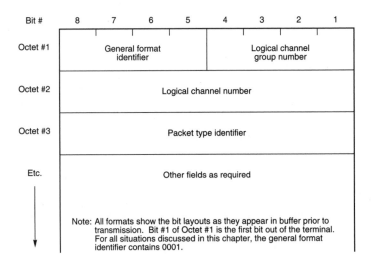

Note: All formats show the bit layouts as they appear in buffer prior to transmission. Bit #1 of Octet #1 is the first bit out of the terminal. For all situations discussed in this chapter, the general format identifier contains 0001.

Data Packets

● Data packets are packets in which Bit #1 in Octet #3 of the header has a value of 0. A data packet can have up to 128 octets of user data.

A packet that has 0 as the value of Bit #1 in Octet #3 of the header is a data packet. Data packet headers normally contain three octets. A standard X.25 data packet contains up to 128 octets of user data following the header. Figure 11.5 illustrates the layout of a typical data packet. This chapter is not intended to cover all possible ramifications and extensions of X.25. There is, for example, the provision for modulo 128 P(S) and P(R) counters, each of which requires seven bits. A data packet header in such a system would require a minimum of four octets.

It was pointed out earlier that X.25 specifies two essential services: Virtual Call and Permanent Virtual Circuit. After a VC has been set up, the operation of data packets under VC service is identical to that under PVC. In the paragraphs that follow, operation under PVC is described first; then the additional concerns of VC, such as call setup, are described.

Theoretically, every X.25 gateway interface can support up to 16 logical channel groups, each containing up to 256 logical channels, for a grand total of 4096 simultaneous logical channels per gateway. It is up to the company that establishes the networks to say how many it will actually support in each type of service—that is, PVC and VC.

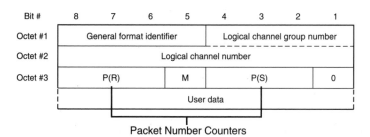

FIGURE 11.5.

A typical ITU-T X.25 data packet.

Notice in Figure 11.5 that Octet #3 of the data packet header contains two 3-bit fields, P(S) and P(R), and a 1-bit field, M. M is the "more data" mark. When M has a value of 1, additional data packets will follow that are to be considered as a unit; when it has a value of 0, no more packet will follow in this unit. P(S) and P(R) are data packet counters, each of which can vary from 000 through 111 (0–7). The counters roll over to 000 again after passing 111. (These are not the same as N(S) and N(R), discussed earlier.) Only data packets have a P(S) counter; there will be a P(S) in each data packet sent across the DTE to DCE interface at the network gateway (Figure 11.1) and a P(S) in each data packet sent from DCE to DTE at the network gateway.

By definition, P(R) is the amount of the next expected value of P(S) from the other direction on that logical channel (this will be explained in a moment). The values of P(S) and P(R) relate to each other within a logical channel at the network level in exactly the same way that N(S) and N(R) relate to each other on a point-to-point link. The Ns are not related to the Ps, however, because the Ns refer to all packets sent in a link, and the Ps refer only to data packets sent in a particular logical channel within that link.

The use of P(S) and P(R) is illustrated in Figure 11.6. A sequence of two-way simultaneous (full-duplex) transmissions of data packets within a logical channel across a DTE/DCE interface at a packet network gateway is shown. In this illustration, each rectangle represents a packet. The first number in the rectangle is the value of P(S), and the second is the value of P(R) in that packet's header. Inspection of the sequence in Figure 11.6 confirms two facts already implied:

● The values of P(S) in a particular direction in a logical channel proceed in numerical order: 0, 1, 2, 3, and so forth.

● The value of P(R) sent in a packet is not updated to i until the entire packet whose value of P(S) is $i - 1$ has been completely received error free. Such an update is an acknowledgment of all packets in that logical channel through P(S) = $i - 1$.

The dynamic establishment and disestablishment of a VC using special packets is very similar to that of placing and terminating a telephone call on the public telephone network, as indicated in Table 11.3 and Table 11.4. Inspection of these tables reveals that seven new packet names have been introduced. An event occurring on one side of the network is usually paired with a complementary event on the other side. For example, a

There are three parts to Octet #3 of the data packet header: two 3-bit fields, P(S) and P(R), and a 1-bit field, M. When M is 1, more data packets are to follow as a single unit.

The values of P(S) and P(R) are related within a logical channel at the network level. P(R) is the amount that P(S) is expected to be in the next packet that is coming from the other direction on that particular logical channel.

Call Request packet from calling DTE to DCE at one interface results in an Incoming Call packet from DCE to called DTE at another interface. Table 11.5 shows the packet type identifiers (Octet #3 of the header) for these pairs of packet types.

FIGURE 11.6.

The values of P(S) and P(R) for a sequence of data packets.

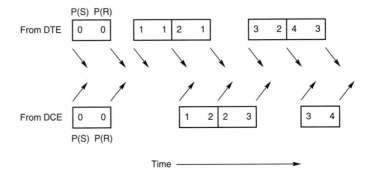

Table 11.3. Network analogies for call establishment.

Telephone Network	X.25 Packet Network
Place call	Send "Call Request" packet
Hear telephone ring	Receive "Incoming Call" packet
Pick up handset of ringing phone	Send "Call Accepted" packet
Hear "Hello"	Receive "Call Connected" packet
Fail to answer ring	Send "Clear Request" packet*
No answer, busy, or fast busy	Receive "Clear Indication" packet
Hang up	Send "Clear Confirmation" packet*
*With causes shown in packet	

Table 11.4. Network analogies after establishment of call.

Telephone Network	X.25 Packet Network
Hang up to disconnect	Send "Clear Request" packet
Hear other person hang up	Receive "Clear Indication" packet*
Hang up after other person hangs up	Send "Clear Confirmation" packet
Call disconnected by network	Receive "Clear Indication" packet*
*With causes shown in packet	

Figure 11.7 shows a "normal" sequence of a VC setup, two-way simultaneous data transfer, and terminal-initiated disconnect. Note that the four packet type identifiers of Table 11.5 are simply passed through the network without the network modifying them.

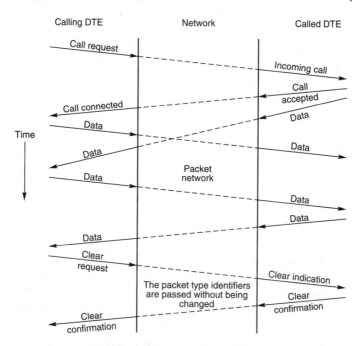

FIGURE 11.7.

A "normal" VC sequence.

Table 11.5. Packet type identifiers for call setup and clearing.

DTE to DCE	DCE to DTE	Octet #3
Call Request	Incoming Call	0 0 0 0 1 0 1 1
Call Accepted	Call Connected	0 0 0 0 1 1 1 1
Clear Request	Clear Indication	0 0 0 1 0 0 1 1
DTE-Initiated— Clear Confirmation	Network-Initiated— Clear Confirmation	0 0 0 1 0 1 1 1

Figure 11.8 shows what happens when a VC does not complete. If the VC is refused by the called DTE, the called DTE sends Clear Request. If the VC is refused by the network, the calling DTE receives Clear Indication.

FIGURE 11.8.

VC not completed.

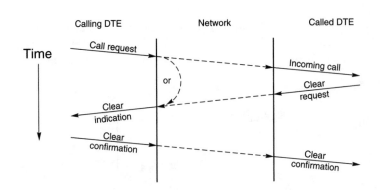

Call Request/Incoming Call Packets

The headers of the Call Request/Incoming Call pair of packets are the most complex of the various header formats. They contain not only the basic three octets shown in Figure 11.4, but also destination addressing and facility selection information. In certain cases, they also contain user data.

- The numbers assigned to the ends of a logical channel do not have to be the same. The intelligent switcher makes the appropriate connection as required regardless of the end numbers.

The logical channel numbers (LCNs) and logical channel group numbers (LCGNs) for PVC service are assigned by the carrier from the ranges of numbers that the carrier decides to designate for PVC service. The numbers assigned to opposite ends of a given logical channel do not have to be the same. Different numbers could be assigned to the opposite ends of the channel, and the intelligent switches within the network would make the appropriate conversions as the packets pass to and fro.

In the case of VC service, the numerical values of logical channels at the opposite interfaces are never the same; the network always converts these numbers to and fro. The channel numbers used are assigned from a pool of numbers available at the time of call setup.

- The logical channel numbers used in VC service come from a pool of numbers available when the call is made. The numbers at the opposite interfaces are different.

In placing a Call Request, a calling DTE selects the highest logical channel number that does not exceed a limit specified by the carrier and that is not already being used on another VC. The network then pairs the selected logical channel number with that VC from that calling DTE. At the destination end, the network selects the lowest logical channel number that is not less than a limit specified by the carrier and that is not already in use with that called DTE. The network then pairs that logical channel number with that VC to that called DTE. The two DTEs engaged in PVC or VC transactions never know (or care) which LCGN or LCN is being used by the other DTE/DCE interface.

VC Destination Addressing

The DTE Address field in the Call Request/Incoming Call Packet format contains digits that are handled much like telephone numbers, with up to 14 digits on international VCs. The arrangement of these 14 digits is given in X.121. For domestic calls, fewer digits are required.

There are many other details in X.25 that cannot be covered here, and the list of facilities and diagnostic codes continues to grow. Refer to the standard for details.

Value-Added Services

X.25 describes a highly flexible basic point-to-point service through a public network. To the user whose terminals operate in the X.25 packet mode, have a significant amount of traffic to send to many locations, and connect via a DTE/DCE serial interface to an X.25 network gateway, X.25 has few shortcomings. For the user who cannot meet all these criteria, X.25 does have limitations. Enhanced (value-added) service offerings, such as those provided by AT&T Information Systems, Sprint (formerly GTE Telenet), BT Tymnet (formerly Tymnet), and others, seek to address these and other matters:

- Broadcast services (sending the same data at the same time to many receivers).
- Dial access. (Because the DTE/DCE interface is intended as a two-way simultaneously synchronous gateway, packet-mode access normally cannot be provided via the public telephone network.)
- Conversion to lower speed start-stop transmission for low-volume terminals.
- Code and protocol conversion services.

The ITU-T has provided guidance with regard to the third item, as will be shown later.

● Enhanced, or value-added, services are provided by some carriers to overcome some of the shortcomings of X.25 that can arise when a terminal does not meet some prerequisites for full X.25 use.

The X Series of Recommended Standards

As stated earlier, X.25 is part of the "X" series of recommended standards for public data networks being made public by the ITU-T. The X series is classified into two categories: X.1 through X.39, which deal with services, facilities, terminals, and interfaces; and X.40 through X.200, which deal with network architecture, transmission, signaling, switching, maintenance, and administrative arrangements. From a packet network user viewpoint, the most important X standards are given in the following list with their titles and brief descriptions:

> X.1—*International User Classes of Service in Public Data Networks.* Assigns numerical class designation to different terminal speeds and types.
>
> X.2—*International User Services and Facilities in Public Data Networks.* Specifies essential and additional services and facilities.
>
> X.3—*Packet Assembly/Disassembly Facility (PAD) in a Public Data Network.* Describes the packet assembler/disassembler that normally is used at a network gateway to allow connection of a start-stop terminal to a packet network.

● Services, facilities, terminals, and interfaces are covered by ITU-T sections X.1 through X.39. Network architecture, transmission, switching, and all remaining areas are covered by sections X.40 through X.200.

X.20bis—Use on Public Data Networks of DTE Designed for Interfacing to Asynchronous Duplex V-Series Modems. Allows use of V.24/V.28 (essentially the same as EIA RS-232).

X.21bis—Use on Public Data Networks of DTE Designated for Interfacing to Synchronous V-Series Modems. Allows use of V.24/V.28 (essentially the same as EIA RS-232) or V.35.

X.25—Interface Between DTE and DCE for Terminals Operating in the Packet Mode on Public Data Networks. Defines the architecture of three levels of protocols existing in the serial interface cable between a packet-mode terminal and a gateway to a packet network.

X.28—DTE/DCE Interface for a Start-Stop Mode DTE Accessing the PAD in a Public Data Network Situated in the Same Country. Defines the architecture of protocols existing in a serial interface cable between a start-stop terminal and an X.3 PAD.

X.29—Procedures for the Exchange of Control Information and User Data Between a PAD and a Packet Mode DTE or Another PAD. Defines the architecture of protocols behind the X.3 PAD, either between two PADs or between a PAD and a packet-mode terminal on the other side of the network.

X.75—Terminal and Transit Call Control Procedures and Data Transfer System on International Circuits Between Packet-Switched Data Networks. Defines the architecture of protocols between two public packet networks.

X.121—International Numbering Plan for Public Data Networks. Defines a numbering plan including code assignments for each nation.

Interrelationships Among X Standards

Many X standard sections give details on other sections or add depth to specific areas of concern. In some cases, a section describes conditions that must be met before other sections become applicable.

Figure 11.9 shows the interrelationships among many of these X standards. In summary: X.25 specifies the relationship between a packet-mode DTE and a packet network. X.28 specifies the relationship between a start-stop (asynchronous) DTE and an X.3 PAD that must reside between a nonpacket DTE and a packet network. X.29 specifies additional relationships above those in X.25 that a packet-mode DTE must satisfy when communicating with a nonpacket mode DTE through a packet network and PAD. X.29 also covers the relationships between two PADs when two nonpacket mode DTEs are communicating through a packet network.

The ITU-T X envisioned the X.3 PAD as being within the packet network—that is, behind the DCE. The 1980 version X.3 covers the PAD only for start-stop (asynchronous) terminals, but it leaves open the future possibility of covering other nonpacket terminals, for example, IBM BSC. Several stand-alone X.3 PADs are now marketed for connection of various start-stop and non-start-stop DTEs to packet networks.

FIGURE 11.9.

Relationships between some X interface standards.

Frame Relay

Although X.25-based packet networks have gained widespread acceptance, their data handling capability in an era of increasing use of fiber-optic cable represents a severe limitation. The growth in the installation of fiber-optic cable for the transmission of voice, data, and video between communications carrier central offices has reduced the potential of transmission errors to fewer than 1 in 10^9 bits from the rate of 1 in 10^5 typically encountered on analog transmission facilities. However, the use of X.25 packet networks results in the flow of packets through numerous data switching exchanges, with each DSE performing error checking and sometimes performing flow control procedures, both of which introduce delays that adversely affect the throughput of data.

Although X.25 error-checking procedures were necessary when packet networks were established using analog leased lines to interconnect DSEs, for many communications applications in which data flows over fiber-optic cable, the use of a series of error checking procedures is both unnecessary and detrimental to developing high-speed transmission that effectively uses available bandwidth. Recognizing this limitation to X.25, a form of fast packet switching referred to as frame relay was developed.

Frame relay can be considered as a logical progression of X.25 packet switching. Under frame relay, most error checking and flow control functions performed in an X.25 network are eliminated. As a result, frame relay transmission occurs at data rates up to the 1.544 Mbps DS-1 rate, which are significantly higher than are obtainable using X.25 packet networks.

Frame Relay Components

The connection of a computer or data terminal to a frame relay network involves the installation of various hardware components as well as knowledge of features unique to this data transport mechanism. From a physical perspective, the connection from a customer premise to a frame relay service provider is quite similar to the connection used for other types of services provided by communications vendors.

Figure 11.10 illustrates a typical connection from a customer premise to a frame relay service provider's nearest serving office. Note that communications equipment located at the customer premise can be any type of frame relay-compliant device, such as a front-end processor, multiplexer, or router. The router illustrated in Figure 11.10 is assumed to provide each workstation on the LAN with access to the frame relay network.

FIGURE 11.10.

Frame relay components.

The CSU/DSU converts unipolar digital signaling into a bipolar format for transmission on the local digital access line as described in Chapter 5, "Synchronous Modems, Digital Transmission, and Service Units." Although there is no reason why an analog local access line cannot be used to provide access to a frame relay service, present service provider policy is to commence the access rate to a frame relay service at 56 Kbps via a digital leased line. The local access line is routed to the serving telephone company office, where it is connected to the frame relay service provider's point of presence (POP), assuming that the service provider is a long-distance carrier. Recently, several local carriers announced frame relay service offerings which enable organizations that require the transmission of data only within a limited geographic area to have their frame relay service requirements performed by a local carrier, assuming that the carrier is cost competitive. Regardless of the frame relay service provider, the local access line can transport (in effect) multiplexed data representing two or more destinations that are routed as virtual circuits by the frame relay service provider.

Similar to the use of an X.25 packet network, the use of a frame relay service enables organizations to route data to many locations via the use of a single leased line. To illustrate this concept, consider the four-site frame relay network shown in the top portion of Figure 11.11. In this example, an organization with four geographically distributed LAN

> Any frame relay-compliant device that is to include a front-end processor, multiplexer, or router can be connected to a frame relay service.

locations installed four frame relay access lines to connect each location to a frame relay access provider. Here, as requirements for transmission between locations occur, the mesh structured network of the service provider is used to get virtual circuits between each location. Note that only four routers, with one port per router, are required to get the capability to transmit between any location. In comparison, the use of leased lines to establish an organizational frame relay service would require six leased lines and 12 router ports, as indicated in the lower portion of Figure 11.11.

Using a Frame Relay Service Provider

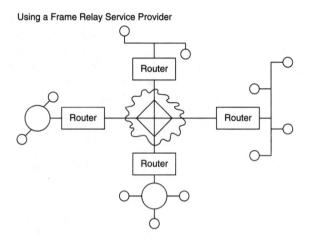

FIGURE 11.11

Comparing the use of a frame relay service to constructing a frame relay network.

Establishing a Frame Relay Network

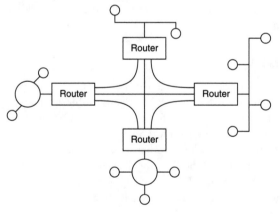

In establishing a frame relay service, it is important to distinguish between the operating rate of the frame relay port connection and what is referred to as the committed information rate (CIR). The port operating rate defines the highest possible speed you can achieve into the frame relay service. That rate also represents the maximum operating rate of any virtual circuit originating from the access line.

The carrier's frame relay network will carry traffic from many organizations. This means that at times the service provider's facilities might not be available to transport the full data rate flowing into the frame relay service.

● The committed information rate represents the minimum data transfer rate obtainable on a frame relay service.

For a fee, frame relay service providers will guarantee a minimum end-to-end transmission rate for each permanent virtual circuit required between your premise and distant locations. That minimum rate is referred to as the committed information rate (CIR). The higher the CIR, the higher the level of performance, albeit at a higher cost.

During most of the day, the data rate transported by the frame relay service might equal the port operating rate of equipment connected to the service. However, during certain periods of time, many users subscribing to the service might require transmission through common portions of the carrier's network facilities that exceeds the capacity of intranetwork circuits. At that time, the carrier periodically drops frames of different subscribers until the aggregate data rate between the congested locations can be carried by the available bandwidth. In doing so, the frame relay service provider will not lower the operating rate of each virtual circuit below the CIR, because the CIR defines the minimum end-to-end transmission rate of each virtual circuit. Because equipment connected to the frame relay service is responsible for end-to-end data integrity, the originating device simply retransmits dropped frames.

To provide equipment connected to the frame relay service with notification that congestion is occurring, bits known as forward error congestion notification (FECON) and backward error congestion notification (BECON) are used within a frame. As congestion occurs, the frame relay service will set the FECON and BECON bit positions before actually dropping frames. Those settings alert equipment to the fact that congestion is occurring in the network.

Cost Comparison

A comparison of the costs associated with the use of a frame relay service can involve an investigation of the pricing structure of many elements. Most frame relay service providers charge a frame relay port fee based on the operating rate of the interface to the service as well as a fee for the CIR subscribed for. Some service providers bill for each CIR for each permanent virtual circuit, whereas other service providers bill for a bandwidth allocation that represents the sum of the CIRs for all virtual circuits. Other charges that frame relay providers might bill for include a fixed charge per virtual circuit, a usage charge based on frames transmitted, and a distance charge based on the length of virtual circuits.

Open Systems Interconnection Reference Model

In 1983, the International Organization for Standardization (ISO) culminated six years of intensive effort to develop and publish a guideline—a reference model—for describing data communications architectures. The resulting document, International Standard #7498, has been redrafted by the ITU-T using its own terminology, and the redraft has been designated ITU-T X.200. The generic name for both documents is Open Systems Interconnection Reference Model (OSI/RM)—usually called simply OSI.

OSI is not a protocol nor does it contain protocols. What OSI does is define a consistent language and boundaries for establishing protocols such that systems that abide by its rules should be "open" to one another—that is, able to communicate.

Decades of frustration caused by incompatibility between competitive or geographically distinct communications systems have created such an appetite for the establishment of cooperative systems that there is a virtual stampede toward global standardization of data communications architectures. Many standard committees in several organizations are now engaged in the development of protocols for the various layers in the numerous systems to which OSI will apply.

OSI Layers

OSI defines a complete architecture having seven layers. There is no specific reason why it is seven rather than six or eight; the functions that must be performed just happened to fall into roughly seven groupings. The lowest three layers (physical, link, and network) correspond closely to the physical, link, and packet levels of X.25. Protocols have been and are being developed for other kinds of systems, such as facsimile, integrated voice/data networks, videotex, and so forth. Even if the protocols were never written, OSI has had a tremendous impact in standardizing the way we view communications.

These are the official names of the seven layers, from top to bottom:

7. Application	3. Network
6. Presentation	2. Link
5. Session	1. Physical
4. Transport	

Each successive step up the list takes one to a higher level of system supervision. In terms of the protocols, lower levels involve successively more embedded headers. Figure 11.12 shows how the seven levels relate for a system whose lower three layers correspond to X.25. (In this case, NH is the packet header.) The concept of layers was previously discussed in Chapter 10, "Alternatives in Local Area Networks."

● OSI/RM is a reference model for data communication architectures. It has been redrafted by the ITU-T and designated ITU-T X.200.

● OSI defines a consistent language and boundaries for protocols so that systems that follow OSI can communicate with one another. However, OSI itself is not a protocol.

● There are seven layers to any architecture as defined by OSI. The three lowest levels correspond roughly to the physical, link, and packet levels of X.25.

FIGURE 11.12.

The seven embedded layers of OSI.

These correspond roughly to the equivalent layers of X.25.

Physical transmission media

An Analogy

The basic requirements to establish, maintain, and terminate communications without error are similar whether verbal or computer communications are being used.

Whenever people communicate, whether by computer or verbally, they invoke protocols at all seven levels of OSI. Without going into the laborious details and vocabulary of the OSI standard, we will illustrate the OSI categorizations of the seven levels from top to bottom for a typical telephone call.

1. *Physical Layer Concerns*—These are the actual sounds being uttered into the mouthpiece and heard from the receiver.

2. *Link Layer Concerns*—Talk when you're supposed to and listen when you're supposed to. Ask for a repeat if there is something you don't understand. Tell the other party to slow down if he's talking too fast.

3. *Network Layer Concerns*—Dial the number and listen for call-progress signals. Redial if you get a busy signal or if cut off. Disconnect when the conversation is completed.

4. *Transport Layer Concerns*—What is the most cost-effective way to handle this call (or these calls) consistent with priorities? What long-distance carriers should be used?

5. *Session Layer Concerns*—Can this situation be handled in one call or several? Will other people need to be brought in at different times? Who will control the discussion in a multiparty conversation? Who will reestablish the call if we're cut off?

6. *Presentation Layer Concerns*—Are we talking the same language and dialect?

7. *Application Layer Concerns*—Am I talking to the right person? Who is paying for this call? Is this the best time to talk, or should I call back later? Does the other party have a pencil and paper to take notes?

Anyone who has used a telephone in everyday business situations can relate to all seven levels of the reference model just described. By reflecting on X.25, the reader should be able to identify the analogies to the packet, link, and physical layer protocols.

What Have You Learned?

1. When protocols are layered, the higher level layers are embedded inside fields of less intelligent layers.

2. Packet switching involves fast store-and-forward computers at each network node.

3. X.25 is an international standard packet switching architecture specifying three layers of protocols at the network gateway.

4. When properly used, X.25 networks provide a fast, reliable, accurate, flexible, and cost-effective data communications alternative.

5. X.25 specifies two services: Virtual Call Service is analogous to a telephone call; Permanent Virtual Circuit service is analogous to a private line.

6. X.25 doesn't provide for dial access or for start-stop transmission, but enhanced services do.

7. A single X.25 interface can handle many logical channels at the same time.

8. X.25 is but a part of a larger group of ITU-T standards on public data networks.

9. X.25/X.121 provides for an extremely large worldwide population of terminals.

10. Frame relay is a form of fast packet switching in which error checking and flow control is minimized.

11. Open Systems Interconnection is a reference architectural model that is revolutionizing the way we view telecommunications.

Quiz for Chapter 11

1. The electrical state of the control leads in a serial interface is a concern of:

   a. The physical-layer protocol.

   b. The link-layer protocol.

   c. The network-layer protocol.

   d. None of the above.

2. The X.25 standard specifies a:

   a. Technique for dial access.

   b. Technique for start-stop data.

   c. Data bit rate.

   d. DTE/DCE interface.

3. The X.25 standard is:

   a. Required for all packet switching networks.

   b. A recommendation of the ITU-T.

   c. A complete description of a public data network.

   d. Used by all packet terminals.

4. The X.25 standard for packet networks is analogous to:

   a. PBX standards for a telephone network.

   b. Handset standards for a telephone.

   c. Local loop standards for a telephone network.

   d. Switching standards for a telephone network.

5. The value of the "A" field in an LAPB frame specifies:

   a. The calling DTE for a virtual call.

   b. The called DTE for a virtual call.

   c. The data sink for a VC or PVC.

   d. One of the two ends of a serial interface.

6. A group of packets from a source through an X.25 packet system to a sink:

   a. Arrives in the same order sent for VC, but not PVC.

   b. Arrives in the same order sent for PVC, but not VC.

   c. Arrives in the same order sent for both VC and PVC.

   d. None of the above.

7. The value of N(S) is related to the value of P(S) as follows:

   a. N(S) – P(S) = number of outstanding packets.

   b. N(S) – P(S) = number of outstanding frames.

   c. N(S) – P(S) = number of active logical channels in a link.

   d. They are not related.

8. A protocol is a set of rules governing a time sequence of events that must take place:

   a. Between peers.

   b. Between nonpeers.

   c. Across an interface.

   d. None of the above.

9. The OSI Reference Model defines the functions for seven layers of protocols:

   a. Including the user and communications medium.

   b. Not including the user or communications medium.

   c. Including the communications medium but not the user.

   d. Including the user but not the communications medium.

10. The X.25 standard covers how many OSI layers:

   a. 3.

   b. 4.

   c. 7.

   d. None.

11. Architecturally, link protocols are at a level:

   a. Lower than physical protocols.

   b. Higher than physical protocols.

   c. The same as physical protocols.

   d. None of the above.

12. A data packet is a packet header together with:

   a. A network layer.

   b. An administrative layer.

   c. User data.

   d. A packet switch.

13. A network node joining three or more links is a:

   a. DSE.

   b. DTE.

   c. DCE.

   d. DTE and DCE.

14. The X.25 standard specifies how many separate protocol layers at the serial interface gateway:

   a. 8.

   b. 2.

   c. 4.

   d. 3.

15. The LAPB frame structure and the frame structure of SDLC are:

   a. Opposite.

   b. Identical.

   c. Reversed.

   d. None of the above.

16. Establishing a virtual "connection" is functionally equivalent to:

   a. Placing a telephone call prior to a conversation.

   b. Connecting a virtual memory.

   c. Physically connecting a DTE and DCE.

   d. None of the above.

17. In X.25 network layer protocol, the data packets normally contain:

   a. One octet of header plus data.

   b. Two octets of header plus data.

   c. Three octets of header plus data.

   d. Four octets of header plus data.

18. The frame relay committed information rate represents:

    a. The maximum data rate on the network.

    b. The steady state data rate on the network.

    c. The minimum data rate on the network.

    d. The interface data rate.

19. The number of circuits required for the interconnection of equipment at four locations is:

    a. 2.

    b. 4.

    c. 6.

    d. 8.

20. The number of ports required for the connection of equipment at four locations to each other is:

    a. 3.

    b. 6.

    c. 9.

    d. 12.

21. Notification of the occurrence of congestion in a frame relay service occurs through the:

    a. Committed information rate.

    b. Forward error congestion notification.

    c. Backward error congestion notification.

    d. Both b and c.

22. The OSI reference model is:

    a. Worthless.

    b. A protocol.

    c. Not a protocol.

    d. None of the above.

23. Layer 1 of the OSI model is the:

    a. Link layer.

    b. Physical layer.

    c. Network layer.

    d. Transport layer.

24. The applications layer of the OSI model is the:

    a. Seventh layer.

    b. Sixth layer.

    c. Fifth layer.

    d. Fourth layer.

Internet

About This Chapter

The Internet represents a network formed by the interconnection of subnetworks. In this chapter, we will examine its evolution, some of the protocols used to transport data, and a few of the applications that resulted in its evolution from an academic-oriented facility to a network used by virtually everyone who has access to a computer. Because the use of the TCP/IP protocol suite is essential for transferring information on the Internet, we will focus on portions of this protocol suite as we examine the Internet and its applications.

Evolution

During the 1960s, the United States Department of Defense sponsored research that resulted in the development of a communications network to interconnect research laboratories and data centers. Funded by the Defense Advanced Research Projects Agency (DARPA), this network was known as ARPANET. It represented one of the first layered communications networks, preceding the development of the seven-layer ISO reference model by approximately a decade.

> **Note:** The evolution of the Internet to include the TCP/IP protocol suite is based on research funded by the U.S. Department of Defense.

The work involved in establishing ARPANET resulted in the development of two specific protocols for the transmission of information: the Transmission Control Protocol (TCP) and the Internet Protocol (IP), commonly referred to collectively as TCP/IP. TCP represents a transport layer protocol that provides end-to-end reliable transmission. To do so, TCP includes such functions as flow control, error control, and the exchange of status information. In comparison, IP represents a connectionless-mode network layer protocol designed to route messages between networks. To do so, IP includes the capability to segment or fragment and reassemble messages that must be routed between networks that support different packet sizes than the size supported by the source and/or destination network.

In addition to TCP, the Internet suite specifies an optional connectionless-mode layer 4 transport protocol known as the User Datagram Protocol (UDP). UDP is used for transaction-based applications, such as the transmission of network management information when transmission efficiency is more important than reliability.

Application Services

Various application services have been developed for transport by the TCP/IP protocol suite. The more well-known applications include the File Transfer Protocol (FTP); an interactive remote terminal access protocol known as TELNET, which enables a terminal to be connected to a remote host as if it were directly connected to the computer; the Simple Mail Transport Protocol (SMTP), which provides a standard method for exchanging electronic mail; the HyperText Transmission Protocol (HTTP), which enables the transportation of World Wide Web (WWW) pages from Web servers to browsers operating on client computers; and the Simple Network Management Protocol (SNMP), which supports the management of network devices.

Figure 12.1 illustrates the layering structure of the TCP/IP protocol suite to include a few of the application services included in the suite. Note that the subdivision of the transport layer in Figure 12.1 is used as a mechanism to indicate which applications are transported by TCP and which are carried by UDP. Later in this chapter, I discuss several of the application services illustrated in Figure 12.1.

FIGURE 12.1.

A portion of the TCP/IP suite.

Applications	File Transfer Protocol	TELNET	HTTP	SMTP	SNMP	DNS
Transport Layer	TCP				UDP	
Network Layer	IP					
Data Link Layer	Data Link Layer					
Physical Layer	Physical Layer					

One of the key reasons for the dramatic growth of the Internet can be traced to the development and structure of the TCP/IP protocol suite. Because TCP/IP was developed using taxpayer funds, its specifications were placed in the public domain, and they are available royalty-free for vendors to develop "protocol stacks" in software to implement TCP/IP's operational features. The growth of the Internet can also be attributed to the structure of TCP/IP, which makes it suitable for both LAN and WAN operations.

For example, on a LAN, TCP/IP can be transported within Ethernet, Token-Ring, FDDI, or another type of local area network frame. Because a considerable amount of effort was expended in developing LAN adapter cards to support the bus structures used in Macintosh, IBM PCs and compatible computers, Sun Microsystem's workstations, and even IBM mainframes, the development of software-based protocol stacks to facilitate the transmission of TCP/IP on LANs provided the capability to interconnect tens of millions of LAN-based computers to one another. This access is normally accomplished by commercial organizations, universities, and government agencies first connecting their networks to the facilities of an Internet access provider.

> TCP/IP specifications are in the public domain, allowing vendors to develop royalty-free software products.

Internet Access Providers

Through the late 1980s when the Internet was primarily used to communicate among colleges, universities, and government agencies, most Internet access providers represented nonprofit associations of schools located within a geographical area. As such, the Internet access provider typically constructed a high-speed backbone network that provided basic connectivity within the geographical area served, and connected that backbone network to other backbone networks. The rapid growth in the use of the Internet by both individuals and businesses resulted in many nonprofit associations becoming commercialized, selling Internet access to both individuals and businesses. Most individuals use a dial-up protocol to access the facilities of an Internet access provider, whereas most businesses use leased lines to connect local area networks to the Internet. Because a LAN can provide support for hundreds to thousands of workstations, there is always a high probability that one or more workstation users require access to the Internet at any particular point in time.

> Most individuals use a dial-up protocol to access the facilities of an Internet access provider, whereas most businesses use leased lines to connect computers on their LANs to the Internet.

Thus, from an economic perspective, it is normally more economical to connect a LAN to the Internet via a leased line than to have individual users use the switched telephone network, because the latter method is commonly billed on an hourly usage basis. In addition, a leased line provides immediate access from the Internet to any application residing on the LAN, such as a Web server, an FTP server, or an electronic mail system. Thus, a leased line connection facilitates bidirectional access to and from the Internet. Figure 12.2 illustrates the two most common methods of Internet access.

FIGURE 12.2.

Common business and individual Internet access methods.

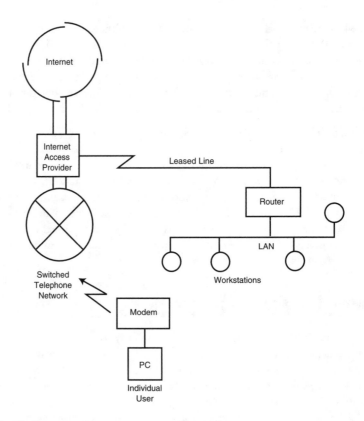

IP Addressing

An IP address is commonly expressed as four decimal numbers with each number separated by a dot.

The routing of information on a TCP/IP network, to include the Internet as well as other public and private networks, is based on IP addressing. An IP address is 32 bits long and is commonly expressed as four decimal numbers ranging from 0 to 255, with each number separated by a dot. Thus, another term used for an IP address is a dotted decimal address.

An IP address is divided into assigned network and host computer sections that together form a unique address. The network portion of the address is assigned by the Internet Network Information Center (InterNIC), whereas network managers and administrators assign the host portion of the address to individual computer users.

To facilitate the assignment of addresses, the format of the 32-bit IP address was structured into five unique network classes, of which three are typically allocated by the InterNIC to Internet access providers, who in turn distribute those addresses to organizations and individuals. IP Address Classes range from Class A through Class E. Figure 12.3 illustrates the structure of the first three IP classes. Class D addresses are reserved for multicast groups, and Class E addresses are reserved for future use.

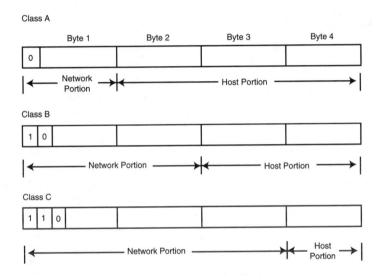

FIGURE 12.3.

IP address formats.

In examining the composition of the IP address classes shown in Figure 12.3, note that the leftmost bits of the address indicate its network class. Also note that the InterNIC assignment of an IP address actually represents the assignment of the network portion of the address, resulting in the manager or administrator of an organization's network that uses an assigned address class being responsible for assigning the host portion of the address.

A Class A address provides the largest range of addresses available for assignment to host computers. Thus, the InterNIC assigns Class A addresses to large organizations and countries that have national networks. Because a Class A address uses the first bit in the first byte as the identifier for this class, a Class A network is restricted to a network number between 1 and 127 for its first decimal number.

A Class B address is evenly split, using two bytes for the network portion and two bytes for the host portion of the address. The availability of two bytes for host computer address assignments enables up to 65,636 hosts to be identified. Thus, Class B addresses are normally assigned to relatively large organizations with tens of thousands of employees.

●

Class A through C addresses are subdivided into network and host portions with the subdivision governing the number of hosts that can be uniquely identified on a network.

A Class C address uses three bytes for the network portion and one byte for host identification. Thus, a Class C network address is restricted to supporting a maximum of 256 hosts. This means that a Class C network address is assigned to small organizations, or multiple Class C addresses are assigned to organizations that require more than 256 distinct host addresses but are not large enough to justify a Class B address.

Domain Name Service

Although IP addresses consist of a sequence of dotted decimal numbers, most readers are probably more familiar with names used to represent Internet addresses, such as www.whitehouse.gov, which represents the address of the World Wide Web server operated by the White House. In this address, www represents the type of service residing on a server, whitehouse represents the name of the organization, and gov indicates that the organization is a government entity.

To facilitate the use of names, each organization registers its name with the InterNIC. The registration process results in the InterNIC assigning the organization to one of six categories referred to as domain names. Thus, the registration process results in a domain name consisting of the organization's name and its domain assignment being registered. In the preceding example, whitehouse.gov would represent the registered domain name. Table 12.1 indicates the current category of domain name suffixes assigned by the InterNIC.

Every organization
that registers its
name with the
InterNIC is assigned
to one of six
domains.

Table 12.1. Domain name suffixes.

Suffix	Type of Organization
COM	Commercial organization
EDU	Educational organization
GOV	Government agency
MIL	Military organization
NET	Networking organization
ORG	Not-for-profit organization

In examining the entries in Table 12.1, note that the domain name suffix indicates the type of organization. Thus, it is entirely possible for two organizations to use the same server host name and have the same organization name yet have separate identities, because each could represent a different type of organization, resulting in their registered names having different endings.

When an organization has a registered domain name, it can prefix that name to indicate specific hosts or applications residing on one host. For example, www.whitehouse.gov and ftp.whitehouse.gov, which could represent a World Wide Web (WWW) server and a File Transfer Protocol (FTP) server, could also represent two applications residing on a common computer. When you enter the IP address in an application as a name, a translation process occurs that converts the name into a 32-bit IP address. This translation process, which is transparent to a user, occurs through the use of a TCP/IP application known as Domain Name Service (DNS).

DNS commonly operates on a separate server on a network and keeps track of the host names on the network. When a user on the network enters a name rather than an IP address when using a TCP/IP application, the name is transported to the DNS server. If the name resides on the network, the DNS server returns the IP address associated with the name. If the name does not represent a computer on the network, but a recent query using that name occurred, the IP address might be in the DNS server's cache memory. If so, it is returned to the requester. If the name is not in the DNS database or in cache memory, the server sends a request to a "higher" DNS server, usually located on another network. To understand why this occurs requires a slight digression to explain the DNS hierarchy.

A top-level domain registers subdomains in its database in the form of the location of the name servers for those domains. Similarly, subdomains keep track of domains under them, in effect creating a naming hierarchy. Thus, if the name server on the current network does not have the name and associated IP address for the name in its database, it forwards the request to a higher-level DNS. This forwarding effort can be replicated several times and traverse areas around the globe until the IP address is found and returned. It is important to note that DNS names play no role in the actual routing of IP packets. Instead, they simply provide the IP address associated with a domain name. It is the router used to connect networks that is responsible for the actual routing of packets. Because we can get a better feel for the flow of data on the Internet by examining IP and TCP, let's turn our attention to those two protocols.

> The DNS is responsible for converting address names into 32-bit IP addresses.

The Internet Protocol (IP)

As briefly discussed earlier in this chapter, IP is a network layer protocol. IP provides for the transfer of a basic unit of information referred to as a datagram. In doing so, IP operates as an unreliable, connectionless protocol. Although your first impression of those terms is negative, they are not as bad as they seem. First, although IP provides an unreliable transmission method, the term "unreliable" should be viewed in the context that delivery is not guaranteed. This means that queuing delays or other problems can result in the loss of data; however, higher layers, such as TCP, can provide error detection and correction that

> IP operates as an unreliable, connectionless protocol that transports datagrams.

results in the retransmission of IP datagrams. Second, the term "connectionless" references the fact that each datagram is treated independently from preceding and succeeding datagrams. This means IP does not require a connection to be established between source and destination before transferring the first datagram or succeeding datagrams.

The routing of datagrams through a network can occur over different paths, with some datagrams arriving out of sequence from the order transmitted. In addition, as datagrams flow between networks, they encounter physical limitations imposed on the amount of data that can be transported based on the transport mechanism used to move data on the network. For example, the Information field in an Ethernet frame is limited to 1500 bytes. Thus, as a datagram flows between networks, it might have to be fragmented into two or more datagrams to be transported through different networks to their ultimate destination.

Figure 12.4 illustrates the routing of two datagrams from workstation A on a Token Ring network to server B connected to an Ethernet LAN. Because the routing of datagrams is a connectionless service, no call setup is required, which enhances transmission efficiency. In comparison, when TCP is used, it provides a connection-oriented service regardless of the lower layer delivery system (for example, IP).

FIGURE 12.4.

Routing of datagrams can occur over different paths.

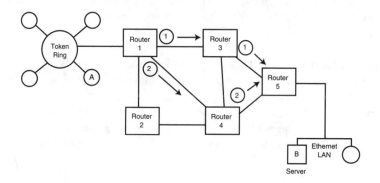

TCP requires the establishment of a virtual circuit in which a temporary path is developed between source and destination. This path is fixed and the flow of datagrams is restricted to the path established. When UDP is used in place of TCP, the flow of data at the transport layer continues to be connectionless and results in the transport of datagrams over available paths rather than a fixed path resulting from the establishment of a virtual circuit.

IP datagrams are transported within the Information field of LAN frames.

Figure 12.5 illustrates the relationship of an IP datagram, a UDP datagram, and a TCP segment to a LAN frame. Note that the IP datagram flowing on a 4 Mbps Token-Ring LAN can be up to 4500 bytes in length because that is the maximum length of a Token-Ring Information field. However, when that datagram flows onto an Ethernet LAN whose

FIGURE 12.5.

Forming a LAN frame.

maximum Information field length is 1500 bytes, the original datagram might have to be fragmented into thirds.

We can gain an appreciation for how datagram fragmentation is accomplished, as well as additional information about the flow of data, by examining the composition of the fields in the IP header.

Figure 12.6 illustrates the fields contained within the IP header. Note that the header contains a minimum of 20 bytes of control information, with Figure 12.6 illustrating the width of each field with respect to a 32-bit word.

The Vers field consists of four bits that identify the version of the IP protocol used to create the datagram. The current version of the IP protocol is 4.

The Hlen field also contains four bits. This field indicates the length of the header in 32-bit words. In comparison, the Total Length field indicates the total length of the datagram to include its header and higher layer information. Because 16 bits are used for this field, an IP datagram can be up to 2^{16}, or 65,535 octets in length.

FIGURE 12.6.

The format of the IP header.

0	4	8	16	31

Vers	Hlen	Service Type	Total Length	
Identification			Flags	Fragment Offset
Time to Live		Protocol	Header	Checksum
Source IP Address				
Destination IP Address				
Options + Padding				

The Service Type field defines how the datagram is handled. Three of the eight bits in this field are used to denote the precedence or level of importance assigned by the sender. Thus, this field provides a priority mechanism for routing IP datagrams.

The Identification field enables each datagram or fragmented datagram to be identified. If a datagram was fragmented, the Fragment Offset field specifies the offset in the original datagram of the data being carried. In effect, this field indicates where the fragment belongs in the complete message. The actual value in this field is an integer that corresponds to a unit of 8 octets, providing an offset in 64-bit units.

> ●
> The Time to Live field provides a fail-safe mechanism that prevents misaddressed datagrams from continuously wandering the Internet.

The Flags field contains two bits that indicate how fragmentation occurs, and a third bit is currently unassigned. The setting of one bit can be viewed as a direct fragment control mechanism because a value of 0 indicates that the datagram can be fragmented, whereas a value of 1 denotes that it can't be fragmented. The second bit is set to 0 to indicate that a fragment in a datagram is the last fragment, and it's set to a value of 1 to indicate that more fragments follow the current protocol.

The Time to Live (TTL) field specifies the maximum time that a datagram can live. Because an exact time is difficult to measure, many routers decrement this field by 1 as a datagram flows between networks, with the datagram being discarded when the field value reaches zero. You can consider this field to represent a fail-safe mechanism because it prevents misaddressed datagrams from continuously wandering the Internet.

The Protocol field specifies the higher-level protocol used to create the message carried in the datagram. For example, a value of decimal 6 would indicate TCP, whereas a value of decimal 17 would indicate UDP. The source and destination address fields are both 32 bits in length. As previously discussed, each address represents both a network and a host computer on the network.

Address Resolution

The physical address associated with a LAN workstation is referred to as its hardware address. For an Ethernet network, that address is 48 bits or 6 bytes in length. In this chapter, I noted that at the data link layer, IP uses a 32-bit logical address. One common problem associated with the routing of an IP datagram to a particular workstation on a network is the delivery of the datagram to its correct destination. To correctly deliver the datagram requires knowledge of the relationship between physical and logical addresses. This relationship is obtained by two protocols that map the physical and logical addresses to each other. One protocol, known as the Address Resolution Protocol (ARP), translates an IP address into a hardware address. The Reverse Address Resolution Protocol (RARP), as its name implies, performs a reverse mapping, converting a hardware address into an IP address.

● The ARP and RARP protocols provide the translation between logical and physical addresses necessary to route datagrams to and from appropriate hardware devices located on the same or on different networks.

To illustrate the use of ARP, assume that one computer user wants to send a datagram to another computer and both computers are located on the same Ethernet network. The first computer broadcasts an ARP packet within an Ethernet frame to all devices on the LAN. That packet contains the destination IP address, because it is known, and sets the hardware address field to zeros, because its value is unknown. Although each device on the LAN reads the ARP packet as it is transmitted as a broadcast packet, only the device that recognizes its own logical address responds. When it does, it transmits an ARP reply in which its physical address is inserted in the ARP address field previously set to zero. To reduce the necessity to constantly transmit ARP packets, the originator records received information in a table known as an ARP cache, allowing subsequent datagrams to be directed quickly to the appropriate address on the LAN. Thus, ARP and RARP provide a well-thought-out methodology for equating physical hardware addresses to IP's logical addresses.

TCP

The Transmission Control Protocol (TCP) is a Layer 4 connection-oriented protocol. This protocol is responsible for providing reliable communications between hosts and processes on different hosts. Concerning the latter, TCP is structured to enable multiple application programs on a host to communicate concurrently with processes on other hosts, as well as for a host to demultiplex and service incoming TCP traffic among different applications or processes running on the host. To accomplish this task, a TCP header includes a destination port number to identify the ultimate destination in a computer. To gain an appreciation for the functionality and capability of TCP, let's turn our attention to its header, which is illustrated in Figure 12.7.

● The destination port number in the TCP header provides the mechanism that enables multiple application processes to be intermixed within a data stream.

FIGURE 12.7.

The TCP header.

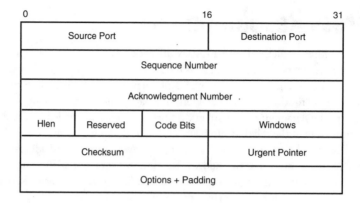

The Source and Destination Port fields are each 16 bits in length and are used to identify a user process or application. The Source Port field is optional and when not used is padded with zeros. The term "well-known port," which is commonly used to denote an application layer protocol or process, actually references the port address used within a TCP header. Table 12.2 lists the well-known ports associated with eight popular TCP/IP application layer protocols. In examining the entries in Table 12.2, you will note that some protocols, such as FTP, use two port addresses or logical connections. One address (21) is for commands and replies and functions as a control path. The second port address (20) is used for the actual file transfer.

Table 12.2. Popular TCP/IP application layer protocols.

Name	Acronym	Description	Well-Known Port
Domain Name Protocol	DOMAIN	Defines the DNS	53
File Transfer Protocol	FTP	Provides file transfer between computers	20, 21
Finger Protocol	FINGER	Provides information about specified user	79
Hypertext Transmission Protocol	HTTP	Conveys information between a Web browser and a Web server	80

Name	Acronym	Description	Well-Known Port
Post Office Protocol	POP	Enables PC users to access mail from a mail server	110
Simple Mail Transfer Protocol	SMTP	Provides electronic mail transfer	25
Simple Network Management Protocol	SNMP	Provides the exchange of management information	161,162
TELNET Protocol	TELNET	Provides remote terminal access to a host	23

If you reexamine Figure 12.5 in conjunction with Figures 12.6 and 12.7, you will note that the use of a TCP/IP application requires three addresses at both source and destination. A port address is required to identify the process or application and is contained within the TCP header. Within the IP header, an IP address is required to identify the network and host computer where the process or application resides. Finally, the delivery of information on a LAN requires the use of a hardware address, which is used within the LAN header shown in Figure 12.5 to deliver the IP datagram.

●
The use of a TCP/IP application requires three addresses: a port address, an IP address, and a device hardware address.

Returning to our examination of the TCP/IP header, the Sequence Number field identifies the position in the sender's byte stream of the data transported in the TCP segment. Thus, this field provides a mechanism to maintain the sequentiality of the data stream.

The Acknowledgment Number field identifies the number of the octet (Sequence Number) that the source expects to receive next. Thus, the Acknowledgment Number verifies the receipt of the prior $n-1$ segment when the Sequence Number is n.

The Hlen field, which is four bits in length, denotes the length of the segment header in 32-bit multiples. The Code Bits field contains six flag bits. Some of those bits, when set, indicate that a specific field in the header is significant and the field value should be interpreted, whereas other bits are used to control the connection and data transfer operation. Table 12.3 summarizes the use of the six Code Bits.

Table 12.3. Code Bit field values.

Code Bit	Code Bit Field Use
URG	Urgent Pointer field significant
ACK	Acknowledgment field significant
PSH	Push function
RST	Reset the connection
SYN	Synchronize Sequence numbers
FIN	No more data from sender

The 16-bit Window field indicates the number of octets, beginning with the one in the Acknowledgment field that the originator of the segment can control. Because TCP represents a full-duplex communications path, each end of the path can use the Window field to control the quantity of data being sent to it. This provides the recipient with the ability to, in effect, have a say over its destiny. That is, if the recipient becomes overloaded with processing or if some other situation results in its inability to receive large chunks of data, it can use the Window field to reduce the size of the chunks of data being sent to it.

The Checksum field provides reliability for the TCP header, the IP header, and data carried in the segment. Thus, this field provides the mechanism for the detection of errors in the segment.

Other than some options beyond the scope of this book, the Urgent Pointer field completes the header. This field enables the position of urgent data within a TCP segment to be identified, and a value in the field is interpreted only when the previously mentioned URG bit is set. When that bit position is set, the value in the Urgent Pointer field indicates the beginning of routine (non-urgent) data.

To illustrate the interrelated role of the Sequence, Acknowledgment, and Window fields, let's examine the transmission of data between two hosts via the use of a time chart that indicates some values for each field. This time chart is shown in Figure 12.8. At the top of Figure 12.8, we will assume that a Window size of 8 segments is in use. Although TCP supports full-duplex transmission, for simplicity of illustration we will use a half-duplex model in the time chart.

Assuming that host A is downloading a program or performing a lengthy file transfer, the first series of segments will have sequence numbers 64 through 71. Assuming that no errors occurred, host B returns an ACK value of 72 to indicate the next segment it expects to receive. Let's also assume that host B is running out of buffer space and that it reduces the window size to 4. Thus, host A uses the Window field value in the TCP header sent to it and reduces the number of units of data it will transmit to four, using an initial SEQ field value of 72 and increasing that value by 1 to 75 as it transmits four units of data to host B. Assuming that all data is received error-free, host B then returns an ACK value of 76 to acknowledge receipt of sequence field numbers through 75.

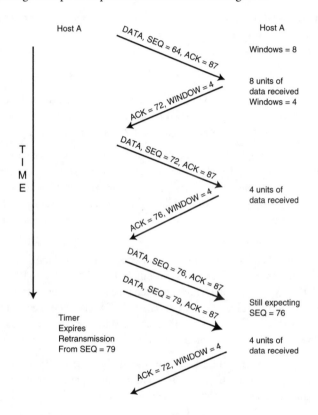

FIGURE 12.8.

A TCP transmission sequence.

Once again host A transmits to host B, this time using sequence field values of 76 to 79. As this transmission occurs, however, let's assume that some type of transmission impairment occurs that sends the data into the proverbial bit bucket so that it is never received at host B. Because host B does not receive anything, it does not transmit anything back to host A. Although host A could wait forever, this would not be a good idea when data becomes lost. Instead, an internal timer clicks down to zero while host A waits for a response. When a response does not appear and the timer expires, host A retransmits the segment, which is then acknowledged at the bottom of Figure 12.8.

● *Through the use of a sliding window, the flow of information between devices can be regulated.*

The altering of the Window field values provides a "sliding window" that can be used to control the flow of information by adjustment of the value of the Window field. In doing so, there are two special field values, 0 and 1, that further control the flow of information. A Window field value of 0 means a host has shut down communications, whereas a Window value of 1 requires an acknowledgment for each unit of data transmitted.

Now that you have a basic understanding of IP and TCP, let's turn our attention to a few of the applications that use the TCP/IP suite.

FTP

The File Transfer Protocol (FTP) was developed as a mechanism to facilitate the transfer of files between computers. As previously mentioned, FTP uses two "well-known ports," port 21 for passing control information, and port 20 for the actual data transfer.

FTP supports approximately 20 commands. Those commands enable a user to change directories (cd), obtain a directory list (dir), initiate a file transfer (get), and transfer a file (put). FTP permits multiple file transfers with the mget and mput commands when used with a filename containing one or more wildcard characters. For example, the command mget *.gif would result in the transfer of all files in the current directory that have the extension .gif.

● *A key advantage of FTP is that it is platform indepen-dent, enabling the transfer of files between different types of computers.*

One of the key advantages associated with the use of FTP is the fact that various imple-mentations exist that operate on a range of computers, from DOS PCs to IBM mainframes. This enables FTP to provide a mechanism to exchange files between computers as long as both computers support FTP and can be reached via a TCP/IP connection. Concerning the TCP/IP connection, FTP relies on TCP at the transport layer to provide a reliable transmission path, ensuring the error-free arrival of data at its destination.

Table 12.4 lists 10 commonly used FTP commands. Because FTP was originally devel-oped as a command-driven application, users had to remember command names and any associated parameter values to effectively use the application.

Table 12.4. Common FTP commands.

Command	Operation
ascii	Perform data transfer using ASCII format (default).
binary	Perform data transfer treating data as binary.
bye	Terminate the FTP session with the remote server and exit the client ftp program.
cd	Change the working directory on the remote server.
delete	Delete a file on the remote server.
dir	List the contents of the current directory on the remote server.

Command	Operation
get	Retrieve a specified file from the remote computer and store it on the local computer.
mget	Retrieve multiple files from a remote computer and store them on the local computer.
mput	Transfer multiple files from the local computer to the remote computer.
put	Transfer a specified file from the local computer to the remote computer.

To facilitate the use of FTP, programs were developed that hide the necessity to know FTP commands through the use of a graphical user interface. Figure 12.9 shows the NetManage Chameleon FTP client program screen displayed when I was using the program to establish a connection to a remote host. Note that the host address, which was entered as ftp.mcom.com, will be converted to a dotted decimal address by the Domain Name Server on my network. Also note that the user name was entered as anonymous. Many FTP servers are configured to accept public access. To facilitate such access, a user account named anonymous is established on the server.

●

An anonymous or guest FTP account enables public access to an FTP server.

FIGURE 12.9.

Using the NetManage Chameleon FTP client program to initiate a connection to an FTP server.

Although many servers with an anonymous or a "guest" account do not require a user to enter a password, other servers might request that a user enter his e-mail address. To provide a level of security and prevent the potential distribution of viruses, many organizations that operate anonymous FTP guest accounts restrict data transfer and prohibit public users from downloading files into the server.

In examining the background of Figure 12.9, note that the screen is subdivided into three sections labeled "Local," "Transfer," and "Remote." The Local section displays the directory structure and the files in each directory on the local or client computer. The Transfer section includes a series of buttons that enable you to perform predefined operations by simply clicking a button. At the top of the Transfer section are two buttons associated with the method of file transfer, with the button associated with Binary shown selected. Thus, clicking either button is the equivalent of entering an `ascii` or a `binary` FTP command. The two columns of buttons in the Transfer section are used to perform predefined operations on the local (button arrow pointing left) host or remote (button arrow pointing right) host, with the capability to perform an operation indicated by the highlighting of the button.

At the time the screen shown in Figure 12.9 was printed, I was in the process of establishing a connection to a remote computer. Thus, no operation in the Transfer section could be performed with respect to the remote computer, and each button in the right column of the Transfer section was not highlighted. However, after a connection to the remote host is established, all the buttons in the transfer section are highlighted. This is illustrated in Figure 12.10, which shows the screen displayed after I connected to a Netscape Corporation FTP site and selected the beta 2.01 version of the well-known browser. Note that by simply entering a filename in the local directory section of the screen and clicking the left-arrow button associated with Copy, one can initiate a file transfer from the remote to the local computer. No muss, no fuss, and no need to remember FTP commands, which is a key attribute associated with the use of different GUI TCP/IP-based application programs.

FIGURE 12.10.

Selecting a file on the remote FTP server.

TELNET

TELNET is an interactive remote access terminal protocol that was developed to enable users to access a remote computer as if they were directly connected to the computer. Similar to FTP, TELNET is based on a client/server model. Although TELNET was developed to provide terminal connectivity to hosts, the client does not have to be a physical terminal, such as one of the popular Digital Equipment Corporation's VT products. Instead, TELNET client programs have been developed that turn PCs, Macintoshes, and even various IBM, Sun, and HP workstations into an interactive terminal.

As previously indicated in Table 12.2, TELNET uses a common TCP connection to transmit both data and control information, with the data flow occurring on well-known port number 23. Similar to other TCP/IP applications, software developers over the past few years concentrated their development efforts on GUI-based applications to include TELNET.

Figure 12.11 illustrates the NetManage Chameleon TELNET Connection Dialog box that is displayed when you select the program's Connect | Connect menu option. Note that you must specify a host address, type of terminal to emulate, and port number when using the NetManage TELNET program. Concerning the port number, although 23 is the default port used for TELNET communications, some organizations select another port number for use by TELNET. Often, the selection of a much higher port number is used to "hide" the presence of a TELNET server from curious wanderers of the Internet.

●
TELNET enables a terminal device to access a remote host as if it was directly connected to the computer.

FIGURE 12.11.

Using the NetManage TELNET program to initiate a connection to a remote host computer.

TN3270

In addition to TELNET, another popular remote terminal program is TN3270. This program was designed to work with the screen control codes used by IBM 3270 type terminals. It enables client computers using TN3270 to access IBM mainframes.

HTTP

Perhaps the most popular Internet TCP/IP application is the HyperText Transmission Protocol (HTTP) that is used to convey information between a Web browser and a Web server. Here the term *browser* represents a software product that uses HTTP to transport information and supports the display of information encoded using the HyperText Markup Language (HTML).

The growth in the use of the Internet can be greatly attributed to the growth of the World Wide Web, the unstructured collection of Web servers containing text, graphics, and audio files whose contents can be viewed and heard through the use of a browser.

Figure 12.12 illustrates the use of the popular Netscape browser to view the Netscape Corporation home page. The address of the page being viewed is shown in the box to the right of the term "Netsite" and represents a file address encoded as a Uniform Resource Locator (URL). URLs provide a mechanism to initiate an FTP or a TELNET session, as well as to access and view predefined files through the use of a browser.

FIGURE 12.12.

Using the Netscape browser to view the contents of the Netscape Web home page.

The file being viewed in Web terminology is referred to as a page. This particular page is the first page displayed when a browser accesses the top-level file on a Web server; thus, it is referred to as a home page.

Web pages can have embedded links to other pages, which are known as hyperlinks. Although the actual addresses of those links are hidden from view, the presence of a link is typically indicated by underlined text in the viewing area of the browser. In the example in Figure 12.12, note that the cursor, which is displayed as a hand with a finger pointing upward, is positioned over the highlighted text "America Online." When you click on that hyperlink, the browser uses the address associated with the link to display a new page of information. You can determine the URL associated with a hyperlink by moving the cursor over the link and viewing the browser's status bar at the bottom of the display. In the example shown in Figure 12.12, note that the following URL is associated with the hyperlink "America Online":

```
http://home.netscape.com/newsref/pr/newsrelease104.html
```

The growth in the connection of Web servers to the Internet has been nothing short of phenomenal over the past few years. By mid-1996, the number of servers connected to the Internet exceeded 200,000, enabling persons to retrieve information about Olympic events, view the latest in automobile designs, and search for jobs, as well as order various products from online catalogs accessible through the use of a browser.

One of the key problems associated with the use of the World Wide Web is the effort involved in locating appropriate information. With more than 200,000 Web servers, each with a distinct URL address, where does one search?

To facilitate the location of information, many companies have set up search sites. Those sites consist of large databases with search engine software that facilitates the location of information stored in the database. To construct the database, the search site typically uses "software robots" that search potential server addresses and index the contents of Web pages, page titles, or categories of information on Web pages. Figure 12.13 shows the use of the Infoseek search guide in an attempt to locate information about Fast Ethernet.

Although the retrieval of Web server-based information is normally without cost, a token-based technology representing digital cash is being developed that could result in requiring Web users to pay for the information. Whether or not digital cash will be successfully implemented, as well as its potential effect on the use of the Web, remains to be determined. In the interim, the use of the Web and the attachment of servers by businesses, government agencies, and educational institutions continues to grow very rapidly.

FIGURE 12.13.

Initiating an Infoseek-based search of the World Wide Web for information about Fast Ethernet.

What Have You Learned?

1. TCP is a transport layer protocol that provides end-to-end reliable transmission, whereas IP is a connectionless-mode network layer protocol designed to route messages between networks.

2. Two key reasons for the growth of the Internet are the fact that TCP/IP is in the public domain and its capability to be used on both LANs and WANs.

3. Most individuals access the Internet via dial-up communications to an Internet access provider, whereas most businesses connect workstations on their LANs via the use of leased lines connecting their offices to an Internet access provider.

4. An IP address is 32 bits long and can be expressed as four decimal numbers separated by dots, or by several names or mnemonics separated by dots.

5. The Domain Name Service is an application that is responsible for converting registered names used to represent Internet addresses into IP addresses.

6. On registering its name with the InterNIC, an organization is assigned to one of six domains.

7. The process of translating the logical IP address into a physical hardware address is referred to as address resolution, and the reverse process is known as reverse address resolution.

8. TCP uses port numbers in its header as a mechanism to enable multiple application processes to be intermixed within a data stream.

9. The use of a TCP/IP application requires three addresses: a port address, an IP address, and a hardware address.

10. The altering of TCP Window field values provides a "sliding window" that can be used to control the flow of information between source and destination.

11. Popular Internet applications built on the use of TCP/IP include the File Transfer Protocol, TELNET, and the HyperText Transmission Protocol (HTTP).

12. A large number of graphical user interface-based TCP/IP applications have been developed to hide the complexities of command-based operations.

Quiz for Chapter 12

1. ARPANET is:
   a. Ralph Kramden's collection of networks.
   b. A network funded by DARPA.
   c. The transport layer protocol.
   d. A connectionless protocol network.

2. The TCP/IP suite connectionless-mode layer 4 transport protocol is:
   a. TCP.
   b. UDP.
   c. IP.
   d. SNMP.

3. TCP/IP:
   a. Is restricted to use on LANs.
   b. Operates only on IBM PCs.
   c. Is in the public domain.
   d. Was developed by Dr. Ethernet.

4. The authority responsible for assigning the network portion of an IP address is the:
   a. NetCen.
   b. Network Center.
   c. Nicnet.
   d. InterNIC.

5. The assignment of the host portion of an IP address is usually the responsibility of:
   a. The TCP/IP coordinator.
   b. The InterNIC.
   c. The local network manager or administrator.
   d. The database administrator.

6. The largest range of addresses available for assignment to a host computer is obtained by:
   a. A Class A address.
   b. A Class B address.
   c. A Class C address.
   d. A Class D address.

7. The address `ftp.moscow.edu` more than likely is:

    a. Located in Russia.

    b. An FTP server.

    c. A military organization.

    d. James Bond's mail drop.

8. The routing of datagrams:

    a. Must follow a fixed path.

    b. Occurs on a virtual circuit.

    c. Can occur over different paths.

    d. Occurs exponentially.

9. The flow of datagrams is efficient due to:

    a. Lack of a need for call setup procedures.

    b. Use of a virtual circuit.

    c. Exponential data flow.

    d. Use of IP.

10. On a LAN, IP datagrams are transported:

    a. In the LAN header.

    b. In the Application field.

    c. In the Information field of the LAN frame.

    d. After the TCP header.

11. The maximum length of an IP datagram is:

    a. 16 bits.

    b. 32 bits.

    c. 65,535 octets.

    d. 32 octets.

12. The field in the IP header that prevents datagrams from continuously wandering through the Internet is:

    a. The Flags field.

    b. The Protocol field.

    c. The Time To Live field.

    d. The Source Address field.

13. The Address Resolution Protocol:

    a. Translates a physical address into a hardware address.

    b. Translates an IP address into a logical address.

    c. Translates a hardware address into a physical address.

    d. Translates an IP address into a hardware address.

14. The port used by a TELNET communications session is:

    a. 21.

    b. 23.

    c. 25.

    d. 27.

15. The receipt of an Acknowledgment Number field value of 27 indicates that:

    a. Destination expects to receive 27 more segments.

    b. Destination expects to receive segment 27 next.

    c. Source expects to receive 27 more segments.

    d. Both source and destination expect to receive 27 more segments.

16. The TCP sliding window:

    a. Can be used to control the flow of information.

    b. Always occurs when the field value is 0.

    c. Always occurs when the field value is 1.

    d. Occurs horizontally.

17. A key advantage of a GUI-based TCP/IP application is that it:

    a. Glues the application to an HP address.

    b. Hides the complexity of commands.

    c. Allows file transfers.

    d. Initiates server protection.

18. TN3270 is:

    a. A terminal emulator designed for asynchronous applications.

    b. An FTP file transfer method.

    c. A terminal emulator developed in 1958.

    d. A terminal emulator for accessing IBM mainframes.

19. The first page displayed when a browser initially accesses a Web server's top-level file is known as:

    a. The master page.

    b. The top page.

    c. The browser page.

    d. The home page.

20. Infoseek represents:

    a. A Web browser.

    b. A TCP/IP protocol.

    c. A Web search tool.

    d. A network layer protocol.

ISDN

About This Chapter

ISDN, which is the acronym for Integrated Services Digital Network, augurs the potential for the development of a universal digital network that provides integrated voice and data on common telephone company facilities. In this chapter, we'll examine the idea behind ISDN, its architecture, and some of the benefits that can be expected from its use.

Concept

The need to transmit human speech resulted in the development of a telephone system that was originally designed for the transmission of analog data. Although the telephone system satisfied the basic need to transmit human speech, its design required the conversion of digital signals produced by computers and terminals into an analog format for the transmission of digital data. This conversion was awkward and expensive because modems were required at both ends of a telephone channel to do the digital-to-analog and analog-to-digital conversions.

A rapid decrease in the cost of semiconductors and the evolution in digital signal processing resulted in the application of digital technology to the telephone network. In the 1960s, telephone companies began to replace the electromechanical switches located in their central offices with digital switches. By the early 1970s, several communications carriers were offering end-to-end transmission services. In these services, unipolar digital data from terminals and computers was converted first into a modified bipolar digital format. Then, through a series of digital repeaters in the network, the data was transmitted to its destination. At its destination, data was converted back to its original unipolar digital format. The unipolar-to-bipolar signal conversion enabled the telephone company to space repeaters farther apart, reducing the construction cost of the digital network. Figure 13.1 illustrates the use of amplifiers and repeaters on analog and digital circuits.

The amplifier used on analog circuits amplifies the entire signal, including any signal impairments. The digital repeater, also known as a data regenerator, regenerates a new digital pulse, eliminating any distortion to the pulse that occurs as it travels on a digital circuit.

Because analog amplifiers increase the size of an analog signal to include any previous distortion, whereas digital repeaters regenerate a digital pulse and eliminate any previous distortion to the digital signal, the error rate on a digital network is significantly lower than that on an analog facility. In addition, the devices required to perform the unipolar-to-bipolar and bipolar-to-unipolar signal conversion are much less expensive than the modems required for signal conversion on analog facilities.

FIGURE 13.1.

Amplifiers versus repeaters.

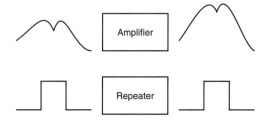

By the mid-1980s, most telephone companies had incorporated a large amount of digital technology into their plant facilities so that a significant portion of the lines connecting telephone company central offices transported speech in digital form, although speech continued to be carried in analog form from the subscriber to the central office. At the central office, speech is digitized for transmission over the backbone network of the telephone system. Similarly, at the central office closest to the destination of the telephone conversation, the digitized speech is reconverted into its analog format, then transmitted to the subscriber's telephone.

The progression of telephone systems in the use of digital technology forms the basis for ISDN. Thus, ISDN can be viewed as an evolutionary progression in the conversion of the analog telephone system into an eventual all-digital network, enabling both voice and data to be transported end to end in a digital format.

Besides integrating voice and data, ISDN provides a level of communications capability above that obtainable with conventional analog technology. When voice and data are integrated, subscribers are able to talk on the telephone and use a computer or terminal at the same time over a common subscriber line. For business, this capability improves the productivity of office workers and reduces the cost of wiring buildings and offices because there should be no need to install separate wires to each desk for voice and data. Thus, ISDN offers subscribers a level of efficiency beyond that obtainable with conventional facilities.

For individual subscribers, ISDN can result in the offering of a series of new functions accessible to their homes over existing telephone wire. Electronic meter reading, slow scan video, Internet access for surfing the World Wide Web and transmitting and receiving electronic mail, and other applications are either offered or can be expected to be offered to individual subscribers and businesses.

ISDN Architecture

Two methods of access to ISDN have been defined—Basic access and Primary access. ISDN Basic access deals with the connection and operation of individual telephone instruments and terminals to the digital network. Primary access governs the method by which many Basic access subscribers can be connected to the network over a common line facility.

Basic Access

Basic access defines a multiple channel connection that is derived by the time division multiplexing of data on twisted pair wiring. This multiple channel connection links an end-user terminal device directly to a telephone company office or to a local private automated branch exchange (PABX). Figure 13.2 illustrates the channel format of the ISDN Basic access method.

F	B1 Channel	D	B2 Channel

B channels are 64 Kbps each.

D channel is 16 Kbps.

2B + D service is a 144 Kbps data stream.

When framing (F) and multiplexing overhead is considered, the actual data rate of a Basic access channel is 192 Kbps, which is the interface transmission rate of the line.

FIGURE 13.2.
The ISDN Basic access channel format.

As shown in Figure 13.2, Basic access consists of two bearer (B) channels and a data (D) channel. The three channels are multiplexed by time onto a common twisted pair wiring media. Each bearer channel can carry one digitized voice conversation or data stream at a transmission rate of 64 Kbps. Digitized voice in ISDN is encoded by sampling voice signals 8,000 times per second and encoding each sample in 8 bits, which results in a 64 Kbps data rate. The inclusion of two bearer channels enables Basic access to provide the subscriber with the ability to transmit data and conduct a voice conversation on one telephone line simultaneously or to be in conversation with one person and receive a second telephone call. In the latter case, assuming that subscribers have an appropriate telephone instrument, they could put one person on hold and answer the second call, all on one line! With analog technology, two physical lines are required. In fact, a Basic access ISDN line can be used to connect up to eight different devices that can be independently accessed via one standard telephone circuit. This expanded access is permissible because the D channel is designed to control the B channels through the sharing of network signaling functions and for the transmission of packet switched data.

Under the Basic access format, up to three channels can be used to provide simultaneous data streams.

To illustrate the expanded capability of ISDN Basic access over conventional telephone service, consider Figure 13.3. Figure 13.3a indicates how you might connect a telephone, fax machine, and computer modem to the public switched telephone network via the installation of three separate telephone lines between your home or office and the telephone central office. Figure 13.3b shows the same equipment connected to a Basic access ISDN line, which, in effect, is one telephone line onto which digitized data is multiplexed. Note that although up to eight devices can share access to the same ISDN Basic access line, only two devices can simultaneously operate at 64 Kbps because only two B channels are contained on a Basic access line. It is anticipated that the capability to transmit packet switched data will enable the D channel to be used to provide many new applications, including monitoring home alarm systems and reading utility meters on demand.

FIGURE 13.3.

ISDN Basic access versus conventional telephone access.

a. Conventional telephone access   b. Using ISDN Basic access

Primary Access

> The T1 carrier used in North America is not the same as that used in Europe due to different methods of signaling.

Primary access is a multiplexing arrangement whereby a grouping of Basic access users shares a common line facility. Primary access is designed to directly connect a PABX or high-speed networking devices, such as inverse multiplexers (described later in this chapter), to the ISDN network. This access method eliminates the need to provide individual Basic access lines when a group of terminal devices shares a common PABX that could be connected directly to an ISDN network via a single high-speed line. Because of the different methods used to multiplex digitized voice conversations between telephone company offices in North America and Europe, two Primary access standards have been developed.

In North America, Primary access consists of a grouping of 23 B channels and one D channel to provide a 1.544 Mbps composite data rate. This data rate is more commonly known as the standard T1 carrier data rate, which was described in Chapter 6, "Multiplexing Techniques." The D channel in Primary access, and each B channel, operates at 64 Kbps. Multiplying 24 channels by 64 Kbps results in a data rate of 1.536 Mbps, which is precisely 8 Kbps fewer than the T1 carrier's 1.544 Mbps data rate.

A North American T1 carrier consists of 24 digitized voice channels. Each voice channel is sampled 8,000 times per second, and 8 bits are used to encode the digitized value of each sample. Thus, a 64 Kbps data rate is required to transmit a digitized voice conversation. To permit synchronization of the T1 signal, a single bit, known as a framing bit, is added to the data stream. The framing bit represents 24 channels, as illustrated in Figure 13.4. One sample of 24 channels of digitized voice is therefore represented by 193 bits. Because the sampling occurs 8,000 times per second, the data rate of a T1 carrier is 193 × 8,000, or 1.544 Mbps.

FIGURE 13.4.
The T1 frame.

In Europe, the T1 carrier consists of 30 digitized voice channels and 2 separate signaling channels. Because each channel operates at 64 Kbps, the resulting T1 carrier data rate is 2.048 Mbps.

ISDN Implementation Standards

ISDN implementation standards address the lower three layers of the OSI Reference Model described in Chapter 11, "Architectures and Packet Networks." The ITU-T defined a series of standards that govern both basic and primary rate physical layer interfaces, as well as the D channel link layer and call setup procedures over the D channel that take place at the network layer level of the OSI Reference Model. Figure 13.5 illustrates the relationship of ISDN implementation standards to the OSI Reference Model. As indicated in Figure 13.5, two sets of standards, I and Q, govern the implementation of ISDN. The I standards govern the physical connection of ISDN-compatible equipment to ISDN circuits, and the Q standards govern the transmission of D channel setup data and information. The Q.921 standard defines the frame structure for transmitting information on the D channel, as well as the contents of the fields of the frame. The Q.931 standard defines the call control procedures used for call setup and teardown, the message structure used to carry call procedure information, and the types of messages that can be transported at the network layer. Readers are referred to ITU-T ISDN Q-series standards for specific information concerning call establishment procedures and data formats on the D channel, as well as the framing format used to transport information on that channel.

FIGURE 13.5.

The relationship of ISDN to the OSI Reference Model.

OSI Reference Model		ISDN Implementation Model	
Application Layer			
Presentation Layer			
Session Layer			
Transport Layer			
Network Layer		Q.931 Call Setup Procedures over the D Channel	
Data Link Layer		Q.921 (LAPD) D Channel Link Layer	
Physical Layer		I.430 Basic Rate	I.431 Primary Rate

Network Characteristics

The major characteristics of an ISDN network follow and form the basis of businesses' and telephone companies' desire for the development of this new network.

ISDN integrates voice, data, and video services.

ISDN has a digital end-to-end connection that provides high transmission quality.

ISDN has improved and expanded services because of B and D channel data rates.

ISDN is more efficient and productive.

ISDN offers advances in device connectivity.

The digital nature of ISDN integrates voice, data, and video services, which eliminates the need for subscribers to get separate facilities for each service. Because an ISDN network is designed to provide end-to-end digital transmission, pulses can be regenerated easily throughout the network, resulting in the generation of new pulses to replace distorted ones.

In comparison, analog transmission facilities use amplifiers to boost the strength of transmission signals, but they also increase any impairments in the analog signal. Because regeneration is superior to amplification, digital transmission has a lower error rate and provides a higher transmission signal quality than an equivalent analog transmission facility.

Basic access provides three signal paths on a common line, and ISDN, too, offers to subscribers the potential of improvements and expansion to existing services. For existing services, current analog telephone-line bandwidth limitations preclude data transmission rates more than 33.6 Kbps occurring on the switched telephone network. In comparison, under ISDN, each B channel can support a 64 Kbps transmission rate, whereas the D channel can operate at 16 Kbps. In fact, if both B channels and the D channel were in simultaneous operation, a data rate of 144 Kbps would be obtainable on a Basic access ISDN circuit, exceeding by a factor of four the current maximum analog circuit transmission rate.

Because each Basic access channel consists of three multiplexed channels, different operations can occur simultaneously without requiring the subscriber to acquire separate multiplexing equipment. Thus, a subscriber could receive a call from one person, transmit data to a computer, and have a utility company read his or her electric meter, all at one time. With the ability to conduct as many as three simultaneous operations on one line, the subscriber gains efficiency and productivity. Efficiency should increase because one line now can support several simultaneous operations, whereas the productivity of the subscriber can increase because of the ability to receive telephone calls and conduct a conversation while transmitting data.

Advances in device connectivity to the ISDN network occurred in two areas. At the physical interface, an eight-pin modular plug and jack provides a common interface that enables devices to be portable between jacks. This eliminates special cabling and, usually, additional telephone company installation charges for the movement of devices between offices. Digital telephones and other instruments can now be manufactured with an intelligent reporting capability. When a telephone is moved from one office to another, simply plugging it into a jack results in its reporting its extension and location to a PBX. This capability enables employees who are moving within an organization to immediately receive telephone calls at their new locations without waiting for the company to reprogram the PBX.

Telephone Equipment and Network Interface

A key element of ISDN is a small set of compatible multipurpose user-network interfaces developed to support a wide range of applications. These network interfaces are based on a series of reference points for different user terminal arrangements that define these interfaces. Figure 13.6 illustrates the relationship between ISDN reference points and network interfaces.

The ISDN reference configuration consists of functional groupings and reference points at which physical interfaces can exist. The functional groupings are sets of functions that can be required at an interface, whereas reference points are employed to divide the functional groups into distinct entities.

The Terminal Equipment (TE) functional grouping is composed of TE1 and TE2 type equipment. Digital telephones, conventional data terminals, and integrated voice-data workstations are examples of TE equipment. TE1 type equipment complies with the ISDN user-network interface and permits such equipment to be connected directly to an ISDN "S" type interface that supports multiple B and D channels.

The Terminal Adapter (TA) can be expected to play a key role in the use of ISDN because it permits equipment with a non-ISDN interface to be connected into an ISDN network.

The NT2 (Network Termination 2) functional group includes devices that do switching and data concentration functions equivalent to the first three layers of the OSI Reference Model. Typical NT2 equipment can include PABXs, LANs, terminal controllers, concentrators, and multiplexers.

FIGURE 13.6.

ISDN reference points and network interfaces.

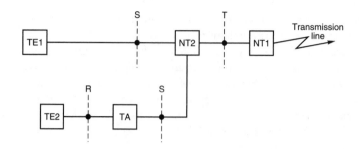

TE1   (Terminal Equipment 1) type devices comply with ISDN network interface.

TE2   (Terminal Equipment 2) type devices do not have an ISDN interface and must be connected through a TA (terminal adapter) functional grouping.

NT2   (Network Termination 2) includes switching and concentration equipment that performs functions equivalent to layers 1 through 3 of the OSI reference model.

NT1   (Network Termination 1) includes functions equivalent to layer 1 of the OSI reference model.

The NT1 (Network Termination 1) functional group is the ISDN digital interface point. It is equivalent to layer 1 of the OSI Reference Model. Functions of NT1 include the physical and electrical termination of the loop, line monitoring, timing, and bit multiplexing. In Europe, where most communications carriers are government-owned monopolies, NT1 and NT2 functions can be combined into a common device, such as a PABX. In such situations, the equipment serves as an NT12 functional group. In comparison, in the United States, the communications carrier can provide only the NT1, whereas third-party equipment would connect to the communications carrier equipment at the T interface.

The last interface that occurs at reference point U is a two-wire connection (Basic access) or four-wire connection (Primary access) between the customer premises (NT1) and the carrier's central office. From this reference point to the central office, data flows in a special compressed transmission format (2B1Q) in which 2 binary bits (2B) are encoded in one quaternary symbol (1Q). When transmission occurs in the 2B1Q format, up to four signal levels can occur, with each level defining the encoding of two bits of data. Table 13.1 indicates the relationship between the four allowed signaling states and the composition of the encoded pairs of bits. Figure 13.7 illustrates an example of 2B1Q coding (top) and the resulting relationship between the quaternary symbol and the encoded binary pairs.

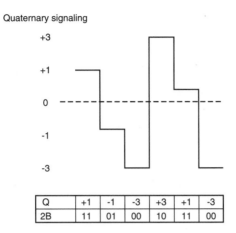

Quaternary signaling

Q	+1	-1	-3	+3	+1	-3
2B	11	01	00	10	11	00

FIGURE 13.7.

A 2B1Q encoding example.

Table 13.1. The 2B1Q relationship.

Quaternary Signal Level	Encoded Bit Values
−3	00
−1	01
+3	10
+1	11

Through the use of 2B1Q encoding, the Basic access 144 Kbps data rate is achieved via a 4 kilobaud rate. This allows the large base of conventional copper pair wiring previously installed between customer premises and communications carrier central offices to be used to support ISDN transmission.

Refer to the ITU-T I recommendation series for detailed information about ISDN reference points and network interfaces.

By providing a set of standardized network interfaces, both pre- and post-ISDN terminals will be able to share the benefits of using ISDN. Pre-ISDN terminal devices will be connected to ISDN facilities by Terminal Adapters, which will convert a non-ISDN interface (R) into an ISDN interface (S).

During the late 1980s, a series of well-publicized field trials of ISDN were conducted in the United States and abroad. Although those trials proved the reliability of technology, it was not until the mid-1990s that ISDN began to acquire a degree of acceptance that could be equated to a few percent of the number of analog telephone lines installed in the United States. The delay in the acceptance of ISDN was based on various factors, with its availability probably the major impediment to its use. To display ISDN, telephone companies

Until the mid-1990s, the availability of ISDN in the United States resembled a series of islands surrounding a few major metropolitan areas.

in many cases had to upgrade or replace older switches in their central offices. In fact, in the late 1980s and early 1990s, a map showing the availability of ISDN in the United States resembled a series of islands surrounding a few major metropolitan areas.

Gradually, over the years, ISDN deployment has been extended so that what appeared to be isolated islands on maps now appears as merged larger areas of availability. Although in late 1996 ISDN was still far from universally available, it was available in more than 70 percent of the United States, and it should be fully available throughout the country by the turn of the century.

Two additional problems that contributed to the slow acceptance of ISDN included problems associated with obtaining ISDN service and a lack of viable applications that could justify the use of this service. As I will shortly note, both of those problems have, to a large degree, been rectified, resulting in a substantial growth rate for the installation of ISDN lines by the mid-1990s.

ISDN Service Codes

For "those who dare," the actual installation of an ISDN line and connection of third-party vendor equipment to that line many times resulted in the proverbial "horror story." The horror story reflected hours or even days of trial-and-error settings and adjustments to make ISDN equipment work with telephone company lines. Until recently, all carriers used their own Service Profile Identification (SPID) codes. The SPID represents a 14-digit telephone number that ISDN equipment transmits to identify itself to telephone company switches that provide ISDN services. That code is also transferred between switches operated by different telephone companies to establish an ISDN call between subscribers of different communications carriers. Due to the lack of ISDN Service Code standards, users had to notify the carrier of the type of device they wanted to connect to an ISDN line, resulting in the carrier making adjustments to its facilities to accommodate the equipment. With a lack of standards, it was often difficult for one carrier to correctly program the central office switch to support third-party ISDN hardware products, as well as to coordinate an agreement for coding among carriers.

The standardization of Service Profile Identification Codes greatly facilitates the interoperability of ISDN equipment manufactured by different vendors and facilities provided by communications carriers.

During 1996, this problem was on the road to elimination as the National ISDN Council—a group of all seven regional Bell operating companies, Cincinnati Bell, GTE Corporation, and Southern New England Telephone Company—agreed to implement a uniform procedure to connect users' ISDN terminal equipment to their ISDN services. All of those companies agreed to use the same SPID codes to connect ISDN terminal equipment to the ISDN switches. Under this agreement, SPID functionality would be moved from central office switches out to network switches by mid-1997, with a totally automated SPID capability scheduled for early 1998. This means that coding errors at the central office and between carrier switches that adversely affect interoperability will be relegated to the past.

Applications

The growth in the use of video-conferencing, a substantial increase in the connectivity requirements for geographically separated LANs, and the literal explosion in the use of the Internet represent three key applications responsible for a significant increase in the use of ISDN.

Until the early 1990s, most video-conferencing systems were relatively expensive, requiring the use of 512 Kbps or greater bandwidth, and they were usually implemented on a point-to-point networking basis via the installation of T1 or fractional T1 leased lines. Although a company might use video-conferencing only an hour or two per day, it had to pay for the 24-hour-per-day use of the leased line. Recognizing this communications cost problem, as well as the requirement of many organizations to perform video-conferencing among many geographically separated locations, communications product manufacturers developed a product known as an inverse multiplexer, or a bandwidth-on-demand multiplexer.

The inverse multiplexer derives its name from the fact that it accepts high-speed input and subdivides the input into two or more output data streams. When the inverse multiplexer's output data streams are connected to an ISDN service, it becomes possible not only to perform video-conferencing on a dial-up basis, but also to adjust the bandwidth used for communications between two video-conferencing systems based on the bandwidth supported by each system and economics. For example, consider Figure 13.8, which illustrates the use of a video-conferencing system via an inverse multiplexer connected to an ISDN Primary Rate Interface (PRI) line operation.

ISDN Primary Rate Interface Frame

Legend

VC   Videoconferencing system

IM   Inverse multiplexer

FIGURE 13.8.

Video-conferencing via an inverse multiplexer and ISDN.

●

Through the use of inverse or bandwidth-on-demand multiplexers, increments of bandwidth in multiples of 64 Kbps can be established via the use of ISDN to support video-conferencing.

Because an ISDN PRI line represents the multiplexing of 23 B channels and a D signaling channel, the inverse multiplexer could be used to support video-conferencing at data rates from 64 Kbps using one B channel to 1.472 Mbps using all 23 B channels. Due to advances in compression technology, most video-conferencing systems require the use of 4 to 6 B channels, in effect requiring four to six calls to be made via ISDN facilities from one video-conferencing location to another location. Although carriers typically bill each call on a per-minute basis, it is often far more economical to pay for several switched dial-up ISDN hours per day than to install a high-speed digital leased line between locations. In addition, through the use of dial-up ISDN, each video-conferencing system in an organization can communicate with other systems by requiring the installation of a mesh structured series of leased lines to connect each system to every other system.

In a LAN connectivity environment, the traditional networking approach was to connect networks via the use of remote bridges or routers and increase the operating rate of the line when users complained about response time delays. Similar to the previously discussed video-conferencing application, inverse or bandwidth-on-demand multiplexers can be used either as a replacement or to supplement the use of leased lines. Concerning inverse multiplexers, if inter-LAN communications are infrequent, ISDN can be used periodically as a replacement for leased lines. One of the key attributes of ISDN is the fact that the time required to set up a call is relatively short in comparison to a call initiated over the analog switched telephone network. This means that transmission delays are more tolerable and do not adversely affect inter-LAN communications. Concerning the use of inverse multiplexers as a supplement to the use of leased lines, this method of communications is highly suitable when an increase in transmission requirements for short periods would otherwise require the installation of a higher-operating-rate and more-expensive leased line. Instead of incurring a higher monthly lease line cost when an increment of 64 Kbps of bandwidth is required for only a small portion of the day, the use of an inverse multiplexer can provide an economical supplement to the use of a digital leased line.

The third major application that has significantly increased the use of ISDN is represented by the explosive growth in the graphics-based World Wide Web. The integration of digital voice, video clips, graphics, and text on Web pages results in a requirement for Web servers to transmit hundreds of thousands to millions of bytes in response to a person clicking an icon on his browser's screen. Because analog modems are limited under the best of connections to a data rate of 33.6 Kbps, whereas ISDN access provides operating rates up to 128 Kbps, the use of ISDN can provide a mechanism for viewing Web pages without irritating delays. Similar to the manner in which *plastics* was used as the all-encompassing word of the future in the popular 1960's movie *The Graduate,* ISDN can be expected to be its replacement for the late 1990s.

What Have You Learned?

1. ISDN can be viewed as an evolutionary process because communications carriers have been converting their facilities to digital technology since the 1960s.

2. Access arrangements to the ISDN network include Basic and Primary access.

3. The multiple channels on one ISDN physical line are obtained through time division multiplexing.

4. Multiple channels on one ISDN physical line permit multiple voice or voice and data transmission to occur at the same time on a common circuit.

5. The Basic access D channel on which data is transmitted in packet form can be expected to be used for such new applications as monitoring of home alarm systems and reading of utility meters, as well as for the transmission of signaling information to control the operation of the B channels.

6. Non-ISDN equipment can be connected to ISDN lines through the use of terminal adapters.

7. The standardization of Service Profile Identification codes facilitates the connection of third-party ISDN hardware to ISDN lines.

8. Such applications as the use of video-conferencing and inter-LAN communications, as well as the increase in the use of the graphics-based World Wide Web, are the driving forces behind the use of ISDN.

Quiz for Chapter 13

1. The data rate of the ISDN Basic access B channel is:
   a. 32 Kbps.
   b. 64 Kbps.
   c. 144 Kbps.
   d. 192 Kbps.

2. The data rate of the ISDN Basic access D Channel is:
   a. 64 Kbps.
   b. 16 Kbps.
   c. 8 Kbps.
   d. 144 Kbps.

3. The equation that defines the composition of an ISDN Basic access line is:
   a. 2B + D
   b. B + D
   c. B + 2D
   d. 2B + 2D

4. In North America, the equation that defines the composition on an ISDN Primary access line is:
   a. 30B + D
   b. 2B + D
   c. B + D
   d. 23B + D

5. The network interface that will permit equipment without an ISDN interface to be connected into an ISDN interface is known as:
   a. TE1.
   b. TE2.
   c. TA.
   d. TE.

6. The number of channels on which different operations can occur simultaneously on one ISDN Basic access line is:

    a. One.

    b. Two.

    c. Five.

    d. Three.

7. Digital telephones and integrated voice-data workstations are examples of what type of ISDN equipment?

    a. TE.

    b. TA.

    c. NT2.

    d. TP.

8. The transmission of data on an ISDN line between a customer's premises and a carrier's central office is encoded using:

    a. Quadrature amplitude modulation.

    b. 2B1Q encoding.

    c. Hexadecimal encoding.

    d. Octal encoding.

9. The Service Profile Identification code:

    a. Identifies the type of ISDN service.

    b. Identifies ISDN equipment to telephone company personnel.

    c. Identifies ISDN equipment to telephone company switches.

    d. Is 12 alphabetic characters in length.

10. The connection of an inverse multiplexer to an ISDN PRI line:

    a. Requires three days for installation.

    b. Uses a SIDIC code.

    c. Enables the use of one to 23 B channels.

    d. Both a and b.

Asynchronous Transfer Mode

About This Chapter

This chapter is focused on a rapidly evolving networking technology that provides the capability to transport voice, data, video, and images. Commonly referred to by the acronym ATM, Asynchronous Transfer Mode provides the opportunity for both end users and communications carriers to transport virtually any type of information using a common format. In this chapter, I examine the rationale for the development of ATM and its underlying technology.

Evolution

Asynchronous Transfer Mode (ATM) represents a relatively recently developed communications technology designed to overcome the constraints associated with traditional, and for the most part separate, voice and data networks. ATM has its roots in the work of a CCITT (now known as ITU-T) study group formed to develop broadband ISDN standards during the mid-1980s. In 1988, a cell switching technology was chosen as the foundation for broadband ISDN, and in 1991, the ATM Forum was founded.

The ATM Forum represents an international consortium of public and private equipment vendors, data communications and telecommunications service providers, consultants, and end users established to promote the implementation of ATM. To accomplish this goal, the ATM Forum develops standards with the ITU and other standards organizations.

The ATM Forum promotes the implementation of ATM via the development of standards with the ITU and other standards organizations.

The first ATM Forum standard was released in 1992. Various ATM Forum working groups are busy defining additional standards required to enable ATM to provide a communications capability for the wide range of LAN and WAN transmission schemes it is designed to support. This standardization effort will probably remain in effect for a considerable period due to the comprehensive design goal of the technology, which was developed to support voice, data, and video on both local and wide area networks.

The Rationale and Underlying Technology

ATM can be considered to represent a unifying technology because it was designed to transport voice, data, and video, including graphics images, on both local and wide area networks. Until the development of ATM, networks were normally developed based on the type of data to be transported. Thus, circuit-switched networks, which included the public switched telephone network and high-speed digital transmission facilities, were primarily used to transport delay-sensitive information, such as voice and video. In comparison, on packet-based networks, such as X.25 and Frame Relay, information can tolerate a degree of delay. Network users can select a networking technology to satisfy a specific communications application, but most organizations support a mixture of applications. Thus, most organizations are forced to operate multiple networks, resulting in a degree of inefficiency and escalating communications costs. By combining the features from both technologies, ATM enables a single network to support voice, data, and video.

The 53-byte ATM cell remains static regardless of changes in the media, operating rate, or framing.

ATM is designed to be scalable, enabling its 53-byte cell to be transported from LAN to LAN via WAN, as well as for use on public and private wide area networks at a range of operating rates. On LANs, ATM support is currently offered at 25 and 155 Mbps, whereas access to WAN-based ATM carrier networks can occur at T1 (1.544 Mbps), at T3 (45 Mbps), or via different SONET facilities at data rates up to 622 Gbps, all based on the transportation of 53-byte cells. A key to ATM's ubiquitous transmission capability is its fixed 53-byte cell length, which remains static regardless of changes in media, operating rates, or framing.

The use of a fixed-length cell enables low-cost hardware to be developed to perform required cell switching based on the contents of the cell header, without requiring more complex and costly software. Thus, ATM can be considered to represent a unifying technology that will eventually become very economical to implement when its development expenses are amortized over the growing production cycle of ATM communications equipment.

Although many organizations merged voice and data through the use of multiplexers onto a common circuit, this type of merger is typically not end-to-end. For example, traffic from a router connected to a LAN might be fed into a port on a high-speed multiplexer with another connection to the multiplexer from the company PBX. Although this type of multiplexing enables a common WAN circuit to be used for voice and data, it represents an interim and partial solution to the expense associated with operating separate voice and data networks. In addition, the emergence of multimedia applications requiring the transmission of video can wreak havoc with existing LANs and WANs due to their requirement for high bandwidth for short periods. ATM represents an emerging technology designed to provide support for bandwidth-on-demand applications, such as video, as well as voice and data. A comparison of the key features associated with each technology can give you an appreciation for ATM technology in comparison to conventional data communications- and telecommunications-based technology. Table 14.1 provides a comparison of nine features of data communications and telecommunications networks to those of an ATM network.

Table 14.1. Comparing network features.

Feature	Data Communications	Telecommunications	ATM
Traffic support	Data	Voice	Data, voice, video
Transmission unit	Packet	Frame	Cell
Transmission length	Variable	Fixed	Fixed
Switching type	Packet	Circuit	Cell
Connection type	Connectionless or connection-oriented	Connection-oriented	Connection-oriented
Time sensitivity	Same	All	Adaptive
Delivery	Best effort or guaranteed	Guaranteed	Defined class
Media and operating rate	Defined by protocol	Defined by class	Scalable
Media access	Shared or dedicated	Dedicated	Dedicated

In a data communications environment, the network can range in scope from a Token-Ring LAN to an X.25 or Frame Relay WAN. Thus, although some features are common to both LAN and WAN environments, there is also some variability. In general, a data communications network transports data by using variable-length packets. Although many WAN protocols are connection-oriented, some are connectionless. Similarly, many LAN protocols are connectionless, whereas others are connection-oriented. Because data communications networks were designed to transport files, records, and screens of data, transmission delay or latency, if small, does not adversely affect users. In comparison, in a

● ATM was designed to adapt to the time sensitivity of different types of applications.

telecommunications network, a similar amount of latency that is acceptable on a data network could wreak havoc with a telephone conversation. Recognizing the differences among voice, video, and data transportation, ATM was designed to adapt to the time sensitivity of different applications. It includes different classes of service that enable the technology to match delivery to the time sensitivity of the information it transports.

Thus, ATM provides a mechanism for merging voice, data, and video onto LANs and WANs. You can gain an appreciation for how ATM accomplishes this by learning about its architecture.

Architecture

ATM is based on the switching of 53-byte cells, in which each cell consists of a 5-byte header and a payload of 48 bytes of information. Figure 14.1 illustrates the format of the ATM cell, including the explosion of its 5-byte header to indicate the fields carried in the header.

FIGURE 14.1.

The 53-byte ATM cell.

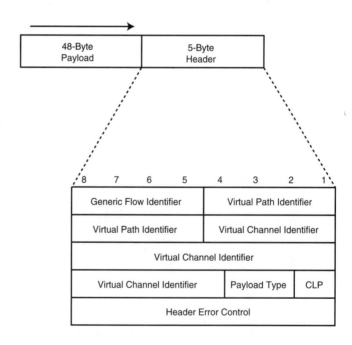

CLP = Cell Loss Priority

ATM uses a two-part connection identifier established through the use of a Virtual Path Identifier and a Virtual Channel Identifier.

The 4-bit Generic Flow Control field is used as a mechanism to regulate the flow of traffic in an ATM network. Currently, the use of this field is under development.

The 8-bit Virtual Path Identifier (VPI) field represents one-half of a two-part connection identifier used by ATM. This field identifies a virtual path that can represent a group of virtual circuits transported along the same route. It is described in more detail later in this chapter.

The Virtual Channel Identifier (VCI) is the second half of the two-part connection identifier carried in the ATM header. The 16-bit VCI field identifies a connection between two ATM stations communicating with one another for a specific type of application. Multiple virtual channels (VCs) can be transported within one virtual path. For example, one VC could be used to transport a disk backup operation while a second VC is used to transport a TCP/IP-based application. Later in this chapter, I will examine the use of the VCI.

The Payload Type Identifier (PTI) field indicates the type of information carried in the 48-byte data portion of the ATM cell. Currently, this 3-bit field indicates whether payload data represents management information or user data. Additional PTI field designators have been reserved for future use.

The 1-bit Cell Loss Priority (CLP) field indicates the relative importance of the cell. If this field bit is set to 1, the cell can be discarded by a switch experiencing congestion. If the cell cannot be discarded, the CLP field bit is set to 0.

The last field in the ATM cell header is the 8-bit Header Error field. This field represents the result of an 8-bit Cyclic Redundancy Check (CRC) code, computed only over the ATM cell header. This field provides the capability for detecting all single-bit errors and certain multiple-bit errors that occur in the 40-bit ATM cell header.

Advantages of the Technology

The use of cell-switching technology in a LAN environment provides some distinct advantages over the shared-medium technology employed by Ethernet, Token-Ring, and FDDI networks. Two of those advantages are obtaining full bandwidth access to ATM switches for individual workstations and enabling attaching devices to operate at different operating rates. Those advantages are illustrated in Figure 14.2, which shows an ATM switch that could be used to support three distinct operating rates. Workstations could be connected to the switch at 25 Mbps while a local server could be connected at 155 Mbps to other switches, either to form a larger local LAN or to connect to a communications carrier's network via a different operating rate.

The selection of a 53-byte cell length results in a minimum of latency in comparison to the packet length of traditional LANs, such as Ethernet, which can have a maximum 1572-byte frame length. By selecting the ATM cell at 53 bytes in length, cells transporting voice, data, and video can be intermixed without the latency of one cell adversely affecting other cells. Because the length of each cell is fixed and the position of information in each header is known, ATM switching can be accomplished via the use of hardware. In comparison, on traditional LANs, bridging and routing functions are normally performed by software or firmware, which executes more slowly than hardware-based switching.

Two additional features of ATM that warrant discussion are its asynchronous operation and its connection-oriented operation. ATM cells are intermixed via multiplexing, with cells from individual connections forwarded from switch to switch via a single cell flow. However, the multiplexing of ATM cells occurs via asynchronous transfer, in which cells are transmitted only when data is present to send. In comparison, in conventional time division multiplexing, keep-alive or synchronization bytes are transmitted when there is no data to be sent. Concerning the connection-oriented technology used by ATM, this means that a connection between the ATM stations must be established before data transfer occurs. The connection process results in the specification of a transmission path between ATM switches and end stations, enabling the header in ATM cells to be used to route the cells on the required path through an ATM network.

FIGURE 14.2.

ATM is based on the switching of 53-byte cells.

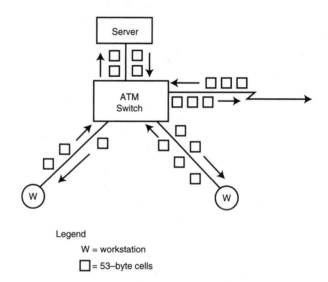

Legend
W = workstation
☐ = 53–byte cells

The ATM Protocol Reference Model

Three layers in the ATM architecture form the basis for the ATM Protocol Reference Model, illustrated in Figure 14.3. Those layers are the physical layer, the ATM layer, and the ATM Adaptation Layer.

FIGURE 14.3.

The ATM protocol suite.

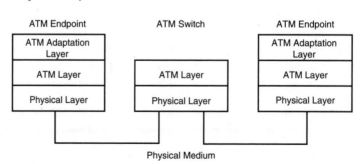

The Physical Layer

As indicated in Figure 14.3, the lowest layer in the ATM protocol is the physical layer. This layer describes the physical transmission of information through an ATM network. It is not actually defined with respect to this new technology. The absence of a physical layer definition results from the design goal of ATM to operate on various physical interfaces or media types. Thus, in place of defining a specific physical layer, ATM depends on the physical layers defined in other networking protocols. Types of physical media specified for ATM include shielded and unshielded twisted pair, coaxial cable, and fiber-optic cable, which provide cell transport capabilities ranging from a T1 rate of 1.544 Mbps to a SONET range of 622 Mbps.

●
ATM depends on the physical layers defined in other networking protocols, resulting in the technology being supported by a range of physical media.

The ATM Layer

The ATM layer represents the physical interface between the ATM Adaptation Layer (AAL) and the physical layer. Thus, the ATM layer is responsible for relaying cells from the AAL to the physical layer for transmission, and in the opposite direction, from the physical layer to the AAL for use in an endpoint. When transporting cells to the physical layer, the ATM layer is responsible for generating the five-byte cell header for each cell. When receiving cells from the physical layer, the ATM layer performs a reverse operation, extracting the five-byte header from each cell.

●
The ATM layer is responsible for generating the five-byte cell header before passing cells to the physical layer for transmission.

The actual manner by which the ATM layer performs its relaying function depends on the location of the layer—at a switch or at an endpoint. If the ATM layer is located in an endpoint, it receives a stream of cells from the physical layer and transmits either cells with new data or empty cells if there is no data to send to the AAL. When located in a switch, the ATM layer is responsible for determining where incoming cells are routed and for multiplexing cells by placing cells from individual connections into a single cell stream.

Cell Routing

The actual routing of ATM cells depends on whether a connection was preestablished or set up as needed on a demand basis. The preestablished type of connection is referred to as a permanent virtual connection (PVC), and the other type is referred to as a switched virtual connection (SVC). In examining the 5-byte ATM cell header shown in Figure 14.1, note the VCI and the VPI fields. The VPI is 8 bits in length, whereas the VCI is 16 bits in length, enabling 256 virtual paths with each path capable of accommodating up to 65,536 (2^{16}) virtual connections.

The use of VPs and VCs results in ATM employing a two-level connection identifier that is used in its routing hierarchy. A VCI value is unique only in a particular VPI value, whereas VPI values are unique only in a particular physical link. The VPI/VCI value assignment has only local significance, and those values are translated at every switch a cell traverses between endpoints in an ATM network.

The actual establishment of a virtual path is based on ATM's network management and signaling operations. During the establishment of a virtual path routing table, entries in each switch located between endpoints map an incoming physical port and a virtual path identifier pair to an outgoing pair. This initial mapping process is known as network provisioning, and the change of routing table entries is referred to as network reprovisioning.

Figure 14.4 illustrates an example of a few possible table entries for a switch where a virtual path was established such that VPI=6 on port 1 and VPI=10 on port 8, representing two physical links in the established connection.

FIGURE 14.4.

Switch operations based on routing table entries.

Routing Table Entries

Received		Transmit	
VPI	Port Number	VPI	Port Number
6	1	10	8
10	8	6	1

The routing of ATM cells between switches is based on the Virtual Path Identifier and the port number routing table entries in each switch.

In examining the entries in the routing table shown in Figure 14.4, note that the table does not include values for VCIs. This is by design because a VP in an ATM network has the capability to support up to 65,536 VC connections. Thus, only one table entry is required to switch up to 65,536 individual connections if those connections all follow the same set of physical links in the same sequence. This method of switching, which is based on the VPI and port number, simplifies the construction and use of routing tables and facilitates the establishment of a connection through a series of switches.

Although VCIs are not used in routing tables, they are translated at each switch. To help you understand the rationale for this technique, I'll focus on their use. As previously noted, a VCI is unique within a VP and is used at an endpoint to denote a different connection within a virtual path. Thus, the VPI/VCI pair used between an endpoint and a switch has a local meaning and is translated at every switch; however, the VCI is not used for routing between switches.

The establishment of a connection between two end stations is known as a Virtual Channel Connection (VCC). To illustrate the routing of cells in an ATM network based on a VCC, consider Figure 14.5, which represents a small two-switch–based ATM network. The VCC represents a series of virtual channel links between two ATM endpoints. In Figure 14.5, one VCC could be represented by VC=1, VC=3, and VC=5, which collectively form a connection between workstations at the two endpoints shown in the network. A second VCC could be represented by VC=2, VC=4, and VC=6. The second VCC could represent the transportation of a second application between the same pair of endpoints or a new application between different endpoints served by the same pair of ATM switches.

FIGURE 14.5.

Connections in an ATM network.

As indicated by the previous examples, each VC link consists of one or more physical links between the location where a VCI is assigned and the location where it is either translated or removed. The assignment of VCs is the responsibility of switches during the call setup process.

The ATM Adaptation Layer

The ATM Adaptation Layer (AAL) represents the top layer in the ATM protocol model. This layer is responsible for providing an interface between higher-layer protocols and the ATM layer. Because this interface normally occurs based on a voice, data, or video application accessing an ATM network, the operations performed by the AAL occur at endpoints and not at ATM switches. Thus, the AAL is shown in Figure 14.3 to reside at ATM endpoints.

The primary function of the ATM Adaptation Layer is format conversion. That is, the AAL maps the data stream originated by the higher-layer protocol into the 48-byte payload of ATM cells, with the header placement being assigned by the ATM layer. In the reverse direction, the AAL receives the payload of ATM cells in 48-byte increments from the ATM layer and maps those increments into the format recognized by the higher-layer protocol.

●
The ATM Adaptation Layer is responsible for mapping a higher-level protocol data stream into the 48-byte payload of ATM cells.

Because it is not possible to address the requirements of the diverse set of applications designed to use ATM within a single AAL, the ITU-T classified the functions required by different applications based on their traffic and service requirements. This classification scheme resulted in four classes of applications being defined based on whether a timing relationship is required between end stations, the type of bit rate (variable or constant), and the type of connection (connection-oriented or connectionless) required. Table 14.2 summarizes the four classes of applications with respect to their timing relationship, bit rate, and type of connection.

In examining the entries in Table 14.2, note that the timing relationship references whether one is required between end stations. Real-time services, such as the transportation of voice or video, represent two examples of applications that require a timing relationship. In comparison, a file transfer represents an application that does not require a timing relationship. When a timing relationship is required, clocking between two end stations must be aligned.

A constant bit-rate application represents an application that requires an unvarying amount of bandwidth, such as voice or real-time video. In comparison, a variable bit-rate application represents "bursty" traffic, such as LAN data.

Table 14.2. The ATM application classes.

Class	Timing Relationship	Bit Rate	Type of Connection
A	Yes	Constant	Connection-oriented
B	Yes	Variable	Connection-oriented
C	No	Variable	Connection-oriented
D	No	Variable	Connectionless

The capability to support connection-oriented or connectionless applications enables ATM to support various existing higher-layer protocols. For example, Frame Relay is a connection-oriented protocol, whereas IP is a connectionless protocol. Through the use of different AALs, both can be transported by ATM.

Based on the four application classes, four different types of AALs were defined: AAL 1, 2, 3/4, and 5. At one time, AAL 3 and AAL 4 were separate types; however, they had a sufficient degree of commonality to be merged. Figure 14.6 illustrates the relationship between application classes and ATM Adaptation Layers with respect to the different parameters used to classify each application class.

FIGURE 14.6.

Application classification and associated AALs.

Application Classification	Class A	Class B	Class C	Class D
Timing Relationship	Required		Not Required	
Bit Rate	Constant	Variable		
Connection Mode	Connection-Oriented		Connectionless	
ATM Adaptation Layer	AAL 1	AAL 2	AAL 5, AAL 3/4	AAL 3/4

ATM Adaptation Layers are distinguished from one another by the method by which the 48-byte cell payload is constructed as a data stream generated by a higher-level protocol is passed to the ATM layer. For example, consider a Class A application represented by a voice conversation. Because the misordering of cells can be viewed as being worse than the loss of cells, the payload is constructed to include a sequence number when Class A traffic is transported. Figure 14.7 illustrates the format of an AAL 1 cell payload. Note that the Sequence Number Protection (SNP) field protects the Sequence Number (SN) field from the effect of bit errors occurring during transmission, in effect providing a forward error detection and correction capability.

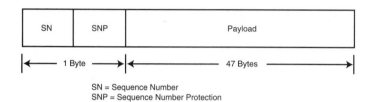

FIGURE 14.7.

AAL 1 cell payload format.

Although several aspects of different AAL operations remain to be specified, the use of different AALs provides the mechanism for the cell-based switching technology on which ATM is based to transport different types of information using a common cell structure.

Although a significant amount of effort has been expended by communications carriers in developing an ATM infrastructure for transporting information between carrier offices, the expansion of this evolving technology to customer premises, as well as its use on LANs, will probably require several years. Currently, several key standards, such as the adaptation of legacy LANs, remain to be promulgated. In addition, as with any new technology, the cost of ATM equipment is relatively high in comparison to the cost of older technology. Over the next few years, we can expect several important standards to be promulgated, and we can also expect to see the cost of ATM equipment become more reasonable as development costs are amortized over a larger base of products. As this occurs, we can anticipate that the use of ATM will considerably expand.

What Have You Learned?

1. ATM represents cell-switching technology designed to transport voice, data, and video by using a common cell format on both local and wide area networks.

2. ATM represents a scalable technology for which 53-byte cells can be transported at a range of operating rates from 25 Mbps on LANs to 622 Gbps via SONET.

3. Recognizing the differences between voice and data transportation requirements, ATM is designed to adapt to the time sensitivity of different applications.

4. A two-part identifier consisting of a Virtual Path Identifier and Virtual Channel Identifier enables multiple connections to be carried on the same path.

5. The ATM Protocol Reference Model has three layers: the physical layer, the ATM layer, and the ATM Adaptation Layer.

6. The routing of ATM cells between switches is based on Virtual Path Identifiers and port number routing table entries in each switch.

7. A Virtual Path Connection (VPC) represents a concatenation of virtual paths between switches, whereas a Virtual Channel Connection (VCC) represents a connection between two end stations via a VPC.

Quiz for Chapter 14

1. The ATM forum is:

    a. A government agency that regulates the use of ATM.

    b. An international consortium that promotes the implementation of ATM.

    c. A branch of the ITU-T involved in the ATM standardization effort.

    d. A debating society involving ATM operations.

2. ATM scalability references the capability of the technology to support:

    a. Different cell lengths.

    b. Different wide area networks.

    c. Different local area networks.

    d. A range of operating rates using the same old format.

3. Latency is a measure of:

    a. LAN operations.

    b. Cell length.

    c. Transmission delay.

    d. WAN operations.

4. The Cell Loss Priority field indicates:

    a. The loss of a cell.

    b. The priority of a cell.

    c. Whether a cell can be discarded.

    d. The capability of a cell to be prioritized.

5. The Header Error Control field in an ATM cell:

    a. Protects user data.

    b. Corrects user data.

    c. Indicates the occurrence of any possible error in the cell header.

    d. Indicates the occurrence of certain types of errors in the cell header.

6. One advantage of the use of ATM over conventional LANs is:

    a. Shared medium access.

    b. Full bandwidth access.

    c. Support of fixed operating rates.

    d. Direct sharing of the medium.

7. The lowest layer in the ATM protocol is the:

    a. ATM Adaptation Layer.

    b. Convergence layer.

    c. ATM layer.

    d. Physical layer.

8. The five-byte ATM cell header is generated by the:

    a. ATM layer.

    b. Physical layer.

    c. ATM Adaptation Layer.

    d. Convergence layer.

9. The routing of ATM cells between switches are based on the:

    a. Virtual Path Identifier.

    b. Port number.

    c. VPI and port number.

    d. Virtual Channel Identifier.

10. A connection between two end stations is a:

    a. Virtual path.

    b. Virtual Channel Connection.

    c. Virtual link.

    d. Virtual LAN.

11. The ATM layer responsible for providing an interface to higher-layer protocols is the:

    a. Physical layer.

    b. Convergence layer.

    c. ATM layer.

    d. ATM Adaptation Layer.

12. The ATM application class that requires a timing relationship, a variable bit rate, and a connection-oriented type of connection is:

    a. Class A.

    b. Class B.

    c. Class C.

    d. Class D.

13. A constant bit rate application represents an application that requires:

    a. An unvarying amount of bandwidth.

    b. File transfer capability.

    c. A varying amount of bandwidth.

    d. A connectionless type of connection.

Network Design and Management

UNDERSTANDING

About This Chapter

The user's terminal device is the source and sink of all user data, but good network design and management is usually necessary to make data communications networks usable and affordable. The term "network design" refers to the selection of various circuit parameters and to the selection and interconnection of various devices to accomplish design goals.

This chapter covers the goals, principles, and tools of efficient network design and management. Many of the administrative principles of network management, such as planning and budgeting, are similar to other kinds of management. The technical aspects to be discussed here include network design goals and throughput timing, networking devices, interconnection, fault isolation, fault correction, and quality assurance.

Any network, no matter how simple or complex, can be incorporated into a larger network. The approach of this chapter is to start with the principles of good network design for basic point-to-point networks, establishing a solid basis for these, and then to discuss some of the technologies for building more complex networks.

Network Design Goals

The greatest motivation for network design is cost. Cost includes a multitude of factors other than the prices of the terminals and networks. For example, the costs of local area networks are usually justified on the basis of higher speed, because the time of the people and computers that use these networks is expensive. In other situations, communications reliability is the basic cost justification. In many cases, the failure of a data communications system to function properly when needed can cost a business far more than the price of the system.

If price were no object, most data networks would be a collection of simple point-to-point channels. Indeed, if a point-to-point channel can be kept busy at a reasonably high bit rate for transmitting data that's worth sending, it might be the most cost-effective way to handle a particular data communications task.

On the other hand, many data applications cannot cost-justify dedicated channels because of insufficient quantity or priority of the data. In such cases, it is sometimes possible to combine data from more than one source into a single long-haul transmission path by use of multiplexers and other networking devices. Although the use of such techniques might allow cost justification of the application, the addition of equipment is likely to reduce reliability and to increase the time and effort required to find and correct a problem.

The underlying objective of data networking is to strike a satisfactory balance between the accurate, timely, and secure delivery of user data and total cost. The term "satisfactory" implies that the user who is paying for the delivery system is satisfied with it.

Accuracy

Previous chapters have discussed the subject of accuracy in terms of error control. Not all data transmissions are required to be error free. For example, electronic mail messages that contain human-language messages do not suffer loss of meaning if a word is occasionally misspelled. On the other hand, the transfer of accounting information between financial institutions requires a high level of accuracy.

Timeliness

Timeliness involves four general aspects: the amount of data to be transmitted, the importance and priority of the information, the average rate of transfer of error-free data, and the availability of the network to the user. These aspects are discussed in the following sections.

The Amount of Data

Obviously, the amount and priority of data will have an impact on the throughput rate required, but cost must be considered in establishing these parameters. In some extreme situations, the amount of data might be so great that the best way to transfer it will be by physically transporting truckloads of magnetic tape! At the other extreme, a satisfactory "networking" solution might be a simple low-speed transmission over a dialed point-to-point telephone channel.

The Priority of the Data

As a general rule, the importance and frequency of testing is directly proportional to the importance and priority of the data. An Italian proverb asserts, "Good things cost less than bad ones." Although this proverb doesn't apply universally to data communications, it does remind us that the best solution isn't always the cheapest. In numerous situations, for example in industrial process control and manufacturing, a total failure of a data link could cost a company more than $10,000 an hour. In such cases, reliability, testing, and planning for alternative methods obviously are of extreme importance.

The Information Throughput Rate

The information throughput rate, properly known as the Transfer Rate of Information Bits (TRIB), is covered in detail in the next section. Basically, TRIB is the average rate of transfer of the actual error-free bits of user data, not counting overhead bits.

The Availability of the Network

The availability of the network is determined by three factors: access time, mean time between failures (MTBF), and mean time to restore service (MTRS). For private lines and permanent virtual circuits, access time is of no concern; for dialed connections and virtual calls, the time delay to establish the call might be significant in comparison with the transmission time if the amount of data is small. MTBF usually refers to the time between "hard" (permanent) failures, but if the error rate becomes high enough, the TRIB can nose-dive even though the connection still exists. MTRS might involve a temporary restoration, as in the case of dialed backup for a private line, or it might simply refer to repair time if no alternative service is available.

Security

Security is receiving increasing attention as data communications is used more and more for significant and important matters of everyday life. Many sources of information are now available that cover this area in detail. Besides the physical aspects of security, data communications security involves both privacy and authentication. Privacy refers to secrecy (use of codes) and protection from unauthorized access (use of passwords). Authentication has to do with ensuring that a data message hasn't been tampered with between source and sink, and verifying that the sender of the message is as claimed.

In certain kinds of transmissions, authentication is more important than any other aspect of networking mentioned so far. For example, a Swiss bank receiving an international telex from another bank containing instructions to transfer funds between accounts will be

As more and more confidential and proprietary information is being transmitted through data communications systems, the security of this information becomes more important.

interested in knowing whether extra zeros have been added to the amount, whether account numbers have been modified, and whether the claimed source of the message is authentic.

In summary, data network design involves a complex series of interrelated judgments involving these and other factors:

Cost of the delivery system	Reliability
Priority of the data	Testing
Response time required	Contingency planning
Throughput rate	Privacy
Accessibility	Authentication

Transfer Rate of Information Bits

As mentioned earlier, TRIB is sometimes called the information throughput rate. By definition,

$$\text{TRIB} = \frac{\text{Number of information bits accepted by the sink}}{\text{Total time required to get those bits accepted}}$$

Due to the burst nature of most data transmission, TRIB has meaning only as an average over a period. Although the data link bit rate has a lot to do with TRIB, other factors might at times have as much or more influence. For example, if the channel is noisy, a higher bit rate might increase the error rate to such an extent that the TRIB actually goes down.

TRIB is almost always less than the bit rate at the serial interface. (In a few sophisticated data compression systems, the TRIB might appear to exceed the actual interface bit rate because the receiver puts out more bits than were actually transmitted.) Two other parameters that usually affect TRIB are transmission overhead and delays. Both of these parameters are closely tied to the coding and blocking of the data and to the protocols used. For example, if the protocol requires that acknowledgment of a block must be received by the sender before the next block is transmitted, round-trip delays are added to the denominator of the TRIB definition given previously. In such instances, block length and delays can have a substantial effect on TRIB. Besides bit rate, these are the factors that should be considered in estimating TRIB:

1. Noninformation bits sent with the data. These include:

   a. Start and stop bits if asynchronous transmission is used.

   b. Parity bits if ASCII code is used.

   c. Redundant (or "stuffed") zeroes if a bit-oriented link protocol (SDLC/HDLC) is used.

   d. Filler bits used by teleprocessing system utilities to fill out partial data blocks, if any.

The TRIB is a result of several factors besides the data link bit rate. In almost all cases, the TRIB is less than the bit rate at the serial interface.

The major parameters that adversely affect the TRIB are transmission overhead and delays.

2. Noninformation characters in the message stream. Depending on the link protocol used, these might include:

  a. Sync characters or flags.

  b. Address characters.

  c. Control characters (STX, ACK, and so on) or control bytes.

  d. Error-checking characters (BCC or FCS).

  e. Transparency characters (DLE) and pads.

3. Noninformation messages required in the administration of the link protocol. These are the initialization, connect, disconnect, polling, and status messages, and so forth. They usually are not counted in TRIB calculations if the sessions are sufficiently long for them to have a negligible effect.

4. Carrier turn-on delay. This is the period between request-to-send from the terminal and clear-to-send from the modem. It is also known as "modem turnaround time." It is required only when a modem is operating with a switched carrier on a circuit that cannot support the bit rate of the modem two ways simultaneously, such as a dialed connection at 4800 bps. It also applies to at least the remote (secondary) stations, and sometimes to all stations, on a multipoint circuit. The amount of the delay, if any, is programmed into the modem at the time of installation, based on the modem manufacturer's recommendations for the particular circuit type and bit rate. It can be from a few milliseconds to a few hundred milliseconds.

5. Modem propagation delay. All synchronous modems operating on voice-grade circuits buffer the data on both transmit and receive. Depending on bit rate, the delay can be in the range of 2 to 10 milliseconds (ms) per modem.

6. Circuit propagation delay. Microwave radio signals, including communication satellite signals, and signals in optical fibers travel nearly at the speed of light. Electrical signals in local wires and cables travel somewhat slower. Also, many local telephone systems contain buffers of various types. As a rule of thumb, estimate 6 ms for local equipment on each end, and 1 ms for every 150 miles of cross-country terrestrial circuit. This gives [12 + (miles/150)] milliseconds for terrestrial one-way delay. Depending on latitude and longitude, satellite signals travel 45,000 to 50,000 miles in propagating from one satellite earth station to another; they also are buffered in the satellite and in the earth stations. Generally, estimate 350 ms from user to user (one way), including terrestrial links between respective earth stations and users.

7. Other propagation delays due to buffering. Most devices used in creating complex networks for data communications store groups of received bits in buffers before retransmitting those bits on the next link. Multiplexers, concentrators, and other types of communications processors are examples of such devices. Depending on the number of bits so buffered and the circuit length, the buffer

●
TRIB also is affected by transmission delays, buffer delays, response time computations, number of filler bits, and the transmission error rate.

delays in some systems can exceed all other propagation delays in the transfer of data. Buffer delays are normally included in the equipment specifications provided by the manufacturer.

8. Computation time for response and other interlock time delays. Although the time for data calculations normally wouldn't be considered in TRIB, the processing time required to check for transmission errors and fabricate an appropriate response should be included because this is a communications function. Also, systems that allow multiple blocks to be sent between acknowledgments often require time gaps or filler bits between successive blocks.

9. Error rate. For blocked data, if the error rate is not large, it is usually sufficient to estimate TRIB by first assuming no errors, then making an adjustment based on the block error rate (BLER). For example, if 1 percent of the blocks contain an error, the block error rate is said to be 1 percent. This means that 1 percent of the blocks will need to be retransmitted; thus, the TRIB will be lowered by approximately 1 percent due to errors.

Example of a TRIB Calculation

Problem: How long will it take to transmit 10,000 records a distance of 500 miles every day on a dialed connection at 4800 bps using BSC protocol? There are 80 EBCDIC characters per record, and two records per block; thus, there are 5000 blocks containing 160 characters. What is the TRIB?

The first step in calculating TRIB is to determine the propagation delays.

Solution: Because the connection is dialed at 4800 bps, the carrier must be switched, which means there will be a carrier turn-on delay in each direction for each block (one for data, one for acknowledgment). From the modem manufacturer's recommendations, this is established as 100 ms. Other delays include the following types:

- Circuit propagation delay, which for a terrestrial 500-mile circuit would be about 15 ms.

- Modem propagation delay, which according to the modem operation manual is 4 ms.

- Computation delay, which according to measurements on the actual terminals is 10 ms for the receiving terminal and negligible for the transmitting terminal.

Assume that each data transmission block includes the following items:

```
  1  leading pad character
  4  sync characters
  1  STX character
160  data characters (2 records at 80 characters each)
  1  EOB or ETX character
  2  character lengths of BCC
  1  trailing pad
───
170  characters
```

Thus, each block has 170 characters including overhead, but not counting DLE characters that would be sent if transparency is required. If each character requires 8 bits, the transmission time actually needed to send a data block at 4800 bps will be this:

$$\frac{170 \times 8}{4800} = 283 \text{ ms}$$

The next step is to determine the character count in the data block and acknowledgment block, and the transmission time required at the data rate.

Assume that each acknowledgment block includes the following items:

```
1  leading pad character
4  sync characters
2  character lengths of ACK0/ACK1
1  trailing pad character
8  characters (all overhead)
```

The transmit time actually needed to send an acknowledgment block will be this:

$$\frac{8 \times 8}{4800} = 13 \text{ ms}$$

Including delays, this will be the round-trip time to send 1 block:

```
100  ms near-end carrier turn-on
283  ms data block transmission
  4  ms transmit modem propagation
 15  ms circuit propagation
  4  ms receive modem propagation
 10  ms sink terminal calculation
100  ms far-end carrier turn-on
 13  ms acknowledgment block transmission
  4  ms transmit modem propagation
 15  ms circuit propagation
  4  ms receive modem propagation
552  ms or 0.552 second round-trip time per block
```

The calculation is completed by combining all delay times to get round-trip time per block, which results in the total time for all blocks. The total time divided into the actual data bits transferred gives the TRIB value.

The total time needed to send 5000 blocks, neglecting retransmissions due to errors, is $0.552 \times 5000 = 2760$ seconds, or 46 minutes. If we assume that 1 percent of the blocks will contain at least 1 bit in error, the time will be lengthened by about 1 percent. The actual number of information bits transmitted is 160 characters per block × 8 bits per character × 5000 blocks = 6,400,000 bits. If errors are not counted, then this is true:

$$\text{TRIB} = \frac{6,400,000 \text{ bits}}{2760} = 2319 \text{ bits/sec}$$

Maximizing TRIB

Note that the TRIB in the example just given is less than half of the modem bit rate of 4800 bps! Major factors contributing to this poor result were the modem carrier turn-on delay (modem turnaround) and the fact that acknowledgment of each block had to be received before the next block could be transmitted. (Note that the total of these times accounted for almost 40 percent of the round-trip time.)

Persons who are unfamiliar with the type of calculation just illustrated often assume that the best way to improve throughput is to increase modem speed. To attempt such a

You can take several actions to improve the TRIB. Installing a two-way simultaneous channel might provide the desired improvement, if the added expense of a private line is justified.

Other possible approaches to improving TRIB performance include changing to a different protocol or increasing block length.

remedy in this example would probably result in lower (not higher) TRIB, because it is likely that the modem turnaround, modem propagation delay, and error rate all would be higher. Not only would the modems cost more, but also the dialing and redialing required to get a connection that would operate satisfactorily at a higher rate would be both time-consuming and frustrating to the operator—if it would work at all.

One possible approach to improvement of TRIB in the example shown might be to eliminate modem turnaround entirely by installing full duplex modems. Still another approach to TRIB improvement might be to change to a different protocol. SDLC is capable of allowing acknowledgment of up to seven frames with only one response. However, to change from BSC to SDLC link protocol would require expensive software and probably hardware modifications in both terminals.

The best way to improve the TRIB in this case would be to increase block length. Assuming sufficient buffer capacity in both terminals, an increase of block length from 2 records to 10 records would result in a total round-trip time of 1.619 seconds per block, with only 1000 blocks required to be sent. The total time needed would be 27 minutes, a daily savings of 19 minutes of long-distance calling. The new TRIB would be 3953 bps, an increase of 70 percent.

Caution: Increasing block length always increases the block error rate because there is a greater exposure to the probability of error in a long block. For a block length increase of 500 percent, the BLER will increase by roughly the same factor. In the example, if the block error rate had really been 1 percent before (very high for such a short block), it would be about 5 percent now. This would erode some of the time savings.

Optimum Block Length

Exact matching to the optimum block length often is not practical because of what the blocking program can accomplish or because long-term changes in error rates and delays cause the optimum block length to change.

Figure 15.1 illustrates how block length affects TRIB, all other factors being equal. For very short blocks, the TRIB is low (as illustrated in the previous calculations) because overhead is a significant proportion of the total transmission. For very long blocks also, the TRIB is low because there is a significant probability of error within the block, and most blocks have to be retransmitted. Somewhere between the extremes, there is a block length, L_M, that yields maximum TRIB. Whether L_M is optimum depends on several factors besides TRIB:

- If the error rate is low, the value of L_M might be so large as to be impractical, particularly for an interactive data system in which fast response is more important than throughput.

- Quite often, the memory capacity of the terminals is not sufficient to handle a block length of L_M.

● The utility programs that actually perform the blocking of data usually won't allow a precise match with L_M.

● Long-term changes in error rates and delays make precise matching impractical anyway.

FIGURE 15.1.

The block length (L_M) for maximum TRIB.

Regardless of these considerations, the network designer should make reasonable estimates of TRIB, be aware of the major impairments to faster TRIB, and ensure that the combination of factors is "best" for each situation.

Networking Devices

Several types of special-purpose devices exist for improving cost-effectiveness of data networks. The basic purposes and advantages of the main types are given in the paragraphs that follow. Refer to Chapter 6, "Multiplexing Techniques," for detailed information concerning the operation and utilization of multiplexers, and to Chapter 10, "Alternatives in Local Area Networks," for details about LAN internetworking devices such as bridges, routers, and gateways.

Multiplexers

Multiplexers are devices that allow the combination of several data channels independently into one physical circuit. Data streams so combined can be separated and recovered at the opposite end of the system. There are two main types: frequency-division multiplexers (FDMs) and time-division multiplexers (TDMs). FDM has the advantage that it can be used on multipoint circuits, but the individual channels usually must each be for start-stop data. TDM can be used if all channels are point-to-point. It generally allows faster bit rates and potentially more channels than FDM at less cost.

● Both the FDM and the TDM have advantages and disadvantages that must be considered to determine which to use in a particular application.

TDMs are of two types: classical (or dumb) TDMs and statistical (or smart) TDMs. Dumb TDMs should be used if the duty cycles of the data channels to be multiplexed are relatively high. A high duty cycle means that the channel is actually carrying bits most of the time. Because dumb TDMs send idle (marking) bits when a channel becomes inactive, they waste a lot of potential capacity when the duty cycles are low.

Whenever usage statistics indicate low duty cycles as the normal mode of utilization of most of the channels to be multiplexed, a statistical multiplexer system is usually a good choice. These devices send only data bits (no idle bits), so they can appear to have a higher total bit rate than the actual rate if a high percentage of idle bits are coming from the terminals.

Modem Sharing Devices

Modem sharing devices allow several terminals to share the serial interface of one modem.

Modem sharing devices (MSDs) do just that: they allow several remote terminals at one site on a common multipoint circuit to share a single modem at that site. MSDs do not multiplex; they simply provide a means of sharing the serial interface of one modem among several terminals.

When a modem sharing unit is used, transmission occurs via polling and broadcast. To understand the operation and utilization of a modem sharing unit (MSU), consider Figure 15.2, in which three terminals share access to a common modem via an MSU.

FIGURE 15.2.

A modem sharing unit enables transmission via polling and broadcasting.

Line Bridging Devices

Line bridging devices allow two or more analog circuits to be shared as one. Bridges are not multiplexers. They allow one modem to be used with circuits to more than one destination. Telephone companies and users can use bridges to create multipoint analog circuits from point-to-point segments.

Modem Eliminators

Modem eliminators are used to connect two DTEs together directly. They also are called null modems.

Protocol Converters

Protocol converters are microprocessors that convert data operating in one protocol, say start-stop ASCII, to another, say IBM BSC. A dial-up X.3 PAD for converting start-stop to X.25 is an example of a protocol converter.

LAN Internetworking

Three communications devices have the primary operational function of interconnecting local area networks. Those devices are bridges, routers, and gateways.

Bridges

Depending on the geographical relationship of LANs, you can consider using a local bridge or a pair of remote bridges to connect LANs. When LANs are in close proximity, you should consider using a local bridge to interconnect the networks. A local bridge consists of a processor, memory, and two LAN adapter cards, with each adapter connected to a separate network. The bridge operates at the Data Link Layer of the OSI Reference Model, examining the source address of each frame on the LAN to which it is attached. This enables the bridge to construct and periodically update a table of known addresses. By comparing the destination address in each frame to the table of known addresses on the LAN, the bridge can decide whether to forward the frame to the other LAN. That is, if the destination address matches a source address in the table of known addresses, the destination of the frame resides on the LAN, and the bridge will not forward the frame onto the other LAN.

A remote bridge operates similarly to a local bridge; however, it is designed to interconnect geographically separated LANs via a wide area network. To accomplish this task, the remote bridge converts frames requiring forwarding into a suitable protocol for transmission via a WAN, such as SDLC or HDLC. Similarly, a remote bridge converts frames received via a WAN link into their appropriate LAN format. Figure 15.3 compares the use of local and remote bridges to interconnect LANs.

●
A useful networking device is the protocol converter— a microprocessor that converts data from one protocol to another.

●
Bridges operate at the Data Link Layer, whereas routers operate at the Network Layer of the OSI Reference Model.

FIGURE 15.3.
Using local and remote bridges.

Local bridging

Remote bridging to connect geographically separated LANS.

Legend:
DSU   data service unit
○   workstations

Routers

●
Routers can be programmed to forward traffic based on several parameters, including line availability and line utilization.

In comparison to bridges, which operate at the Data Link Layer, a router operates at the Network Layer of the OSI Reference Model. This means that routers make their forwarding decisions based on network addresses rather than media access control (MAC) addresses used by bridges. Although the installation of routers normally requires more effort than the installation of bridges, routers provide a significant increase in functionality and operational capability. For example, routers can be programmed to forward traffic via different paths through a network based on line availability, line utilization, and other parameters.

Figure 15.4 illustrates the use of routers to interconnect three LANs. Note that data transferred from a workstation on LAN A to a workstation on LAN C can flow on the path A–C or the paths A–B and B–C. Thus, routers can be used to construct backup communications paths in the event a primary path becomes inoperative.

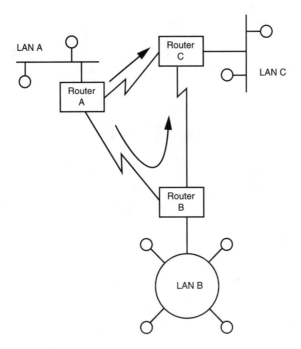

FIGURE 15.4.
Routers support the use of alternative paths on a dynamic or predefined basis.

Gateways

A gateway represents a special type of protocol converter that operates at all layers of the OSI Reference Model. The primary function of a LAN-based gateway is to convert application data transported at the Data Link Layer on a LAN for transmission to a mainframe computer. This conversion is twofold. First, application data generated by a workstation on the LAN is encoded into an application data stream used by a particular type of mainframe computer. Next, the LAN-based data stream is converted into the transport protocol recognized by a mainframe computer. The actual transmission of data from a gateway to a mainframe commonly occurs via a serial transmission link, with the gateway connected to a LAN via a network adapter card. Thus, a gateway commonly provides a series of conversions from the Physical Layer through the Application Layer.

Interconnection of Networking Devices

The preceding section contained only a partial listing of devices intended to interconnect different types of networks and network components. Space does not allow a discussion of the numerous possible alternative requirements in the actual interconnection of leads between devices, terminals, modems, and so forth.

> When actually making the physical connections between the various types of networking devices, be sure that you thoroughly understand all equipment manuals and interface standards.

Probably the best advice that can be given is to study the equipment manuals and the interface standards themselves. As an alternative, refer to the book *Data Communications Networking Devices, Third Edition,* by Gilbert Held, published by John Wiley & Sons, for specific information concerning the operation and utilization of more than 25 networking devices.

While you are selecting appropriate networking equipment, ordering necessary transmission lines, and developing an equipment installation schedule, you should also consider policies, procedures, and equipment you might need in order to maintain your network. Although often overlooked, testing, troubleshooting, and capacity planning are important network management issues that every network manager and administrator can eventually expect to face. Thus, in concluding this chapter, I will focus on different tests and test equipment that can be used to isolate network problems, procedures that can improve network operations, and two standards supported by many networking devices that facilitate the management of TCP/IP-based networks.

Fault Isolation

The process of recognizing the failure of a device or circuit is commonly referred to as fault detection. Fault detection usually is pretty easy; fault isolation is more complicated. The first question is, Is the problem in a terminal device or in the communications system? Troubleshooting data terminals and LAN workstations is beyond the scope of this book, but one book you can refer to is *LAN Testing and Troubleshooting,* by Gilbert Held, published by John Wiley & Sons. If terminals and workstations pass self-test procedures but still will not communicate, chances are good that the problem is in the communications system.

Loopback Tests

> In the loopback test, which is a basic data communications fault isolation technique, faults are successively isolated by the process of elimination.

One of the basic techniques for isolation of faults in data communications is the loopback test. In a loopback, the output at the far end of a system or subsystem is connected to the input of the return path. Then the output of the return path is examined in relation to the input to the outgoing path.

Figure 15.5 illustrates how successive loopbacks can be used to isolate a fault on a single point-to-point data link that uses an analog circuit. The local modem is first self-tested using an analog loopback at its far terminals (point A). If it passes the test, the loop is removed from the local modem. Then the local modem and the analog circuit are tested together using a remote analog loopback at the near terminals (point B) of the remote modem. If that test also appears satisfactory, the remote analog loop is removed, and the entire data link is tested end-to-end round trip using a digital loopback at the far terminals (point C) of the remote modem. (Loopbacks at points B and C are useful only if the channel is full-duplex.) Using a process of elimination, the location of the fault can be narrowed to the local modem, the analog circuit, or the remote modem.

FIGURE 15.5.
Loopback test points.

Loopbacks cannot determine which side of a path, outgoing or return, is faulty, but only the person who has to repair it really needs that information. End-to-end tests can distinguish the direction of the fault, but that often requires at least modest training of a person at the remote site.

Caution Number One

Know what is being tested when performing a self-test on a device. As with terminals, no self-test ever tests all the circuitry. For example, Figure 15.6 shows that a self-test of a modem doesn't check data continuity through the line transformers and through the RS-232 interface circuitry. The latter problem can be very treacherous. Whenever practical, use external tests to be sure.

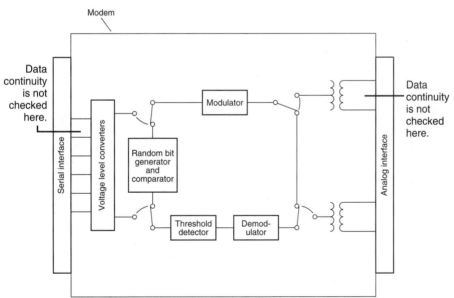

FIGURE 15.6.
Some modem circuitry is not tested in self-test.

Switches are shown in self-test position

●
One should not only know what parameters of the faulty device can be tested, but also know the capabilities, limitations, and special requirements of the test system/equipment.

Caution Number Two

Most analog data circuits are designed to operate with a substantial drop in signal level from input to output; for example, there is a 16 dB loss each way in a private-line voice-grade circuit to be used for data. When an analog loopback is performed at the remote end without gain being inserted at that point, the input signal for the return path is 16 dB lower than it should be. Such a low-level signal can cause both the analog return path and the local modem receiver to operate improperly, perhaps giving a false indication. Many systems that provide for remote analog loopbacks automatically insert gain in the loopback path to avoid this problem. If the modems used in the test depicted in Figure 15.5 are not so equipped, a different procedure should be used. For example, perform a self-test on each modem, and then with an assistant at the far end, perform an end-to-end test.

Data Communications Test Equipment

Many kinds of test equipment are available to assist in the detection and isolation of faults in data communications systems.

Test equipment enables network technicians and users to observe the state of the DTE-DCE interface circuits, as well as the composition of data on a circuit. In this section, I will examine the operation and initialization of several types of test equipment.

Amplifier-Monitor

The self-contained, battery-operated audio amplifier-speaker-monitor, sometimes called a "watergate box," is readily available at retail electronics supply stores for around $20 or less. Not only is it useful for detecting the modem carrier and changes in modem output signals, but it's also the easiest way to detect a noisy circuit or to tell whether a modem is putting out tone-dial or pulse-dial signals. It can also be used to monitor call progress and answer-back tones on dialed data links.

Breakout Box

The basic specialized data testing device is the breakout box, so named because it provides access to individual leads in the serial interface between a DTE (such as a terminal) and a DCE (such as a modem). Prices range from about $60 to $250 for breaking out the 25 leads of an RS-232 interface, to $100 to $500 or more for devices that test high-speed interfaces. Price depends on ruggedness, whether the unit is programmable (leads can be crisscrossed), and whether data activity can be observed directly without a voltmeter. The higher-priced units feature built-in battery power, full tri-state LED monitoring of leads, programmability, ruggedness, and DIP switches to open the circuits of individual leads. They might also provide positive and negative test voltages.

Bit Error Rate Tester

The next step up in acquisition of specialized data test equipment would be a bit error rate tester (BERT). RS-232 BERTs range in price from under $250 to around $1000, depending on whether block error (BLERT) and error-second measurements are to be included, whether start and stop bit insertion/deletion is required (if asynchronous multiplexers are in the circuit), and whether various automatic indicator features are present. Some models also feature programmable message generators for checking out terminal devices. High-speed BERT/BLERTs in the multimegabit-per-second range can cost much more.

Decibel Meter

If analog voice-grade circuits are used extensively, a decibel (dB) meter is a wise invest-ment for checking transmit and receive levels. A basic dB meter costs around $200. Per-sons considering purchase of a dB meter should consider a combination unit. Excellent portable meters with digital display are available. Such a meter that can read dBm, relative dB, frequency, relative frequency, voltage, current, and resistance costs about $400 to $500. Such an expenditure is not recommended unless testing on analog circuits is expected to be a common occurrence.

Oscilloscope

A multichannel oscilloscope (or "scope") with x-y inputs can be used with a breakout box for observing serial interface signals or with a modem for detecting certain impairments on analog circuits. Examples of the use of a dual-trace scope in the RS-232 interface would be to measure modem turnaround time, to check for crosstalk interference between tim-ing leads, and to observe degradation of signals in long serial interface cables.

With synchronous modems having signal-space (constellation) pattern generators, an x-y oscilloscope becomes a powerful instrument for detecting phase hits, phase jitter, ampli-tude hits, harmonic distortion, dropouts, and impulse noise in analog circuits. With other modems, a scope can be used to observe eye patterns for harmonic distortion, phase jitter, and certain types of hits.

Scopes that are suitable for these purposes generally cost in the range of $800 to $3000, depending on compactness, maximum data rate, and number of channels.

●
An oscilloscope, used within a breakout box for access, is an important error isolation and testing tool.

Voice Frequency Test Set

For the really serious user of data over voice-grade analog circuits, a voice frequency test set is a device that can quantify the major parameters of a voice-grade analog circuit. Stan-dard capabilities include frequency response (amplitude received versus frequency for con-stant amplitude transmitted), C-message noise in dBrnc, C-message notched noise (S/N) in dB, and audio monitoring. Costs can range from $1000 upward, depending on the degree of automation in the tests and additional test functions provided. Although the less-expensive units do not provide for measurement of envelope delay distortion (one of the two parameters affected by C-conditioning), large amounts of delay distortion often are accompanied by large amounts of attenuation distortion, which is much easier to measure. Voice frequency test sets normally should be used in pairs to provide end-to-end testing.

●
A voice-frequency test set enables measurement of frequency response, noise, and distortion of voice-grade analog circuits.

Data Link Content Monitor

Many large users of data communications have painfully discovered that the general pur-pose computer is not an efficient device for debugging data link and network protocols.

Nor is it the best device for bit error rate testing of wideband data channels, T1 multiplexers, and the like. The computer time, programmer time, and other expensive resources saved in a single project often can pay for the purchase of test equipment to cover these areas.

A data link content monitor monitors and displays signals crossing the serial interface. Some allow specified sequences to be stored for later analysis.

One equipment category is the basic RS-232 data link content monitor. This device simply monitors and displays signals passing across the serial interface. The display is normally in terms of characters, if appropriate, or it can be in binary or hexadecimal in the case of uncoded data. Pricing varies with the number of codes, the type of display, the capability to trap (or freeze) and display specific sequences, the amount of memory, scrolling of trapped memory contents, speed of the device with and without recording in memory, and whether the conditions of various nondata leads in the serial interface are recorded with the data for later analysis.

Simulator

Because a simulator is actually a special-purpose computer, it can be programmed to simulate a computer port, remote terminal, or network gateway for system development.

Monitor devices are excellent for diagnosing protocol problems in data links, but they are not efficient for system development. This function is best handled by a simulator. Such a device can be user-programmed to simulate a computer port, remote terminal, or network gateway in order to "exercise" the hardware/software system being developed. Simulators are actually special-purpose computers utilizing easy-to-learn high-level programming languages. They also can be programmed to operate effectively as content monitors, BERTs, and BLERTs. Prices range from $1000 to $25,000, depending on protocols supported, speed, serial interfaces supported, amount of memory, type of display, ease of programming, and portability. The more sophisticated units provide simulation up through the packet level (OSI Level 3) of X.25/X.75 protocols or through all ATM layers.

Protocol Analyzer

The protocol analyzer is the most sophisticated type of data communications test equipment currently marketed. The protocol analyzer gets its name from the major function it performs—protocol analysis. In doing so, the protocol analyzer monitors the bit stream flowing on a communications circuit or a LAN cable and decodes the bits into characters that represent the format and information content of the protocol. When designed explicitly for use on LANs, the protocol analyzer is usually referred to as a LAN analyzer. When designed for use on LANs and WANs the protocol analyzer is referred to as an enterprise analyzer. For example, a protocol analyzer monitoring an HDLC transmission would convert the bit sequence 01111110 to a flag character and then indicate the start or end of a frame of information. Other features incorporated into most protocol analyzers include the capability to analyze several communications protocols, perform data simulation, and carry out BERT and BLERT testing.

Most protocol analyzers include a built-in breakout box, a keyboard, online storage, and a display in a common housing. Due to the almost ubiquitous status of personal computers, some protocol analyzer manufacturers designed their products as adapter boards that are inserted into the system unit of a PC. When acquired as an adapter board, the protocol analyzer uses the keyboard, online storage, and display of the computer, significantly reducing the cost of the analyzer. Prices of protocol analyzers range from $1000 for devices manufactured on adapter boards for use in personal computers to more than $25,000 for stand-alone protocol analyzers designed to decode the most recent protocols, such as signaling on the ISDN D channel.

Figure 15.7 illustrates a Digilog 800 protocol/performance analyzer. This device contains a color monitor, hard disk, and floppy disk, as well as a full function keyboard. In addition to decoding a number of protocols, the Digilog 800 provides numerous performance statistics based on line monitoring of different protocols. The screen shown in Figure 15.7 is a "fill in the blank" menu system that enables operators to easily develop programs and get performance measurements or decode different protocols.

FIGURE 15.7.

A Digilog 800 protocol/performance analyzer.

Figure 15.8 illustrates a hand-held and very portable protocol analyzer manufactured by Frederick Engineering of Columbia, Maryland. Referred to as the ParaScope 64M, this protocol analyzer can be cabled to any PC DOS computer's parallel port to use the processing power of the computer to execute the vendor's software, which turns the computer into a protocol analyzer.

The ParaScope 64M illustrated in Figure 15.8 can be used to monitor standard RS232 communications at data rates up to 19,200 bps or V.35/RS-449 communications at data rates up to 64,000 bps. The light-emitting diodes and switches located in columns in the middle of the ParaScope 64M provide users with a breakout box capability to monitor and open and close circuits on a monitored interface. However, the primary use of the ParaScope 64M is as a protocol analyzer, providing users with the ability to monitor the flow of data, create programs to operate on the monitored data, and display the results of the execution of programs.

FIGURE 15.8.

The Frederick Engineering ParaScope 64M protocol analyzer.

The Frederick Engineering ParaScope 64M was developed as an extension of that vendor's Feline series of protocol analyzers. The Feline series was developed as adapter cards designed for insertion into conventional PCs and laptop and notebook computers, as well as software that operated on each computer. A special hardware interface box referred to as a pod is cabled to the adapter card installed in the computer. The pod is very similar to the ParaScope 64M in that it contains connectors for monitoring the interface between a DTE and DCE and converts the voltage level of the monitored circuit to the transistor-to-transistor logic (TTL) voltage level used internally by computers. The ParaScope 64M differs from the Feline pod in that it incorporates the adapter card logic, alleviating the necessity to install an adapter card in a computer. This makes the ParaScope 64M ideal for use with modern notebook computers that lack an expansion slot to accommodate the insertion of an adapter card.

●

The ParaScope 64M is cabled to the parallel port of a DOS computer, and it executes Feline software that results in the computer becoming a protocol analyzer.

The integration of the Feline adapter card into the ParaScope 64M results in its capability to be used with Feline software. To illustrate the utility of the system obtained from the use of Feline software and ParaScope 64M hardware, I'll examine some of the features of the software. Figure 15.9 illustrates a split-screen Feline display in which the upper portion of the screen defines information about the interface being monitored and the status of timers and counters. In the computer operating Feline software, timers and counters can be considered as memory locations that accumulate specific timing or counting values based on the execution of a program you create using Feline. In the next section, we will examine the creation of a small program and illustrate its execution on monitored data. The lower portion of Figure 15.9 contains a window that indicates the DCE and DTE data flow across the monitored interface.

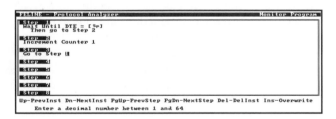

FIGURE 15.9.

A Feline protocol analyzer software split-screen display.

If you examine Figure 15.9, you will note that control and nonprintable characters are indicated by mnemonics, such as L_F for line feed, and Sp for space character. The lower line across every Feline display screen indicates the function key values assigned to a specific screen. For example, to remove the split screen and display monitored data in a full screen, you would press the F7 key, which is assigned to the generation of a full-screen display.

Program Development

Figure 15.10 illustrates the creation of a program that counts the number of spaces encountered on the DTE side of a monitored interface. When you select Feline's program mode of operation, your display is initially filled with a series of blank steps and function key value assignments. As you press appropriate function keys when the cursor is placed in a step, you assign one or more program instructions to the step. In Figure 15.10, step 1 waits until a space is encountered on the DTE side of the line, and then the program jumps to step 2. In step 2, counter 1 is incremented, and step 3 simply branches the program back to step 1. Thus, when data is monitored using this program, the value in counter 1 indicates the number of spaces encountered on the DTE side of the line.

FIGURE 15.10.

Creating a program to count spaces on the DTE side of the line.

Now that we have created a program, I'll again monitor the line and examine the value assigned to counter 1. Figure 15.11 illustrates the Feline split-screen display resulting from monitoring a 9600 bps line after we created the program previously illustrated in Figure 15.10. Note that when the screen was captured for printing, a total of 2810 spaces on the DTE side of the line were encountered because that is the value assigned to counter 1. Although the program is not very sophisticated, it provides an indication of how you can create a program and use the program when monitoring a line. If users were reporting throughput problems on a particular circuit during a file transfer operation, you might consider developing a program to count negative acknowledgments (NAKs). Because each

NAK results in the retransmission of a previously transmitted block, a high level of NAKs would indicate that retransmissions due to line errors are resulting in a low level of data throughput.

FIGURE 15.11.

Monitoring with a program that counts spaces on the DTE side of the line and assigns the number of spaces to counter 1.

LAN Analyzers

Today, network managers and administrators can select from a wide range of local area network analysis tools. Some LAN analyzers are designed to provide users with traffic- and network-related error information, whereas other products are designed to decode packets and provide data important for isolating errors resulting from improper hardware or software configurations or application problems. To help you gain an appreciation for the functionality and capability of a LAN analyzer, I will examine the use of TokenVision, a software product developed by Triticom, Inc., of Eden Prairie, Minnesota, for operation on IBM PC or compatible computers connected to a Token-Ring network.

TokenVision

TokenVision is a software product that turns an IBM PC or compatible personal computer into a LAN analyzer. Although this product requires the installation of a Token-Ring adapter card in the personal computer and the connection of that adapter card to a Token-Ring network, you can use the PC for other applications when you are not analyzing the data flow on the network. Another product from Triticom is EtherVision, which requires the installation of an Ethernet adapter card in a PC and the connection of that adapter card to an Ethernet network. EtherVision provides a traffic monitoring and analysis capability for Ethernet LANs.

TokenVision operates at the Data Link Layer, enabling a user to monitor traffic based on either the source or the destination address contained in MAC frames that flow on the network. Figure 15.12 illustrates the Triticom TokenVision Source Address Monitoring Screen display. Note that at the time the screen was captured, the program had identified 187 distinct network stations. To do so, the program constructs a table of source addresses in memory. As network stations become active, the program recognizes their source address in frames placed on the network, adds their address to the table, and increments a counter that defines the number of distinct network stations recognized at a particular point in time.

FIGURE 15.12.

A TokenVision Source Address Monitoring Screen display.

The main window of the Source Address Monitoring Screen display shown in Figure 15.12 contains four columns listing source MAC addresses encountered and the number of frames containing that source address. Thus, the program provides a real-time count and display of locations originating traffic. In examining the MAC addresses shown in Figure 15.12, note that some addresses indicate the name of a vendor, whereas other addresses have the prefix Vend?. Because the IEEE assigns blocks of MAC addresses to different vendors, the program reads the first three bytes of the six-byte address to determine the vendor that manufactured the Token-Ring card. Those addresses with the prefix Vend? represent adapter cards produced by a vendor that received a block of MAC addresses from the IEEE after the program was developed.

By pressing the F4 key, you can sort MAC addresses by their count. Thus, from this screen you can easily determine those stations that are generating a large percentage of network traffic. This fact can be important if your LAN utilization is high and you want to investigate who is heavily using the network and what they are doing before considering a potential and probably costly network upgrade.

From the TokenVision station monitoring window, you can display network utilization on a percentage basis via a Skyline display. Figure 15.13 illustrates the network utilization Skyline display on a per-second basis. Note that during the 60-second interval shown in Figure 15.13, the maximum network utilization was 5%, which indicates that during the monitoring period visually shown on-screen, the network was not heavily used. Because a 60-second period represents a small amount of time on which to base a decision concerning network utilization, the program provides users with several methods to monitor utilization and other parameters over a prolonged period. First, by pressing the F5 key, you can change the Skyline display to a per-minute basis, and the past hour of utilization is displayed.

●

Knowing the IEEE MAC block assignment for different vendors enables TokenVision to display the manufacturer of adapter cards based on source addresses that flow on the network.

FIGURE 15.13.

*A Triticom
TokenVision Skyline
display of network
utilization.*

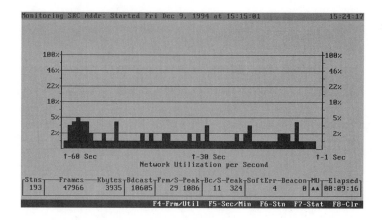

A second method you can use is to set a threshold that will generate an alarm when the threshold is exceeded. Thus, you can use the threshold method to determine whether during a certain period the utilization exceeded a predefined level. A third method you can use to track network utilization is obtained from the program's Statistics display, which is shown in Figure 15.14. In examining the Statistics Screen display shown in Figure 15.14, note that in addition to denoting average, current (now), and peak utilization, the display notes the time when the network utilization peak occurred. Also note that the display provides a distribution of frames based on their length or size. This information can be very important in attempting to determine the type of traffic carried on the network and whether a certain type of traffic is hogging network bandwidth. For example, small frames typically transport interactive traffic, whereas relatively long frames transport files. Thus, if the frame size distribution indicates a large number of relatively long frames and network utilization is very high, this could indicate that one or more network users are transferring large files, which represents a major contributing factor to the use of network bandwidth.

FIGURE 15.14.

*A Triticom
TokenVision Statistics
display.*

Network Control System

Many companies that operate large complex data networks have found the timely isolation of faults to be so important as to cost-justify the installation of a centralized network control system, as depicted in Figure 15.15. When based on the use of analog leased lines, such systems commonly use the low end of the frequency spectrum of the voice-grade circuit to carry a signal interrogation and reporting "side channel." Such systems add significantly to the cost of each modem in the system.

In a large, complex data network, it might be cost effective to add a centralized network control system to assist in fault detection and isolation.

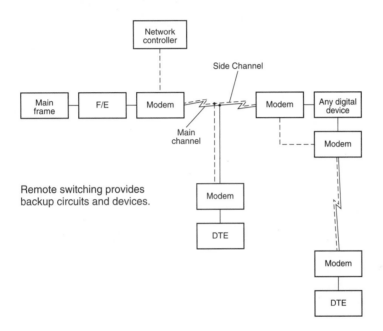

FIGURE 15.15.

A network control system.

A modem that is addressed by the central unit can be commanded to perform certain tests and report the results back for display or recording. Such tests as continuity, level of received signal, and condition of an RS-232 lead can be accurately conducted without interrupting or modifying data flow. Other tests, such as self-tests and loopbacks, do cause interruption of data flow. Many of the more sophisticated systems can be user programmed to perform interruptive tests automatically during off-hours when actual interruption of data is unlikely. Test results can be automatically logged and compared with former test results to detect changes in circuit parameters.

When digital transmission circuits are used in a network device, control cannot be effected by the use of a side channel of frequency to convey control information and return statistics and device status data. Instead, both data and control information are transmitted on the same digital channel. This requires managed devices to interpret data and respond to recognized commands imbedded in the data stream.

Although network control systems were originally developed for use with analog circuits, most modern systems are now produced to operate with digital circuits, and some systems support both types. Regardless of the type of transmission circuitry supported, the network control system can be characterized by the inclusion of a scheme for remote switching of circuits and devices to provide backup in the event of failures. The combination of remote testing and remote backup of data communications network control systems based on digital interrogation and reporting is now beginning to replace the analog systems.

Restoration of Service

Providing reliable service restoration promptly and economically is a challenging task.

Given enough planning and money, prompt and reliable restoration of data communications service is easy, but to make it economical is a little harder.

The planner for data communications backup should consider the following questions:

- What is the frequency and length of downtime to be expected?
- Can steps be taken to decrease the frequency and length of downtime without incurring additional costs; that is, are you getting what you already are paying for?
- What will be the extra costs incurred due to complete outage of the service for the frequency and duration indicated?
- Can these extra costs be reduced by a reduced-capability backup—for example, backing up a 56 Kbps private line using a 9600 bps dialed connection?
- What are the actual costs of all relevant backup schemes? Include the cost of personnel time as well as the cost of backup. The cost of backup must include the operating costs, such as dialed connection charges, as well as initial investment and installation costs.

Getting the Most for the Money

You can often improve existing systems' performance by closely examining the existing system and established procedures.

Before a backup technique is designed and implemented, a review of current procedures might improve the frequency and duration of downtime.

- Is there ongoing positive communication not only with the people in the user's own organization, but also with suppliers of equipment and services?
- Do users have a thorough knowledge of the capabilities and limitations of all data communications system facilities, software, and hardware at their disposal, particularly the capabilities and limitations of self-contained test features?
- Are there well-designed restoration procedures that are agreed to in advance by all concerned and that are strictly followed?
- Are new systems benchmark-tested as they are placed in service, and then tested on a regular schedule to detect changes in circuit parameters?

● Are exceptions (failures) documented, and are repeat offenders discovered?

● Is there an ongoing in-house training program to ensure that each individual in the organization can properly handle all appropriate parts of the above five points for those portions of the system within his or her purview?

Rapport with Suppliers

Central to any cost-effective service-restoration program is a firmly established positive rapport with all major suppliers of equipment and services—especially with key individuals such as telephone company (telco) personnel. Many data-link failures can be traced directly or indirectly to a breakdown in people-to-people communications between vendors and users. For example, in the case of an organization like a telephone company with many levels of personnel that deal with the customer, the rapport between supplier and customer must exist at all levels: Data technicians should be on a first-name basis with telco testboard personnel, technician supervisors with testboard supervisors, the data communications operations manager with the telco network operations manager, and so on. When such rapport exists, several symptoms will be apparent:

● Employees on both sides will be more helpful and understanding, especially in high-pressure situations.

● Information on new testing and quality assurance techniques will flow easier. The user will gain a better understanding of the built-in test capabilities in the vendor's services and equipment. In fact, technicians on both sides will be eager to share their excitement over some new piece of test gear or a new discovery.

● Better confidence in each other's abilities will emerge and will give rise to more of a supplier-user team approach.

● The vendor employee will often render assistance above and beyond what is required and expected.

Data communications managers who succeed in cultivating this kind of rapport with their major vendors consider it among their greatest assets. In particular, they are careful to establish and follow good procedures for the testing of systems and proper reporting of problems to the vendor. Inherent in this process is the careful development of an escalation and reporting system.

Escalation and Reporting

Through meetings with all concerned, the data communications manager should develop a very specific escalation schedule. This schedule should show exactly who becomes involved at increasing levels of authority, what calls are placed, and at what levels when a particular type of problem fails to show progress toward resolution after a specific time lapse. All persons involved in this schedule should be involved in its development, should "sign-off" on it, should have a personal copy of the finished product, and should have a cause for negative feelings whenever it is invoked.

●
Close personal rapport between supplier and customers at all levels is of utmost importance to the smooth, efficient restoration of service of a communications system.

●
Clearly established procedures must be developed to ensure that the proper level of management is involved in the correction of problems in a timely manner.

Before asking for help from higher levels or from the vendor, it is absolutely vital that the user exhaust all means at his disposal to make use of test facilities available to him—especially self-tests. Remember the story about the little boy who cried "wolf"? Nothing can damage credibility and rapport faster than to blame the vendor when the problem is with another vendor or is in-house.

Personnel responsible for data subsystem and system testing must be thoroughly familiar with self-tests and their limitations, and with the meaning of any other tests for which they have equipment. Troubles should be reported only after such testing has been adequately documented, and escalation should be invoked only after the lack of progress in problem resolution has been documented.

> The personnel involved in system and data subsystem testing should be thoroughly familiar with the capabilities and limitations of the tests and the test equipment.

Such documentation of problems and their resolutions should be permanently recorded and reviewed with the vendor at regular intervals. This review aids in spotting areas of recurring difficulties and possibly degrading facilities and components, so these can be serviced before a "hard" failure occurs. This is why the benchmarking of newly acquired facilities is important.

Finally, appreciation should be expressed when appropriate. Nothing will make an employee of a vendor work harder for a user than an appreciation letter to his boss for good work done on the user's behalf.

Standards

As with other aspects of data communications, network management has both de facto and de jure standards associated with it. One popular example of a de facto standard is IBM's NetView product, which can be used to control and manage NetView-compliant products used in an IBM mainframe-based network. Two popular examples of de jure network management standards are the Simple Network Management Protocol (SNMP) and Remote Monitor (RMON), both of which were developed to facilitate the management and control of TCP/IP-based networks. In concluding this chapter, I will provide an overview of both standards.

Simple Network Management Protocol

The Simple Network Management Protocol (SNMP) represents a de facto standard for managing TCP/IP-based networks. Developed by the Internet Engineering Task Force (IETF) as a mechanism to facilitate the management of multivendor products used in TCP/IP networks, SNMP uses a client-server architecture for monitoring and controlling SNMP-compliant devices.

Architecture

SNMP architecture is based on the interrelationship of three basic components: a manager, an agent, and a database. The SNMP manager represents a software program that turns the computer executing the program into a Network Management Station (NMS).

The agent represents software or firmware residing in a managed network device, such as a bridge, router, or host. Each agent stores management data and responds to SNMP manager queries for one or more data items.

The third component of SNMP is the database, which is formally referred to as the Management Information Base (MIB). In actuality, the MIB represents a collection of databases for the set of all managed devices supported by SNMP. This means that each agent has its own database of relevant objects for which it collects statistics and performs other functions. Figure 15.16 illustrates the general relationship between an SNMP manager, an agent, and the agent's MIB. Although only one agent is shown in Figure 15.16, the SNMP manager can theoretically control an infinite number of agents.

● SNMP consists of three basic components: a manager, an agent, and a database.

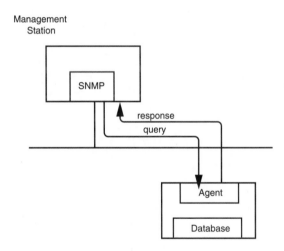

FIGURE 15.16.

The SNMP architecture.

The ability of a manager to control an agent is based on the use of two addresses. The first address is the IP address of the agent, which enables the manager to send requests to distinct agents. The second address represents the location in the Management Information Base of an object to be set or the counter value to be retrieved. To facilitate the ability of vendors to develop products that interoperate with each other, objects in the MIB are assigned addresses based on a tree structure. Thus, a network manager developed by one vendor can set or retrieve information from an agent developed by another vendor as long as the user knows the agent's IP address and the location of the object in the MIB to be set or retrieved.

● SNMP sets and retrieves data using the IP address of an agent and the location in the MIB of an object to be set or the counter value to be retrieved.

Figure 15.17 illustrates the operation of SimpleView, an SNMP Manager program from Triticom, Inc. This program turns an IBM PC or compatible computer into a TCP/IP network manager. In the left portion of Figure 15.17, note two network map entries labeled `Ethernet probe` and `Token Ring`, with an IP address assigned to each entry. Here each entry represents a special type of agent known as a Remote Monitor probe, whose use I will discuss shortly. To set or retrieve an object associated with a selected agent, you need to specify the location of the object in the MIB. To do so, you can either directly enter a numeric sequence of digits and dots, which are hard to remember, or you can use the program's MIB walk facility to locate a selected object. Using the window labeled MIB Walk, you can click on higher-level MIB entries referred to as groups to explode the objects contained in a particular group. For example, the System group contains seven objects, which were displayed by double-clicking on the `system` entry in the MIB Walk window. By moving a highlighted bar over a selected object and clicking the Select button, you cause the selected object to be used as the MIB Variable entry in a selected SNMP command. Because the `Get` command is shown selected in Figure 15.17, selecting the `sysDescr` object from the MIB Walk window and using that object in the `Get` command would result in the retrieval of the system description of the agent whose IP address is `198.78.46.41`.

FIGURE 15.17.

Using SimpleView's MIB Walk window to select an object from an agent's database as the variable to retrieve.

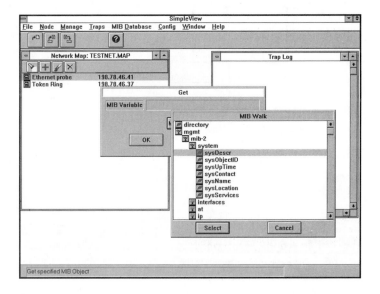

SNMP is based on the use of a limited number of commands. In addition to `Get`, SNMP supports the `Get Next`, `Set`, `Get Response`, and `Trap` commands. The `Get Next` command enables you to "walk" through an MIB, one variable at a time. Agents provide results using a `Get Response` command. The `Set Request` command is used to alter the setting of an agent, such as a router table, and a `Trap` represents an unsolicited command that an agent sends to a manager after sensing the occurrence of a predefined condition, such as a line failure.

RMON

A Remote Monitoring (RMON) set of standards was developed by the IETF to facilitate the collection and retrieval of information on remote networks from a management platform. In an RMON environment, remote agents, known as probes, are configured to automatically collect predefined information about the operating characteristics of the network they are connected to. Information to be collected is defined by different RMON standards. For example, the RMON standard for Ethernet defines nine groups that an Ethernet RMON probe would be designed to support. An RMON probe maintains statistical tables for each group and can manipulate tables independently, which reduces the amount of data required to be transmitted between a probe and a manager. This feature can be extremely valuable, especially when LANs are interconnected by relatively low-speed 56 Kbps circuits. Otherwise, if all traffic were passed from a probe to a distant manager, the management traffic could saturate the WAN connection between LANs.

The RMON standard for Ethernet defines nine groups, and a tenth group was added to the Token-Ring RMON standard. Table 15.1 lists the RMON MIB groups and describes the contents of each group.

Table 15.1. RMON MIB groups.

Group	Description
Statistics	Provides information for quantifying the operation of a network, such as packets, octets, and different errors.
History	Provides historical data on Statistics group variables for trend analysis.
Hosts	Collects information for each host on the network.
Host Top N	Enables a user to define information about the most active hosts on the network.
Traffic Matrix	Provides traffic and error reports that occur between pairs of stations.
Alarms	Reports changes in network characteristics when a preset condition is reached.
Events	Generates SNMP traps based on the previously set Alarms group thresholds.
Filters	Allows selection of packets to be captured, letting managers isolate traffic for review based on a predefined criteria.
Packet Capture	Copies packets into the probe for transfer to the manager later. Packet capture is based on filtering specifications in the Filters group.
Token Ring	An extension to the basic RMON MIB to provide Token-Ring-specific information, such as ring station information.

Figure 15.18 shows the screen display of Network General's Foundation Manager when it was used to retrieve information from the statistics group of an RMON probe. Note that the top window contains eight bar charts that identify such performance elements as bytes/sec and frames/sec, and the lower window provides bar charts of the distribution of frames by frame length and by different error conditions. Foundation Manager isolates many SNMP and RMON details from the user by allowing most operations to be performed by a simple point-and-click operation. For example, clicking on different icons at the top of the screen results in the automatic display of values for different RMON groups. Today, network managers and administrators can select from a wide range of network management products that can greatly facilitate the operation of national and international networks. By selecting appropriate network management products, you can isolate and rapidly correct network-related problems, as well as gain knowledge of potential problems before they become actual problems. Thus, SNMP and RMON can be used for network planning as well as problem isolation.

FIGURE 15.18.

Using Network General's Foundation Manager to retrieve statistical information from an RMON probe.

What Have You Learned?

1. The underlying objective of data networking is to strike a balance between the accurate, timely delivery of user data and total cost.

2. Any network, no matter how simple or complex, can be incorporated into a large network. A larger network cannot be optimized until its component parts are individually optimized.

3. Information throughput rate involves many factors besides the modem bit rate.

4. Classical time division multiplexers provide a powerful tool for combining data transmission link requirements into a smaller number of higher-speed links. Statistical TDMs can be even more powerful if the duty cycles of individual links to be combined are low.

5. Frequency division multiplexers can be useful if the links involve low-speed multipoint data transmission.

6. Other useful networking devices include sharing devices, modem eliminators, and protocol converters.

7. Loopbacks are a common and simple technique for testing data communications components and networks.

8. Test equipment for data communications falls into two generic categories: digital testing and analog testing.

9. The capability to create programs that operate against monitored data can be used to isolate different types of communications problems.

10. Good network design includes appropriate planning for contingencies and procedures for restoring service.

11. Dialed backup is a common technique for restoring service on analog and digital transmission systems.

12. SNMP and RMON are the network management standards that facilitate network planning and problem isolation.

Quiz for Chapter 15

1. Which of the following is not considered a primary objective of data networking?
    a. Security.
    b. Packet switching.
    c. Timeliness.
    d. Accuracy.

2. On a point-to-point data channel using an analog circuit, TRIB is:
    a. Higher than the modem bit rate.
    b. Equal to the modem bit rate.
    c. Lower than the modem bit rate.
    d. Not related to the modem bit rate.

3. The block length that gives maximum TRIB:
    a. Increases as the error rate increases.
    b. Decreases as the error rate increases.
    c. Isn't related to error rate.
    d. Is called the optimum block length.

4. Smart TDMs:

  a. Are always better than dumb TDMs.

  b. Are always better than FDMs.

  c. Are the same as modem sharing devices.

  d. Might be better than dumb TDMs if the data terminals have a low duty cycle.

5. FDM devices can operate:

  a. On multipoint analog data channels.

  b. More efficiently than dumb TDMs.

  c. More efficiently than smart TDMs.

  d. Like modem sharing devices.

6. Protocol converters are:

  a. The same as multiplexers.

  b. The same as TDMs.

  c. Usually operated in pairs.

  d. Usually not operated in pairs.

7. Null modems are a type of:

  a. Modem eliminator.

  b. Modem.

  c. Multiplexer.

  d. Protocol converter.

8. A basic technique for isolating data communications faults is:

  a. Calling the telephone company.

  b. Performing a loopback test.

  c. Calling the DTE service department.

  d. Simulating the system on a special-purpose computer.

9. Bridges operate at:

  a. The Data Link Layer.

  b. The Network Layer.

  c. The Transport Layer.

  d. The Application Layer.

10. Routers make forwarding decisions based on:

  a. MAC addresses.

  b. Network addresses.

  c. Source addresses.

  d. MAC address tables.

11. The device that can make forwarding decisions based on line availability and line utilization is the:

  a. Local bridge.

  b. Remote bridge.

  c. Gateway.

  d. Router.

12. The main purpose of a data link content monitor is to:

  a. Determine the type of switching used in a data link.

  b. Determine the type of transmission used in a data link.

  c. Detect problems in protocols.

  d. Measure bit error rates.

13. The most sophisticated type of data communications test equipment is the:

  a. Simulator.

  b. Protocol analyzer.

  c. DTE.

  d. Breakout box.

14. An example of a portable protocol converter is the:

   a. ParaScope.

   b. Datascope.

   c. UniScope.

   d. UltraScope.

15. An example of a protocol converter counter value is:

   a. Bit delay.

   b. ACK/NAK delay.

   c. ACK/NAK count.

   d. Data rate.

16. The organization that assigns blocks of MAC addresses for use in network adapter cards is the:

   a. IEEE.

   b. ITU-T.

   c. CCITT.

   d. AAA.

17. Knowing the distribution of frames by their length is important in attempting to determine the:

   a. LAN speed.

   b. LAN type.

   c. Type of traffic.

   d. Type of user.

18. The SNMP Management Information Base is:

   a. Located in the network manager.

   b. Based on time.

   c. Based on the manager used.

   d. A database.

19. To set or retrieve data from an SNMP agent, you must have:

   a. The agent's IP address.

   b. The address of the agent's object to be set.

   c. An SNMP manager.

   d. All the above.

20. The RMON standard for Ethernet has:

   a. 9 groups.

   b. 10 groups.

   c. 11 groups.

   d. 12 groups.

Glossary

2B1Q   An encoding technique used on ISDN lines in which two binary bits (2B) are encoded in one quaternary (1Q) symbol.

amplifier   A device used to increase the strength of an analog signal.

analog signal   A signal, such as voice or music, that varies in a continuous manner. Contrast with *digital signal.*

ASCII (American Standard Code for Information Interchange)   A 7-bit code established by the American National Standards Institute to achieve compatibility between data services. Equivalent to the international ISO 7-bit code.

ATM Adaptation Layer   The ATM layer responsible for translating higher-level protocol data into the 48-byte ATM cell payloads.

ATM endpoint   The location in an ATM network where a connection is either initiated or terminated.

attenuation   The difference between transmitted and received power due to transmission loss through equipment, lines, or other communication devices.

bandwidth   The frequency range between the lowest and highest frequencies that are passed through a component, circuit, or system with acceptable attenuation.

baseband   The frequency band occupied by a single or composite signal in its original or unmodulated form.

baseband signaling   A method of signaling in which only one signal occurs on the transmission media at any point in time.

Basic access   The method whereby individual telephone instruments and terminals will be connected to a digital network.

baud   A unit of signaling speed equal to the number of signal events per second. Not necessarily the same as bits per second.

binary coded decimal (BCD)   A system of binary numbering in which each decimal digit 0 through 9 is represented by four bits.

Binary Synchronous Communications (BSC or BiSync)   A communications protocol developed by IBM that has became an industry standard. It uses a defined set of control characters and control character sequences for synchronized transmission of binary coded data between stations in a data communications system.

bis   Meaning "second" in Latin, this term is used as a suffix to denote a secondary version of a CCITT modem standard.

bit   Contraction of *binary digit*. The smallest unit of information. A bit represents the choice between a one or zero value (mark or space in communications terminology).

bit rate   The speed at which bits are transmitted, usually expressed in bits per second. Not necessarily the same as baud rate.

block   A sequence of continuous data characters or bytes transmitted as a unit. A coding procedure is usually applied for synchronization or error-control purposes.

bps (bits per second)   A measure of the information transfer rate of a data channel.

bridge   A device that connects LANs at the ISO data link level.

broadband signaling   A method of signaling in which multiple signals share the bandwidth of the transmission media by the subdivision of the bandwidth into channels based on frequency.

buffer   A storage device used to compensate for a difference in rate of data flow, or time of occurrence of events, when data is being transmitted from one device to another.

byte   A binary element string operated on as a unit and usually shorter than a computer word. Eight-bit bytes are common.

carrier   A signal suitable for modulation by another signal containing information to be transmitted. The carrier is usually a sine wave for analog systems.

CCITT (Consultative Committee for International Telephone and Telegraph)   A standards-making body whose recommendations are more closely followed in Europe than North America.

cell   A 53-byte-long transmission unit used by ATM. Each cell has a 5-byte header and a 48-byte payload.

channel, voice grade   A channel, generally with a frequency range of about 300 to 3400 Hz, suitable for transmission of speech or data in analog form. Data transmission rates of 9600 bps can be achieved by modulation techniques that produce a baud rate of 2400.

character   A letter, figure, number, punctuation, or other symbol contained in a message or used in a control function.

character set   The characters that can be coded or printed by a particular machine.

code   A set of unambiguous rules specifying the way in which characters can be represented.

committed information rate   The minimum operating rate supported by a frame relay service.

common carrier   A company that furnishes communications services to the general public and that is regulated by appropriate state or federal agencies.

conditioning, line   The addition of equipment to a leased voice-grade channel to improve analog characteristics to allow higher rates of data transmission.

connection-oriented   A type of communications in which a connection must be established between the sender and receiver before transmission occurs.

constellation pattern   The pattern gotten from plotting the location of each bit combination modulated by a modem through phase and amplitude changes.

contention   The facility provided by the dial network or a port selector that allows multiple terminals to compete on a first-come-first-served basis for a smaller number of computer ports.

data communications equipment, also data circuit-terminating equipment, (DCE)   The equipment that provides the functions required to establish, maintain, and terminate a connection, and that provides the signal conversion required for communication between data terminal equipment and the telephone line or data circuit.

data terminal equipment (DTE)   A computer or business machine that provides data in the form of digital signals at its output.

dBm   Decibel referenced to one milliwatt. Used in communications circuits as a measure of signal power. Zero dBm equals one milliwatt into a specified impedance, often 600 ohms.

decibel (dB)   A logarithmic measure of the ratio between two powers, P_1 and P_2. The equation is $dB = 10 \log_{10} P_2/P_1$.

delay equalizer   A corrective network that is designed to make the phase delay or envelope delay of a circuit or system substantially constant over a desired frequency range.

delay, propagation   The time required for a signal to travel from one point to another in a component, circuit, or system.

demodulation   The process of recovering data from a modulated carrier wave. The reverse of modulation.

dial-up line   A communications circuit that is established by a switched circuit connection using the telephone dial network.

dialing directory   A module in a communications program that enables telephone numbers and descriptions of those numbers to be entered. Selecting an entry in the dialing directory results in the program dialing the number associated with the entry.

dibit   A group of two bits. In four-phase modulation, such as Differential Phase Shift Keying (DPSK), each possible dibit is encoded as one of four unique carrier phase shifts. The four possible states for a dibit are 00, 01, 10, and 11.

digital repeater   A data regenerator that, on the detection of the rise of a digital pulse's leading edge, regenerates the pulse.

digital signal   A discrete or discontinuous signal; one whose various states are identified with discrete levels or values.

distortion, delay   Distortion resulting from non-uniform speed of transmission of the various frequency components of a signal through a transmission medium. Also called group delay.

distortion, harmonic   The result of nonlinearities in the communication channel that cause harmonics of the input frequencies to appear in the output.

distortion, linear (or amplitude)   An unwanted change in signal amplitude such that the output signal envelope is not proportional to the input signal envelope, but no frequency-related distortion is involved.

echo suppressor   A device that allows transmission in only one direction at a time. Echo suppressors are inserted in telephone circuits to attenuate echoes on long-distance circuits. They are not desirable in data communications circuits because they increase the turn-around time.

equalization   The process of reducing the effects of amplitude, frequency, or phase distortion of a circuit by inserting networks to compensate for the difference in attenuation or time delay at various frequencies in the transmission band.

filter   A network designed to transmit electrical signals having frequencies within one or more frequency bands and to attenuate signals of other frequencies.

flow control   The orderly regulation of the flow of data by the use of special characters (inband signaling) or control signals at the RS232 interface (outband signaling).

frame relay   A packet switched service that does not provide for error detection and correction, resulting in minimal routing delays.

frequency division multiplexer (FDM)   A device that divides the available transmission frequency range into narrower bands, each of which is used for a separate channel.

frequency response   The change in attenuation with frequency relative to the attenuation at a reference frequency. Also called attenuation distortion.

frequency shift keying (FSK) A form of frequency modulation commonly used in low-speed modems in which the two states of the signal are transmitted as two separate frequencies.

full-duplex Refers to a communications system or equipment capable of simultaneous two-way communications.

gateway Hardware and software that enables devices located on a local area network to access the facilities of another network.

half-duplex Refers to a communications system or equipment capable of communications in both directions, but in only one direction at a time.

handshaking Exchange of predetermined codes and signals between two data terminals to establish a connection.

inband signaling A method of flow control in which a device transmits a character (usually an XOFF) to inform another device to suspend transmission and another character (usually an XON) to resume transmission.

interface A shared boundary defined by common physical interconnection characteristics, signal characteristics, and meanings of interchanged signals.

intermodulation noise Spurious frequencies, such as sum and difference frequencies, which are the products of frequencies transmitted through a nonlinear circuit.

IP address A 32-bit address that identifies the network and host in a network.

ISDN (Integrated Services Digital Network) A future offering designed to provide a universal digital network that will enable the integration of voice and data on a common telephone company facility.

jitter A tendency toward lack of synchronization caused by mechanical or electrical changes.

kilostream A digital network that operates in the United Kingdom.

line (1) A circuit between a customer terminal and the central office. (2) The portion of a transmission system, including the transmission media and associated repeaters, between two terminal locations.

link A circuit or transmission path, including all equipment, between a sender and a receiver.

local area network (LAN) A communications network that is restricted to a small geographical area, usually within a building or on a campus, and that has cabling normally installed or controlled by the organization that operates the network.

local loop The pair of wires between a customer terminal and the central office.

loopback test   A test of a communications link performed by connecting the equipment output of one direction to the equipment input of the other direction and testing the quality of the received signal.

mark   One of the two possible states of a binary information element. The closed circuit and idle state in a teleprinter circuit. See *space*.

modem (MOdulator/DEModulator)   A type of DCE that at the transmitting end converts digital data to an analog signal for transmission on telephone circuits. A modem at the receiving end converts the analog signal to digital form.

modulation   The process of varying some characteristic of the carrier wave in accordance with the instantaneous value or samples of the intelligence to be transmitted. Amplitude, frequency, and phase are the characteristics commonly varied.

multiplex   To interleave or simultaneously transmit two or more messages on a single channel.

multistation access unit (MAU)   A device that enables workstations on a LAN to be cabled in a star configuration.

noise   Random electrical signals, introduced by circuit components or natural disturbances, that tend to generate errors in transmission.

outband signaling   A method of flow control in which an RS232 control signal (usually Clear to Send) is lowered to inform a device to suspend transmission and raised to inform a device to resume transmission.

PABX (private automatic branch exchange)   A device that is installed on a customer's premises and that enables a large number of telephones to automatically access the switched telephone network by using a smaller number of lines connecting the PABX to the telephone company network.

PBX (private branch exchange)   Telephone switching equipment dedicated to one customer and connected to the public switched network.

permanent virtual circuit (PVC)   A logical connection between endpoints in a network that remains in place until the network administrator tears it down.

personal computer   A computer with processing power based on a microprocessor and designed primarily for use by one person.

polling   The individual selection of multiple terminals by a controller to allow transmission of traffic to and from all terminals on a multidrop line in an orderly manner.

port   An interface on a computer configured as data terminal equipment and capable of having a modem attached for communication with a remote data terminal.

primary access   A multiplexing arrangement whereby many ISDN Basic access subscribers can be connected to a digital network over a common line facility.

protocol   The rules for communication between like processes, giving a means to control the orderly communication of information between stations on a data link.

protocol analyzer   A device that decodes a bit stream being monitored into characters that represent the format and information content of a transmission protocol.

redundancy   The portion of the total information contained in a message that can be eliminated without loss of essential information.

repeater   A communications system component that amplifies or regenerates signals to compensate for losses in the system.

serial transmission   A method of information transfer in which the bits that compose a character are sent in sequence one at a time.

slow scan video   The process whereby still video images are transmitted frequently to provide the appearance of video motion.

space   One of the two possible states of a binary information element. The open circuit or no current state of a teleprinter line. See *mark*.

start bit or element   The first bit or element transmitted in the asynchronous transmission of a character to synchronize the receiver.

statistical multiplexer   A multiplexer that uses the idle time of connected devices to carry data traffic from active devices.

stop bit or element   The last bit or element transmitted in the asynchronous transmission of a character to return the circuit to the at-rest or idle condition.

switched virtual circuit   A logical connection through a network established on a demand basis for a temporary period.

symbol   The graphical representation of some idea that is used by people. Letters and numbers are symbols.

TA (terminal adapter)   A device that is used to enable equipment with a non-ISDN interface to be connected to that digital network.

TE1 (terminal equipment 1)   Devices that comply with the ISDN network interface and that can be connected directly to the digital network.

TE2 (terminal equipment 2)   Devices that do not have an ISDN interface and must be connected by using a TA (terminal adapter) to the digital network.

ter   Meaning "third" in Latin, this term is used as a suffix to denote a third version of a CCITT modem standard.

terminal emulation   Software or firmware that enables a personal computer or terminal to duplicate the screen attributes of a specific terminal.

time division multiplexer (TDM)   A device that allows the transmission of two or more independent data channels on a single high-speed circuit by interleaving the data from each channel on the circuit by time.

transmission, asynchronous   Transmission in which each information character is individually synchronized, usually by the use of start and stop elements.

transmission, synchronous   Transmission in which the sending and receiving instruments are operating continuously at substantially the same frequency and in which the desired phase relationship can be maintained by means of correction.

Trellis-coded modulation   A modem modulation process in which one or more redundant bits are added to each group of bits used to generate a signal change. The extra bit (or bits) allows only certain sequences of signal points to be valid, resulting in a lowering of the error rate.

Turnaround time   The actual time required to reverse the direction of transmission from sender to receiver or vice versa when a half-duplex circuit is being used. Time is required for line propagation effects, modem timing, and computer reaction.

UART (universal asynchronous receiver/transmitter)   A device that performs asynchronous communications functions by converting parallel digital output from a DTE into serial bit transmission and vice versa.

virtual channel connection (VCC)   A concatenation of virtual channel links between two endpoints in an ATM network.

virtual path connection (VPC)   A concatenation of virtual path links between two or more switches in an ATM network.

XMODEM   A half-duplex file transfer protocol limited to transmitting one file at a time.

YMODEM   A half-duplex file transfer protocol that supports the transfer of multiple files.

ZMODEM   A full-duplex file transfer protocol that supports the transfer of multiple files and enables a previously interrupted transmission to be resumed at the point of interruption.

Bibliography

B

A History of Engineering & Science in the Bell System: The Early Years (1875-1925), Whippany, NJ: Bell Telephone Laboratories, Inc., 1975.

Bell Laboratories Record, Whippany, NJ: Bell Telephone Laboratories, Inc., November 1980.

Bellamy, John. *Digital Telephony,* New York: John Wiley & Sons, Inc., 1982.

Bigelow, Stephen. *Understanding Telephone Electronics, 3rd Ed.,* Carmel, IN; Sams, a division of Macmillan Computer Publishing, 1983.

Black, Uyless. *Computer Networks Protocols, Standards, and Interfaces,* Englewood Cliffs, NJ: Prentice Hall, Inc., 1993.

Black, Uyless. *Data Networks,* Englewood Cliffs, NJ: Prentice Hall, Inc., 1989.

Doll, Dixon. *Data Communications; Facilities, Networks and Systems Design,* New York: John Wiley & Sons, 1978.

EIA Standard RS-232-C (and others), Electronic Industries Association.

Freeman, R.L. *Telecommunication System Engineering,* New York: John Wiley & Sons, Inc., 1980.

Freeman, R.L. *Telecommunication Transmission Handbook, 2nd Ed.,* New York: John Wiley & Sons, Inc., 1981.

General Information—Binary Synchronous Communications, IBM Publication Nr. GA27-3004, IBM Systems Development Division, Publications Center.

General Information—IBM Synchronous Data Link Control, IBM Publication Nr. GA27-3093-2, IBM Systems Development Division, Publications Center.

Held, Gilbert. *Data and Image Compression, 4th Ed.,* New York: John Wiley & Sons, 1996.

Held, Gilbert. *Data Communications Networking Devices, 3rd Ed.,* New York: John Wiley & Sons, 1993.

UNDERSTANDING

Held, Gilbert. *Digital Networking,* New York: John Wiley & Sons, 1991.

Held, Gilbert. *Ethernet Networks, 2nd Ed.,* New York: John Wiley & Sons, 1996.

Held, Gilbert. *LAN Management with SNMP and RMON,* New York: John Wiley & Sons, 1996.

Held, Gilbert. *Mastering PC Communications Software,* New York: Van Nostrand Reinhold, 1993.

Held, Gilbert. *Protecting LAN Resources,* New York: John Wiley & Sons, 1995.

Held, Gilbert. *Testing and Troubleshooting Data Communications Networks, 2nd Ed.,* New York: Van Nostrand Reinhold, 1992.

Held, Gilbert. *The Complete Modem Reference, 3rd Ed.,* New York: John Wiley & Sons, Inc., 1996.

IEEE Transactions on Communications, IEEE Communications Society, August 1980, Vol. COM-28.

ITU-T Recommendations V.29, X.21, and X.25, ITU-T, Geneva, C.H.

Kreager, Paul. *Practical Aspects of Data Communications,* New York: McGraw-Hill Book Co., 1983.

Martin, James. *Telecommunications and the Computer,* Englewood Cliffs, NJ: Prentice Hall, Inc., 1969.

McNamara, John E. *Technical Aspects of Data Communications, 2nd Ed.,* Digital Press, 1982.

Members of the Technical Staff and the Technical Publications Department. *Engineering and Operations in the Bell System,* Whippany, NJ: Bell Telephone Laboratories, Inc., 1977.

Members of the Technical Staff. *Transmission Systems for Communications, Revised 4th Ed.,* Whippany, NJ: Bell Telephone Laboratories, Inc., 1971.

Notes on the Network, American Telephone & Telegraph Co., 1980.

Owen, Frank E. *PCM and Digital Transmission Systems,* New York: McGraw-Hill, Inc., 1982.

Parameters of Telephone Network Design, IBM Publication Nr ZZ-11-3201-0, IBM World Trade Corp., Jan. 1977.

Sherman, Kenneth. *Data Communications: A User's Guide,* Reston Publishing Co., 1981.

Stauffer, J.R. *IEEE Journal on Selected Areas in Communications,* Vol. SAC-1, No. 3, April 1983.

Tanebaum, Andrew S. *Computer Networks, 2nd Ed.,* Englewood Cliffs, NJ: Prentice Hall, Inc., 1995.

Answers to Quizzes

Chapter 1

1. d	**8.** a
2. b	**9.** c
3. a	**10.** c
4. c	**11.** c
5. c	**12.** b
6. b	**13.** ~~b~~ a
7. b	

Chapter 2

1. c	**14.** c
2. a	**15.** c
3. b	**16.** a
4. b	**17.** b
5. c	**18.** c
6. ~~c~~ d	**19.** d
7. c	**20.** a
8. c	**21.** c
9. d	**22.** b
10. a	**23.** a
11. a	**24.** c
12. b	**25.** a
13. c	

Chapter 3

1. c
2. a
3. b
4. d
5. d
6. b
7. b
8. d
9. b
10. c
11. a
12. c
13. c
14. b
15. c
16. c

Chapter 4

1. c
2. a
3. b
4. a
5. b
6. c
7. c
8. c
9. b
10. a
11. c
12. b
13. c
14. c
15. c
16. c
17. b
18. b

Chapter 5

1. d
2. b
3. c
4. c
5. d
6. c
7. a
8. c
9. b
10. c
11. d
12. d
13. b
14. b
15. c

Chapter 6

1. b
2. c
3. c
4. c
5. a
6. d
7. c
8. d
9. b
10. a
11. c
12. c
13. a
14. d
15. a

Chapter 7

1. a and c
2. c
3. b
4. d
5. d
6. c
7. d
8. b
9. c
10. c
11. c
12. b
13. c
14. d
15. c
16. b
17. b
18. c
19. a
20. c
21. f
22. a
23. c
24. b
25. c

Chapter 8

1. a
2. c
3. c
4. d
5. d
6. c
7. c
8. b
9. d
10. c
11. b
12. b and d
13. a
14. b
15. c
16. d

Chapter 9

1. a		**7.** d
2. c		**8.** b
3. b		**9.** d
4. d		**10.** a
5. d		**11.** d
6. b		**12.** d

Chapter 10

1. c		**14.** b
2. a		**15.** d
3. d		**16.** d
4. b		**17.** a
5. c		**18.** d
6. d		**19.** a
7. a		**20.** d
8. a		**21.** c
9. b		**22.** b
10. b		**23.** d
11. b		**24.** c
12. d		**25.** b
13. a		

Chapter 11

1. a
2. d
3. b
4. c
5. d
6. c
7. d
8. a
9. b
10. a
11. b
12. c
13. a
14. d
15. b
16. a
17. c
18. c
19. c
20. d
21. d
22. c
23. b
24. a

Chapter 12

1. b
2. b
3. c
4. d
5. c
6. a
7. b
8. c
9. a
10. c
11. c
12. c
13. d
14. b
15. b
16. a
17. b
18. d
19. d
20. c

Chapter 13

1. b
2. b
3. a
4. d
5. c
6. d
7. a
8. b
9. c
10. c

Chapter 14

1. b
2. d
3. c
4. c
5. d
6. b
7. d

8. a
9. c
10. b
11. d
12. b
13. a

Chapter 15

1. b
2. c
3. b
4. d
5. a
6. d
7. a
8. b
9. a
10. b

11. d
12. c
13. b
14. a
15. c
16. a
17. c
18. d
19. d
20. a

Index

UNDERSTANDING

E

G-H

I

Q-R

S

Teach Yourself Java in 21 Days

Laura Lemay, et al.

Introducing the first, best, and most detailed guide to developing applications with the hot new Java language from Sun Microsystems.

CD-ROM includes the Java Developer's Kit.

Provides detailed coverage of the hottest new technology on the World Wide Web.

Shows readers how to develop applications using the Java language.

Includes coverage of browsing Java applications with Netscape and other popular Web browsers.

Covers Java.

Price: $39.99 USA/$53.99 CDN   *Casual–Accomplished–Expert*   *Internet/Programming*
ISBN: 1-57521-030-4   *500 pp.*   *7 3/8×9 1/8*   *01/01/96*

HTML, JAVA, CGI, VRML, SGML Web Publishing Unleashed

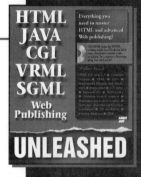

William Stanek

Includes sections on how to organize and plan your information, design pages, and become familiar with hypertext and hypermedia. Choose from a range of applications and technologies, including Java, SGML, VRML, and the newest HTML and Netscape extensions.

CD-ROM contains software, templates, and examples to help you become a successful Web publisher.

Teaches how to convey information on the Web using the latest technology, including Java.

Readers learn how to integrate multimedia and interactivity into their Web publications.

Covers the World Wide Web.

Price: $49.99 USA/$67.99 CDN   *Casual–Accomplished–Expert*   *Internet/Web Publishing*
ISBN: 1-57521-051-7   *960 pp.*   *7 3/8×9 1/8*   *03/01/96*

Teach Yourself Web Publishing with HTML 3.2 in 14 Days, Professional Reference Edition

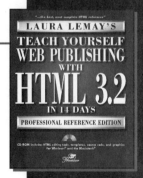

Laura Lemay

This is the updated edition of Lemay's previous bestseller, *Teach Yourself Web Publishing with HTML in 14 Days*, Premier Edition. In it, readers will find all the advanced topics and updates—including adding audio, video, and animation to Web page creation.

CD-ROM included.

Explores the use of CGI scripts, tables, HTML 3.2, the Netscape and Internet Explorer extensions, Java applets and JavaScript, and VRML.

Covers HTML 3.2.

Price: $59.99 USA/$81.95 CDN   *New–Casual–Accomplished*   *Internet/Web Publishing*
ISBN: 1-57521-096-7   *1,104 pp.*   *7 3/8×9 1/8*   *06/01/96*

Paul McFedries' Windows 95 Unleashed, Premier Edition

Paul McFedries

Completely updated and revised. Bestselling author Paul McFedries has created a Windows 95 user's masterpiece. In the traditional style of the Unleashed series, every new feature is discussed in detail, leaving the reader fully informed and completely functional within the new operating system. It also includes coverage of soon-to-be-released Microsoft Internet products, such as VBScript, Internet Studio, and Microsoft Exchange—coverage not found anywhere else.

CD-ROM contains an easy-to-search online chapter on troubleshooting for Windows 95.

Covers Internet topics, including the Microsoft Network.

Discusses multimedia topics, internetworking, and communication.

Price: $59.99 USA/$83.95 CDN   Accomplished–Expert
ISBN: 0-672-30932-7   1,376 pp. 7 3/8×9 1/8   07/01/96

Add to Your Sams Library Today with the Best Books for Programming, Operating Systems, and New Technologies

The easiest way to order is to pick up the phone and call

1-800-428-5331

between 9:00 a.m. and 5:00 p.m. EST.
For faster service please have your credit card available.

ISBN	Quantity	Description of Item	Unit Cost	Total Cost
1-57521-030-4		Teach Yourself Java in 21 Days (Book/CD-ROM)	$39.99	
1-57521-051-7		Web Publishing Unleashed (Book/CD-ROM)	$49.99	
1-57521-096-7		Teach Yourself Web Publishing with HTML 3.2 in 14 Days, Professional Reference Edition (Book/CD-ROM)	$59.99	
0-672-30932-7		Paul McFedries' Windows 95 Unleashed, Premier Edition (Book/CD-ROM)	$59.99	
❏ 3½" Disk		Shipping and Handling: See information below.		
❏ 5¼" Disk		TOTAL		

Shipping and Handling: $4.00 for the first book, and $1.75 for each additional book. Floppy disk: add $1.75 for shipping and handling. If you need to have it NOW, we can ship product to you in 24 hours for an additional charge of approximately $18.00, and you will receive your item overnight or in two days. Overseas shipping and handling adds $2.00 per book and $8.00 for up to three disks. Prices subject to change. Call for availability and pricing information on latest editions.

201 W. 103rd Street, Indianapolis, Indiana 46290

1-800-428-5331 — Orders   1-800-835-3202 — FAX   1-800-858-7674 — Customer Service

Book ISBN 0-672-30934-3